The Final Days of
Edgar Allan Poe

Perspectives on Edgar Allan Poe

General Editor: Barbara Cantalupo,
Pennsylvania State University, Lehigh Valley

The Perspectives on Poe series includes books on new approaches to Edgar A. Poe, his work and influence; all perspectives—theoretical, historical, biographical, gender studies, source studies, cultural studies, global studies, etc.—are invited.

TITLES IN THIS SERIES

The Final Days of Edgar Allan Poe: Nevermore in Baltimore by David F. Gaylin (2024)

Poe and Women: Recognition and Revision edited by Amy Branam Armiento and Travis Montgomery (2023)

Anthologizing Poe: Editions, Translations, and (Trans)National Canons edited by Emron Esplin and Margarida Vale de Gato (2020)

Poe and the Idea of Music: Failure, Transcendence, and Dark Romanticism by Charity McAdams (2017)

The Lovecraftian Poe: Essays on Influence, Reception, Interpretation, and Transformation edited by Sean Moreland (2017)

Translated Poe edited by Emron Esplin and Margarida Vale de Gato (2014)

Deciphering Poe: Subtexts, Contexts, Subversive Meanings edited by Alexandra Urakova (2013)

Poe's Pervasive Influence edited by Barbara Cantalupo (2012)

https://lupress.cas.lehigh.edu/

The Final Days of Edgar Allan Poe

Nevermore in Baltimore

David F. Gaylin

LEHIGH UNIVERSITY PRESS
Bethlehem

Published by Lehigh University Press
Copublished by The Rowman & Littlefield Publishing Group, Inc.
4501 Forbes Boulevard, Suite 200, Lanham, Maryland 20706
www.rowman.com

86-90 Paul Street, London EC2A 4NE, United Kingdom

Copyright © 2024 by The Rowman & Littlefield Publishing Group, Inc.

All rights reserved. No part of this book may be reproduced in any form or by any
electronic or mechanical means, including information storage and retrieval systems,
without written permission from the publisher, except by a reviewer who may quote
passages in a review.

British Library Cataloguing in Publication Information Available

Library of Congress Cataloging-in-Publication Data
Names: Gaylin, David, 1955– author.
Title: The final days of Edgar Allan Poe : nevermore in Baltimore / David F. Gaylin.
Description: Bethlehem : Lehigh University Press, [2024] | Series: Perspectives on Edgar
  Allan Poe | Includes bibliographical references and index. | Summary: "The Final
  Days of Edgar Allan Poe contains an in-depth examination of the circumstances of
  Edgar Allan Poe's death in 1849. Beginning with a chronology of the poet's life, the
  book then delves into the many myths and theories that have become attached to the
  poet's mysterious demise"—Provided by publisher.
Identifiers: LCCN 2023057764 (print) | LCCN 2023057765 (ebook) | ISBN
  9781683933939 (cloth) | ISBN 9781683933946 (epub)
Subjects: LCSH: Poe, Edgar Allan, 1809–1849—Death and burial. | Poe, Edgar Allan,
  1809–1849—Last years. | Authors, American—19th century—Biography. | Baltimore
  (Md.)—Biography. | Baltimore (Md.)—History.
Classification: LCC PS2632 .G39 2024 (print) | LCC PS2632 (ebook) | DDC
  818/.309—dc23/eng/20240206
LC record available at https://lccn.loc.gov/2023057764
LC ebook record available at https://lccn.loc.gov/2023057765

♾️™ The paper used in this publication meets the minimum requirements of American
National Standard for Information Sciences—Permanence of Paper for Printed Library
Materials, ANSI/NISO Z39.48-1992.

To the memory of Thomas "Tucker" Gaylin Jr.,
this book is lovingly dedicated.

Glad should I be . . . as an enthusiastic admirer . . . [that] the assignment of such an agency as the actual cause of his death be made with truthfulness.

— Joseph Evans Snodgrass, "The Facts of Poe's Death and Burial," *Beadle's Monthly*, May 1867, p. 285

Contents

Illustrations		ix
Acknowledgments		xiii
Abbreviations		xv
Introduction		1
1	Peaks and Pits, and Pendulum Swings	13
2	On to Richmond	63
3	Missing in Mobtown	87
4	"The Worse for Wear"	103
5	Beware the Ward Heelers	115
6	Hospital on the Hill	131
7	The Island of Dr. Moran	149
8	"Congestion of the Brain"	167
9	Premature Burials, an Epilogue	187

Appendices

A	Proposed and Popular Causes of Poe's Death	203
B	Timeline of Poe's Final Days	223
C	Notes on Relevant Individuals Mentioned in the Text	225
D	Dr. Moran's Letter to Maria Clemm, November 15, 1849	239

Notes	243
Bibliography	295
Index	303
About the Author	311

Illustrations

FIGURES

1.1.	Miniature of Elizabeth "Eliza" Poe	14
1.2.	Holliday Street Theater in Baltimore	15
1.3.	Rosalie Mackenzie Poe	17
1.4.	Jane Stith Stanard's Richmond gravesite	21
1.5.	University of Virginia	24
1.6.	Maria Clemm	27
1.7.	John Pendleton Kennedy	29
1.8.	Engraving of Poe, c. 1843	31
1.9.	Virginia Clemm Poe	31
1.10.	Thomas Willis White	33
1.11.	George Rex Graham	38
1.12.	Edgar Allan Poe, after 1844	45
1.13.	Nathaniel Parker Willis	47
1.14.	Frances Sargent Osgood	49
1.15.	Marie Louise Shew	52
1.16.	Sarah Helen Whitman	55
1.17.	Daguerreotype of Poe, c. 1848	58
1.18.	"Annie" Daguerreotype of Poe, c. 1849	60
2.1.	Poe cottage at Fordham, New York	64
2.2.	Moyamensing Prison, Philadelphia	65

2.3.	John Sartain	66
2.4.	Engraving of the Fairmount Water Works	68
2.5.	View of Richmond from Church Hill	69
2.6.	George Lippard	71
2.7.	Richmond home of Sarah Elmira Shelton	74
2.8.	Swan Tavern, Richmond, Virginia	79
2.9.	"Thompson" daguerreotype of Poe	81
2.10.	Rockett's Landing, Richmond	84
3.1.	1845 steam packet advertisement	88
3.2.	Map of Poe's movements within Baltimore City	90
3.3.	1849 view of Baltimore's harbor	92
3.4.	Widow Meagher's oyster bar, Baltimore	93
3.5.	Contemporary view of Nathan C. Brooks' home	94
3.6.	Baltimore and Calvert Streets, c. 1850	95
3.7.	Lexington Market	96
3.8.	Philadelphia, Wilmington & Baltimore Railroad station	98
3.9.	East Baltimore, c. 1849	100
4.1.	912 East Lombard Street, Baltimore	104
4.2.	William Hand Browne	105
4.3.	Richard Hart at 912 East Lombard Street, Baltimore	107
4.4.	Richard Hart points to the spot of Poe's discovery	109
4.5.	Henry Herring	110
4.6.	Hacks for hire advertisement, c. 1849	112
5.1.	"Ward agents" on Election Day	117
5.2.	John R. Thompson's original lecture manuscript	121
5.3.	John Reuben Thompson	122
5.4.	Fourth Ward newspaper ad	124
5.5.	Poe as a cooping victim	126
6.1.	1845 Washington University advertisement	132
6.2.	Baltimore City and Marine Hospital, c. 1852	134
6.3.	Photo of Church Home and Infirmary	137
6.4.	Engraving of Poe's hospital	140
6.5.	Daguerreotype showing Poe's hospital in 1849	142

Illustrations

6.6.	Baltimore City and Marine Hospital advertisement	143
6.7.	Neilson Poe	144
6.8.	Dr. William M. Cullen	146
7.1.	Old Capitol Prison, Washington, DC	151
7.2.	Dr. John J. Moran	152
7.3.	Gravesite of John and Mary Moran	153
7.4.	Poe's steamer trunk	155
7.5.	Merchants Exchange Building, Baltimore	158
7.6.	Program for Dr. Moran's Washington, DC, lecture	159
7.7.	YMCA Hall, Baltimore	160
7.8.	Moran's 1885 book on Poe's death	161
7.9.	New York actor's monument to Poe	165
8.1.	1850 federal census record	168
8.2.	Judge Neilson Poe	169
8.3.	Rufus Griswold	170
8.4.	Elizabeth Rebecca Herring	173
8.5.	Thomas Dunn English	174
8.6.	Dr. John C. S. Monkur	178
8.7.	"Ultima Thule" daguerreotype of Poe	179
9.1.	Church Home and Infirmary, c. 1870	188
9.2.	George Spence	190
9.3.	Westminster Presbyterian Church	193
9.4.	Miss Sara Sigourney Rice	195
9.5.	Concordia Hall, Baltimore	195
9.6.	Western Female High School, Baltimore	199
9.7.	Engraving of the monument's dedication ceremony	200
9.8.	Poe's Monument, 1875	201

Acknowledgments

As anyone who has ever produced a book understands, it can never be done alone, and appreciation must always be given to those who help authors find their way out of the wilderness. I must first acknowledge my obligation to the writers and scholars who have preceded me; even in this age of electronic information and digitized archives, it is certain that without their work, much of the material presented here would not have been found. In particular, *The Poe Log*, by Dwight Thomas and David K. Jackson (1987); *Edgar Allan Poe: A Critical Biography* (1941), by Arthur Hobson Quinn; and *The Collected Letters of Edgar Allan Poe* (2008), edited by John Ward Ostrom, Burton R. Pollin, and Jeffrey A. Savoye, proved absolutely critical to this project.

Other resources upon which I heavily relied included the Enoch Pratt Free Library, Baltimore, Maryland, through which access to the *Baltimore Sun* archives was achieved; many new details on Poe's time in the city were found there. I must also voice my appreciation of Google Books for their digitization of (and access to) obscure titles; their service saved me from many evening trips to the Goucher College Library, and book purchases on Amazon.

Without question, the single most important resource used in the creation of this work was the website of the Edgar Allan Poe Society of Baltimore, Maryland (https://www.eapoe.org). There I found magazine articles on Poe that were not on Google Books, as well as crucial volumes, long out of print. Even those titles that matched examples in my collection were easier exploited in the digital form found there. It is not an overstatement to say that without the Poe Society website, this book may have ended being little more than a graphic novel, by comparison.

It is also necessary to thank several individuals who unselfishly gave their time, material, and expert advice. I am indebted to Michael McGlasson for the discovery of Dr. Moran's medical school thesis. Brian Shipley graciously xiv *Acknowledgments*

allowed the first-time use of a Neilson Poe tintype; his Poe-family collection undoubtedly holds more "firsts." Another photograph that is being published here for the first time is that of Dr. William M. Cullen. Having been alerted to its existence, I spent many unsuccessful hours in its search, and only after my capitulation was it located by Eben Dennis, the head of the Special Collections Department at the Enoch Pratt Free Library, who probably spent more time in its pursuit than I did. Christopher P. Semtner, the curator of Edgar Allan Poe Museum in Richmond, Virginia, allowed access to the museum's extensive library which holds the original manuscript of John Thompson's lecture. Mr. Semtner also gave kind permission for use of some of the museum's images. Ms. Sam Brawand structured and formatted the raw manuscript to comply with the publisher's requirements while schooling me in the Chicago Manual of Style. Dr. Katherine Crassons and Tricia Moore at Lehigh University Press demonstrated extraordinary patience with my inexperience of the academic publishing process; I will be grateful *evermore* for the sacrifices they made for this project. And I am indebted to Charlotte Gaylin, for her technical assistance with parts of the typescript; it is a handy thing to have an English teacher as your daughter.

Finally, I would like to offer a special appreciation to Poe scholar Jeffrey A. Savoye, without whose knowledge, guidance, and timely assistance the finished work would certainly have been a great deal poorer. Jeffrey is also the creator of the Edgar Allan Poe Society of Baltimore website which now contains the most complete collection of Poe's works, and related titles, ever assembled. But still he found time to come to my rescue, and more than once.

* * *

Regarding the images that accompany the text, every effort was made to identify the sources and assign the correct attributions. For uniformity, photographs taken by the author and those in the author's collection, as well as those in the public domain, are simply credited "Author."

Abbreviations

Allen   Hervey Allen, *Israfel: The Life and Times of Edgar Allan Poe*, rev. ed. (New York: Farrar & Reinhart, 1934).

CL   John Ward Ostrom, Burton R. Pollin, and Jeffrey A. Savoye, eds. *The Collected Letters of Edgar Allan Poe*, 2 vols. (New York: Gordian Press, 2008).

H   James A. Harrison, ed., *The Complete Works of Edgar Allan Poe*, 17 vols. (New York: Thomas Y. Crowell, 1902).

M   Thomas Ollive Mabbott, *The Collected Works of Edgar Allan Poe*, 3 vols. (Cambridge, MA: Belknapp Press of Harvard University Press, 1969; 1978).

Miller   John Carl Miller, *Building Poe Biography* (Baton Rouge: Louisiana State University Press, 1977).

Moran   John J. Moran, *A Defense of Edgar Allan Poe: Life, Character and Dying Declarations of the Poet* (Washington, DC: William F. Boogher, 1885).

Phillips   Mary E. Phillips, *Edgar Allan Poe the Man*, 2 vols. (Philadelphia: John C. Winston, 1926).

PL   Dwight Thomas and David K. Jackson, *The Poe Log: A Documentary Life of Edgar Allan Poe 1809–1849* (Boston: G. K. Hall, 1987).

Powell   Michael A. Powell, *Too Much Moran: Respecting the Death of Edgar Poe* (Eugene, OR: Pacific Rim University Press, 2009).

Pratt	Edgar Allan Poe Collection, Enoch Pratt Free Library, https://collections.digitalmaryland.org/digital/collection/poe.
Quinn	Arthur Hobson Quinn, *Edgar Allan Poe: A Critical Biography* (New York: D. Appleton-Century, 1941).
Stoddard	Richard Henry Stoddard, *Select Works of Edgar Allan Poe, Poetical and Prose* (New York: W. J. Widdleton, 1880).
Weiss	Susan Archer Weiss, *The Home Life of Poe* (New York: Broadway Publishing, 1907).
Woodberry	George E. Woodberry, *The Life of Edgar Allan Poe*, 2 vols. (Boston: Houghton Mifflin, 1909).

Introduction

Sometime around 1967, I was gifted a hardbound copy of Edgar Allan Poe's works by my grandmother, who had a lifelong appreciation of poetry. The book was Doubleday's *Complete Stories and Poems of Edgar Allan Poe* that she had found in a thrift store, and it came to me without a dust jacket. I cannot recall why she gave it to me or if I had done something to make her think I had an interest in poetry at that time, but I can remember her repeated readings of "Annabel Lee" to us as children; it became my sister's favorite poem. For some reason I decided to keep the book. When in high school a few years later, I was tasked to write some poems as a class assignment and retrieved the dusty old volume to use its contents as a pattern. I cared little for Poe's gory stories that had been thrust upon me in class, but his poetry had a music to it that I, still an adolescent, could grasp; I thought the rhythm as important in conveying the message and mood as the lyrics that provided its staff. As I turned in my silly lyrics at school, something had been disturbed inside me that would ultimately cause a desire to continue this form of expression on paper, perhaps more for therapeutic reasons than a creative need.

But it was not until the 1976 release of the Alan Parsons Project record album, *Tales of Mystery and Imagination*, that my enthusiasm for all things "Edgar Allan Poe" really took flight. With Poe's poems and short stories put to music, here at last was a compelling adaptation of his works. Now I *wanted* to read his tales and discover all I could about him. I blew the dust off the old Doubleday again and binged on Poe. I could not put the tattered book down, and the tease of a biography that I found on the final pages was just gasoline on the fire.

I had to know more about the man's life, and death, but in the days before Barnes and Noble box stores, and the internet, acquiring a book on a specific topic, let alone a specific title, was somewhat arduous by comparison. I first

2 *Introduction*

found a discarded and well-defaced library copy of William Bittner's *Poe: A Biography* (1962) that gave what I thought to be an accurate and adequate record of the poet's life. However, the *description* of his death was confined to six paragraphs (not counting citations) in the book's appendix. Next, I found the revised 1934 edition of *Israfel: The Life and Times of Edgar Allan Poe*, by Hervey Allen, which covered his life in much greater depth albeit through flowery, rose-tinted glasses. Yet within this 748-page tome, only six pages are given to Poe's final days, with the imprecise account generating more questions than answers. In due course, I purchased a new, paperback copy of Arthur Hobson Quinn's magnificent, no-stone-unturned, *Edgar Allan Poe: A Critical Biography* (1941). Quinn produced an exhaustive and highly accurate examination of Poe's life but still furnished barely five pages on his death. After close reading this third biography, I considered myself sufficiently conversant with the poet's life; but as to his death, I was like most other students of Poe, still malnourished. I found it difficult to accept that more was not known, and then focused my search on anything published on the cause and circumstances of his demise. I acquired and read the biographies by George Woodberry, Mary Phillips, John Ingram, Thomas Mabbott ("Annals"), and others—probably in the wrong order. From all these I had distilled somewhat of a consensus of what had happened to Poe but there was little new information or anything conclusive. By the time of Kenneth Silverman's excellent *Edgar A. Poe: Mournful and Never-Ending Remembrance* in 1991, there was yet no standalone title on the subject.

Eventually some works relating only to Edgar Poe's death emerged but these, for the most part, were written to promote a predetermined theory. In John Walsh's *Midnight Dreary* (1998), Poe does not die an organic death but was murdered by relatives of his fiancée, who wanted to prevent the marriage. Following this book was Matthew Pearl's *The Poe Shadow* (2006), a novel in which the poet is murdered to prevent publication of his literary magazine. While researching his story, Pearl found significant new information on Poe's final days, although he used it only as gingerbread for his fictional tale. In *Decryption of the Death of Edgar Allan Poe* (2017), its author, Dr. Ralph Giorno, makes a compelling case for malaria as the cause of death, while not adequately explaining how Poe could have been misdiagnosed by the various doctors examining him during his many illnesses. The most important work directly addressing the subject is Michael Powell's *Too Much Moran: Respecting the Death of Edgar Allan Poe* (2009). Benefiting from the arrival of the internet, Powell uncovered much new information on the circumstances of that fateful week in October 1849; but here again, the author used much of the material to support his preconceived theory that because of an allergic reaction to alcohol, Poe could not have died from its abuse, and

Introduction 3

instead succumbed from the consequences of neglect by the staff of the hospital to which he was taken. The most recent (2023) book on the topic, Mark Dawidziak's *A Mystery of Mysteries: The Death and Life of Edgar Allan Poe*, is stylishly written, but as the title implies, the publication does not focus solely on the poet's demise. Yet the author ultimately advocates a *theory* of tubercular meningitis as Poe's cause of death. As I discuss in this work, some of these ideas have a degree of plausibility, but to begin with a hypothesis and then go in search of facts to support it does not make for sound journalism, or a persuasive argument.

In time, my enthusiasm for Poe became such that I volunteered as a docent and tour guide at the Edgar Allan Poe House in Baltimore, Maryland. Despite its intimidating location, the little structure at 203 North Amity Street has become a literary shrine and is visited each year by thousands of Poe devotees and students of American literature from around the world. After only a short time there, I realized that many coming to the house had the same hunger for information on the poet's death. Indeed, there were a marked number coming to the house only to ask the question, "How did Poe die?" In reply, I sometimes quipped, "Badly." Some of these literary pilgrims had theories of their own and wanted them validated; others simply wanted to get an official answer, but I grew increasingly uncomfortable with my ability to provide a definitive explanation. So, in the spring of 2019, I began this book project, *hoping* to offer an objective examination of the poet's shadowy demise: if I could not nail down the facts, once and for all, I would at least gather as many as I could, and quell some of the hunger pangs.

* * *

Anyone attempting to offer a solution to the riddle of Edgar Allan Poe's death must recognize it as two separate and distinct mysteries: How did he come to be discovered at a tavern in East Baltimore, and what illness or condition actually brought him down? While a malady such as encephalitis, pneumonia, or delirium tremens may have killed him, these medical conditions lend little insight into what occurred before his discovery. And when some have espoused "cooping" (the practice of kidnapping and compelled voting) to be the cause of death, it is difficult to see how one can die directly from being forced to participate in the political process.[1] Of course, it can be argued which of the two questions is the more important, but a straightforward discussion of the cause has been made difficult and needlessly ambiguous by admirers of Poe who refused to consider that the genius also had human weaknesses.[2] These devotees, who have been blind to his flaws and failings, have done as much to abuse the truth of his life, and death, as those in a second group who

4 *Introduction*

would have everyone believe that he was nothing but an unprincipled inebriate. Of these two opposing camps, one of Poe's contemporaries, Thomas Dunn English, said: "One . . . is made up of those who like to expose the darkest part of personal history to public view; the other of the injudicious admirers of the dead poet who try to prove that he was a saint, and think they aid their object by abusing every one with whom he ever had a quarrel."[3] By rejecting his vulnerabilities, these well-meaning supporters have muddied the story of Poe's passing, and in doing so opened the door to an embarrassment of maladies, afflictions, and preposterous ideas on its cause. To illustrate this ever-growing field of speculative study, I have appended to this work a register of more than forty formally proposed theories on his death, a list that is certain to be obsolete in the not-too-distant future, if not already.

It should be stated that at the time of Poe's death, there were no arguments, public or private, as to its cause. At the hospital in which he died, there seems to have been no deliberation among those who had cared for him. This is evident in the letter sent to his aunt, Maria Clemm, a little over a month after his passing by the facility's administrator, Dr. John J. Moran, in which he stated, "Presuming you are already aware of the malady of which Mr. Poe died" (appendix D), clearly indicating an accepted cause—no mystery. Those who would have raised any question, especially those who were acquainted with his reputation, were satisfied by prevalent rumors of a drunken debauch. Indeed, all those who rendered aid to Poe, at the tavern and the hospital—all eyewitnesses to his condition—remarked about his apparent intoxication. Even those who had no personal knowledge of the circumstances, such as his mentor and patron, John Kennedy, were convinced at the time that Poe's death resulted from an alcoholic binge. It is true that some would later reverse their original statements in an effort to decontaminate the poet's name, while others would exaggerate his condition to promote a personal cause or enmity. But the *mystery* of Poe's death would not be generated until years after its occurrence, and mostly by those seeking to rescue his reputation.

When I began this project, I resolved to let the research and the retrieved facts guide my course. Having read most of the known accounts of his death, I had a fair grasp of what *could* have caused it but was not a subscriber to any particular theory. However, after evaluating the entirety of available evidence and testimony, it became increasingly difficult for me to accept that alcohol played no role in the death of Edgar Allan Poe. Support for this is irresistible and can be found in the many demonstrations of his growing instability and cumulative alcoholic episodes as his life drew to its close. Although there are fewer contemporaneous descriptions of his drinking during his early years,[4] there seems to have been a discernible change in Poe around the time of his wife's symptomatic confirmation of tuberculosis in 1842, after which the

Introduction 5

record provides us with increasing examples of reckless intemperance. Yet, for the greater part of his life, he was apparently not a habitual drunkard. There are testimonials from those who knew him and were intimate with his habits that would seem to confirm this.

Clouding the picture further is the tradition, seemingly disseminated by Poe himself, that he was constitutionally unsuited to liquor and incapable of drinking any more than a single glass at a time.[5] After his death, biographers, and even some who knew him during life, would perpetuate this explanation of Poe's intolerance to alcohol, some going as far to say that he exhibited an allergic (or pathologic) reaction to it.[6] However, in a January 1848 letter to his admirer, George W. Eveleth, Poe sabotages the myth; when attributing his "irregularities" to the fluctuating health of his wife he wrote, "I am constitutionally sensitive—nervous in a very unusual degree. I became insane, with long intervals of horrible sanity.[7] During these fits of absolute unconsciousness I drank, God only knows how often or how much." Other than well-meaning followers wanting to defend the poet's reputation, I discovered no empirical evidence of Poe's elevated sensitivity to alcohol; the support for it being largely tradition and hearsay.

Furthermore, there is much to indicate that Edgar Poe's capacity for drink became such that he ultimately descended into a state of dependency. Some have argued that, in obedience to his pledge made to a temperance organization, he abstained from all drinking during the final three or four weeks in Richmond, but there is evidence, even photographic, that this may not have been the case.[8] Although Poe could have avoided *binging* during that final month in Virginia, complete abstinence for an individual who had developed an addiction could only have occurred involuntarily, with the results being the equally unwanted experience of delirium tremens, a consequence of alcohol withdrawal. Symptoms of this nightmarish condition include confusion, elevated heart rate, fever, profuse sweating, and restlessness; with the more progressed cases augmented by visual (and auditory) hallucinations, uncontrolled vocal outbursts, and violent, bodily tremors.[9]

In his final months, it appears that Edgar Poe experienced more than one episode of delirium tremens, perhaps the first occurring after landing in Philadelphia on his way to Richmond. There *he* described a state of panic and paranoia in which he was being pursued by assassins, and horrific hallucinations of ghostly figures, torture, and dismemberment, with a resulting period of prostration consuming several more days. A second, and perhaps even a third attack, is reported to have taken place while he was in Richmond during which he was informed by his attending physician that another such occurrence would be fatal.[10] And it is also possible that Poe was suffering these attacks before he started for Virginia.[11] It must be understood that only those who have acquired a chemical dependence on alcohol suffer these attacks caused by its deprivation, and to predicate delirium tremens as the cause of Poe's death is to accept that he ultimately developed such an addiction.

The symptoms that he exhibited after his admittance to the hospital in Baltimore, as described by the physician of record, John J. Moran (before he thought to deny them), are classic manifestations of the disorder.[12] Yet they are also consistent, in whole or part, with several other conditions that could have caused his death. Encephalitis is an inflammation of brain tissue usually the result of a viral, or bacterial infection and those suffering can demonstrate symptoms that include fever, confusion, seizures (or tremors, if you like), and loss of consciousness. Moran would eventually claim that he consulted with Washington University Professor John C. S. Monkur, who, after examining Poe, articulated a diagnosis of encephalitis.[13] Whether Moran's story is true or not, the short, seven-day incubation period of the illness confers to it a degree of plausibility. Malaria is another potentially fatal illness that is not easily dismissed here. Although often a chronic condition, a relapse or an attack can appear without warning. The flu-like symptoms include fever, perspiration, irregular breathing and heartrate, and exhaustion. During his time in the US Army, Poe was stationed at Fort Moultrie in South Carolina where he could have contracted the disease.[14] And a misdiagnosis during his time would not have been uncommon, especially in northern climes where the sickness is not normally anticipated. If Poe was critical, or had an underlying condition (or conditions), when brought to the hospital, an opportunistic infection such as pneumonia could have actually been the coup de grace, and the inability of infected lungs to metabolize oxygen could have caused a cardiopulmonary collapse. Some of his symptoms, as given by Moran, are descriptive of the illness: labored breathing, fever, perspiration, shaking (tremors), and confusion or a change in mental awareness.

Obviously, Poe was not suffering all of these illnesses at the time of his death, but there is a very real possibility that he had experienced a comorbidity of more than one condition: the trauma of delirium tremens to someone afflicted with heart disease certainly could be enough to end someone's life. Or, if neglected and given less than adequate attention (by the hospital staff) while struggling with a respiratory infection, there can be little wonder that someone so plighted did not survive.

Unfortunately, a death certificate or hospital case-record that establishes the cause of his death has never been found. When writing to Poe's aunt in the weeks following his death, Moran seems to have been transcribing from a case-record (appendix D). During this time in Baltimore City when a patient died, it was the practice to send the hospital record, or a copy, to the Board of Health that compiled and categorized all fatalities within interment reports.

Introduction 7

This data was subsequently presented to the city council, after which the individual reports were discarded. With regard to a death certificate for Poe, exhaustive searches have been conducted without success; and as the state and local governments were not then requiring them, it appears unlikely that such a document was ever produced for Poe, leaving the door open for those who would come later with exculpatory explanations.

* * *

If the cause of Edgar Allan Poe's death can be established, a second group of questions then bid to be answered: Was the condition in which he was found self-induced or thrust upon him by others? How did he come to be at Gunners' Hall in East Baltimore? What transpired in the hours, or days, preceding his discovery there? Here we find no shortage of theories either. One of the first to be circulated, that Poe's death was the result of a drunken debauch, was endorsed by his patron and mentor, John Pendleton Kennedy, who wrote in his diary a couple days following it, "He fell in with some companion here who seduced him to the bottle. . . . The consequence was fever, delirium, and madness, and in a few days a termination of his sad career in the hospital."[15] It is not known how Kennedy came by his information or if he was simply perpetuating an existing rumor but this explanation, of which there is no reliable evidence, nevertheless would become the most widely accepted in the immediate aftermath.

Many years after his death, stories would be told of an intoxicated Poe wandering around north of the city's business district in the area of Lexington Market. The son of Nathan Brooks, a literary colleague, would maintain that while his father was away, the poet called at their home nearby.[16] Others would claim to have seen him passed out inside the market. Still another of these unsubstantiated accounts, that would later become a Poe family tradition, described an encounter by one of Edgar Poe's cousins at the Baltimore Museum (at the corner of Calvert and Baltimore Streets) where the author of "The Raven" was seen sleeping beneath its staircase—the relative not stopping to help.[17]

One of those Baltimoreans whom Poe knew and who probably *would* have provided him with assistance, or perhaps just a dry place to sleep, lived only steps away from where he was eventually found. Dr. Joseph Evans Snodgrass had been a literary colleague and at the time was apparently still on friendly terms with the poet. It has been suggested that Poe was attempting to reach Snodgrass's house but got no closer than the tavern. Indeed, the doctor would later claim that Poe asked for him by name when finally recognized; but he (Poe) could have just ended up in that neighborhood after missing his train

8 *Introduction*

to Philadelphia. From Poe's surviving correspondence it has been presumed that his purpose in Baltimore was only to make a travel connection on his way north where he planned to fulfill an agreement to edit a collection of poems before ultimately returning to Richmond with his aunt.[18] The railroad terminal in Baltimore, for passengers heading to the northeast, was only a few blocks from the Lombard Street inn where he was discovered. If the train was at capacity, or he was without the fare to continue his trip, Poe may have lingered in the area hoping to find someone who would help him to get aboard a later departure, as he had done in Philadelphia three months earlier; in this Snodgrass also fits the bill.

In yet another story, Poe succeeded in leaving Baltimore by train but was afterward returned to the city in a state of delirium and left to wander in the vicinity of the station. This tale, emerging many years after his death, appears to have been generated by a publicity-seeking train conductor claiming to have assisted Poe personally. However, I discovered that although this man had in fact worked as a train attendant, it was not for the line Poe would have used and it appears he was not working for any railroad at the time of the poet's death.[19]

The most widely believed hypothesis on Poe's presence at the tavern is one in which he was kidnapped by political partisans, stupefied with a continuous supply of alcohol, and then made to perform as a repeat voter in the congressional elections taking place on the day he was discovered. The practice, which was well established by the election of 1849, was dubbed "cooping" for the coop-like settings in which the victims were imprisoned: firehouse backrooms, basements, backyards, etc. That Poe was found at a polling place (public houses then served such functions) in a semiconscious or stupefied condition, and wearing someone else's clothing, would seem to conform with the idea almost perfectly. But the theory, that his condition resulted from such abuse, again was not put forth immediately: it would not be until ten years after Poe's death that a Richmond acquaintance would incorporate the idea as part of his public lectures on the poet.[20] I should also confess that this explanation, above all the others, is the one I wanted to believe; like many I thought the circumstances too great for coincidence. Yet after almost three years of in-depth study, I found no credible eyewitnesses or trustworthy testimony to give the theory adequate support. However, the idea has become so prevalent that a separate chapter is provided for its analysis.

In the end I found no satisfactory account of Poe's movements or whereabouts in Baltimore City before his discovery there on October 3, 1849. How he came to be at the tavern at the Fourth Ward Hotel that rainy afternoon, and for what purpose, has several intriguing and credible explanations as shown,

Introduction 9

but ultimately none that can be substantiated. That second part of the mystery, for now, appears to be safe.

* * *

This book consists of nine chapters, beginning with a *brief* look at Edgar Allan Poe's life that concentrates on the people, places, and events that would come to play a significant role in those closing weeks. This biographical study may appear intrusive and extraneous to the work's main topic, but an explanation of his circumstances, as well as the individuals involved, is essential in providing context to the poet's final days. The examination of his death begins with chapter 2 and his departure from New York in late June 1849. Poe's health and habits during this trip not only demonstrate that his final disappearance in Baltimore was part of an existing pattern, but also that his experiences almost certainly hastened his demise. Of Poe's activities immediately following his arrival in Baltimore, little or nothing is known, and chapter 3 explores his *possible* movements around the city, and the encounters claimed by others. This is followed by a description in chapter 4 of his discovery and retrieval at the tavern, and continues with a discussion of the cooping theory in chapter 5.

Chapter 6 describes the hospital in which the poet died, its troubled history, and the many myths associated with Poe's brief admittance there. No other person has done more to mislead and confound Poe's biographers than the hospital's administrator, Dr. John Moran. It is widely accepted that Moran fabricated most, or all, of what he related about Poe's final moments.[21] Yet he remains such an important figure in the poet's death that an entire chapter 7 was needed to explain Moran and his actions. That some of his claims were actually found to be true is reported here for the first time.

In chapter 8, some of the plausible causes and popular theories of Poe's death are explored. And finally, chapter 9 serves as an epilogue to chronicle the aftermath of the poet's passing. In particular, the myths and traditions associated with his burial, the cemetery, and the creation of his monument in Baltimore are examined here. The general text is then followed by four appendices that include: a comprehensive listing of the many theories of Poe's death (appendix A); a timeline of what is known of his final days (appendix B); a directory of the relevant individuals mentioned (appendix C); and a transcription of Moran's letter to Maria Clemm (appendix D). It is my hope that in this arrangement, this book will adequately address the subject as well as provide a useful reference for those hungering for answers.

* * *

10   *Introduction*

In closing, I believe a few disclaimers with regard to this work would not be out of place. First, let me say that I am no doctor, as will be crystal clear to those readers who are. Any medical observations (or descriptions) offered herewith are not the result of a formal study of medicine but rather are from a layman's eye and provided for the purposes of explanation—often for the benefit of *my* understanding.

In addition to exploring the possible causes of Poe's death, it was another purpose of this work to address the myths and traditions that have become ensconced in his biography or put forth in other scholarly accounts. As a consequence of this game of whack-a-mole, some given details may be digressive or disconnected from the immediate text. In some instances, detours of considerable length were necessary in order to expose longstanding legends. For this and any other inconsistencies to the narrative flow, I offer my sincere apology.

As with any biographical study, some observations are inevitable; however, I have tried (my best) to consign them to the introduction and notes, where they belong. Even though I am currently serving as president of the Edgar Allan Poe Society of Baltimore and relied heavily on its resources for the creation of this work, it must be clear that any views or opinions offered here are mine alone, and not to be construed as those of the association, or any of its members. With regard to the endnotes that comprise a substantial part of this work, and where much of the newly discovered information is authenticated, it is hoped that readers will methodically consult the cited sources and details contained therein to gain a fuller understanding of the given narrative—I have always found the use of a second bookmark the easiest way to manage this.

Naturally, what Edgar Allan Poe was made to endure during his life could have shaped the things he wrote, but to explain his compositions, or his creativity, as the product of his mental or physical health is not the object of this study. I made no attempt here to correlate the circumstances of his death with his work or to interpret how his demise, now clouded in so much mystery, could have facilitated his posthumous fame as a writer. And I dared no analysis of what the preoccupation with his death may say about our culture—these discussions must be left to the better equipped. This work explores only the possible cause, or causes, of his death and in that effort focuses on a single aspect, and brief interval, of the poet's life. Furthermore, although we may find fascination in the mysterious circumstances of Poe's passing, it must be understood that how he died is certainly not as important as how he lived, or more accurately, how he applied his all-too-short life—we notice his death now only because he was great while alive.

Introduction 11

Finally, I want to say that as disconcerting as some may find this account to be, it is not to be interpreted in any measure as a depreciation of the beautiful lyrics and brilliant tales Poe produced while he lived. Indeed, I would not have given so much of my existence to such an endeavor but for a profound appreciation of Edgar Allan Poe's genius, and the importance of his journey:

By a route obscure and lonely,
Haunted by ill angels only,
Where an Eidolon, named Night,
On a black throne reigns upright,
[reaching] these lands but newly
From an ultimate dim Thule—
From a wild weird clime that lieth, sublime,
Out of Space—Out of Time[22]

Chapter One

Peaks and Pits, and Pendulum Swings

Sometime during the early days of autumn in 1849, Edgar Allan Poe disappeared into the lawless, overcrowded city of Baltimore, Maryland, a place that had grown even more dangerous since he had moved away a decade and half earlier.[1] For an undetermined amount of time he would not be seen or heard by anyone that he knew, only to be discovered[2] by chance on a rainy afternoon, semiconscious and muttering to himself at a tavern on East Lombard Street—a scenario made only the more improbable by the fact that he had become by then one of the more famous men in America. Of course, before the widespread availability of photography, he would have gone unrecognized to most, but Poe had resided in Baltimore for more than five years during different periods of his life and since his departure he regularly passed through the town when traveling in the eastern United States. The city was known to him, and he would have been familiar to many in the city, especially to those he visited and to others that sought his acquaintance. Still, he managed to avoid anyone that could have helped him, perhaps for a number of days, and after being transported to a nearby hospital, died there among strangers on October 7.

To understand how a man celebrated during his time for crafting some of the most brilliant and beautiful things written in the English language could have ended up in such pitiful surroundings, a brief account of his life concentrating on his health and habits, as well as the people, places, and events that would come to play a significant role in those closing weeks, should succeed in providing some context. To demonstrate that Poe's disappearance in Baltimore was not an isolated occurrence, it will be necessary to also discuss aspects of his private life and practices, as well as these can be determined.

Like the title of one of his tales,[3] Edgar Poe's is a story of peaks and pits, and pendulum swings—a life of privilege and abject poverty, a tale of academic accolades and public humiliation, and a saga of forbidding anonymity that would ultimately burst into international fame—the cumulative effect of which could not help but alter his spirit, character, and ability to cope with the world.

Edgar Poe was the second of three children born to parents who were engaged in what passed for show business in early nineteenth-century America: dramatic, comic, and musical theater. Poe's parents were itinerant players in various acting companies who traveled between cities of the infant republic as theatrical seasons and employment opportunities dictated. His English-born mother, Elizabeth "Eliza" Arnold, was the child of married London actors and she seems to have been groomed for the stage. Soon after her family's relocation to Boston, Massachusetts in 1796,[4] she made her theatrical debut playing (convincingly) the comedic role of Biddy Bellair, a character much older than her nine years—precocity, it seems, was a family trait. Given a delightful singing voice and the ability to play both male and female characters, Eliza quickly became one of the darlings of the fledgling American theater. At the age of fourteen she married fellow actor, Charles Hopkins, who would make her a widow only three years later when it is believed he succumbed to yellow fever while the couple was working in Washington, DC.[5]

As is the case with Poe's mother, little is certain of Edgar's American father, David Poe Jr., before being chronicled in theatrical records. He was born in Baltimore in 1784, three years before Eliza, to David Poe Sr. and Elizabeth Cairnes, both of whom were Irish immigrants who had settled in that city. Although later described as temperamental and highly strung,[6] David showed intelligence and was sent to law school by his father; but exhibiting the same rebelliousness that his son would also show in later years, David Jr. rejected the study of law in favor of a career in the theater, a choice that brought disapproval and expulsion from his family.[7] Yet

Figure 1.1. As a traveling theater performer, Elizabeth "Eliza" Poe maintained a tumultuous if not instable lifestyle. The influence of her profession on the infant Poe has been widely discussed. *Courtesy of the Enoch Pratt Free Library, Special Collections*

he was committed to the profession and seemed to have worked hard at it. In addition, he was handsome and had a commanding voice; theater managers almost immediately cast him in leading parts, often as Eliza's lover or husband. Therefore, it probably came as little surprise that after only a short five months following the death of Charles Hopkins, David Poe married the young widow in April 1806.[8] The newlyweds finished the season in Richmond and during the ensuing summer traveled north to appear with theatrical companies in Philadelphia and New York, finally settling in Boston where they were to largely remain for the next three years.

While Elizabeth was a talented and much-loved performer, David, apparently without any formal training, was inconsistent and often tentative. According to biographer Geddeth Smith, "for every good theatrical notice, there seemed to be two bad ones."[9] Still, during their first season together at the Federal Street Theater, they became an important part of the company there and were inseparable even when not cast in the same productions. By the fall, the couple was expecting their first child and through most of January and February 1807, Eliza was not mentioned in theatrical notices while she took time to give birth; Edgar's older brother, William "Henry" Leonard Poe, was born on January 30, 1807.

The life of itinerant actors in America at that time was a precarious one indeed. Even those of an ensemble company who were relied upon could find their assignments unexpectedly curtailed or suspended altogether by the lack of public favor or because of the closure of a theater due to an outbreak of contagious disease. The pressures of life with a newborn could have easily exacerbated the difficulties the couple faced in pursuing such an unpredictable career. Perhaps there is evidence of such pressure in David Poe's reaction to a theater critic who belittled one of Eliza's performances soon after giving birth. When she returned to the stage to play the role of a young boy, a critic for the monthly theatrical journal, *Polyanthos*, pointed out

Figure 1.2. Edgar Allan Poe's mother, Eliza, gave many performances in Baltimore at the New Theater on Holliday Street. It was replaced by this larger structure in 1813 which stood only a few blocks from the Lombard Street tavern where he was found. *Author (print from author's collection)*

16 *Chapter One*

the inadequacies of her costume to hide feminine contours by calling her character a hermaphrodite. In response to this remark, David stormed to the writer's residence.[10] As biographer, Arthur Hobson Quinn, points out, he then became the second of three generations of Poes who would attempt "to answer the criticisms of objectionable editors by force."[11] The actors had of course been subjected to unfavorable reviews before this, but David's ill-conceived reaction seems to suggest an increased sensitivity or level of anxiety.

How long little Henry, as he would later be known, remained with his parents is unclear. Family tradition holds that during their summer vacation following Edgar's birth two years later, the couple traveled down to Baltimore where the infant (Edgar) was placed with his grandparents for several months,[12] but very possibly it may have been during this visit that the older boy was left in their care instead. If indeed David's parents looked after either child for any length of time, it would indicate that their position toward their son had softened.

BIRTH

In any event, David and Eliza returned to Boston for the theater's opening in September and remained there, visiting the South only during the summer months for much needed off-season employment. Eliza was then "in the zenith of her powers,"[13] but David continued to struggle on stage even though he still garnered important roles. His difficulties did not pass unnoticed, and critical, sometimes abusive, reviews of his performances became more frequent. The few positive reviews he received were qualified with comments on his apparent nervousness, rushed delivery of his lines, and instances of mispronunciation. Added to David's ineptness was his growing unreliability perhaps caused by, or resulting in, increased drinking.[14] There were also the increased demands stemming from his wife's subsequent pregnancy—the Poe's second child, Edgar, was born on January 19, 1809, in a house near the Federal Street theater.[15]

Eliza's missed acting assignments consequent to her maternity leave apparently exacerbated the family's dire financial situation.[16] In the days immediately following the poet's birth, David traveled south to seek assistance from at least one relative. From a later account of this trip, we are given another view of David Poe's temperament and probable drinking. Cousin George Poe Jr. reported to William Clemm Jr. that the actor initially showed up at his house at Stockerton, Pennsylvania, but did not make any requests, instead asking for a later meeting to discuss his purpose. According to George, David

Poe failed to show at the appointed time but days after sent him an "impertinent" note. An excerpt of this communiqué reads as follows:

> Sir, You promised me on your honor to meet me at the Mansion house on the 23d—I promise you on my word of honor that if you will lend me 30, 20, 15 or even 10$ I will remit it to you immediately on my arrival in Baltimore. Be assured I will keep my promise at least as well as you did yours and that nothing but extreem [sic] distress would have forc'd me to make this application.[17]

Quinn has observed that the note seems to describe traits of the father that could have been transmitted to his son: instability and a propensity for the bottle, as well as appeals for money that were coupled with ultimatums. But as the biographer also points out, it would be unwise "reading too much into one letter," which survives only through a transcription by its angered recipient.[18]

It is evident that David had, by this time, acquired a reputation for drinking as an abusive lampoon of him in the theatrical journal, *Rambler's Magazine*, shows. Under the title, "Sur un Poe de Chambre," French doggerel identifies David Poe's relatives as vessels or quantities of alcohol.[19] That fall, on October 18, 1809, David made his last recorded stage appearance while then engaged at the Park Theatre in New York. When he was advertised to appear in a play scheduled two days later, it was announced at the last minute that due to his indisposition, the production had been cancelled. The word "indisposition" was often used in theatrical notices at the time to cover intoxication,[20] but was also a polite way to explain illness. Although his withdrawal from the profession could have been expedited by the unceasingly cruel critical notices,[21] there is no evidence that actually confirms David Poe immediately left his wife and family.[22] It has been suggested that he was suffering from tuberculosis and remained with Eliza until succumbing during her final engagement in Norfolk, Virginia, two

Figure 1.3. Along with her older brother Edgar, Rosalie Poe was with her mother in Richmond, Virginia, at the time of her death. Afterward she was raised by the family of Mr. and Mrs. William Mackenzie. *Edgar Allan Poe Museum, Richmond, VA*

18   *Chapter One*

years later.[23] However, their separation, well before July 2, 1810, would seem to be confirmed by an advertisement for her theater benefit that evening in New York, explaining the event "for the purpose of extricating herself from *embarrassments* occasioned by having two small children to support out of the scanty pittance of her weekly wages,"[24] the statement indicating that she was then the sole provider for the family without any qualification of being widowed.

In later years, Edgar Poe would state that his father died shortly after his mother, but the rationale for this claim was perhaps more for the benefit of his younger sister's reputation. There has been some speculation as to the actual date of Rosalie's birth, although the date of December 20, 1810, is said to have been recorded in the Mackenzie family bible. This would *seem* to eliminate David Poe as her father if he had left the family during the fall of 1809, or even during the ensuing winter. Certainly John Allan, Poe's foster-father, had accepted this state of affairs as a letter he later wrote to Poe's brother, Henry, demonstrates:

> I must end[,] and this with a devout wish that God may yet bless him [Edgar] & you & that Success may crown all your endeavors & between you [bothers] your poor Sister Rosalie may not suffer. At least She is half your Sister & God forbid my dear Henry that We should visit upon the living the Errors & frailties of the dead.[25]

The ordeal of a third birth (and requisite nursing) to a woman who was perhaps experiencing the symptoms of late-stage tuberculosis would have had a disastrous effect on Eliza's stamina, and probably her appearance as well. As an appeal for her theater benefit appearing in the *Norfolk Herald* of July 26, 1811, makes clear, her once youthful form had changed:

> She was said to be one of the handsomest women in America; she was certainly the handsomest I had ever seen. She never came on the stage but a general murmur ran through the house, What an enchanting creature!
>
> But now, "the scene is changed,"—Misfortunes have pressed heavy on her. Left alone, the only support of herself and several young children—Friendless and unprotected she no longer commands the admiration she formerly did . . . though grief may have stolen a few of the roses from her cheeks, still she retains the same sweetness of expression and symmetry of form and feature.[26]

Somehow Eliza continued to perform during most of the final year of her life, the last record of her appearance on stage being on October 11, 1811.[27] If she was indeed suffering from consumption, the spontaneous and persistent coughing would have made public performances impossible. Finally on December 8, 1811, Elizabeth Poe died at Richmond, in a rented room to which she had been confined. Some have recorded that her death resulted from pneumonia;[28] however, surviving communications, as well as a newspaper notice for one of her theater benefits, indicate that she had been suffering from a persistent, identifiable illness.[29]

Although much has been written about the potential influence of his mother and her profession on Poe, it is unlikely that any such impressions would be more than subliminal on a toddler not yet three years old.[30] At that age, it would have been unusual for a child to retain any conscious memory even of the stormy surroundings to which he was exposed. In Poe's case, such circumstances would have included frequent uprooting, histrionic personalities, and a changing cast of caregivers. Additionally, at that time the acting profession was widely viewed, especially among many "respectable citizens," as a disreputable one—the era of the Jenny Linds, Lillie Langtrys, and Booth family was still decades away—and it carried a social stigma that even the offspring of those so engaged would find difficult to escape, if not embrace.[31]

FOSTER PARENTS

With their mother's death, and the father no longer a member of the family, Edgar and his siblings became orphans. He and his younger sister were taken in by separate Richmond families. Henry ended up in the care of his paternal grandparents in Baltimore, but it is not certain when this occurred. While Rosalie was claimed by William and Jane Mackenzie, Edgar Poe was taken into the home of John and Frances Allan; both families, being regular theatergoers, would have been apprised of the orphans' plight.[32] That the Virginians would have assumed the children's maintenance without at least informing their relatives in Baltimore seems improbable. Based on Edgar Poe's mention of a letter in the possession of his grandparents' family, it is suggested that Poe's relatives had been consulted. Poe claimed the letter contained John Allan's written promise of "adoption" and a "liberal education" in order to "induce" their permission of his care.[33]

It has been commonly assumed that John Allan was a wealthy man at the time, but as a partner in the mercantile of Ellis and Allan, an import/export firm of which tobacco was the chief commodity, his circumstances then could only be described as comfortable.[34] Unfortunately his wife, Frances, seems to have been perpetually uncomfortable or "never clear of complaint," as John Allan would later confide. She suffered from chronic illnesses and was purported to be temperamental and often irritable.[35] Despite her difficulties, whether based in neurosis or a physical malady, Frances' condition did not

20   *Chapter One*

prevent her from extending shelter to Poe as a two-year-old child. Indeed, such demonstrations of charity were quite fashionable, especially in the South, and Frances Allan was nothing if not fashion-minded. But it quickly became apparent that little Edgar would be more than a social ornament to the childless couple. The record of John Allan's expenditures undertaken for his ward provides ample proof that "he conceived a pride and a tenderness for the little lad whom he came to regard as his son."[36] It should also be pointed out that although the Allans, as a married couple, were childless at the time of Poe's "adoption," John Allan had already fathered a son through a prior extramarital liaison.[37] It is believed that Frances subsequently became aware of the affair (and the consequence), and may have eventually communicated this knowledge to her godson.[38]

After only a few weeks in the custody of his new family, Poe was baptized in the Episcopal faith as "Edgar Allan Poe."[39] With his dark, curly hair and enormous eyes, he was an adorable child who exhibited a cleverness that his godparents loved to show off to friends and family. They provided him with an exceptional education that included private academies in Richmond and schools in England while the family was living abroad—in the spring of 1815, John Allan and his family sailed to England and remained there for five years while John operated a branch office of his business there.[40] Surviving records suggest that little was spared in the toddler's upbringing, and there is adequate testimony to indicate that he was even spoiled by the Allans. When later asked about his young pupil, Poe's London schoolmaster, Reverend John Bransby, would assert, "Edgar Allan [as he was then known] was a quick and clever boy and would have been a very good boy if he had not been spoilt by his parents . . . the Allans allowed him an extravagant amount of pocket-money, which enabled him to get into all manner of mischief."[41] Quinn has explained the consequences of such inconsistent discipline for Poe by saying, "If there were varying degrees of affection shown him by John Allan and his foster-mother, this difference would have had its influence upon a sensitive child."[42] There can be no question that Frances was devoted to Edgar, and he to her, but how much of his personality (and behavior) was shaped by her emotional volatility will probably never be known.

In 1820, the Allans returned to Richmond and to a period of forced austerity. John's overseas branch of the business had ultimately been unsuccessful, and home operations had suffered as well. As a result, accommodations with creditors became necessary in order to keep the concern of Ellis and Allan afloat. Yet Poe's guardian still found money for the boy's schooling which would seem to demonstrate not only John Allan's continued regard for his ward but also his appreciation for higher education in general. Poe was enrolled in Joseph H. Clarke's preparatory academy where he excelled and impressed his classmates with his advanced scholarship, but according to Colonel (CSA) John T. L. Preston,[43] who recalled his time with Poe there many years later, the poet was apparently not fully accepted by his aristocratic comrades at the school:

> Of Edgar Poe it was known that his parents had been players, and that he was dependent upon the bounty that is bestowed upon an adopted son. All this had the effect of making the boys [at the school] decline his leadership and on looking back on it since, I fancy it gave him a fierceness he would otherwise not have had.[44]

How his classmates learned of his lineage and subsequent guardianship is not known but biographer, John Ingram, has stated that by that time Poe had resumed the use of his own surname, a choice that suggests willfulness, if not feelings of independence.[45]

It is not known precisely when or why Poe's relationship with his fosterfather began to decay but it seems to have been more than just the natural rebelliousness of adolescence. When writing to Poe's older brother in the fall of 1824, perhaps looking for an explanation or even advice on how to repair relations, John Allan seemed to be genuinely disturbed by the change.[46] He also indicated that the bitterness between them had been ongoing for some time. Allan was obviously one of those who "kept score" and he viewed the fifteen-year-old's hostility in terms of ingratitude, while his foster son, with a sensitive nature and unbroken spirit, regarded every constraint from his guardian as an insult. One can imagine vicious exchanges between the two, with Allan reminding his charge that he was nothing more than the offspring of "gypsies," and Poe retaliating with Allan's "whoremongering" and *his* "offspring."

Into this stormy household came an enormous financial windfall which would change the lives of all

Figure 1.4. As a sensitive adolescent, Poe found a kindred spirit in Jane Stith Stanard, the mother of his classmate. With her tragic early death in 1824, Poe grieved deeply and was said to frequent her grave at Shockoe Hill Cemetery in Richmond. He would later write the poem, "To Helen," in her memory. *Author (author photograph)*

22 *Chapter One*

concerned. Upon his death in March 1825, William Galt Sr. left the bulk of his estate to John Allan, his nephew, which immediately made him one of the wealthiest men in Virginia.[47] This of course gave Allan the means to continue Poe's educational support, something he chose to do in spite of the teenager biting his master's hand, seemingly at every turn. Nevertheless, the responsibilities and amount of time needed to manage his new fortune, with its financial holdings, three landed estates, and myriad residential and commercial properties in Richmond (Galt had also been one of the city's noteworthy landlords), undoubtedly consumed much of Allan's attention, and it could only have worked to exacerbate the deteriorating relationship between him and his ward. How Edgar viewed this change in the family's fortune is not directly recorded. In view of the fact that Allan had still made arrangements for Poe's enrollment at the new university in Charlottesville, the boy may have assumed that he would receive a trickledown inheritance of his own. But, as will be discussed, Poe seemed to have an inability to appreciate the depth of animosity that his words could cause in others, and his standing in the Allan household at this time was anything but assured.

Among Allan's first purchases with his new riches was a substantial brick mansion at Main and Fifth Streets, then a fashionable part of Richmond. Undoubtedly, this would have been an exciting time for the family as they spent the summer relocating to, and outfitting, their new home. For Poe, it would have been an especially memorable time. Not only was he being tutored in preparation for the university, but he also began his first serious romance with a fifteen-year-old neighbor, Sarah Elmira Royster.[48] In short order, the two secretly pledged themselves to marry but, according to "Elmira," her father strongly objected to their plan and succeeded in sabotaging the affair after Poe left for college. The two would try again, many years later.

UNIVERSITY OF VIRGINIA

On February 14, 1826, Edgar Allan Poe matriculated at the newly created University of Virginia at Charlottesville. Poe's achievements at the college are a matter of record, and his time there has been carefully examined, but of concern to this study are the first accounts we have of his habits. Not that he would have been receptive to any advice coming from John Allan, someone who had no college experiences of his own, it was probably without much guidance that the seventeen-year-old was "thrown suddenly, a mere boy, into the free-and-easy set of University students over whom, at the time, no restraints had been set."[49] Unlike the boarding school in England, Thomas Jefferson's experimental university of student self-government provided little supervision of the students. Among his fellow young aristocrats, Poe was exposed to practices and behaviors to which his familiarity would have been expected. Adding to his difficulties there were costly personal expenses for which no consideration was made by Allan, either through ignorance or deliberate design.[50] Poe would claim that he resorted to gambling only as a device to meet these unforeseen obligations—gambling, and in particular card-playing among the students, on and off school property, became an immediate and serious problem for the university's administration such as it was.[51] However, his frolics with cards produced debts that far exceeded the primary cause; by one estimate the amount was $2,500, which would have been extraordinary at the time.[52] When later trying to soften John Allan (for another cause), Poe would confess his responsibility in the fiasco: "I have no excuse to offer for my [con]duct except the common one of youth[fulnes]s."[53]

It is also during his time at university that we have the first mention of his experiences with alcohol. Whether the result of peer pressure or lack of supervision, there is testimony to *suggest* that the seventeen-year-old engaged in some amount of social drinking while at Charlottesville. According to his classmate, Thomas Goode Tucker,

> His passion for strong drink was of a most marked and peculiar character. He would always seize the tempting glass, generally unmixed with either sugar or water—in fact, perfectly straight—and without the least apparent pleasure swallow the contents, never pausing until the last drop had passed his lips.[54]

And there is also this observation from another of his college companions, Dr. Miles George:

> To calm & quiet the excessive nervous excitability under which he labored, he would too often put himself under the influence of that "Invisible Spirit of Wine."[55]

It is important to recognize that these reports of Poe's drinking by his classmates at the university were offered only after many years had passed, and by which time he had gained celebrity (and reputation), giving the aged storytellers incentive to embellish, and perhaps even invent, their recollections. Of course, even if the accounts are accurate, these would not have described Poe's first acquaintance with liquor. Although he was presumably not of drinking age during his time with the Allans, Poe would have certainly been a witness to frequent demonstrations of Southern conviviality, especially when included at social events organized by them. That John Allan himself was no stranger to the bottle is implied not only by Poe's calculated accusation that "Mr. A is not very often sober,"[56] but also by his subsequent defense of the

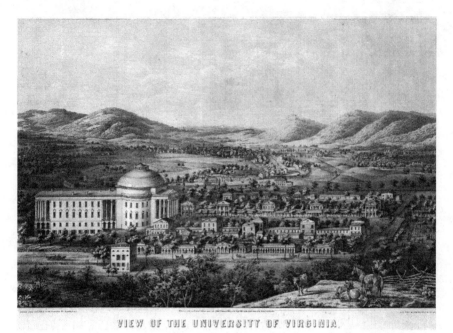

Figure 1.5. Poe attended the University of Virginia where he excelled. However, his inexperience, lack of guidance and John Allan's parsimony caused Poe's accrual of insurmountable financial debt forcing his removal from the school after the first year. *Library of Congress, Geography and Map Division*

same accusation after Allan had learned of the slur.[57] However, no reliable evidence has been found to support the idea that Poe's guardian ever indulged more than socially.

Without intercession from his foster-father, Poe had no hope of satisfying all the debts he had accrued while at the university. Allan subsequently went to Charlottesville but arranged to settle only the accounts that *he* considered legitimate,[58] afterward returning with Poe to Richmond, presumably to celebrate Christmas.[59] It is unclear whether Allan immediately decided to remove Edgar from the university. Initially, Allan may not have been aware of the extent of Poe's debts and as the promissory notes (and warrants) began to accumulate, he may have then told his "son" that another college session was out of the question.[60] What Poe did for the next several months is not certain; some biographers held that he was put to work in Allan's office but it seems he did little more than cloister himself at the family's mansion.

Finally, on March 19, 1827, after an apparent vicious exchange of words between John Allan and his ward, which included Allan's order for Poe to leave the house, the young poet took a room at the nearby Court House Tavern. His departure seems to have been precipitous, as indicated by a letter Poe wrote to Allan on the following day, asking him to send the trunk of clothes he had left behind.[61] Based on subsequent correspondence, it appears that Allan did not comply,[62] but Poe's repeated requests for his trunk here will be shown to have some significance during his final days in Baltimore.

In his initial letter to Allan, Poe also confided that he intended to relocate to Boston, Massachusetts, where he would "engage in some business." Most of Poe's early biographers presumed that he sailed directly to New England from Richmond; however, it appears that before reaching Boston, he spent some days, or weeks, in Baltimore.[63] There he would have visited his older brother and his aunt's family with whom Henry Poe was living.[64] The household, headed by his father's sister, Maria Clemm, also consisted of Poe's invalided grandmother, Elizabeth Cairnes Poe, who was being cared for by Maria and her two children, Henry and Virginia. It may also have been during this stop in Baltimore that Poe was introduced to Lambert Wilmer,[65] who became a close acquaintance, and in 1866, would also publish his recollections of their time together during the poet's later stay in that city.[66]

MILITARY CAREER

By the first week in May 1827, Poe had reached Boston,[67] but his movements and means of survival there immediately after his arrival have not been established conclusively. He may have found work as a shipping clerk for which he was inadequately paid, but after a few weeks, on May 26, Poe enlisted in the United States Army. In an apparent attempt to remain hidden from those who may have been pursuing him, he gave his name as "Edgar A. Perry." While Poe was born in Boston, the city also figures in his story as the place in which he was first published. Before his enlistment, he succeeded in coaxing a young printer to produce the very first collection of his poems, *Tamerlane and Other Poems*.[68] Review copies of the small, unimpressive pamphlet by its anonymous author were sent to literary publications; however, no contemporaneous critical notice of it has been found, and it is believed that the bulk of the fifty or so booklets printed were thrown away. Today (2021), it is one of the most sought-after first editions of American literature, with surviving examples valued in excess of $600,000.[69]

In November, Poe's artillery outfit was transferred to Fort Moultrie at Charleston, South Carolina, and late the following year, underwent another reassignment to Fort Monroe at Old Point Comfort, Virginia. As described by writer and West Point librarian J. Thomas Russell, the army during this period "was not keyed to a wartime pitch," and "while [military] life was ordered and rigorous, it was neither extremely harsh nor characterized by

26   *Chapter One*

violent disruptions."[70] There appears to have been much opportunity (and acceptance) for drinking while serving in the US military at that time, especially among the enlisted men.[71] Poe seems to have abstained, or at least convinced his superiors that he did, as evidenced by the letters of recommendation he received upon leaving the regular army in 1829. For example, Lieutenant Joshua Howard, his company commander, noted that, "his habits are good, and intirely [*sic*] free from drinking." Additionally, Fort commandant Lt. Colonel W. J. Worth, wrote that the Poe "appears to be free from bad habits."[72]

After completing eighteen months of a five-year enlistment, Poe seemed weary of army life as a regular soldier but decided, for whatever reason, that he wanted to obtain a commission instead—his final promotion to sergeant-major appears to have been in preparation for an application to West Point.[73] Lieutenant Howard agreed to Poe's discharge only on the condition that he arrange for a substitute (a practice that was then allowed) and obtain the permission of his foster-father, something that John Allan apparently initially resisted. It was only after Frances Allan's death on February 28, 1829, that Poe's guardian agreed to help him with his plan to become a cadet.[74] Poe, impatient to find his substitute, ultimately promised Sergeant Samuel Graves a $75 "re-enlistment bonus," an exorbitant amount when the usual fee for such a transaction was $12. Graves agreed to act on an initial payment of $25 and accepted Poe's note for the balance.

Poe was discharged in April and after a short visit with his foster-father of perhaps a couple of weeks, he went to Baltimore. Although John Allan was again communicating with his ward and providing him some financial support, he did not invite the young man to stay with him in Richmond. Poe spent the time in Maryland pursuing his application to West Point and making attempts to get a second volume of poems printed. Where he resided while there is not certain; when writing to John Allan he indicated he had been staying at a hotel and that his grandmother's family was unable to provide him accommodation. However, it is clear that Poe developed a close relationship with them as evidenced by his agency in the reassignment of a slave for Maria Clemm, as well as her willingness to make clothes for her nephew.[75] That he also spent a great deal of time with his brother Henry is indicated by a financial obligation that he took in concert with him, and for which he may have later been jailed because of nonpayment.[76]

In December 1829, Poe succeeded (possibly with the financial backing of John Allan) in getting his collection of poems, *Al Aaraaf, Tamerlane and Minor Poems*, printed by Baltimore publisher Hatch and Dunning.[77] Unlike his first volume, this one garnered a small amount of critical notice, some of which was favorable. Perhaps impressed by Poe's literary accomplishment and his resolve to gain entrance to West Point, Allan relented and allowed him to return to Richmond sometime during the winter.[78]

Edgar Poe ultimately secured his admission to the military academy on July 1, 1830, but his tenure there would be short—he was surprised by the discipline, rigid curriculum, and dearth of free time. Poe had also expected that his previous military service and time at the university would confer to him special consideration, and he was unhappy when he learned otherwise.[79] Of the many fables of Poe's West Point time, his drinking there has arguably been given the widest circulation, due, in no small part to the "reminiscences" of Thomas W. Gibson, who had for a time been the poet's roommate. In an 1867 article for *Harper's Magazine*, Gibson stated that, "the unfortunate habit that proved the bane of his [Poe's] after-life had even at that time taken strong hold upon him . . . the more dangerous habit of constant drinking."[80]

Yet here again is a questionable description of Poe's drinking that seems to have been volunteered only for sensation and to exploit Poe's posthumous reputation. As writer and West Point alumnus Carlisle Allan explained, "drunkenness was a very serious offense against the regulations, and as cadets were being court-martialed almost weekly throughout the fall of 1830 for merely having liquor in their possession, it is not likely that Poe ever appeared at West Point 'roaring drunk.'"[81] Poe's court-martial and subsequent expulsion from the academy were not the result of drinking; rather these were the product of a self-engineered dismissal that was triggered by John Allan's denial of his request to resign honorably. Poe undoubtedly followed the example of another roommate, Timothy Jones, who only a month before, in November, had affected *his* discharge by simply neglecting duties.[82]

The rupture with his foster-father had by then become irreparable. Shortly after Poe's admittance to the military academy, John Allan learned of his ward's outstanding debt to Sergeant Graves, an obligation that Poe claimed (to Allan) he had already settled. But Graves informed Allan of

Figure 1.6. After breaking with his foster family in Richmond, Poe eventually went to live with his father's sister in Baltimore. Maria Clemm would become the most important woman in the poet's life. *Edgar Allan Poe Society of Baltimore*

28   *Chapter One*

Poe's excuse that he was unable to get the money from "Mr. A" because he "is not very often sober."[83] Perhaps nothing illustrates Allan's anger more vividly than the abrupt denial and shunning of his "son." Allan stopped answering Poe's letters, even when Edgar wrote that he was suffering from starvation and sickness. When Allan had traveled to New York City for his wedding to Louisa Patterson on October 5, 1830, he made no attempt to contact Poe who was only a short distance away at West Point.[84] At this point, the young poet probably realized that his guardian had completely cut him loose. John Allan died four years later at his Richmond home and while he made bequests even to his illegitimate offspring, there was no mention of Edgar Poe in his will.[85]

In February 1831, Edgar left the academy and went to New York City where he arranged for the printing of a third edition of his poems. Poe secured funding for the publication by soliciting subscriptions from his fellow cadets while he was still at West Point. They had apparently been expecting to see poetic lampoons of academy personnel, but they received a very different book. Simply titled *Poems*, the cheaply made booklet was published by Elam Bliss and to the disappointment of his classmates, it was anchored largely by the pieces appearing in *Al Aaraaf, Tamerlane and Minor Poems* (1829).[86] Although Poe anticipated some notoriety from the work, it received limited critical attention and, like his two earlier volumes, the book generated no profits.

BALTIMORE

With no money or prospects, Poe had little choice but to return to his aunt's impoverished household in Baltimore. There he found his brother "entirely given up to drink & unable to help himself."[87] Henry's incapacity did not help the family's dismal financial circumstances; their income consisted primarily of Elizabeth Poe's $20-a-month pension, bestowed by the state of Maryland for her husband's service during the War of Independence. It appears that Poe immediately set out to find employment, asking (without success) his friend Nathan C. Brooks for a position at his newly opened school at Reisterstown, Maryland.[88] He also approached the editor of the *Baltimore Gazette*, William Gwynn, asking for *any* work that he or anyone else in the city had.[89] It is not known whether Gwynn helped in any way although it is suggested that Poe was given some employment in the months following his arrival in the city.[90]

There is a story assigned to this period that, *if true*, would seem to provide one of the first records of Poe's abuse of alcohol.[91] After returning to Baltimore, he made the acquaintance of Mary Starr, a seventeen-year-old girl who lived near his aunt's East Baltimore address. Although the duration of their relationship is unclear, it became a romantic one and, according to Mary, their "final lovers quarrel" may have been aggravated by her suitor's inebriation.

> One night I was waiting in the parlor for Eddie, and he didn't come. . . . Eddie arrived, shortly after my mother spoke to me, and had been drinking. . . . He said he had met some cadets from West Point [that] took him to Barnum's Hotel, where they had a supper and champagne. . . . A glass made him tipsy. He had more than a glass that night. . . . We then had a quarrel, about whose cause I do not care to speak . . . and he went away.[92]

While the couple's subsequent estrangement was likely caused by reasons other than Poe's drinking, this account appears to show in him an abandonment of decorum (and punctuality) when intoxicated.

Edgar Poe had barely settled in with his new family before his older brother died on August 1, 1831. According to Poe, Henry had become an alcoholic; however, it is believed that he had also contracted tuberculosis and ultimately succumbed to it.[93] The following year, the Poe-Clemm family moved from their Wilks Street tenement to a new house at the western edge of the city. With its remote location, and alternate water source, the residence spared them from an outbreak of cholera then raging in Baltimore.

Perhaps at the encouragement of his friend, Lambert Wilmer, who was then editing the Baltimore literary magazine, *Saturday Visiter*, Poe began to write fictional stories. In response to contests offering cash prizes by magazines in Philadelphia and Baltimore, he feverishly churned out a dozen tales, some of which are considered to be his early masterpieces. The *Saturday Courier* (Philadelphia) advertised an award of $100 for the best "American Tale" for which Poe submitted at least five of his compositions. Although none of his short stories secured the top prize, the *Courier* duly published all of them, albeit without attribution.[94]

He had better luck with a promotion organized by the *Visiter* in Baltimore

Figure 1.7. John Pendleton Kennedy was a Baltimore lawyer and published novelist when he served as a judge in a literary contest that gave Poe his first recognition. He became an early patron and mentor to Poe, facilitating his first employment in professional literature. *Poe Baltimore*

30   *Chapter One*

that had advertised a $50 premium for the best original short story and $25 for the most accomplished poem. Poe again bombarded the publisher with six of his tales and one poem. The panel of distinguished judges appointed by the magazine to evaluate the submissions consisted of John H. B. Latrobe, Dr. James Henry Miller,[95] and prominent Baltimore lawyer and novelist John Pendleton Kennedy. Of the triumvirate, Kennedy was the only one at the time with recognized *creative* writing credentials, having just published *Swallow Barn* (1832), and the other two would have been by necessity reliant on his judgment. Poe's fantastic nautical tale titled "MS Found in a Bottle" was pronounced by them to be the best, and was duly published in the magazine. Poe believed that his submitted poem, "The Coliseum," was also thought by the judges to be the best in that category but was instead supplanted by one penned by the magazine's editor, John H. Hewitt, who had replaced Poe's friend, Lambert Wilmer. According to Hewitt, Poe was waiting for him outside of the *Visiter* office a couple of weeks later, and as the new editor reported, "assail[ed] me on a public thoroughfare."[96] There is no independent confirmation of the affair but the two writers never reconciled even after Hewitt claimed to have later assisted Poe during a chance encounter in Washington, DC.[97] The magazine's award of $50 to Poe was not, as Latrobe would say, "inopportune"; more importantly, the success brought him recognition within the literary community and also introduced him to John Kennedy who would become his friend and patron.

The short-lived windfall notwithstanding, the family continued a precarious existence, their survival depending largely on the grandmother's allowance from the state. Maria Clemm is believed to have made some money by sewing and dressmaking while her son, Henry, may have also contributed financially by working as a stonecutter. How much, if anything, Poe was able to add to the family coffers is unknown; he continued an industry of writing and submitting his work for publication but without consistent or substantive reward.[98] But if he did not offer a steady income, Edgar at least contributed the scholarship and culture he had acquired by tutoring his young cousin Virginia.[99]

That Poe's health was not perfect at the time is suggested in a letter that he wrote to the publisher of the *Southern Literary Messenger*, Thomas White: "I am glad to say that I have entirely recovered—although Dr. Buckler . . . assured me that nothing but a sea-voyage would save me"; the poet's malady was not specified.[100] The fixed view of Edgar Allan Poe that has come to us is of a man with a weak constitution and tenuous health, but this was probably not always the case. Although we cannot be certain about Poe's physical fitness during his early life, especially when relying on anecdotes of his youthful vitality given years after he achieved fame, there is no reason to

Figure 1.8. This accurate engraving of a circa 1843 daguerreotype of Poe, showing him with mutton chop sideburns and no mustache, bears little resemblance to his more celebrated portraits. Yet he appeared this way for most of his adult life. *Author (printed engraving from author's collection)*

Figure 1.9. Virginia Clemm was Poe's first cousin and living with his aunt when they met. After her premature death in 1847 Poe would write the beautiful ballad, "Annabel Lee." *Courtesy of the Enoch Pratt Free Library, Special Collections*

doubt his much-touted decathlon swim in the James River when he was fifteen. According to classmate, Mr. Andrew Johnson, Poe swam, accompanied by friends in two boats, "from Richmond to Warwick, a distance of five or six miles . . . and it took him several hours to accomplish the task, the tide changing during the time."[101] It is also said that as an adolescent he was a formidable boxer and swift runner. Yet even if these stories are true, how he could have retained this vigor during his adult years of perpetual poverty and malnourishment remains open to question. Because many people expressed concerns for his physical welfare near the end of his life, it is likely that Poe's health, even if once robust, had declined to a more precarious state.

Perhaps resulting from their shared adversity, the Poe-Clemm family became very intimate, tagging each other with pet-names: "Muddy" was short for mother (Maria), "Eddie" for Edgar, and "Sissy" being short for sister, which is how Poe had viewed Virginia. This period of four years in Baltimore also gave Poe an intimacy with the city that only someone who *walks* its streets everyday can acquire—knowledge not just of street names, but of their direction and the order in which they fell. He learned the locations of the libraries, magazine offices, and bookstores;[102] and he also knew the markets,

32 *Chapter One*

restaurants, and watering holes, especially those frequented by local writers. The Seven Stars Tavern on Water Street was said to have been a favorite.[103] His extended residency in Baltimore during the early 1830s allowed him to become acquainted with the city's ways; such familiarity would have removed any hesitation of visiting or traveling through it at a future date.

RICHMOND AGAIN

When Edgar Poe's grandmother, Elizabeth, died on July 7, 1835, her state pension and the family's primary source of income perished with her. Through the auspices of John Kennedy, Poe had the prospect of employment in Richmond with the newly established publication, *Southern Literary Messenger*, and within a few weeks, he quit Baltimore for the Virginia capitol.[104] He had at first attempted to gain a teaching position that had been advertised there,[105] but when the job was conferred to another he showed up at the magazine office to find a position that was defined by proofreading and technical support, not the editorial responsibilities he had envisioned.[106]

It is believed that Poe intended to leave the Clemm family only for a short time while he could establish himself in his new situation, and bring them to Richmond later. But after only a couple of weeks with the *Messenger*, Poe was in trouble with the magazine's owner, Thomas White, over his drinking and erratic performance. Most biographers believe that this episode was triggered by the offer of Edgar's Baltimore cousin, Neilson Poe, to assume the care and education of Virginia Clemm, which would have thwarted Poe's plan of reuniting with the family that he still obviously needed.[107] However, this was also the first time in almost two years that Poe was on his own, without the supervision of an authoritative figure. Flush with his first "paycheck," he may have precipitously embarked on a drinking spree. This possibility is indicated in a letter written at the time by Thomas White, to his friend, Lucian Minor, in which he states, "He [Poe] is unfortunately rather dissipated,—and therefore I can place very little reliance upon him."[108] Two weeks later, White wrote again to Minor saying that "Poe has flew [*sic*] the track already. His habits were not good. . . . I am now alone."[109] Although there are indications that this may not have been Poe's first drinking binge, it is the earliest for which satisfactory evidence is provided.

Whether Poe was actually dismissed by the publisher or left on his own accord is unclear. In any event, by the time White was reporting his break with Poe, the poet had already returned to Baltimore, and to his still intact family. He then *apparently* married his cousin Virginia in a ceremony kept secret from his relatives there who had tried to prevent the union.[110] It should be noted, however, that other than a record of the Baltimore County marriage license, dated September 22, 1835, and an early statement given to Poe's biographer, John Ingram, conclusive evidence for the wedding is still lacking.[111] Poe also, in an exchange of letters, asked White for reinstatement and made promises to reform his habits.[112] White, who desperately needed help with the magazine, agreed only on the condition that there would be no more drinking:

> Separate yourself from the bottle, and bottle companions, for ever! Tell me if you can and will do so—and let me hear that it is your fixed purpose never to yield to temptation.
>
> If you should come to Richmond again, and . . . be an assistant in my office it must be especially understood by us that all engagements on my part would be dissolved, the moment you get drunk.[113]

By October 3, Poe had brought his aunt and cousin to Richmond. Their reappearance in his daily life appeared to restore him to the straight and narrow, and he was soon back in the office of the *Southern Literary Messenger* assisting White. What became of Henry Clemm, Maria's son, is unknown. He stayed behind in Baltimore working for (or as) a stonecutter, after which it is said he went to sea. In a letter to his second cousin, George W. Poe, written in 1839, Edgar Poe included a genealogical table that indicated Henry was then still alive.[114]

During the ensuing year, Poe worked diligently at the magazine, undertaking its editorial duties and successfully establishing a reputation as a ferocious but informed literary critic. The resulting publicity increased the monthly's circulation and helped both the magazine and Poe gain national prominence. Outwardly at least, things seemed to be going his way at last. He was earning a steady salary for the first time

Figure 1.10. Thomas White was the first owner and publisher of the *Southern Literary Messenger*, a monthly periodical ostensibly devoted to literature and the fine arts. In 1835, White hired Poe to help him with the magazine. *Edgar Allan Poe Museum, Richmond, VA*

34 *Chapter One*

in his life and working in the field of his choice. In May, a public marriage ceremony was conducted between Poe and his cousin Virginia Clemm at the boarding house in which they were living. According to Neilson Poe, "this second marriage . . . took place to save all comments, because the first one had been so private."[115] Biographer, Hervey Allen, provided a somewhat cynical explanation for a second, "real wedding" that according to him was performed to protect the family from charges of deception and soliciting charity from relatives under false pretenses.[116] In any event, the springtime ceremony was undoubtedly welcomed by mother and daughter. White's wedding present to the couple was said to have been an increase of Poe's wages to $20 a week.

For much of his time with the *Messenger* the poet appears to have remained temperate. In December 1836, when writing again to his friend, White would state, "Poe . . . I rejoice to tell you, still keeps from the bottle."[117] Yet within a year the publisher was reporting that Poe had been breaking his promise of abstinence and that he intended to discharge him:

> Highly as I really think of Mr. Poe's talents, I shall be forced to give him notice, in a week or so at farthest. . . . Three months ago I felt it my duty to give him a similar notice,—and was afterwards overpersuaded to restore him to his situation on certain conditions—which conditions he has again forfeited.[118]

Poe's drinking bouts were sometimes followed by periods of indisposition that disrupted the publication's production.[119] White was often late in getting out his magazine on time, as he would explain, "Owing to sickness among my most material hands."[120] Poe would later admit to such lapses, saying,

> While I resided in Richmond and edited the Messenger, I certainly did give way, at long intervals, to the temptation held out on all sides by the spirit of Southern conviviality . . . it sometimes happened that I was completely intoxicated, For some days after each excess, I was invariably confined to bed.[121]

White's disenchantment with Poe was not solely over his personal habits; he had grown increasingly concerned about the fallout from Edgar's savage literary reviews, and the two also squabbled over the publication's content. Furthermore, White was having financial difficulties of his own, and the shedding of Poe's salary may have also factored into his decision.[122] During the first week in January 1837, Poe was told that although he would still be paid for written contributions, his editorial duties on the magazine were no longer needed.[123] He was aware of the desperate circumstances that his departure created for White, and there is some indication that Poe vacillated before searching for work elsewhere, believing (or hoping) that the publisher would rehire him yet again. But this time White was resolved, and the consequences be damned.

In February 1837, Poe and his family removed to New York City. It is difficult to believe that he would have committed to such a major change without the presumption of employment, or at least a plan of some type. He had been communicating with Francis L. Hawks who indicated that the soon-to-be-published *New York Review* would have a position for him; however, their exchange may have been at Poe's initiation. In any event, the *Review*, intended as a theological publication, was probably inconsistent with Poe's aspirations and there is no evidence of an association with the magazine other than his published review of a travel log of biblical sites in the Middle East. In May, a financial collapse occurred that precipitated a nationwide economic depression, and the resulting lack of discretionary income hit the publishing industry particularly hard. No matter how unique Poe's gifts were, few periodicals could afford to pay for them. Other than his limited contributions to magazines and bound anthologies, little is known about the sources of Poe's income or his family's means of survival during the year that they spent in New York. Poe's biographer, Arthur Quinn, wrote that Maria Clemm operated (or managed) a boarding house for part of the time. One of her guests, William Gowans, later wrote of his frequent contact with Poe which remains the only account of the poet during that time:

> For eight months, or more, "one house contained us, us one table fed." During that time I saw much of him, and had an opportunity of conversing with him often, and I must say I never saw him the least affected with liquor, nor even descend to any known vice, while he was one of the most courteous, gentlemanly, and intelligent companions I have met.[124]

It should be observed that Gowans offered this description of Poe in 1870, after more than thirty years had passed and at a time when Poe's fame was ascending.

PHILADELPHIA

During the middle part of 1838 (the exact date has not been established), Poe and his family moved from New York to Philadelphia where he would eventually have better luck in finding employment for his pen. Unfortunately, the relocation did not immediately assuage the family's desperate circumstances. According to author, James Pedder, after landing in Philadelphia the Poe family was "literally suffering for want of food" and forced to live "on bread and molasses for weeks together."[125] Poe was then shifting his family between

36   *Chapter One*

boarding houses and attempting to borrow money from whomever he could: merchants, publishers, and relatives. In addition, he was peddling his works to several publications including the *American Museum of Literature and the Arts* that had been started in Baltimore by his friends Nathan C. Brooks and Dr. Joseph Snodgrass. Poe was also busy arranging the publication of his novel, *The Narrative of Arthur Gordon Pym* by Harper & Brothers (1838),[126] and revising a textbook on conchology for which he collected a single fee; however, proceeds from all these efforts were sporadic, providing only a fraction of what the family needed to survive.[127] In the pursuit of a steady income, Poe would make several attempts at obtaining a federal clerkship during his time in Philadelphia. In making his first request to James Kirke Paulding, one of his admirers who had just received an appointment as Secretary of the Navy, Poe found it necessary to deny reports of his drinking. He assured Paulding, "Intemperance, with me, has never amounted to a habit; and had it been ten times a habit it would have required scarcely an effort on my part to shake it from me at once and forever."[128] How Paulding, a New Yorker who was then living in Washington, DC, became aware of Poe's reputation is not certain but as a novelist and story writer he had occasion to correspond with many who knew the poet including those at the *Southern Literary Messenger*.[129]

In May 1839, Poe joined (at his instigation) *Burton's Gentleman's Magazine*, a monthly literary publication, for a $10 weekly wage (increased to $50 per month in 1840). The situation and duties he performed there were similar to those he found at the *Messenger*. He served as critic, chief contributor, and the magazine's untitled editor, while suffering under a proprietor whose abilities were questionable, or in this case, mitigated by other pursuits.[130] Poe remained with the magazine for an entire year before being acrimoniously dismissed in May 1840. The owner, William "Billy" Burton, would claim not only that Poe was frequently intoxicated but also that he neglected his duties and disappeared from the office altogether during his (Burton's) absence— allegations to which the publisher gave circulation.[131] Poe, on the other side, would claim that Burton, wanting to divorce himself from the business, was cutting expenditures, had underpaid him, and advertised the magazine's sale without notice. That Poe was by then gaining a reputation for intemperance among the Philadelphia literati, there can be little doubt, but Burton may have exaggerated his editor's habits in order to minimize his own neglect of the periodical.

It was at this time that Poe first announced (publicly) a plan to start his own magazine, an idea that he first proposed to Lambert Wilmer when they both resided in Baltimore.[132] Since his earliest experiences with periodicals, Poe had dreamed of publishing a magazine of his own, but his idea was of a monthly literary journal targeting the most sophisticated readers in the country and supporting it with only the finest writers. His would be an expensive publication that would not necessarily attract popular readership, and as such, its prospects for success would not have been assured. After learning of Burton's intent to offer his magazine for sale, Poe, while still employed there, printed a prospectus for his publication and circulated it among the city's newspaper editors. The potential appearance of yet another literary journal was viewed by Burton as an impediment to the sale of his product and was perhaps the real reason for Poe's dismissal. In any event, despite a well-organized campaign of advertisements, Poe was unable to get his magazine off the ground at the beginning of 1841 as he had planned. The delay was announced in December: "*The Penn Magazine*—owing to the severe and continued illness of Mr. Poe . . . is postponed until the first of March next."[133] It is not improbable that Poe had feigned his illness to buy more time for the magazine's launch; however, it may have been during this time that he first sought the medical care of Dr. John Kearsley Mitchell.[134] The forty-two-year-old Philadelphia doctor was also an amateur poet and songwriter, and as the subsequent owner of a chess playing automaton (robot) that Poe had earlier exposed as having a concealed operator,[135] it is likely that he sought out the poet after his arrival in the city.

How Edgar Poe and his family survived the period following his departure from the *Gentlemen's Magazine* is unclear. When writing to a relative, he indicated that Maria Clemm had traveled to New Jersey, perhaps seeking assistance from an acquaintance there.[136] It is also possible that Poe was diverting some of the support solicited for his magazine project although there is no evidence that such a scheme had been his original intent.[137] In February 1841, Poe took a position with *Graham's Magazine* as a book review editor, citing the financial crisis that had then closed Philadelphia banks as the reason for the suspension of his magazine project. George Rex Graham, who had much greater publishing ambitions than William Burton, purchased the stage actor's magazine (and subscription list) in October 1840, four months after Poe's dismissal.[138] The magnate then combined the *Gentleman's Magazine* with another periodical that he had purchased the previous year to form *Graham's Magazine*. Poe's hard-hitting literary reviews,[139] and quality submissions (by him and many others), along with some of the finest engravings and color plates then in existence, catapulted the new publication almost overnight into one of the most widely read in America at the time. Both Poe's annual salary of $800 and the payments he received as a contributor to *Graham's,* and other publications, allowed him a measure of financial stability for the first time since leaving John Allan.

While Graham seems to have been more lenient than William Burton as an employer, the enterprise was still his to command. Poe may have at first believed that Graham would subsidize *his* magazine project, but the poet eventually came to understand that it would not happen.[140] From the early months of his tenure at *Graham's*, he privately expressed a desire to acquire a government clerkship to his friend Frederick Thomas who had secured an office in the Department of the Treasury. However, a similar, full-time position would seem to be at odds with Poe's plan of starting his own magazine, especially the prestigious publication that he was proposing. At the same time he was acquiring some of the fame he so desperately sought. His controversial book reviews and features on autography and cryptography had made him the talk of the literary world, and his short stories, such as "The Murders in the Rue Morgue" and "A Decent into the Maelstrom," brought Poe recognition with the reading public.

Yet the pendulum was sweeping back again, and any domestic or financial contentment that Edgar Allan Poe had found would prove to be short-lived. That January of 1842, his wife Virginia became spectacularly symptomatic of tuberculosis when, during the middle of a recital at their home, she began to cough up blood. It is believed that Mitchell was called upon to treat her and that he diagnosed bronchitis, perhaps for the benefit of both *husband* and wife. For the next five years her condition would fluctuate, with relapsing hemorrhages and periods of recovery, until she finally succumbed to the "bronchitis" in January 1847.[141] Tuberculosis was epidemic in the nineteenth century and after claiming so many close to the family, it is difficult to believe that Edgar and his aunt had not detected the signs in Virginia before her pulmonic rupture.[142] Nevertheless, he fell apart at the sudden appearance of the disease in his beloved little "wifey," and in the days that followed, he apparently lost his ambition to thrive. It has been reported that Mitchell also treated Poe at this time, although the exact nature of his ailment and related care remains uncertain.[143] He later resigned his post at the magazine and would fall back into a financial abyss.

Figure 1.11. After his break with Burton, Poe joined the staff of *Graham's Magazine*. George Rex Graham was more appreciative of Poe's genius and paid him a better wage allowing the poet a measure of financial stability for the first time since leaving John Allan. *Author (printed engraving from author's collection)*

His circumstances and emotional state at the time are best described in his own words:

> The state of my mind has, in fact, forced me to abandon for the present, all mental exertion. The renewed and hopeless illness of my wife, ill health on my own part, and pecuniary embarrassments, have nearly driven me to distraction. My only hope of relief is the "Bankrupt Act", of which I shall avail myself as soon as possible. . . . Mrs Poe is again dangerously ill with hemorrhage from the lungs. It is folly to hope.[144]

Although it is not proven that Virginia's condition immediately triggered an increase in Poe's drinking, it is not so difficult to establish that the habit became more difficult to hide from others. After being given hope of his wife's recovery,[145] Poe emerged from his creative and motivational stalemate. Within the following year, 1842, he would produce "The Masque of the Red Death," "The Pit and the Pendulum," and "The Tell-Tale Heart," all now seen as literary masterpieces. But his break with *Graham's* meant that he no longer had a standing outlet for his tales and magazine articles which then became more of a chore to place. In June 1842, he made an unaccompanied trip to New York City in order to sell some of his work and perhaps find employment. Unfortunately, while there, he embarked on another drinking spree and apparently showed up at the offices of the *Democratic Review* intoxicated, an escapade that would elicit from him a written apology to the editors:

> Will you be kind enough to put the best possible interpretation upon my behavior while in N-York? You must have conceived a queer idea of me—but the simple truth is that Wallace would insist upon the juleps, and I knew not what I was either doing or saying.[146]

Poe is believed to have made the rounds of several other publishing offices, and if he made these calls while under the effects of alcohol, it is difficult to believe that word of his condition would not have been privately shared among those who traded in stories for a living; certainly Poe thought this to be the case as indicated by his request for the "best possible interpretation" of his behavior.[147] When discussing this trip to New York, some of his biographers have written that Poe also paid a visit, while intoxicated, to his onetime sweetheart, Mary Starr, who lived across the river in New Jersey at that time. Although the story's chronology agrees with the record, it relies on her recollections given (through a relative) almost fifty years later, the veracity of which must be viewed in that context.[148] In any event, after his return to Philadelphia, it appears that Poe was ill and in bed for almost a week;[149] as with most of his prolonged drinking episodes, a period of indisposition followed.

40 *Chapter One*

With full-time employment no longer standing in the way, Poe rekindled his plan for a literary magazine of his own. For sound reasons he changed the name of the proposed publication to *The Stylus* and commenced a search for a financial partner. Among those he considered were Robert Tyler, the president's son, Thomas Holley Chivers,[150] a financially well-off Georgia landowner and Thomas Cottrell Clarke, who had begun the publication of the *Philadelphia Saturday Museum* on December 10, 1842. Ultimately, Poe would convince Clarke to go in with him. He described his vision of this potential arrangement to Frederick Thomas:

> I have managed, at last, to secure, I think, the great object—a partner possessing ample capital, and, at the same time, so little self-esteem, as to allow me entire control of the editorial conduct. He gives me, also, a half interest, and is to furnish funds for all the business operations—I agreeing to supply, for the first year, the literary matter.[151]

This agreement may have been contingent on Poe becoming the assistant editor of Clarke's magazine, as announced in the edition of March 4; but he would never fill the position for unspecified reasons.

In support of the *Stylus* project, Poe made another unaccompanied trip, this time to Washington, DC, during the first week of March 1843. Ostensibly, the purpose of the journey was to secure subscriptions and contributors for the magazine, or at least that appears to be the reason given to Clarke, who had advanced the poet travel money.[152] Poe may have even promised to lecture while in the capitol to recover expenses. However, *his* primary objective for the trip was to secure a government appointment (in the Customs Office at Philadelphia) and to meet with Robert Tyler, the president's son, who he believed could pull the appropriate strings.[153] Poe was counting on Frederick Thomas, then a Washington resident and an acquaintance of Tyler, to be his guide while in the city and to arrange an introduction to the president's son. Unfortunately, upon his arrival Poe found his friend bedridden and unable to accompany him around town, upending the poet's plans and not improbably, his confidence in the trip's outcome. Instead, he had to rely on another colleague, Jessie Dow, who would report to Clarke that Poe went on a drinking binge:

> He arrived here a few days since. On the first evening he seemed somewhat excited, having been over-persuaded to take some Port wine. On the second day he kept pretty steady, but since then he has been, at intervals, quite unreliable.[154]

We have been given some hint of what took place during this episode from a letter that he wrote after returning to Philadelphia. He offered apologies for

Peaks and Pits, and Pendulum Swings 41

his "petulance" and "vexation" to no less than five individuals including his bedridden host, the owner of the hotel at which he (Poe) was staying, and Jessie Dow's wife. He also asked Dow not to say a word "about the cloak turned inside out."[155] Apparently, Poe had soiled his coat in some manner or perhaps just unwittingly wore it reversed for a period of time. Afterward, Poe became so ill that he was unable to return home, requiring treatment from Thomas's physician for several days. When it was thought he had recovered sufficiently, Dow made arrangements for his trip back to Philadelphia: "We will see him on board the cars bound to Phila., but we fear he might be detained in Baltimore and not be out of harm's way."[156]

One result of this tragic affair was Clarke's withdrawal from Poe's magazine project,[157] although Clarke's financial difficulties at the time with the *Saturday Museum* could have also played a part in the decision. Had Poe just disappeared when in Washington and suffered his lapse among strangers, the outcome would have been harmful enough; however, his drinking took place among acquaintances, and his behavior was observed by some who would not forget what they saw. One of these witnesses is thought to have been his old nemesis, John Hewitt, who claimed to have encountered Poe while walking on Pennsylvania Avenue:

> He came boldly up to me, and, offering me his hand, which I willingly took, asked me if I would forget the past. He said he had not had a mouthful of food since the day previous, and begged me to lend him fifty cents to obtain a meal. Though he looked the used-up man all over—still he showed the gentleman. I gave him the money—and I never saw him afterwards.[158]

Another of those believed to have engaged with Poe in Washington was writer, novelist, and politician Thomas Dunn English, who had first met Poe in 1839 while the latter was on the staff of *Burton's Gentleman's Magazine*. English, then a Philadelphia resident, was at first impressed with the poet and, for a while became his frequent companion, but being a firm advocate of alcohol abstinence, he grew disenchanted with Poe after discovering his drinking habit. Thomas English's antipathy toward his onetime companion during the time of his Washington visit is evident by his temperance tale, "The Doom of the Drinker," a narrative that included a cruel and thinly veiled caricature of Poe as a "wino," among other things.[159] Clarke, who was also a staunch advocate for the temperance movement, would publish English's tale not long after the incident.

That Poe's personal reputation was then being discussed among literary associates is evidenced by a letter written by his longtime friend, Lambert Wilmer, on May 20, 1843. In the letter, Wilmer confided his concerns to their shared acquaintance, John Tomlin, the postmaster of Jackson, Tennessee:[160]

42   *Chapter One*

It gives me inexpressible pain to notice the vagaries to which he has lately become subject. Poor fellow! he is not a teetotaller by any means, and I fear he is going headlong to destruction, moral, physical, and intellectual.[161]

Wilmer may have also "delicately" alluded to Poe's drinking in print which would explain how the poet learned the tattler's identity.[162] He would never speak to his friend again.

Relatives of the poet were also becoming aware of his difficulties, whether indirectly or from Poe himself. In a letter written to him by his second cousin, William Poe, Edgar was cautioned against, "a great enemy to our family, I hope, however, in yr [your] case, it may prove unnecessary, 'A too free use of the Bottle.' Too many & especially Literary Characters, have sought to drown their sorrows & disappointments by this means."[163] That his Baltimore cousin thought it necessary to offer this counsel could indicate that he had by then gotten wind of Poe's reputation; and the mention of "a great enemy to our family" also conveys William's belief of a hereditary predisposition to alcoholism. Indeed, Poe would also imply a familial susceptibility to the disorder when publicly answering a slanderous rejoinder made by Thomas Dunn English in 1846.[164]

From Poe's family would also come the claim that he had acquired an opium habit while living in Philadelphia. Although during his lifetime there seems to be no reliable testimony indicating his drug use, this pronouncement, coming from a family member in 1884, was given weight by some biographers.[165] Poe's cousin, Elizabeth Herring Tutt, who was widowed in 1835, went along with her family to live in the Quaker City sometime around 1840, and after learning that Poe and his family were also there, she made frequent visits to their home.[166] In her dotage, "Miss Herring" would relate to Professor George Woodberry that during this time "she had often seen him decline to take even one glass of wine, but that, for the most part, his periods of excess were occasioned by a free use of opium."[167] In a second deposition, Herring would reiterate that the family "did all possible to conceal his faults" and that after each recovery "he made good resolutions only to be broken."[168] It must be pointed out however, that her recollections were given to Woodberry secondhand through a relative, Amelia Fitzgerald Poe,[169] at a point more than forty years after the period described. Herring's motivation for claiming Poe's aversion to alcohol and supplanting it with an opium habit can only be guessed at, if indeed she made the allegations.

Incredibly, the most convincing repudiation of Poe's potential drug use would be provided by none other than the poet's sworn enemy, Thomas Dunn English:

Had Poe the opium habit when I knew him (before 1846) I should both as a physician and a man of observation, have discovered it during his frequent visits to

Peaks and Pits, and Pendulum Swings 43

my rooms, my visits at his house, and our meetings elsewhere—I saw no signs of it and believe the charge to be a baseless slander.[170]

It is true that during his time in Philadelphia, Poe befriended several eccentric writers that had, or would later acquire, notorious habits. Henry B. Hirst was a close companion and frequent drinking partner who seems to have preferred brandy; but it was only after Poe's death, when the absinthe fad began, that Hirst became addicted to *La fee Verte* (the green fairy), which ultimately ruined his mind. The engraver, John Sartain, was also said to have been a frequent drinker of the licorice-flavored potion but would claim that it was only at Hirst's insistence.[171] George Lippard was another of Poe's Philadelphia acquaintances who became notable for his odd habits, but his eccentricities seem to have been limited to his dress and bohemian lifestyle. In any event, there is no proof that Poe himself became a habitué of anything other than the alcoholic beverages that were available during *his* time.[172]

After leaving *Graham's Magazine*, Poe would not find employment with any other publication in Philadelphia, yet he continued to write, almost manically, and peddled his works wherever he could. In addition to his submitted reviews and magazine columns, Poe wrote at least a dozen tales during 1844, his last year in that city; among these were, "The Spectacles," "The Oblong Box," "The Premature Burial," "The Purloined Letter," "The System of Doctor Tarr and Professor Fether," and "The Balloon Hoax." Some scholars have stated that he was also working on "The Raven" during this time.[173] The income, even from so many submissions, was sporadic and certainly inadequate, but Poe found that he could earn some money by presenting lectures, and he gave as many as six talks on American poetry between November 21, 1843, and March 12, 1844. The lectures, in Pennsylvania and Delaware, were all well attended and for the most part well reviewed; however, he used his pulpit as an opportunity to publicly criticize Rufus Wilmot Griswold's anthology, *The Poets and Poetry of America* (1842), "in not the most gentle manner."[174] Reports of these brutal attacks on Griswold's work were inevitably communicated to the anthologist, who would take the censures as a personal affront and never allowed them to pass from his memory. Edgar Poe's inability to recognize the bitterness his words caused in others would ultimately yield catastrophic results.

It appears that Poe made these lecture trips unaccompanied, but there is no *reliable* record of him using the time away from home to indulge in drinking sprees. However, an episode may have occurred during his Baltimore lecture when it is believed that he bunked with the Herrings and became abusive with members of the family while intoxicated. Although Henry Herring did not say when they transpired, he would subsequently imply that more than one incident took place. When finding Poe at Gunners' Hall five years later,

44   *Chapter One*

Snodgrass asked Herring why he would not take the stricken poet to his house, to which he replied "that Poe had 'so frequently abused his hospitality by the rudeness as well as vulgarity of his bearing while drunk, toward the ladies of his household,' that he 'couldn't think, for a moment, of taking him to his house in his present besotted condition.'"[175]

Ultimately, Poe came to recognize that the lectures and freelance work were insufficient to sustain his family. He had been borrowing money prodigiously and selling off possessions but was still seriously in arrears with the house rent.[176] At the beginning of April 1844, he left Philadelphia without informing his friends, many of whom were correspondents inclined to save such communications among their autographs; if he confided the reason for his departure to anyone, it does not survive. Thomas Dunn English would later claim that he was "the sole possessor of the scandalous secret" that drove Poe from the city but that he was too much the gentleman to reveal it.[177] From all appearances, it seems that Poe had made no plans, other than escape.

NEW YORK

Edgar Allan Poe's second period in New York City is arguably the most intriguing part of his story, a comprehensive study of which is long overdue. It was during these five years that Poe achieved international fame and published the poems for which he would be best known: "The Raven," "The Bells," and "Annabel Lee." His lectures during this period were attended by hundreds, if not thousands, who paid to hear him recite his works, and for a moment he even realized the long-held dream of conducting his own magazine. But New York would also serve as a stage for Poe's tragic final acts, and it would become a place where he would be as those *he* had pilloried and skewered in print. Here the poet would engage in a misguided attack on a beloved literary figure, entangle himself in humiliating public scandals, and suffer a tidal wave of poverty—all of which would frame the death of his wife as he watched helplessly. While his time in New York makes for an absorbing story, it is mainly the effects of these pendulum swings on Poe, and how they may have hastened his death, that will be of concern to this study.

When Poe arrived in New York City, he had his wife Virginia on his arm. Perhaps from lessons learned during previous relocations, this time Maria Clemm did not permit him go ahead unaccompanied. If he had no plan, Poe was inexplicably upbeat when he first arrived; perhaps it was the presence of his wife. On his first day in the city, he dutifully reported their status to Maria:

> We arrived safe at Walnut St wharf. . . . I went up Greenwich St and soon found a boarding-house. . . . The landlady seemed as if she could'nt [im]press us

enough. . . . Sis [Virginia] is delighted, and we are both in excellent spirits. She has coughed hardly any and had no night sweat. . . . I feel in excellent spirits & have'nt drank a drop. . . . We are resolved to get 2 rooms the first moment we can. In the meantime it is impossible we could be more comfortable or more at home than we are.[178]

It is not clear whether the second room was intended for Virginia or her mother (or perhaps both). Maria Clemm had stayed behind in Philadelphia presumably to settle affairs there, but it may have been a month or more before she managed to join them in Gotham.

This of course was not Poe's first time in New York, but he seemed to treat the move as an adventure as suggested by his energetic explorations of Manhattan that he chronicled for an obscure periodical in Columbia, Pennsylvania.[179] Notwithstanding these and other feature articles, Poe was still hard at his creative writing and found that he needed a measure of seclusion. He, along with Virginia and her mother, moved in with a larger family that operated a farm five miles north of the city. There he found the solitude to write new things and complete others that had been in the works. At the same time, he needed to engage editors. Although well known to most of the magazine proprietors in the country, he was apparently having difficulty placing his fiction or at least convincing them to publish it in a timely manner. Inevitably, he needed a steadier income. In October, he joined the staff of the newly created *Evening Mirror* as a critical editor and "mechanical paragraphist," as the publisher, Nathaniel Parker Willis, would later describe his position there.[180] It is from Willis that we are given a snapshot of Poe's time at the paper.

Figure 1.12. This early daguerreotype of Poe is believed to have been made while he was living in New York sometime after 1844. Most of the photographic images of Poe, such as this example, are shown in reverse confirmed by the button orientation on his clothing. *Edgar Allan Poe Society of Baltimore*

He resided with his wife and mother . . . a few miles out of town, but was at his desk in the office, from nine in the morning till the evening paper went to press . . . he was invariably punctual

46   *Chapter One*

and industrious . . . through all this considerable period, we had seen but one
presentment of the man,—a quiet, patient, industrious, and most gentlemanly
person, commanding the utmost respect and good feeling by his unvarying
deportment and ability.[181]

During this first year in New York, it appears the isolation and "quality-
time" that he spent with his family kept Poe focused and mostly out of trouble, but his world would be turned upside down at the end of January 1845
with the publication of his lyrical poem, "The Raven."[182] The piece became an
immediate sensation, and along with the fortuitous publication of a flattering
biography of the poet appearing in *Graham's Magazine*, Poe was catapulted
onto the public stage. The poem was immediately printed, reprinted, and
parodied in magazines and newspapers around the country. Even his enemies
could not withhold their praise. When noticing the second number of the
American Review, Lewis Gaylord Clark, editor of the *Knickerbocker Magazine*, would state, "The very best thing in its pages is a unique, singularly
imaginative, and most musical effusion, entitled 'The Raven.'" Clark would
then add, "We have never before, to our knowledge, met the author, Mr.
EDGAR A. POE, as a poet; but if the poem to which we allude be a specimen
of his powers in this kind, we shall always be glad to welcome him in his new
department."[183] Poe had always viewed himself principally as a "poet," and
by 1845, he had published a number of works in verse, including "To One
in Paradise," "Bridal Ballad," and "Dream-Land." However, most knew him
only as a caustic literary critic and a writer of imaginative stories. With the
publication of "The Raven," he at last acquired the coveted emblem.

Virtually overnight, Edgar Allan Poe became one of the most sought-after
figures in New York where people who were unknown to him asked for his
autograph, and magazine editors now approached *him* for contributions. He
was invited to (and eagerly attended) evening parties where the author of
"The Raven" would mix among other notable writers and poets, there to be
seen and heard for the first time by some who showed up only for that purpose. Poe may have anticipated this rise in his status or at least the necessity
of restoring his social presence. Several weeks before the poem was published, he confided to his Washington friend, Frederick Thomas, "In about
three weeks, I shall move into the City, and recommence a life of activity
under better auspices, I hope, than ever before."[184] Sometime in February,
he moved back to lower Manhattan to be near his place of work and the
addresses of those who sought his company.

Poe exploited his notoriety even further by resuming his lectures and on
February 28, he delivered an address on American poetry at the Society
Library building in New York that drew, amazingly, no more than 300
people. Two months later he was encouraged to give an encore lecture at

the same venue but owing to the evening's severe weather, was forced to cancel the talk. He apparently became upset over the cancellation and, by one account, had to be ushered to work the following morning after spending the night drinking.[185] If true it may have been the first such incident in almost a year's time.

Fame, like money in his pocket, seemed to have a destabilizing effect on Poe. When preoccupied by composition, or under the watchful eye of his aunt, he stayed on the rails, but when on his own he was vulnerable to impulses that were normally kept in check while he remained at home. With full-time employment, he was away from the family during daytime hours; however, with his new status as a celebrity, he was often absent in the evenings. From this period in the spring of 1845 until the final months before his death in October 1849, the record is adequately filled with corroborative accounts of his drinking, though only those occurrences deemed necessary to demonstrate a pattern have been added to the chronology.

Figure 1.13. In the fall of 1844, N. P. Willis was editing the *Evening Mirror* in New York and gave Poe employment there when he desperately needed it. After Poe left the paper Willis consistently promoted his interests and numbered among the poet's staunchest defenders after his death. *Library of Congress*

Edgar Poe's rising fame was also appropriated by others. In February 1845, he was offered a partnership in the newly begun *Broadway Journal* by one of its founders, Charles Briggs. Believing he would be the publication's editor, Poe left his position at the *Evening Mirror*. How much editorial control he actually had at first is a matter of question but by giving him an interest in the weekly magazine, Briggs secured a celebrated name for the masthead and was not required to pay Poe a wage; instead, he was to receive a third of the profits, should any materialize. They did not.[186]

Poe had nurtured a lingering resentment of what he thought was the inordinate attention given to New England poet, Henry Wadsworth Longfellow, and while he was with the *Mirror*, published a contemptuous review of Longfellow's anthology, *The Waif* (1845).[187] Perhaps as a device to attract attention and increase the paper's subscription, he continued the campaign against Longfellow when editing the *Broadway Journal*. "The Longfellow War," as it became known at the time, certainly put a spotlight on Poe and the periodical, but his ill-advised charges of plagiarism against America's most popular poet created a new nest of enemies, especially in the northeast.[188] One consequence of this was a lecture he delivered on October 16 for the Boston Lyceum, during which he found an audience that can be politely described as "curious."[189] Instead of a new poem that he had been paid to provide, Poe recited the inscrutable, and ponderous, "Al Aaraaf," retitled for the occasion. At some point during the evening Poe became intoxicated; it is not clear whether it was from fortifying himself prior to speaking or afterward during a reception held in conjunction with the lecture. When his condition was reported in the press, he responded by saying that his drinking was strategic, and that the presentation had been intended as a hoax. This unfortunate affair appears to have been a repeat of the circumstances described by Thomas Dunn English, when earlier that year, Poe failed to appear with a new poem before a group at New York University.[190] Whether a unique occurrence or not, the Boston Lyceum episode would hound him (publicly) during the following year and do much to stain his growing fame.

While at the *Broadway Journal*, the author of "The Raven" not surprisingly received regular requests from aspiring writers. After publishing an early essay by Walt Whitman, titled "Art-Singing, Heart-Singing" (1845), Poe got a visit from the poet to discuss the composition, and the possibility of further submissions. Whitman later recalled Poe as being "very kindly and human, but subdued, perhaps a little jaded."[191] Another caller was not so fortunate. During the course of a campaign to have his poem, "Ode on a Grecian Flute" published, a young Richard Henry Stoddard showed up at the *Journal* to find a belligerent Edgar Poe accusing him of literary theft. He was then rudely ejected from the magazine's office by its editor who Stoddard claimed was "in his cups" at the time.[192] The experience would undoubtedly skew Stoddard's handling of Poe's posthumous reputation when it became his turn to sit in an editor's chair.

In October 1845, Poe's final partner on the *Journal* withdrew from the struggling enterprise, leaving him as the sole owner and editor. At long last, he had a magazine of his own to conduct as he wished, but his tenure as a publisher would be a short one. In trying to keep the magazine afloat single-handedly, he succeeded only in the accrual of insurmountable personal debt, and by the end of the year, Thomas H. Lane, Poe's newly acquired financial backer, had little choice but to cease publication. Edgar Poe's pendulum had reached another apex and was now heading back in the other direction.

At this time, he still enjoyed some currency among a coterie of literary women of New York, some of whom engaged in romantic flirtations with the celebrated poet. During a visit to his Manhattan home in January 1846, one of these women, Mrs. Elizabeth Ellet, noticed a letter (to Poe) from a rival poetess lying carelessly exposed, after which she contacted the sender, Mrs. Frances Osgood, and convinced her to retrieve all of her communiqués.[193] The appearance of Osgood's emissaries at his door demanding the return of the letters angered Poe and prompted him to rashly declare that "Mrs. Ellet had better come and look after her own letters."[194] His indiscrete remark suggesting that Ellet was also sending him love letters was communicated to her, which put in motion a chain of events that not only saw his life threatened by the woman's brother, but also led to a fistfight with Thomas Dunn English (then editing a magazine in New York) after he had voiced disbelief in Poe's version of the affair.[195] Poe ultimately offered a written conciliation to Mrs. Ellet stating that he had been subject to a fit of insanity;[196] it was then duly reported in the newspapers that he had become deranged.[197] The fiasco succeeded in poisoning his relationship with the circle of bluestockings, and he was subsequently excluded from their literary gatherings.[198] In addition, Poe's widening indebtedness and reputation for the bottle made him a social pariah to others in New York who saw him as many things, but certainly not "deranged."

Figure 1.14. Frances Sargent Osgood was one of the New York bluestockings with whom Poe became enamored. They addressed love poems to each other in periodicals of the day; however, there is no corroborative evidence that the relationship was anything other than platonic. *Author (printed engraving from author's collection)*

Sometime immediately following the Ellet episode, Poe moved out of the city and boarded with his family at a farmhouse near the East River, in the vicinity of what is 47th Street today. The area at the time was still undeveloped and viewed as "the country."[199] He may have been trying to put some distance between himself and his embarrassments; if so, he found that even Turtle Bay was not private enough. During that spring, after returning from a trip to Baltimore where he suffered another

50 *Chapter One*

"illness,"[200] Poe took his family to live in the village of Fordham, then a remote area thirteen miles north of lower Manhattan. There he cloistered himself in a little cottage amid persistent reports that he had been suffering bouts of "brain fever," a lingering souvenir of the Osgood/Ellet scandal and his claim of temporary insanity.[201]

Without a steady source of income, Poe earned what he could by continuing to write and submit magazine features. "Marginalia" was a series of random critiques, opinions, and witticisms, often no more than a couple of paragraphs in length, that were intended as column fillers in the periodicals to which they were sent. Published in various papers from 1844 to 1849, they yielded little return, but it appears that Poe had also planned them for a collection at some point. In April, he began a different series of vignettes describing "The Literati of New York City" in highly personal terms, not only discussing the published works of various authors, but also their private histories and physical appearances. Although intended only as a gossip column,[202] Poe seemed to have had difficulty determining the boundary lines of propriety. Perhaps thinking that his sketches were humorous, these vignettes included exaggerated and fabricated shortcomings of the authors, material that was understandably viewed as personal attacks by some of the individuals he targeted. Considering Poe's then well-known personal reputation and his vulnerability to reciprocal exposure, the choice to undertake such a project seems incredible, but as biographer Arthur Quinn observed, "Poe must have had mental resiliency to a remarkable degree, for he remained undaunted after defeat."[203] Nevertheless, whether motivated by the need for money or publicity, the series proved wildly popular and succeeded in sustaining his relevancy.

One of the authors with whom he went too far was the hot-blooded Thomas Dunn English, who seemed equally powerless to restrain himself. In a vicious, no-holds-barred reply to the "Literati" sketch addressing him, English made public the details of the Osgood/Ellet Scandal and the resulting fistfight he had with Poe, declaring himself, not unsurprisingly, to be the victor.[204] He also added an account of Poe's Boston Lyceum fiasco as well as an allegation that the poet used a drinking binge to escape his obligation at the New York University. English capped his fusillade by accusing the poet of forgery and of obtaining money under false pretenses. Poe answered the libelous recriminations with a lawsuit; he would eventually win his case and receive a settlement albeit at the continued expense of his reputation.[205] Yet it was in his reply to English's rejoinder that Poe not only acknowledged a drinking *habit* publicly for the first time but also hinted that it was hereditary:

> The errors and frailties which I deplore, it cannot at least be asserted that I have been the coward to deny. Never, even, have I made attempt at extenuating a

Peaks and Pits, and Pendulum Swings 51

weakness which is (or, by the blessing of God, was) a calamity, although those who did not know me intimately had little reason to regard it otherwise than as a crime. For, indeed, had my pride, or that of my family permitted, there was much—very much—there was everything—to be offered in extenuation.[206]

THE PITILESS PENDULUM

The little money trickling in from his writing was not enough to sustain one person, let alone a family of three, and their growing reliance on charity was not aided by Poe's reputation and all the bridges that he had burned. At some point during the late autumn of 1846, Mary Gove, an advocate for health reform and one of the writers Poe had sketched in his Literati series, paid a visit to his home at Fordham. There she found the family "living in the greatest wretchedness,"[207] without adequate food or clothing. She also discovered that Poe and his wife were desperately ill, although from different maladies: while both were certainly malnourished, Virginia was shivering through the closing stages of tuberculosis, whereas her husband, immobilized by depression, may have also been suffering a persistent gastrointestinal imbalance from his drinking.[208] Gove would later recall, "As soon as I was made aware of these painful facts, I came [returned] to New York, and enlisted the sympathies and services of a lady, whose heart and hand were ever open to the poor and miserable."[209] The woman she recruited was Marie Louise Shew, an unpaid practical nurse with some medical training (probably informally from her doctor-father) who dedicated her services to the impoverished. Living in the city, Shew untiringly traveled up to Fordham, almost daily, ministering to Virginia throughout her final weeks, and also to her husband after the girl died.

When the poetess Mary E. Hewitt learned of the family's plight from Mrs. Gove, she immediately—before visiting Fordham in person—approached newspaper editors for donations to assist the Poes; the editors in turn published descriptions of the family's grim circumstances and requests for contributions:

> We regret to learn that this gentleman and his wife are both dangerously ill with the consumption, and that the hand of misfortune lies heavy upon their temporal affairs.—We are sorry to mention the fact that they are so far reduced as to be barely able to obtain the necessaries of life. This is, indeed, a hard lot, and we do hope that the friends and admirers of Mr. Poe will come promptly to his assistance in his bitterest hour of need.[210]

As with the published reports of Poe's insanity, the declaration that *both* were "dangerously ill with the consumption" was unsupported—the poet may have been confined to bed at the time but there is no evidence that he was also stricken with tuberculosis.[211]

The poor health and acute pecuniary distress of Poe and his family became *the* topic of discussion at the bluestockings' literary gatherings. Among those who responded to the published appeals for relief were some who did not attend, including Mrs. Jane Ermina Locke, a Massachusetts poetess and relative of Frances Osgood, and Brooklyn housewife Sarah "Estelle" Anna Lewis. In sending financial assistance, these women also offered their poems, asking for their work to be "objectively" evaluated. Poe's impoverishment provided little escape from these unwholesome arrangements, but his subsequent advocacy of these mediocre poets shows that when given the means, he paid his debts.

Whatever the cause of his illness, Poe had recovered sufficiently by the middle of December to correspond with magazine editors about his personal situation and future projects. Virginia's condition, however, continued to worsen, and six weeks later, on January 30, 1847, her short life came to an end. Although her death was not unexpected, Poe suffered a relapse, requiring the continued presence of Marie Shew at the cottage. A recurring fever, and Maria Clemm's voiced fear that the "illness will be a serious one," seem to indicate that his condition may not have been psychosomatic. Indeed, his state of health was such that he did not attend the court proceedings of his libel suit against the *Evening Mirror* that had been postponed until February 17. It may have been around this time that Shew took him to see Dr. Valentine Mott, who was then on the staff of the University Medical College of New York. The charity nurse believed the poet was suffering a brain disease:

Figure 1.15. Marie Louise Shew was an unpaid practical nurse who traveled up to Fordham from Manhattan, sometimes daily, to nurse the dying Virginia Poe. She would claim that Poe was suffering from a brain lesion and then later, a heart ailment. *Poe Baltimore*

I decided that in his best health, he had leasion [lesion] on one side of the brain, and as he could not bear stimulants or tonics, without producing insanity, I did not feel much hope, that he could be raised up from a brain

Peaks and Pits, and Pendulum Swings 53

fever, brought on by extreme suffering of mind and body . . . sedatives even had to be administered with caution.[212]

Shew would claim that the eminent surgeon concurred with her diagnosis; although the reliability of her reminiscences, written down almost thirty years later, has proven to be more than a little questionable, and a formal record of such a verdict by Mott remains to be found.

Under the care of Marie Shew and his aunt, Poe recovered. Initially, he was able only to answer the correspondences that had been accumulated during his indisposition, but he was soon able to receive callers at the cottage and pay visits to acquaintances in the city. In June 1847, it was reported in the *Evening Mirror* that Poe "staggered" into their publishing office and that his behavior was such that the police were needed "to take him away."[213] Although this account was eagerly provided by Poe's bitter enemy, Hiram Fuller, the paper's editor, it is difficult to accept that Fuller would have published a story that could not have been substantiated, especially in light of the money damages that the poet had just collected from him; Poe's motivation for such a visit can only be guessed.

While the award from his lawsuit temporarily relieved some of the financial pressure, Poe soon found that he needed to sell more of his writings. In late July, he undertook a trip apparently for the purpose of reestablishing channels for his work and making arrangements for its publication. It appears that Poe first went to Washington, DC, where he visited his friend Frederick Thomas. It may have also been on this trip that he saw Robert D'Unger again while passing through Baltimore. D'Unger was then working for the daily newspaper, the *Baltimore Patriot and Commercial Gazette*, and on this occasion, he claimed a chance encounter with Poe in the vicinity of the Exchange Building on Gay Street where they discussed books that D'Unger had just purchased, the latter giving no indication that the poet was anything but sober.[214]

However, on his final stop in Philadelphia, it appears there may have been another drinking episode. In an effort to place some of his work, Poe called at the publishing offices of magazines including *Godey's Ladies Book*. Of this visit, Louis A. Godey would report to a friend, "Mr. Poe has been on here—but it were better for his fame to have staid [stayed] away . . . he called on me quite sober—but I have heard from him elsewhere, when he was not so."[215] Immediately after his return to Fordham, Poe wrote an apologetic letter to Robert T. Conrad, associate editor for *Graham's Magazine*, thanking him for coming to his rescue while in Philadelphia, and stating that, "without your aid . . . it is more than probable that I should not now be alive to write you this letter."[216] In the note, Poe would also confess to having been "exceedingly ill" while there and without money for the train fare back to New York. The proof

54   *Chapter One*

in this case is (understandably) only circumstantial; yet, as will be seen, there were more of such occurrences during the poet's final period.

For the rest of that year, Poe seems to have stayed mostly at home creating new work and endeavoring to get it published. How he and his aunt survived over the winter is unclear but their reliance on charity had not diminished. That his confinement to Fordham had worked to restore his health and keep him out of trouble is indicated in a long letter to his pen pal from Maine, George Eveleth:

> My habits are rigorously abstemious and I omit nothing of the natural regimen requisite for health:—i.e—I rise early, eat moderately, drink nothing but water, and take abundant and regular exercise in the open air. But this is my private life . . . and of course escapes the eye of the world.[217]

He then gave his correspondent a plausible explanation for the public perception of his intemperance:

> The desire for society comes upon me only when I have become excited by drink. Then only I go—that is, at these times only I have been in the practice of going among my friends: who seldom, or in fact never, having seen me unless excited, take it for granted that I am always so.

If Poe was being truthful, his statement would indicate that he was, at that time, able to achieve extended periods of abstinence. This possibility is upheld by testimony from a visitor to the cottage during that summer. Eighteen-year-old Mary Elizabeth Bronson was among a party that spent a day at Poe's Fordham home, and she would later record her memory of the encounter as well as subsequent meetings with the poet: "I never saw him excited by liquor or any other stimulant. He was always, when I have seen him, a gentleman in the highest sense of the term; of manners most agreeable."[218]

Poe's plan to launch a prestigious literary magazine of his own had not gone away, and by the beginning of 1848 he seemed reenergized by the possibility. He printed a revised prospectus and planned a promotional tour of the southern and western states to acquire subscriptions; Richmond, Virginia, was the planned starting point. To fund the expedition, he would organize lectures along the way but there was no design (or enough money) to take Maria Clemm along as chaperone; Poe would go on his own. To raise the capital needed just to start his tour, he returned to the Society Library in New York City and presented a lecture there on the evening of February 3, although his topic, "The Universe," had little correlation to his aim of establishing a literary journal of *belles-lettres*. The small attendance, due probably to inclement weather rather than to the abstract advertising the lecture, did not generate the hoped-for money to cover travel expenses, and his departure would suffer a series of delays. He had originally planned to leave for Richmond in March,[219] but postponed his departure ostensibly to expedite the publication of "Eureka," his treatise on the creation of the universe from which his lecture was derived. It is also evident that he simply did not have the money to begin the trip; the $14 advance that he had requested (and received) from the publisher for "Eureka" would have been inadequate even for immediate necessities, if not diverted elsewhere.[220]

That Poe was still without the means to leave New York as late as June is evident by his brazen request for assistance from Charles Astor Bristed, a writer he had admonished in one of his Marginalia columns that year.[221] In his appeal to Bristed, Poe reveals that another reason for his trip to Virginia was in "going personally to a distant connexion [sic] near Richmond and endeavoring to interest him in my behalf." Edward Valentine Jr., who was a first cousin of his foster-mother, Frances Allan, was at that time living in Buchanan, Virginia (west of Lynchburg). He may have been the "distant connection" referenced by Poe in the letter. Unable to reach Valentine after his arrival in Richmond, Poe would send him a written request for $200 later that year, indicating that he would use the money as start-up capital for the *Stylus* project.[222] It appears that Valentine gave no more assistance than the price of a subscription.

After receiving a visit at the cottage from Mrs. Jane Locke, Poe agreed to lecture in her hometown of Lowell, Massachusetts; she also offered to provide his lodging while there. The advertised topic of his presentation that he gave on July 10 was "The Poets and Poetry of America," which apparently garnered better attendance than his former talk on the theory of the universe.[223] It was while staying with the Locke family in Lowell that Poe was introduced to their neighbor, Mrs. Nancy Richmond, a married woman with whom he inexplicably developed a deep emotional attachment that would last until his death.

Sometime around the middle of July, Poe left for Richmond. Whether the receipts from his lecture in

Figure 1.16. Sarah Helen Whitman was a widow and poetess from Rhode Island who became spellbound by Poe's writings. After a brief and turbulent courtship, the two became engaged. *Courtesy of the Providence Athenaeum*

56   *Chapter One*

Massachusetts provided the needed travel expenses is unclear; he may have gotten some additional assistance from the Lewises or even Thomas Chivers who had been trying to meet with Poe in New York before he left. Likewise, there are no *confirmed* reports of his drinking before he arrived in Virginia.[224] If Edgar Poe generated much correspondence during this brief trip, little of it has survived, and as a consequence, his movements in the southern city during the summer of 1848 are *suggested* mostly by what others wrote. It is evident that he met with John R. Thompson, then the editor of the *Southern Literary Messenger*, and arranged for the publication of both "The Rationale of Verse" and a review of Mrs. Lewis's book of poems.[225] However, Thompson would write that their meeting occurred only after Poe had recovered from a drinking spree in the Rockett's Landing district, east of the city:

> Edgar A. Poe had been, for a fortnight, in a debauch, in one of the lowest haunts of vice upon the wharves in this City. . . . I learned that such a person had indeed been there, drunk, for two weeks, and that he had gone . . . without hat or coat, to the residence of Mr. John Mackenzie, some three miles distant in the country, alone & on foot.[226]

Although this story is in keeping with an established pattern, it must be stated that there is no independent confirmation of it; Thompson, whose testimony has been shown to be often infused with exaggeration, remains its only authority.

One letter that Poe wrote to his aunt during this trip has survived, and from it we learn that he had indeed been staying at the home of John Mackenzie and perhaps that of John's mother also, where the poet's sister, Rosalie, was then living.[227] It is also apparent that while in Richmond he had some interaction with John M. Daniel of the *Semi-Weekly Examiner*. His exchange with Daniel could not have been a pleasant one as Poe would claim to have challenged him to a duel at the time; however, a supporting account of the incident, as given to J. H. Whitty more than sixty years later by Robert W. Hughes (a writer for the *Examiner*), appears derivative, if not altogether fictional.[228] Daniel himself never acknowledged the *affaire d'honneur* [an affair of honor] with Poe but would later indicate that their encounter may have taken place while the poet was inebriated.[229]

For reasons not adequately demonstrated, Poe's stay in Richmond was cut short, and by September 5 he had returned to Fordham. According to Thompson, Poe's friends "were compelled at last to reship him to New York" after efforts "to get him sober" failed.[230] Many biographers have offered a different theory about his departure in citing Poe's possible romantic motivation. Accordingly, after receiving a letter from Sarah Helen Whitman containing an excerpt of a romantic poem, Poe summarily abandoned his southern

Peaks and Pits, and Pendulum Swings 57

campaign and rushed home in order to pursue her acquaintance. Mrs. Whitman was an attractive widow and a talented poetess whom Poe had noticed when delivering his lectures on poetry. She became enthralled with his writings and communicated her admiration in ways that he could not miss. That Poe was contemplating an introduction with her before he left for the South is indicated in a letter he wrote to Whitman's friend, Anna Blackwell, on June 14:

> Do you know Mrs Whitman? . . . Can you not tell me something about her—any thing—every thing you know—and keep my secret—that is to say let no one know that I have asked you to do so?[231]

Upon his return to the North, he wasted little time in calling on Mrs. Whitman at her home in Providence, Rhode Island, and after spending a few days there in late September romancing her, Poe impetuously made a proposal of marriage. Whitman gave no definite reply; although it appears she seriously considered it, she became wary after receiving reports of his drinking from those trying to prevent the marriage. Her equivocation, along with her family's vehement opposition to the union, surprised and unnerved Poe. He wrote her long, gushing letters declaring his love, and he continued to urge the marriage, yet his efforts had the ring of expedience rather than heartfelt romance. During return visits ostensibly made to convince her, Poe appears to have had difficulty in abstaining from drink and hiding the lapses.[232]

Toward the end of October, he had been invited to repeat his lecture in Lowell, and on his way there he stopped to see Mrs. Whitman to make another pitch of matrimony. However, when the lecture was cancelled, Poe vanished for a time from both Lowell and Providence. In a long letter written to "Annie" Richmond after, he claimed his disappearance was the result of a suicide attempt in which he endeavored to swallow a lethal amount of laudanum. According to Poe, while in Boston he downed an ounce of the potion only to become sick and in need of several days to recover, all while Sarah Whitman had been awaiting his return to Providence. Although many biographers have trusted this story, others are skeptical. Poe did not provide the explanation (to Mrs. Richmond) until two weeks had passed which was more than enough time to concoct an alibi for another drinking binge.[233] He would give Whitman a different reason for the disappearance, though she later indicated her distrust of the explanation. She wrote that he likely had "fallen under the old temptation, which he vainly endeavored to persuade me was caused only by the restless anxiety my silence had occasioned in him."[234] Nevertheless, supporting evidence for either scenario remains to be discovered.

Equally disturbing was an apparent panic attack on November 9 that he suffered in front of Sarah Whitman and her mother. According to the poetess, it occurred on the same day that he sat for the iconic "Ultima Thule" daguerreotype:

> Soon after he left the office [the daguerreotype studio of Samuel Masury and S. W. Hartshorn], he came alone to my mother's house in a state of wild & delirious excitement, calling upon me to save him from some terrible impending doom.... The tones of his voice were appalling & rang through the house. Never have I heard anything so awful, even to sublimity.... It was long before I could nerve myself to see him. My mother was with him more than two hours before I entered the room.... When my mother requested me to have a cup of strong coffee prepared for him, he clung to me so frantically as to tear away a piece of the muslin dress I wore.... In the afternoon he grew more composed, & my mother sent for Dr. A. H. Okie, who, finding symptoms of cerebral congestion, advised his being taken to the house of his friend Wm. J. Pabodie, where he was kindly cared for.[235]

It has been presumed that the breakdown was the result of his drinking during the prior evening;[236] however, this uncontrolled emotional spasm seems to suggest that Poe was afflicted with something beyond, or in addition to, conventional alcoholism.[237]

Figure 1.17. Edgar Allan Poe poses for a daguerreotypist at the behest of his fiancée, Sarah Helen Whitman, in November 1848. Whitman would end the engagement after Poe broke his pledge of abstinence. *Brown University Archives*

Incredibly, Sarah Whitman still agreed to marry Poe but only on the conditions that they could secure her mother's approval and that he would observe complete abstinence, from then on. After taking measures to protect the family estate from someone she thought a fortune hunter, Whitman's mother finally gave her consent to the union on December 22. But on the following day, after receiving a report that Poe had broken his pledge of abstinence that very morning, Whitman called off the wedding.[238] While pleading his defense to her, Mrs. Power (Whitman's mother) intervened and expelled him from their house, upon which he immediately departed for New York. That Poe would permit his drinking to destroy an association with Sarah

Peaks and Pits, and Pendulum Swings 59

Helen Whitman, and the potential for an improvement of his circumstances that she represented, indicates that he had by then lost the ability to control it.

FINAL YEAR

With the New Year came somewhat better prospects for Poe. Just prior to Christmas of the previous year, he delivered a lecture at the Franklin Lyceum of Providence, Rhode Island that may have attracted his largest attendance, which by one estimate, was almost 2,000 people.[239] If his compensation had been derived from ticket sales, Poe would have had quite a bundle of money to sustain him (and his aunt) during the ensuing weeks. In addition, he was energetically producing more work and, as the record indicates, he was becoming more aggressive in his efforts to get it placed.[240] Among the masterpieces that he finished during this period were "Eldorado," "The Bells," and the ballad, "Annabel Lee."

But in spite of this increased productivity, some of his usual publishing outlets returned Poe's submissions after having gone out of business, while other periodicals "pleaded poverty" and were no longer paying for any contributions. And then there were magazines such as the *Southern Literary Messenger* that withheld what they owed him without explanation. Notwithstanding any funds remaining from his last lecture, Edgar and his aunt were forced to continue a life of pecuniary desperation. His persistent advocacy of Estelle Lewis's tedious poetry during this time suggests that he was still receiving assistance from her.[241] In a letter to Annie Richmond, Poe revealed the despair he was feeling at the time:

> It is not so much ill that I have been as depressed in spirits—I cannot express to you how terribly I have been suffering from gloom. . . . You know how cheerfully I wrote to you not long ago—about my prospects—hopes—how I anticipated being soon out of difficulty—well! all seems to be frustrated.

Poe's attachment to the married woman was deepening and he hinted that he and his aunt were discussing a move to be near her:

> We have told our landlord that we will not take the house next year. Do not let Mr. R. [Richmond], however, make any arrangements for us in Lowell, or Westford—for, being poor, we are so much the slaves of circumstances. At all events, we will both come & see you & spend a week with you in the early spring or before.[242]

In late May, or early June, Poe traveled by himself to visit with Annie and her family where he stayed a week or more perhaps trying to lift his spirits.[243]

Figure 1.18. While Poe was staying with the family of Mrs. "Annie" Richmond at Lowell, Massachusetts, in the spring of 1849, his hostess commissioned this daguerreotype of him. Arguably the most revealing of the eight known photographic images of the poet, one biographer would describe his countenance as "pained and apprehensive." *J. Paul Getty Museum*

There he also spent time among the villagers, even beginning a flirtation with a young teacher at the school in which Annie's brother, Bardwell Heywood, was the principal. It was during this trip to Lowell that Mrs. Richmond convinced him to sit for a pair of photographic portraits, arguably the most revealing of the poet. The "Annie" and "Stella" daguerreotypes, as they would become known, depict a "visibly older, more haggard Poe: . . . the effects of time and dissipation far more evident than in the Providence photographs."[244] Still another biographer would describe his appearance as "pained and apprehensive."[245] If Poe derived any measure of comfort from this visit with Annie, it does not show in the images.

Yet another sweep of the pendulum held the promise of financial rescue for Poe in the form of a mislaid communication from a well-off admirer. Edwin H. N. Patterson was a young newspaper owner from the West (Oquawka, Illinois), who had sent Poe an offer to fund his long-dreamed-of national literary magazine. According to the terms of Patterson's proposal, Poe would have complete editorial control and also an equal share in its proceeds.[246] Patterson's letter, mailed before Christmas, was not received by Poe until the end of April, but he immediately jumped at the idea and made plans to pick up where he left off in Richmond the year before.[247] He would conduct a tour of the South and West, promoting the new magazine while gathering the needed subscriptions and arranging for possible contributors. To cover his travel costs, Poe planned to give lectures along the way, but money would be needed to start the expedition. He asked Patterson to forward half of a $100 allowance to John Thompson at the *Southern Literary Messenger* that he could collect upon his arrival there around the first of June.[248]

Peaks and Pits, and Pendulum Swings

As with the trip to Virginia of the previous year, the original date of his planned departure in 1849 was postponed because he lacked the necessary funds just to leave Fordham. Poe makes this predicament clear in his last known letter to Annie Richmond: "When I can go now, is uncertain—but perhaps I may be off to-morrow, or next day:—all depends upon circumstances beyond my control."[249] He had also written to John Thompson asking him to send a small amount of money, or to forward Patterson's letter (containing the $50 stipend) if he had already received it. But all his efforts to acquire traveling money seemed to find little success, and by the end of June, he was still sitting in New York.

During these final months before he left for the South, there are no *confirmed* accounts of drinking episodes; however, earlier in the spring, Poe wrote to Mrs. Richmond saying that he was recovering from an illness. Before posting the letter, Maria Clemm appended her own postscript:

> Eddy; he has been very ill, but is now better. I thought he would die several times. God knows I wish we were both in our graves. It would, I am sure, be far better.[250]

Of course, without further information, we cannot be certain as to the precise nature of Poe's ailment, but Clemm's ominous remark—which was in regard to the illness and not their wider circumstances—raises the possibility that he had suffered another, and perhaps more fearful, episode of the frenzied panic he experienced in Providence. According to Clemm, her nephew was then "under an impression that he might be called suddenly from the world," and he gave her a written request to have the anthologist, Rufus W. Griswold, act as his literary executor.[251] Whether Edgar Allan Poe actually left such a document, or articulated his fatalism, has never been proven, but Clemm's pursuit of Griswold to superintend a collection of the poet's works after his death would have far-reaching consequences.[252]

Chapter Two

On to Richmond

Edgar Allan Poe finally managed to leave for Richmond, Virginia, on Friday, June 29, but not from the cottage at Fordham. He, along with Maria Clemm, had traveled down to Brooklyn, and during the day they dined with Mrs. Lewis and her husband before the poet departed on his southern lecture tour. There could have been several reasons for the visit, not the least of which was Poe's desire to reduce his presence at the cottage—apparently, he was in arrears there and being pressed for the rent money.[1] They also got a meal at the Lewis's, no small matter to the cash-starved poet and his aunt. And the location of the Lewis residence, at 125 Dean Street in Brooklyn, was not too far out his way and certainly much closer to the point of departure than Fordham, which was thirteen miles above the city.

However, the most important reason for visiting the Lewises before leaving was perhaps financial. As discussed, they had provided Poe and his aunt with material assistance during the previous eighteen months. In exchange, Poe worked to get her poetry published and to provide favorable notices. He also cashed in what little influence he had to arrange a publication of her collected works, which he also praised publicly. In describing this arrangement, Poe's biographer, Arthur Hobson Quinn, would write, "There is something especially artificial in Poe's friendship with 'Stella.' She was evidently a vain woman, whose husband, Sylvanus D. Lewis, was able and willing to pay for her vanities."[2] The surrender of his critical integrity nauseated him, but entrapped by his circumstances, he had little choice. That the Lewises also aided him at this time with some amount of his travel expenses may have been the real purpose of the stopover. Following dinner with the couple, there were hugs and handshakes at the front door after which Poe and Maria Clemm climbed into the Lewises' carriage for the short trip over to the Fulton Ferry.[3] There, Poe bid a prolonged and tearful farewell to his "Muddy," who

Figure 2.1. By 1849, Poe and his aunt were planning to move from their cottage in Fordham, New York. After leaving there in the early summer for a tour in support of a planned literary magazine, he would never see her or the house again. *Author (printed engraving from author's collection)*

then returned to the Lewises' home to spend the night. She would never see her "Eddie" again.[4]

After parting with Maria, Poe paid the two-cent fare and was ferried across the East River. He then made his way over to Liberty Street on the other side of Manhattan where another ferryboat would have taken him across the Hudson River to Jersey City and the "cars" to Philadelphia. The afternoon train left at 4:30 p.m., and it is probable that Poe arrived too late, necessitating a layover in New York or Jersey City.[5] If he made the afternoon connection, he would have boarded with at least one piece of luggage, perhaps just a valise with clothing, manuscripts, and his written lecture. Although the train had multiple stops on the way to Philadelphia, the trip was usually completed in five hours and Poe would still have arrived there well before midnight, or if delayed, midafternoon the following day.

He successfully reached the train depot on Market Street probably on June 30, although the date has not been firmly established. Poe could have spent the prior evening (or evenings) in Manhattan, Jersey City, or in the area around the Philadelphia train station. Sometime before, or after his arrival, he lost his valise, a calamity suggesting that he had already begun to drink. He would later claim in a letter to Maria Clemm that he recovered the bag at the train depot, but that the papers it contained had been stolen. There is some question to this tale of the valise's retrieval without his written lectures; it appears to have been invented to portray a theft of the case instead of its abandonment during a spree.[6]

Where he went and what he did after his arrival in Philadelphia can only be supposed. At that time, the conspicuously intoxicated were not left on the street but sent to the county prison for a fine or confinement. Poe confessed in a letter to Maria Clemm, and to others, of having been taken to Moyamensing Prison on a charge of public drunkenness; however, it appears his internment may have been abbreviated when he was recognized and "dismissed without the customary fine."[7] When recalling these events in 1889, Poe's friend John Sartain stated that Poe next showed up at his engraving studio on a Monday afternoon (possibly July 2) "looking pale and haggard and with

Figure 2.2. After arriving in Philadelphia on June 30, 1849, Poe may have been detained on a charge of public drunkenness and taken to Moyamensing Prison, shown here. That Poe was familiar with its design is indicated by his confessed hallucination of a glowing banshee perched on its "granite battlements." *The Library Company of Philadelphia*

a wild expression in his eyes." Poe was in "terror of his life" and informed Sartain that he had overheard two men plotting to kill him while on the train *to* New York and, after "giving them the slip," returned to Philadelphia. Much has been made of this mistaken detail stating that Poe was on his way to New York, but recalling events forty years after they transpired, it is likely that Sartain's memory was less than perfect. As subsequent testimony (even by Poe) will demonstrate, he was indeed traveling *from* New York at that time, and there is no evidence to support the idea that he had attempted to double-back.[8]

Sartain tried to calm Poe, who, still panicked with paranoia, asked for a razor to remove his mustache in order to disguise himself from those *he said* were pursuing him. Sartain, fearing that Poe's thoughts were turning toward suicide, scraped the mustache off with a pair of scissors: "Taking him to the rear of the office I sheared away until he was absolutely barefaced."[9] Poe's attempt to disguise himself here will be shown later to have significance.

He remained with Sartain while he worked in his office, but in the early evening Poe decided to go out to the Fairmount Water Works, a reservoir overlooking the Schuylkill River. Sartain, still concerned that Poe might try to do himself harm, went along. According to the engraver, it was during their evening stroll that Poe confided about both his detention at Moyamensing and his nightmarish vision of conversing in whispers with a luminous female form that was perched high up on the prison's stone parapet. Poe then told of an attempt there by guards to immerse him in a giant cauldron of boiling water and other tortures, such as making him watch while Maria Clemm was slowly dismembered. Sartain eventually returned Poe, probably still debilitated, to his house where he was put to bed, his friend sleeping in the same room to keep a watchful eye. The following morning (or perhaps on July 4, after a second night), Sartain claimed that Poe had sufficiently recovered to be trusted to go out

Figure 2.3. John Sartain was an engraver and publisher who met Edgar Poe in 1840 while they were both involved in the Philadelphia magazine trade. He was among those who came to Poe's rescue during the poet's final trip through the city in the summer of 1849. *Author (printed engraving from author's collection)*

On to Richmond 67

alone. After an hour or two, he returned to tell Sartain that the experiences he described, including the pursuing assassins, "had been a delusion and a scare created by his own excited imagination,"[10] although his detention at Moyamensing Prison was probably factual.[11] While there is no visible reason to doubt Sartain's version of events, Poe would later attribute his rescue in Philadelphia largely to two other men, Chauncey Burr and George Lippard.

How many days elapsed from the time he left John Sartain's custody until he climbed the four flights of stairs to George Lippard's newspaper office is unclear. If he had another bout of drinking after leaving Sartain, he came back to the surface long enough to get an emotional (and unsigned) letter off to Maria Clemm on July 7.[12] According to Lippard, Poe was totally destitute and had been making the rounds the day before to homes of literary acquaintances asking for assistance. He dramatically appealed to Lippard for help in getting some money that would see him out of Philadelphia. Being low on funds himself at the time and recognizing that Poe was, at the very least, unprepared to travel (he was inadequately dressed and wearing only one shoe), Lippard offered to go out and canvass for contributions in his place; Poe would stay behind and rest in the office.[13] The young editor did not fare much better than Poe at first: there was a cholera epidemic then raging in Philadelphia that had chased many out of town, and those he did find would not help when they discovered the beneficiary's identity. Lippard, dispirited and not feeling well, went home without returning to work. The next morning, he hurried back to the printing office to find Poe still there, perhaps even more upset and telling Lippard that he thought he had deserted him. Lippard redoubled his efforts and had better luck on the second day. He induced Louis A. Godey and Samuel D. Patterson, the latter then publishing *Graham's Magazine*, to give five dollars each. He then convinced John Sartain and his clerk, William Miskey, to put up a few dollars. Chauncey Burr had also offered to pitch in personally and returned with Lippard. Burr invited Poe to his home, where the three spent the afternoon preparing him for the journey to Richmond. Finally, in the evening, the pair accompanied Poe to the depot on Market Street and placed him on the 10 p.m. train to Baltimore, Burr paying the three-dollar fare.[14]

Poe had by then spent almost two weeks in a city that should have delayed him only a few hours. When first reporting to Maria Clemm, he blamed his breakdown on a bout of cholera: "I have been so ill—have had the cholera, or spasms quite as bad."[15] Later, after landing in Richmond, he would tell her, "All was hallucination, arising from an attack which I had never before experienced—an attack of mania-a-potu. May Heaven grant that it prove a warning to me for the rest of my days."[16] Poe may have indeed become ill while in Philadelphia which then raises a question of how and where he would have recovered. Nevertheless, his latter explanation is probably more truthful

Figure 2.4. After spending an afternoon at John Sartain's engraving studio in Philadelphia, Poe decided to visit the Fairmount Water Works, a favorite scenic spot on the Schuylkill River. Sartain, concerned that Poe might try to jump from the bridge that spanned above the river, went along as a precaution. *Library of Congress*

as the nightmare of *mania-a-potu* [delirium tremens] can be the result of alcohol withdrawal to someone who has developed a chemical dependence. If Poe had such a condition and drank until his pockets were dry, or ended up at a place where he could not be treated, the torture of delirium tremens would soon follow. The ghostly images, graphic mutilations, and pursuing assassins that he related to John Sartain are traditional manifestations of such an attack.[17]

When comparing this episode to events in Baltimore three months later, the parallels are easy to see. In both instances, he was traveling alone, without supervision, and had started out with some money in his pockets. Like his return trip later in the fall, here he was just passing through Philadelphia with no particular goal other than to make a travel connection. However, when traveling back north through Baltimore, he would find no friends to come to his aid until it was too late, with the result being much different.

Although probably not fully recovered, Poe left Pennsylvania on his own with at least ten dollars in his possession, heading for Baltimore and its reputation for lawlessness.[18] After a six-hour journey on the train that involved a wait for a ferry at the Susquehanna River, he disembarked during the early morning hours at President Street on the east side of town. During this time of day, even in Baltimore, the taverns and oyster houses were all shuttered; the timing, and perhaps his lingering sickness, probably kept Poe out of trouble.

One of the Saturday steam packets bound for Richmond left Baltimore's harbor at 4 p.m. from the wharf on Light Street, about twelve blocks to the west.[19] How he spent the ten to twelve hours in Baltimore before his departure is unknown; perhaps he got much needed sleep on the boat (which was permitted) or he may have used the time to write to his aunt.[20] As the name suggests, these boats carried mail as well as freight, and they made many scheduled and unscheduled stops along the way. The cruise down the Chesapeake Bay and up the James River, against the current, usually took more than twenty hours on the direct boat, which would have deposited him at Ludlam's Wharf, a mile below Richmond, in the early afternoon of July 15.[21]

At last, back in the Old Dominion, Poe was far enough away from New York where the scandals and gossiping tongues had, for the most part, not been given large circulation. Yet for all the practical reasons for coming to Richmond, Poe had a genuine enthusiasm for the place. When in Philadelphia, he told George Lippard, "I am homesick for Virginia. I don't know why it is but when my foot is once in Virginia, I feel myself a new man. It is a pleasure to me to go into her woods—to lay myself upon her sod—even

Figure 2.5. This view of Richmond from Church Hill depicts the city as it appeared during the time of Poe's final visit in the summer of 1849. That he was planning to resettle there is not certain. *Library of Congress*

70   *Chapter Two*

to breathe her air."[22] Now he was again among those with familiar thinking, and familiar accents.

He first took a room at the American Hotel on the corner of Eleventh and Main Streets and immediately wrote again to Maria Clemm in an attempt to allay her fears. The letter is filled with emotion and a lament of the lost lectures, and it is not likely she reaped much relief from it other than the single dollar he enclosed:

> Oh, Mother, I am so ill while I write—but I resolved that come what would, I would not sleep again without easing your dear heart as far as I could. My valise was lost for ten days. At last I found it at the depot in Philadelphia, but (you will scarcely credit it) they had opened it and stolen both lectures. Oh, Mother, think of the blow to me this evening, when on examining the valise, these lectures were gone. All my object here is over unless I can recover them or re-write one of them. . . . I got here with two dollars over—of which I inclose [*sic*] you one. Oh God, my Mother, shall we ever again meet? If possible, oh COME! My clothes are so horrible, and I am so ill. Oh, if you could come to me, my mother. Write instantly—oh do not fail. God forever bless you.[23]

That he still had any money to send to his aunt establishes that he did not linger in Baltimore; nor let "his feet slip" while on the steamboats.[24]

Within a day or two, Poe finally received his first communication from Clemm after leaving her in New York more than two weeks earlier, and the effect her words had on him was nothing short of miraculous as can be seen in his reply:

> My Own Beloved Mother—
> You will see at once, by the handwriting of this letter, that I am better—much better in health and spirits. Oh, if you only knew how your dear letter comforted me! It acted like magic. Most of my suffering arose from that terrible idea which I could not get rid of—the idea that you were dead. For more than ten days I was totally deranged, although I was not drinking one drop; and during this interval I imagined the most horrible calamities. . . . All is not lost yet, and "the darkest hour is just before daylight." Keep up heart, my own beloved mother—all may yet go well. I will put forth all my energies. When I get my mind a little more composed, I will try to write something. Oh, give my dearest, fondest love to Mrs. L. Tell her that never, while I live, will I forget her kindness to my darling mother.[25]

Edgar Allan Poe was finally "himself" again.

Outwardly, his purpose for the return to Richmond was to raise funds and build a subscription list for the magazine venture in which he was to be partnered with Edwin H. N. Patterson, and he followed his reply to Clemm with a brief note to him acknowledging and expressing thanks for the $50 advance he had waiting for Poe (at the *Southern Literary Messenger*) when he arrived.[26] His funding strategy for the magazine project involved lecturing to pay his travel expenses, but he was now painfully aware that he was without his written manuscripts. He dashed off yet another letter to George Lippard back in Philadelphia explaining their loss and imploring him to conduct a search, but even with the assistance of Chauncey Burr, the effort would prove unsuccessful.[27] Poe would undoubtedly spend his first weeks in Richmond feverishly reconstructing the lecture, as evidenced by an announcement at the end of the month that he would deliver a talk on "The Poetic Principle" at the Exchange Hotel.

Figure 2.6. George Lippard was a writer and magazine editor who had befriended Poe during the time of his residence in Philadelphia. He was among those who rescued the poet from the streets there during his final visit in 1849. *Library of Congress*

From this burst of activity, and attention to purpose, it is clear that Poe had recovered his health. In short order he removed to the Swan Tavern on Broad Street. He explained to an acquaintance that in "choosing it—it was cheap, well kept in 'the old Virginia style,' associated with many pleasant memories of his youth, and, lastly and chiefly, nearest Duncan Lodge," a place where he would direct much of his attention during this last visit to Richmond.[28]

Duncan Lodge, located approximately two miles northwest of the city's center, was the home Mrs. Jane Mackenzie and her family, who had taken in and raised Poe's sister, Rosalie; during the time of Poe's final visit to Richmond she was still a member of the family. Shortly after his arrival in town, he paid a call to the Mackenzie family and at some point, asked for an introduction to Susan Archer Talley, a twenty-seven-year-old poetess who had been published and even recognized in Rufus Griswold's anthology, *Female Poets of America* (1849). Poe had previously corresponded with her in regard to her uncle, Edward Valentine (also a first cousin of Frances Valentine, Poe's foster-mother), and his possible financial support of the *Stylus* project.[29] The Talley family lived near the Mackenzies, so Poe's request for an introduction would not have been unexpected.[30] It may have been the

72   *Chapter Two*

following day that Poe and Rosalie made a call on them—Susan would later look back on their first meeting through infatuated eyes:

> Poe was seated near an open window, quietly conversing. His attitude was easy and graceful, with one arm lightly resting upon the back of his chair. . . . He rose on my entrance, and, other visitors being present, stood with one hand resting on the back of his chair, awaiting my greeting. So dignified was his manner, so reserved his expression, that I experienced an involuntary recoil, until I turned to him and saw his eyes suddenly brighten as I offered my hand; a barrier seemed to melt between us, and I felt that we were no longer strangers.[31]

According to Talley, Poe spent much time with her, and a significant portion of the information concerning his last days in Richmond is derived from her reminiscences of it. However, her account of him and his activities during those final weeks must be viewed with caution; her admiration of (and perhaps romantic interest in) Poe certainly colored some of her recollections, and the attention he showed her in return may have been "sponsored" by her relationship with Edward Valentine.

Yet another motive for Poe's return to Virginia was a hoped-for reestablishment of his relationship with his teenage sweetheart, Elmira Royster, now the widow, Mrs. Elmira S. Shelton, a woman of independent means. It is not clear when the idea to pursue her arose in Poe; Susan Talley indicated that John Mackenzie suggested the union while Poe was in Richmond during the summer of 1848.[32] Although he may have intended to see her at that time, Shelton makes it clear in a letter to her cousin, Dr. Philip Fitzhugh, that they did not meet during Poe's brief visit to the Virginia capitol. He *reportedly* cut that trip short in order to commence a courtship with Sarah Whitman in Rhode Island.[33]

There can be little doubt as to the reason for Poe's newfound interest in Mrs. Shelton as his remarkable letter to Maria Clemm on August 29 reveals:

> Her property is not so large as I was told—but is ample for all our wants. Mr. Shelton left property to the amount of $60,000, and since his death it has much increased in value and is now worth at least 70,000. . . . But she has had charge of the estate now for 9 years; and as she is said to be a notable manager, no doubt she has laid by many thousand dollars in money.[34]

At the age of thirty-nine years, Elmira Shelton had given birth to four children and no longer had the bloom of youth. Susan Talley [Weiss] would describe Shelton's appearance at the time as having, "large, deep-set, light-blue eyes and sunken cheeks, her straight features, high forehead and cold expression of countenance." She also added: "Doubtless she [Shelton] had been handsome in her youth, but the impression which she produced upon me was that of a sensible, practical woman, the reverse of a poet's ideal."[35]

Yet as soon as he was settled, and suitably clothed, Poe made a beeline for Shelton's house on Church Hill. His determination and brazen impatience for a marriage is depicted in Elmira Shelton's account of his first visit:

> I was ready to go to church and a servant told me that a gentleman in the parlour wanted to see me. I went down and was amazed to see him—but knew him instantly—He came up to me in the most enthusiastic manner and said: "Oh! Elmira, is this you?" That very morning I told him I was going to church, that I never let anything interfere with that, that he must call again and when he did call again he renewed his addresses [proposal]. I laughed at it; he looked very serious and said he was in earnest and had been thinking about it for a long time. Then I found out that he was very serious and I became serious. I told him if he would not take a positive denial he must give me time to consider of it. And he said a love that hesitated was not a love for him.[36]

Shelton would have been well aware of her former beau's celebrity, perhaps she had even followed his career, but it is likely that she was not, at first, acquainted with his reputation. Nevertheless, Shelton would indeed consider his *addresses*.

Now "himself" again, Poe had to (or at least try to) follow through on some of the promises he made in order to fulfill the original objectives of his southern tour. He visited the office of the *Southern Literary Messenger* where he had been sending contributions prior to his arrival.[37] These submissions consisted largely of reviews, notices of poems and installments for his Marginalia series, the latter of which had been previously published. Poe's compensation from the editor, John R. Thompson, may have been slow in coming, prompting the visits. But Thompson wanted something more substantial; he wanted a new tale, and now that Poe was in town, he expected to get one. When writing to Rufus Griswold immediately following Poe's death, Thompson claimed that he paid for a new composition: "I lost nearly as much by his death as yourself, as I had paid him for a prose article to be written, and he owed me something at that time."[38] Thompson would state, in his ever-changing recollection of events, that he advanced Poe a small amount for the work a day or two before his departure for New York.

Poe finally wrote a substantive letter to Edwin Patterson, giving cholera and a prolonged recovery as the reason for the delayed reply. In his earlier letter, Patterson had suggested a three-dollar price for their proposed magazine, but Poe replied that it should remain a more expensive publication as they had discussed. He added that a July (1850) launch for the magazine

Figure 2.7. During his final months in Richmond, Poe began a courtship with his adolescent sweetheart (then a widow) Sarah Elmira Shelton, who was living in this house at 2407 East Grace Street. The house survives today in private hands. *Edgar Allan Poe Museum, Richmond, VA*

was more workable than the coming January, and Poe also promised to visit him in St. Louis before then. These details appeared to demonstrate, outwardly at least, that he was still planning to move forward with the venture.[39]

He would also (eventually) visit the offices of the *Richmond Semi-Weekly Examiner* and make peace with its editor, John M. Daniel. Daniel had been critical of Edgar Poe in his newspaper. Given that Poe claimed to have challenged him to a duel during his visit of the previous summer, it is not clear why Daniels started warming to the poet.[40] In his publication, he now penned lengthy and objective reviews of Poe's lectures. Daniel also included friendly notices of Poe's anticipated marriage and seemed eager for his pending relocation to the area. After their meeting, it had even been rumored that Poe was to join the staff at the *Examiner*.[41] Indeed, when Poe finally left for New York, his departure was deemed newsworthy by Daniels, and when word came of his death on October 9, the editor appeared stunned, and penned a *mostly* sympathetic obituary.[42]

When he was not visiting newspaper offices, Poe was making social calls, often in tandem with his sister Rosalie, who was energized by her older brother's visit. Edgar Poe was indeed a genuine celebrity and his rumored betrothal to a Richmond blue blood endowed him with a social currency that had many seeking his company who otherwise would not. The long list of those who received him during these weeks also included old acquaintances and childhood playmates who still saw him as their friend, including Robert Stanard, his schoolmate and the son of perhaps his first infatuation, Mrs. Jane Stith Stanard, whom he immortalized in his poem, "To Helen." He visited Robert Sully, renowned portrait painter and school chum; and he saw an ill Eliza Lambert who was staying with the family of J. H. Strobia, also intimate acquaintances of Poe and the Allans. Dr. Robert Cabell was another childhood friend who hosted, along with his wife, a gathering one evening in which Poe was the star attraction.[43] Poe reportedly also paid visits to Thomas Alfriend, Mrs. Peter Chevalie, and Dr. John Carter.

Of course, Poe and his sister were also regulars at the Mackenzie's Duncan Lodge and Talavera, the home of Susan Talley who would write that Poe thought this time to be the most enjoyable of his mature life: "the last few weeks in the society of his old and new friends had been the happiest that he had known for many years." She added that "when he again left New York he should there leave behind all the trouble and vexation of his past life. On no occasion had I seen him so cheerful."[44]

Several of those who saw him at this time provide an illuminating snapshot of the poet's appearance and demeanor. According to the twenty-year-old Oscar P. Fitzgerald, Poe was, "A compact, well-set man about five feet six [eight] inches high, straight as an arrow, easy-gaited, with white linen coat and trousers, black velvet vest and broad Panama hat, features sad yet finely cut, shapely head, and eyes that were strangely magnetic as you looked into them . . . a man bearing the stamp of genius and the charm of a melancholy that drew one toward him with a strange sympathy."[45]

From Johns Hopkins University Professor, Basil L. Gildersleeve, comes this recollection of the poet: "Poe himself I saw and heard in Richmond during the last summer of his life. He was lodging at some poor place in Broad Street, if I am not mistaken. At least I saw him repeatedly in that thoroughfare—a poetical figure, if there ever was one, clad in black as was the fashion then—slender—erect—the subtle lines of his face fixed in meditation."[46]

Perhaps the best, if not the most romanticized, description of Poe at this time comes from Miss Talley again:

His dark curling hair was thrown back from his broad forehead—a style in which he habitually wore it. . . . He always carried a cane,[47] and upon entering the shade of the avenue would remove his hat, throw back his hair, and walk lingeringly, as if enjoying the coolness, carrying his hat in his hand, generally behind him. Sometimes he would pause to examine some rare flower, or to pluck a grape from the laden trellises . . .

Poe's eyes, indeed, were his most striking feature, and it was to these that his face owed its peculiar attraction. I have never seen other eyes at all resembling them. They were large, with long, jet-black lashes,—the iris dark steel-gray, possessing a crystalline clearness and transparency, through which the jet-black pupil was seen to expand and contract with every shade of thought or emotion . . .

Apart from the wonderful beauty of his eyes, I would not have called Poe a very handsome man. He was, in my opinion, rather distinguished-looking than handsome . . . but at the period of my acquaintance with him he had a pallid and careworn look,—somewhat haggard, indeed.[48]

76 *Chapter Two*

Talley also added that "his dark, scrupulously kept mustache did not entirely conceal a slightly contracted expression of the mouth and an occasional twitching of the upper lip." Poe was also known to smoke a pipe or chew tobacco as the situation, and funds, would allow.

Another of those offering him a place to stay on this visit was the family of Mr. and Mrs. W. A. R. Nye. Mr. Nye was connected with the newspaper, the *Richmond Daily Whig*, and the families had apparently met during the time of Poe's previous residence in Richmond twelve years earlier. It is not clear how much time, if any, he spent with them during this visit, but they felt close enough to contact Maria Clemm on his behalf. Mrs. Nye wrote to Clemm in August apparently asking her to come to Richmond, which would suggest that they thought Poe needed her help.[49]

Early in August, prior to his first lecture, Poe appears to have fallen ill after another drinking episode. Susan Talley, who claimed that Poe made a deliberate effort to hide such things from her, remarked on an occurrence that she only heard about from a friend:

> All that I knew of the matter was when a friend informed me that "Mr. Poe was too unwell to see us that evening." A day or two after this he sent a message by his sister [Rosalie Poe] requesting some flowers, in return for which came a dainty note of thanks, written in a tremulous hand. He again wrote, inclosing a little anonymous poem which he had found in some newspaper and admired; and on the day following he made his appearance among us, but so pale, tremulous and apparently subdued as to convince me that he had been seriously ill. On this occasion he had been at his rooms at the "Old Swan" where he was carefully tended by Mrs. Mackenzie's family.[50]

This account would seem to be confirmed independently by a letter to Professor James A. Harrison from William J. Glenn, once associated with the Sons of Temperance (Richmond), in which he wrote that "[Poe] boarded at the old Swan Tavern, on Broad Street, between Eighth and Ninth. Dr. George Rawlings, an intimate friend of mine, told me he attended him there in an attack of delirium tremens, and before he had ceased to visit him, he left the tavern."[51] It may have been during this episode that he made a call on the family of his childhood playmate, Catherine Elizabeth Poitiaux, but was refused admittance to the house by her family because of his perceived condition.[52]

If the Mackenzies and Dr. Rawlings came to Poe's aid, they had him restored in time to deliver his scheduled lecture at the Exchange Hotel on August 17. Despite the oppressive heat forcing many out of town to cooler retreats, the Concert Room of the hotel was filled. Poe gave a solid, steady performance that was well received by those in the building and for the most part, well reviewed in the papers, with at least two writers asking for an encore.[53]

In the audience was Elmira Shelton who, in spite of warnings from family and friends, now appeared to have become receptive to his marriage proposal. Perhaps as a consequence of others cautioning her, she asked Poe if they could postpone the ceremony until January; certainly, a reasonable suggestion given their circumstances and the gravity of such a commitment. The request had the expected result on Poe, who became irritated and stopped calling on her.[54] It is difficult to understand how Shelton would have still wanted to marry Poe—by then she would have been apprised of his drinking, if she had not witnessed it firsthand. Both her mother and children were vociferous, and relentless, in their opposition to the union, and she would be sacrificing three quarters of her husband's estate—a stated condition of his will, should she remarry. Yet Elmira Shelton appeared to have fallen once again for the man, who was now a celebrated author and poet.

According to Susan Talley Weiss, reports of the marriage now became public, even appearing in the papers, but all against the poet's wishes.[55] The effect this publicity would have had on Poe can only be guessed at. Perhaps he secretly felt some relief after Shelton had asked for the delay, allowing a reprieve from the potential enslavement of a loveless marriage. Annie Richmond seems to have been on his mind constantly, and a church merger with Shelton would have raised "yet another terrible bar" between him and the Massachusetts lady.[56] He was also yearning for the company of his aunt who was far away in the North as well. That she herself was in dire need of help did not appear to be as important to Poe as his separation from her. He wrote to her that his lecture, although well attended, had not generated enough profit to settle his bill at the Swan Tavern, let alone allow anything to be sent up to her.[57]

That he eventually became depressed and sank below the surface a second time is almost assured. From here Susan Weiss picks up the story again:

On a second and more serious relapse he was taken by Dr. [Thomas] Mackenzie and Dr. Gibbon Carter to Duncan's [sic] Lodge, where during some days his life was in imminent danger. Assiduous attention saved him, but it was the opinion of the physicians that another such attack would prove fatal. This they told him, warning him seriously of the danger. His reply was that if people would not tempt him, he would not fall. Dr. Carter relates how, on this occasion, he had a long conversation with him, in which Poe expressed the most earnest desire to break from the thralldom of his besetting sin, and told of his many unavailing struggles to do so. He was moved even to tears, and finally declared, in the most solemn manner, that this time he would restrain himself,—would withstand any temptation.[58]

78   *Chapter Two*

As biographer Arthur Quinn would observe, "How difficult it was for Poe to withstand that temptation in a society, where conviviality was a matter of course, can well be imagined. To refuse to drink with an acquaintance was almost an insult, and few were good enough friends to help him in his struggle."[59]

In the August 29 letter to his aunt, Poe reported that he had left the Swan Tavern and registered at the Madison House (Tenth and Bank Streets).[60] This relocation was probably not by choice as he wrote, "forced by circumstances to remain at an expensive hotel." The reason for this is not known but it is possible that after settling his bill and redeeming his trunk at the Swan he may have been asked to leave. There are also the negative associations of residing at a tavern, especially when you are about to wed someone of the upper society; Poe may have simply sought a more eminent address.

Or perhaps his vacating the inn was a condition of his admittance into the Sons of Temperance, a nineteenth-century version of Alcoholics Anonymous, the announcement of which appeared in August 31 edition of the *Banner of Temperance*, the organization's newsletter:

> Edgar A. Poe, Esq.
>
> This gentleman who has been in our city for some weeks past, and who has been ministering to the delight of our citizens in several highly interesting lectures, was initiated as a Son of Temperance in [the] Shockoe Hill Division, No. 54, on last Monday night [August 27]. We mention the fact, conceiving that it will be gratifying to the friends of temperance to know that a gentleman of Mr. Poe's fine talents and rare attainments has been enlisted in the cause. We trust his pen will sometimes be employed in its behalf.[61]

William Glenn, then the presiding officer who administered the oath to Poe, would later write, "There had been to us no intimation that Mr. Poe had violated his pledge before leaving Richmond."[62]

Poe's membership was picked up and printed in papers around the country, and it is certain that Elmira Shelton (and everyone in her family) was given the news as the wedding was back on now, at least as far as Poe was concerned. By the end of August, Poe was back on his feet again, making the rounds socially as well as arranging another lecture in Norfolk, Virginia. He was also visited by John Loud, a Philadelphia piano manufacturer, who asked Poe to edit a number of poems written by his wife who sought to have her work published in book form. Poe accepted the task for which Loud would pay him $100, an exorbitant amount of money, but he would have to appear in Philadelphia.[63]

Back in New York, Maria Clemm was doing without even the basic necessities to survive, and she turned both to those she knew, and to strangers for

Figure 2.8. Shortly after arriving in Richmond on his final visit, Poe boarded at the Swan Tavern on Broad Street, depicted here in its original settings. However, before leaving for Philadelphia, it appears he was forced to relocate to the nearby Madison House. *Author (printed engraving from author's collection)*

help. She desperately wanted to join Poe in Virginia and had undoubtedly asked the Lewises to provide for her travel expenses. However, they would have been reluctant, at the very least, to bankroll a severing of their relationship with Poe that was likely to become permanent.[64] The Lewises' cautiousness is suggested by their withholding of a letter that Poe sent to Clemm, when he was still in Philadelphia, asking her to join him.[65]

Several days in advance of his advertised lecture there on September 14, Poe made his way down to Norfolk, apparently at the request of Mrs. Susan Maxwell who also provided his lodging.[66] Taking in the ocean air, he seemed to have become more at ease, no doubt reminiscing about his time at Fortress Monroe. Poe was the toast of the tidewater, and in the evenings he was "entertained by the first families of Norfolk." After the lavish dinners, Poe would have been expected to sing for his supper, and there would have been recitals of "The Raven," "Ulalume," and perhaps "Annabel Lee." There, as anywhere in the South, correct hospitality prescribed social drinking, but according to Susan Ingram, then a young ingénue of eighteen years, he gave no hint of inebriation: "There were no indications of dissipation apparent when we saw Poe in Virginia at that time. I think he had not been drinking for a long time. If I had not heard or read what was said about his intemperance I should never have had any idea of it from what I saw in Poe."[67]

80   *Chapter Two*

On September 14, Poe delivered his lecture on "The Poetic Principal" at the Norfolk Academy, but the audience was small, and even with the tickets increased to 50 cents, the receipts could not have been great. After returning to Richmond, Poe wrote again to his aunt explaining why he was still unable to send her anything: "I lectured at Norfolk on Monday [Friday] & cleared enough to settle my bill here at the Madison House with $2 over. I had a highly fashionable audience, but Norfolk is a small place & there were two exhibitions the same night. . . . My poor poor Muddy I am still unable to send you even one dollar—but keep up heart—I hope that our troubles are nearly over."[68] In this final surviving letter to his aunt, Poe appears to be making plans to resettle in Richmond (after the marriage) and that the trip back North was only to oversee Mrs. Loud's poems and retrieve her. It must be observed that had there been no offer from Loud, and had Maria Clemm managed to come south on her own, Poe could have stayed in Virginia and avoided (or at least postponed) the fateful events in Baltimore that would take place four weeks later.

Poe apparently had promised Mr. Loud that he would be in Philadelphia by September 7 to work on his wife's poems, but after a third lecture was organized in Richmond, it became necessary to postpone his departure. He wrote directly to Mrs. Loud informing her that he could not leave before the twenty-fifth, due to "circumstances beyond my control."[69] That he felt the pressure of obligation suggests that he had taken an advance on the work from her husband.

In the meantime, Poe continued his campaign to gather names (and actual subscriptions) for his planned magazine venture. He also visited newspaper offices and the homes of friends and acquaintances. On one of these mornings, while passing William Pratt's Virginia Skylight Daguerrean Gallery, Poe was invited by the proprietor to sit for a photographic image. Poe at first demurred, claiming he was not dressed for it, but Pratt, reminding him that he had promised earlier to sit for the photographer, managed to get him upstairs.[70] Two slightly different daguerreotypes were made of Poe that day, after which he quickly left the studio without either in his possession. With the preceding weeks spent visiting old friends and the potential of prosperity before him, Poe should have been the picture of happiness. Yet in the photos he is shown as the man that Susan Weiss described as having "a pallid and careworn look,—somewhat haggard, indeed." These remain as the last known photographic images of the poet.

On the eve of his *originally* planned day of departure, Poe delivered an encore lecture at the Exchange Hotel. According to John Carter, who claimed to have attended, there were only thirteen people in the hall, including Carter's party of four and the doorman.[71] Johns Hopkins University professor, Basil L.

Figure 2.9. In this photographic image taken of Poe at Richmond in the weeks before his death he is shown glassy-eyed, and with a careworn appearance. That he had been wearing a hat just prior to the sitting is apparent. *Rare Book and Manuscript Library, Columbia University*

Gildersleeve, was also there that night and recalls the night to have been a benefit for Poe: "some of his friends got up a reading for his benefit, and I heard him read the 'Raven' and some other poems before a small audience in one of the parlors of the Exchange Hotel."[72] Twenty-year-old journalist Oscar P. Fitzgerald, who was covering the lecture for the *Richmond Examiner*, also remembers it as a benefit for Poe, but claimed the room was full: "The tickets were placed at five dollars each, and at that price three hundred

82   *Chapter Two*

persons were packed into the assembly rooms of the old Exchange Hotel. The net proceeds of the lecture amounted to fifteen hundred dollars. There was a touch of old Virginia in the way this was done."[73] A ticket price of five dollars is not likely, but even at 50 cents, there would have also been the expenses of securing the venue, printing advertisements, hiring a doorman, and so forth. If the performance had been poorly attended, the receipts would not have been significant, certainly not the $1,500 that Fitzgerald would claim that Poe had in his pocket when he left Richmond.[74] Sitting in the front row was Elmira Shelton who was now giving all the appearances of an enamored fiancée—it seemed she was now throwing caution, and her inheritance, to the wind. Although many years later she would tell an interviewer that at the time of his departure, she was not engaged to Poe, a letter she penned to Maria Clemm two days before the lecture indicates otherwise:

> You will no doubt be much surprised to receive a letter from one whom you have never seen.—Although I feel as if I were writing to one whom I love very devotedly, and whom to know, is to love—Mr. Poe has been very solicitous that I should write to you, and I do assure you, it is with emotions of pleasure that I now do so—I am fully prepared to love you, and I do sincerely hope that our spirits may be congenial—There shall be nothing wanting on my part to make them so—I have just spent a very happy evening with your dear Edgar, and I know it will be gratifying to you, to know, that he is all that you could desire him to be, sober, temperate, moral, & much beloved.
>
> It is needless (I know) for me to ask you, to take good care of him when he is, (as I trust he soon will be) again restored to your Arms—"I trust a kind Providence" will protect him, and guide him in the way of truth, so that his feet slip not.[75]

This remarkable outreach to Mrs. Clemm, made at Poe's urging, from someone that she had never met, seemed to be laying a foundation for living arrangements after the marriage, yet it should be noted that the words "marriage" and "engagement" appear nowhere in her letter. And of course, if the date for the ceremony had not been confirmed before he left, she may have used that as the basis for her later renunciation of an agreement with Poe.[76] She may have also made the denial for the benefit of family members, especially her children, who probably viewed her dalliance with the poet as a depreciation of Mr. Shelton. In any event, Poe seemed convinced that the wedding would take place upon his return to Richmond, and this prospect had to be weighing on him when he was leaving. How he dreaded the union is revealed by his own hand: "I confess that my heart sinks at the idea of this marriage. I think, however, that it will certainly take place."[77] Albeit through drastic measures, Poe ultimately found a way to get out of it.

On September 26, his departure now apparently planned for the following morning, Poe was very busy making necessary travel arrangements and bidding his goodbyes. During the day, or perhaps the day before, he apparently spent some time with his sister and the Mackenzies, and it may have been on this visit that he left his steamer trunk with them. This was followed by a final stop at the home of the Talley family. As Susan Talley would recall, Poe seemed to be buoyed by his time in Richmond; he was in good spirits when they said their farewells and gave no indication of being ill.[78]

In writing to Rufus Griswold later on October 10, John Thompson stated that on the eve of his departure, Poe stopped by the office of the *Southern Literary Messenger*, and while there, he was given a personal letter to deliver to Griswold when he reached Philadelphia.[79] Thompson also described Poe as being in good spirits, making no mention of illness. During this visit Poe presented, or sold, to Thompson a manuscript copy of "Annabel Lee," although the editor would say the five dollars that changed hands was borrowed by Poe for travel expenses. If true, it would suggest that he had retained little money from his final lecture.[80]

In the early evening, he made his last call on Elmira Shelton. As she would report in her letter to a distraught Maria Clemm on October 11, 1849,

> He came up to my house on the evening of the 26th Sept. to take leave of me. He was very sad, and complained of being quite sick. I felt his pulse, and found he had considerable fever, and did not think . . . he would be able to start the next morning, (Thursday). . . . I felt so wretchedly about him all of that night, that I went up early the next morning to inquire . . . when much to my regret, he had left in the boat for Baltimore.[81]

Coming from Shelton only two weeks after Poe left her parlor, there is no reason to question her timeline. Nevertheless, this account of his illness, which seems to be at odds with later descriptions of his good health given by John Thompson and Susan Archer Talley, and Shelton's subsequent search the following morning, could have easily been added for Clemm's comfort, especially in light of the scandalous cause of death that was then already being circulated.

Poe's next steps in Richmond (as described here) are reconstructed through the remembrances of an acquaintance given more than fifty years after they occurred, and by which time a person's stature could be elevated by even a brief association with the poet; the veracity of this testimony must be evaluated in that light. It has been the tradition that on the evening before his departure, Poe stopped at the office of Dr. John Carter to chat and to look through the day's newspapers.[82] When he left there for a late-night dinner at Sadler's Restaurant, he had Carter's walking stick with him. Apparently, his cane and

Carter's were similar in appearance and Poe may have grabbed the doctor's by mistake, or perhaps he preferred it and thought the exchange would not be noticed. Much has been made of this, but it is important now only in establishing how Carter would later recover the cane and in the process, call in to question his version of events.

When traveling, the disposition of a person's baggage can reveal their intentions, if not their movements and locations. However, even Poe's luggage on this trip has become a matter of dispute, as will be shown. From all the available evidence, it appears that Poe left a trunk containing his belongings in Richmond, either with the Mackenzies or at the Madison House where he had been staying. It is not likely that Poe would have kept the hotel room, and the attendant financial obligation, during his absence; the inn would probably have offered short term storage for Poe's baggage, especially if expecting his quick return.

It is more likely that he would have left his belongings in the custody of his sister and the Mackenzies, for which there would certainly have been no storage fees. This scenario would seem to be supported in a letter written by Rosalie Poe to Rufus Griswold the following year in which she complained, "I think and do say that I have been unjustly treated since his death, his trunk is taken from me which he gave to me himself. Mr. Poe [Neilson Poe] of

Figure 2.10. In 1849, travelers leaving Richmond by boat departed the capitol at Rockett's Landing, an industrial and warehouse district south of the city. Poe's date of departure from there is not certain. *Library of Congress*

On to Richmond 85

Baltimore has it & will not give it to me until I administer for it."[83] Biographer Hervey Allen would write in 1926 that Poe removed his trunk from Duncan Lodge and had it carried down to the Swan Tavern (Poe was actually staying at the Madison House by that time), even breaking one of Mackenzie's lamps in the process.[84] In her book of collected letters by Edgar Allan Poe, Mary Newton Stanard would seem to infer that this was the very same travel trunk that Poe had asked John Allan to send to him when leaving Richmond in 1827.[85] Indeed, it appears that Poe had no baggage with him when he arrived in Richmond on that last trip and he probably would have acquired the trunk during his time there.[86] Given his pecuniary circumstances, it is more likely that he would have found a secondhand item, if not one borrowed or retrieved from the Mackenzies after leaving it with them during one of his earlier stays.[87]

This is not to suggest that he left for Baltimore without any luggage. Even for the short trip north that he planned, Poe would have needed the basics, a change of clothing, grooming accessories, and similar items. For these, and his necessary papers, a valise or satchel would have sufficed.[88] If heading for the boat directly after his dinner party, as Carter claimed, he would have had this bag with him. Yet Carter would recall it differently. According to him, Poe met some friends at George Sadler's restaurant in the Old Market Hotel and did not leave there until midnight; some of the group then accompanied him down to the Rockett's Landing area where the departing steamers were tied up. Carter would further state, without any firsthand knowledge, "it is certain that he [Poe] had been drinking and that he seemed oblivious of his baggage, which had been left in his room at the Swan Tavern [Madison House]."[89] However, this was probably not the case as it appears that Poe had a piece of luggage with him when he landed in Baltimore.[90] If Poe had sent his baggage ahead to the dock at Ludlam's Wharf before visiting Carter that evening, the question then becomes, how did the doctor's pilfered walking stick come to be with the trunk he left behind? Because Carter would report that his cane was eventually returned to him by the people who had recovered Poe's trunk in Richmond following his death, it would appear that at some point after leaving Sadler's, he had attended to his belongings and stowed the walking stick at that location. And if Poe had left his trunk at Duncan Lodge with the Mackenzies, along with Carter's cane, it is not probable that he called on the doctor on the evening before his departure: the Mackenzies' house was too remote a location for Poe to have visited after leaving the restaurant if he had hoped to return in time to catch his boat.[91] Considering this *possibility*, Poe's long-assumed date of departure of September 27, or his visit to Carter's office the evening before, can be legitimately questioned. Although the poet may have been informing acquaintances that he was leaving on the twenty-seventh, it must be observed that there are no surviving eyewitness accounts confirming that he boarded a steamer in the small hours of Thursday morning.

No matter the actual date, Edgar Poe would eventually manage to push away from the pier at Ludlam's Wharf. In doing so, he was putting distance between himself and the impending bondage to Elmira Shelton, as well as his pledge to the temperance society—and Poe also had some money in his pocket.

Chapter Three

Missing in Mobtown

"On 1 November 1849 Neilson Poe wrote Rufus W. Griswold: The history of the last few days of his [Poe's] life is known to no one so well as to myself, and is of touching & melancholy interest, as well [as] of the most admonitory import."[1] Notwithstanding the boast, and sympathy for his cousin, there are no *reliable* accounts of Edgar Allan Poe's movements in Baltimore in the days before his discovery on October 3. Unlike his time in Richmond, and even Philadelphia, there remains a vacuum of evidence and eyewitness testimony for his activities in the city; given this void, we can only hope to examine the possibilities, and expose the fictitious. It should first be pointed out that we cannot be certain of what Poe had planned after reaching the city. From his surviving correspondence, it appears that he intended only to make a travel connection in Baltimore on his way north, but if he had at some point decided on a stopover, perhaps to visit acquaintances in pursuit of his magazine project, his movements within the city become even more perplexing.

As discussed, there may be some question as to Edgar Poe's actual date of departure from Richmond, Virginia. It is widely believed that he left the city on Thursday morning, September 27, 1849, aboard the steamer *Pocahontas*, one of two boats then operated by the Powhatan Line offering direct service to Baltimore, the second vessel being the *Columbus*. However, on this trip back to Maryland, Poe may not have been on either one. The *Pocahontas* left from Henry Ludlam's wharf at Rockett's Landing on Tuesdays, while the *Columbus* was a Saturday boat, and both were afternoon departures at 4 p.m. If he left from Richmond on the twenty-seventh, he could not have used either of these.[2]

It is more likely that Poe traveled on one of the steamers operated by the same line, but with a more convenient shuttle service to Norfolk.

Figure 3.1. This advertisement for steamboat transportation to southern states appeared in the 1845 Matchett's Directory for Baltimore. Three of the named vessels that serviced Baltimore from Norfolk were still in use at the time of Poe's final trip. *Author (print from author's collection)*

These departed on three days of the week (Tuesdays, Thursdays, and Saturdays) at 5:30 a.m.[3] This possibility appears to be supported by Dr. John Carter who would later produce a copy of Thomas Moore's *Irish Melodies* that he claimed Poe had left in his office before heading north.[4] On the top of the title page is written (apparently in Carter's hand) the word "Augusta," perhaps as a notation of the boat that Poe had said he was taking. The *Augusta* was indeed one of the Norfolk steamers in the Powhatan Line's James River fleet, along with the *Curtis Peck* and *Mount Vernon*. This would also seem to confirm Carter's assertion that Poe departed Richmond on the morning of September 27. Of course, the doctor could have easily written the boat's name in the book at a later date to support his story.[5]

From Norfolk, Poe would have reached Baltimore on one of three boats operated by the Baltimore Steam Packet Company. These were conveniently scheduled for the northern traveler, to leave ninety minutes after the arrival of the Richmond packets, and were advertised to dock at Baltimore in time for the "morning trains" the following day.[6] Had Poe managed to leave Richmond on Thursday morning, his connecting boat to Baltimore would have been the *Jewess*. If, however, he waited until Saturday, he could have arrived there aboard the *Herald*,[7] or even the *Columbus*. No matter which boat he took, all the passenger steamers that plied the Chesapeake Bay had dining saloons as an advertised convenience; the lucrative concession was usually operated by the boat's captain or purser.[8] Depending on the level of accommodation that a traveler purchased, the boat fare could have included meals, but drinks at the bar were for cash, and although there is some question as to the amount, when Poe left Richmond he had money in his pocket. Traveling alone, without any

Missing in Mobtown

supervision, it is not hard to image that Poe had started drinking during his leisurely, thirteen-hour cruise up the Chesapeake.[9]

Richmond boats operated by the "Old Bay Line," as it would later be called, landed at Spear's Wharf in Baltimore, where Pier 3 is today.[10] From there, if taking the 9 a.m. train to Philadelphia, Poe would have had to board it at President Street, nine blocks to the east, assuming passage was available. However, the ticket depot for the Philadelphia, Wilmington & Baltimore Railroad (PW&B) was then on Pratt Street (just beyond Light Street), approximately four city blocks to the west; they were at that time sharing a building with the Baltimore & Ohio Railroad.[11] Before boarding his train east of town, Poe would have had to head in the opposite direction to the ticket depot. There is some reason to believe that Poe gave his luggage to a porter upon his arrival at the dock, the bag would have then been forwarded to the depot or directly to President Street.[12] If this is correct, it would suggest that he was aware of his surroundings when he landed. It would also help to explain why he was without any belongings when eventually found.

Baltimore was not like Richmond. By 1849 it had become a major center of international commerce, and the city was still a boomtown, moaning from the growing pains. The Virginia capitol then had a population of approximately 27,000, while Baltimore's 170,000 citizens made it the second largest city in the union, behind only New York.[13] "The basin," as the city's inner harbor was then known, was a commercial port choked with local fishing boats, steamers from the eastern regions, and ocean-going vessels from other continents.[14] On the streets surrounding the waterfront, the horse and cart traffic was incessant. The stevedores jockeying their wagons for access up-and-down the piers, and along Light Street, created a never-ending commotion; and on Pratt Street they had to dodge occasional parades of horse-drawn omnibuses that were shuttling their passengers between hotels, train stations, and boat docks.[15]

The Maryland seaport was a noisier, and certainly nastier, place than the town Poe had just left, and its reputation for lawlessness was righteously won. Known disparagingly as "Mobtown," the city was a hotbed of criminality, political corruption, and perennial rioting. As writer Francis Beirne would observe, "when the populace was in the mood for going on a rampage almost any reason would do."[16] The principal cause of the disorder was the lack of adequate law enforcement, a consequence of the city's explosive growth and the council's failure to keep pace.[17] In 1849, there were still no formalized police patrols in Baltimore City. The constabulary, consisting of a crew of night watchmen and fewer daytime constables, spent much of their time in the watch-houses located in six wards throughout the city.[18] Although the streets in the downtown area were gas-lit at night, ostensibly to combat crime, no

Figure 3.2. The encircled numbers on this 1848 plan of Baltimore City identify the places associated with Poe's final visit as mentioned in the text—the reported location of the Widow Meagher's oyster stand is included for reference purposes. Some of the streets and rail lines shown in this plan were not then completed. *Author (print from author's collection)*

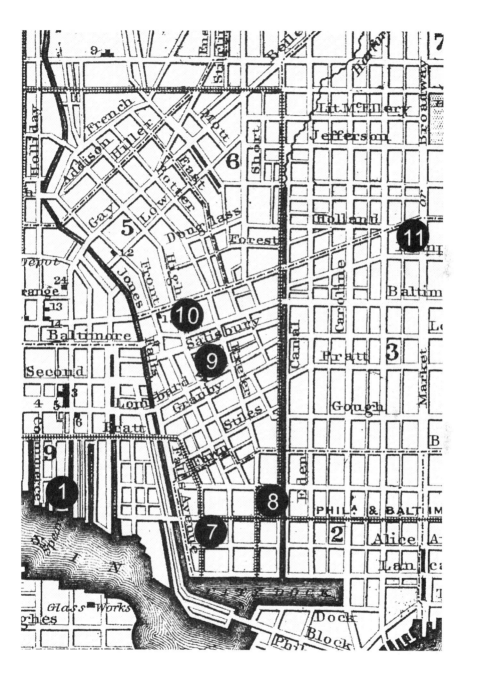

Figure 3.3. This early daguerreotype of Baltimore's harbor was taken in 1849. It shows the steamer, *Herald*, docked at the bottom of Spear's Wharf (Pier 3 today) where Poe could have disembarked. *Author (print from author's collection)*

one profited more from the modernization than the tavern owners, who could then extend the hours of their patrons' disorderly behavior.

Yet Poe was no "babe in the woods" here; he was well acquainted with the city and its ways. He knew the streets intimately, having walked them for more than five years. He knew the harbor, the docks, and the location of the train depots; but he also knew the locations of the city's groggeries and oyster houses. If Poe had to kill time before his train departure, he would not have had to step far from the waterfront to find such an establishment. A morning arrival would have normally precluded such a detour—during the early hours these places would have been locked up, and his task of transferring to the train should have been straightforward. However, if Poe took a later boat from Richmond, he could have had an afternoon landing in Baltimore, making his passage through the city during the time of day when the taverns were wide open. There is also the possibility that the train going north was at capacity when Poe tried to purchase a ticket, imposing a layover and unanticipated *opportunities* in the city.

One of several parables of Poe's whereabouts after he arrived involves an oyster bar called the "Widow Meagher's Place," believed to have been located on the northeast corner of Pratt and Hollingsworth Streets directly across from the harbor.[19] In this tale given by an anonymous California man to Poe biographer Eugene Didier, the oyster stand was a favorite of the poet's where he would plant himself and rattle off "witty couplets and at times, poems of some length" for the old woman. It is not certain where the testimony of his informant stops and Didier's begins, although it is not likely the biographer would propose that Poe wrote his 1843 tale, "The Gold Bug," there as his storyteller claimed. Most scholars believe this account to be a fabrication.[20] A search made in period directories revealed no one doing business under the name "Meagher," "Meagle," "Widow Meagher," or similar spellings and pronunciations, although it was not uncommon for locals to refer to a store, or tavern, by the name of someone who worked there, especially if that person was popular. It is possible that Mary Meagher had at one time been a server at Sawkins' Ale & Oyster House or perhaps one of the many other seafood bars located near the harbor.[21]

Perhaps a more trustworthy account of his whereabouts was given by Professor George Woodberry who, in his 1909 revised biography, stated that "Poe wandered in Baltimore or its neighborhood for five days. It is known that he called on his old friend, Dr. Nathan C. Brooks, partially intoxicated, and not finding him at home went away."[22] Unfortunately, Woodberry provides no authority for this statement, but there is still reason to give it some measure of credibility. Author Matthew Pearl believed the source for this anecdote was none other than Nathan Brooks' son whom Woodberry had befriended while working in Baltimore. Young Brooks was a reporter for the *Baltimore Sun* at the time, a status that confers some integrity to any information he would have provided.[23] Pearl wrote that Edgar Poe may have left a calling card communicating his attempted visit which would explain how Brooks and his son knew of it. The author then made the assumption that Poe "went away" based on the testimonial that Brooks placed in the *Baltimore Sun* thanking the Liberty (Fire) Company for their prompt response to a fire at his home. Pearl presumed that Poe arrived at the house to find it fire-damaged and empty of inhabitants.[24] This was a logical supposition except that the

Figure 3.4. The establishment shown here is reputed to be the Widow Meagher's oyster bar. An unidentified man claimed that he spent time here with Poe on the evening before his discovery in East Baltimore. *Edgar Allan Poe Society of Baltimore*

Figure 3.5. After his arrival in Baltimore, Poe may have tried to call on his friend, Nathan C. Brooks, who at the time was living in this townhouse that still stands at 657 West Lexington Street. *Author (author photograph)*

fire, taking place on September 22, was actually at a structure on Fayette Street that Brooks was leasing, or perhaps just occupying, for the newly created Baltimore Female College. As reported in the September 24 edition of the *Baltimore Sun*, "the fire being discovered in the upper part of the building on Fayette near Liberty Street, occupied by N. C. Brooks, Esq. The damage sustained was trifling."[25] Irrespective of the amount of destruction to his new school, Brooks would have had his hands full and an evident reason to be away from home when Poe could have made his visit, but he was not out of town as some biographers have written.

There is no indication as to why Edgar Poe may have tried to see Brooks, but it is not improbable that the poet had spent too much money in the boat's saloon and afterward needed assistance to continue his trip. Nathan Brooks was an old Baltimore friend and a well-known member of the literary scene in the city when Poe was a resident. Brooks' poetry and prose tales had been published in anthologies and in leading literary magazines such as the *New York Mirror* and the *Southern Literary Messenger*. In 1838, Brooks, along with Dr. Joseph Snodgrass, put out the short-lived *American Museum of Science, Literature, and the Arts*, a literary magazine to which Poe also contributed some of his works.[26] Matthew Pearl suggested that another possible reason for the visit was Brooks' connections to the literary community in Baltimore and the subscription leads he could have provided for Poe's proposed magazine. Pearl even hinted that Poe may have called on others in the city for the same purpose, but this is unlikely as these would have been literary people inclined to write of (and record for posterity) an encounter with Poe.[27] In any event, Poe would not have been seeking medical assistance from Brooks who, by avocation, was an educator and not a doctor of medicine.[28]

Woodberry furnished no support for his claim that Poe was partially intoxicated during the attempted visit. Pearl also offered no evidence, and it is hard to see how Poe's condition could have been established from a calling card that he may have left behind. Perhaps a clue may be found in the description of "partially" intoxicated, a characterization that could suggest Poe was observed or encountered by a neighbor when he had reached Brooks' house on Lexington Street.[29] Yet Woodberry's belief of Poe's friend not being at home is well placed, as Brooks unquestionably would have come to the poet's rescue and written about the encounter afterward, just as his Philadelphia protectors did.

Another unconfirmed sighting of Edgar Poe in the same section of the city became a tradition within the Poe family in Baltimore. In a magazine article published many years after his death, the poet's cousin, Elizabeth Ellicott Poe, claimed that another relative of Poe's (George Poe) came across the writer while walking in front of Barnum's Baltimore Museum on the night of October 3. There, he noticed a man lying in a stupor beneath the steps to the second-floor entrance, on the Calvert Street side of the building. After having a closer look, he was surprised to discover that the man was his cousin, Edgar Poe. It was also the family's story that George Poe immediately alerted his brother Neilson who failed to go to Poe's rescue that night.[30] One of the

Figure 3.6. The busy intersection of Baltimore and Calvert Streets around the time of Poe's death—in an unconfirmed account of Poe's last days, he was seen lying beneath the steps to the second floor of the Baltimore Museum, at the far right. *Author (printed engraving from author's collection)*

obvious problems with this account is the date and time given: by the evening of October 3, Poe was already lying in a hospital bed two miles away, east of the city. Of course, as with any oft repeated tradition, the date may shift with each retelling. The Poe family apparently blamed Neilson for his minimal involvement after his famous cousin had been hospitalized and this story could have been hatched in an effort to reinforce their position. Nevertheless, there remains no independent confirmation of it.

Still another unflattering account of Edgar Poe's whereabouts, in the days after he arrived, was given by Mrs. D. H. Carroll in an undated letter to Sara Sigourney Rice. Rice had solicited stories from those who had known (and claimed to have known) the poet for a tribute book she was putting together as a companion to the 1875 monument of Poe in Baltimore.[31] The letter consists of transcriptions Mrs. Carroll made of two statements given to her in which Poe was said to have been seen at Lexington Market. The first was by the Reverend W. T. D. Clemm, a relative of Edgar's wife Virginia and the presiding clergyman at Poe's burial. In his statement, Clemm recalls what

Figure 3.7. In yet another unsubstantiated account of Poe's whereabouts after arriving in Baltimore, he was seen passed out on a butcher's block at Lexington Market, shown here many years later. *Library of Congress*

he believed Dr. John J. Moran, the administrator of the hospital where Poe was taken, had told him on the day prior to Poe's funeral: "He was found in Lexington market, lying on a butcher's block dead drunk."[32] Clemm would also add that Poe was taken directly from there to the hospital on Broadway. The second version by Mr. John S. Macher told of two acquaintances that were passing through the market and "saw a man lying there covered with flies." One of the men, a "Mr. Turner from East Baltimore," recognized the unfortunate individual as "the poet, Edgar Allan Poe."[33]

There are too many difficulties with the veracity of these statements; in addition to the convoluted chain of hearsay and secondhand accounts relayed to Miss Rice, there is also the problem of the unidentified sources who originally provided the information. After his discovery, Poe was indeed sent to a hospital but it was from a location on Lombard Street, not Lexington Market. And any testimony emanating from Moran must be questioned, as will be demonstrated. Although these stories must be counted among the fictitious accounts of Poe's final days, and are only included here in the pursuit of diligence, it should be pointed out that the home of Nathan C. Brooks, which Poe may have tried to visit, was only two city blocks away from Lexington Market.

THE MAYBE TRAIN

In addition to these unconfirmed sightings of Poe in the city, stories would emerge many years later that he actually made his train connection and headed for Philadelphia, only to return to Baltimore later in a delirious state. Most, if not all, of these accounts seem to have been spawned from a single magazine article appearing in the September 1872 edition of *Harper's Monthly* and written by Richard H. Stoddard.[34] The source for his information was Edgar's cousin, Neilson Poe, who was interviewed (for Stoddard) a year earlier by his friend, George B. Coale, a Baltimore photographer.[35] In his letter to Stoddard, Coale seems to be summarizing Neilson Poe's testimony, not quoting him, and it is difficult to know how much of the statement actually came from the poet's cousin. Yet when paired with other details in Coale's transcription, Neilson's entire account appears untrustworthy and derivative. Working backward in his timeline, Neilson starts by saying that *he* found Edgar Poe on October 4 (the day after he was actually discovered) and personally conveyed him to the hospital. Neilson then includes the suspicion that Edgar had been kidnapped by "ward managers" and used as a repeat voter around the city, the day before—a ten-year-old theory that had by then become well circulated. He next incorporates Moran's fantastic deathbed conversation with Edgar

Poe, suggesting acquiescence to, or possible collaboration in, the doctor's version of events. He then concludes with the story of Poe's abortive travel beyond Baltimore saying, "He [Edgar Poe] had unfortunately taken a single drink with a friend, between trains, and in consequence was brought back by the conductor on the Philadelphia train from Havre de Grace in a state of delirium." Neilson provided no source for this information at the time, nor did he identify the train official that returned Poe to Baltimore.

It is probable that this story was making the rounds before Neilson Poe sat for his interview with Coale; he may have even heard it from Moran, who would repeat the scenario in an article for the *New York Herald* a few years later.[36] In this version, Moran infers that Poe could have traveled most of the way to Philadelphia before being turned back: "He [Poe] was seen to go to the depot to take the cars for Philadelphia, and that the conductor, on going through the cars for tickets, found him lying in the baggage car insensible. He took him as far as Havre de Grace, where the cars then passed each other, or as far as Wilmington, I forget which, and placed him in the train coming to Baltimore." Later in his book, *A Defense of Edgar Allan Poe* (1885), Moran would give more detail, declaring he interviewed the conductor and giving his name as "Capt. George W. Rollins" [Rawlings].[37] The doctor would also add that the conductor claimed to have seen two "sharks" following Poe when he

Figure 3.8. In 1849, the Philadelphia, Wilmington & Baltimore Railroad shared a depot with the Baltimore & Ohio Railroad at what is today, 1 East Pratt Street. The station shown here was built the following year on President Street, where Poe's train would have departed the city. *Library of Congress*

got off the train and "expressed his thorough belief that those two men went through him" (robbing him of everything including his clothing).[38]

In 1849, there was still no bridge over the Susquehanna River, and train cars were ferried across and connected to a locomotive on the other side before continuing. The PW&B railroad had a well-practiced routine that usually insured a straightforward crossing, but if the river was angry, a delay of hours or even days would not have been uncommon.[39] Other than depositing him at one of the stations along the line, the river crossing would have provided the only opportunity to shuttle Poe directly to cars going back to Baltimore; the conductor would later claim that he escorted Poe back to the city.[40]

One of the problems with this story is that Rawlings does not appear to have been employed by the PW&B Railroad at the time of Poe's death. He had indeed been a train conductor but with the Baltimore and Ohio (B&O) Railroad, yet was apparently working as the Baltimore agent for a maritime freight company during most of 1849.[41] The other difficulty with Rawlings is his notoriety: Moran describes him as "well-known" and he appears to have been (like Moran) a bit of a publicity hound, often shown in the newspapers receiving awards and citations from his railroad employer. That he could have simply concocted this encounter with Poe would not have been out of character.

According to Moran, Rawlings came forward with his story immediately during the weeks following Poe's death, but there remains no independent verification of this. It is clear that Moran had heard the conductor's claims before Moran's article appeared in the *New York Herald* (1875), which included mention of Poe's train ride north. The story then quickly found its way into the 1876 Widdleton edition of *The Works of Edgar Allan Poe*; John Ingram later copied the account (without attribution) in his landmark 1880 biography of Poe.[42] Many of Poe's subsequent biographers would derive their versions (of this story) from Stoddard and Ingram.

Another writer who gave the idea some weight was Michael Powell, author of the indispensable, *Too Much Moran: Respecting the Death of Edgar Poe* (2009). Powell wrote that "Poe appears to have been discovered ill between Philadelphia and Havre de Grace" after secreting himself in a baggage car, which infers that Poe actually made the river crossing but as a stowaway on the train. Powell then writes that he was "shepherded back to Baltimore in the belief he had family and friends there who would take care of him" which could suggest Poe was lucid enough to speak with the conductor.[43] The writer also proposed that Poe could have returned to Baltimore as early as the afternoon of the same day he left, and that he remained in the Old Town section of the city until his discovery on October 3.

Figure 3.9. This image shows an area of East Baltimore Street stretching into the Old Town section of the city around 1850; it was less than three blocks from where Poe was found. Most of the businesses on the north side of these streets erected awnings to shade their entrances. *Author (Printed photo from the author's collection)*

In another book, *Midnight Dreary: The Mysterious Death of Edgar Allan Poe* (1998), John Walsh would expand upon Stoddard's train story as a crucial component for his theory that Poe was murdered. According to Walsh, Poe was followed from Richmond by three brothers of Elmira Shelton, who wanted to prevent her marriage to someone they thought to be a fortune hunter, and in that pursuit, were unanimous in their resolve to make an attack on him. In the story, Poe is not taken off the train at Havre de Grace but succeeds in reaching Philadelphia where he is confronted by the Shelton brothers. Poe then flees, grabbing a train back to Baltimore, only to be caught again by the trio, beaten, and forced to drink an entire bottle of whiskey, after which they assumed that he would continue to drink and thereby provide them with evidence of intemperance to present to their sister. It should be pointed out that Walsh's premise also relies on John Sartain's mistaken recollection (see chapter 2) that Poe was on his way to New York when, in a delusional state, he encountered pursuing assassins.[44]

Biographer Arthur Quinn was another who believed that Poe had made it to Philadelphia only to wind up back in Baltimore a day later without visiting the Louds. In a letter to Quinn from his college friend, Dallet Fuguet, dated

October 20, 1927, Poe is said to have visited other acquaintances in the city, and after falling ill was afterward taken to the home of James P. Moss at 70 South Fourth Street. Moss was married to the aunt of Thomas H. Lane, Poe's partner, when he became owner of the *Broadway Journal* in New York; Lane was a cousin of Fuguet from which Quinn received the letter. As told to him, Quinn writes, "The next morning, against their protests, Poe left, in poor condition, saying that he was going on to New York. Lane believed that Poe must have taken the wrong train and gone back to Baltimore."[45]

Here again is a tenuous sequence of hearsay and traditions recalled many years after Poe's death. One difficulty with this version is the six-hour trip back to Baltimore (with many stops) and the opportunities Poe would have had to get off the train once realizing he was heading in the wrong direction. Lane was claiming that all these events took place on the days immediately preceding Poe's death, but he could have easily confused this alleged trip with the poet's visit to Philadelphia while on his way to Richmond a few months earlier, a scenario that is a better fit.[46]

If Poe had reached Philadelphia, it is certain that he did not call on Marguerite Loud based on a later advertisement for her book of poems, which mentions that Poe was prevented from serving as the project's editor. Printed in Rufus Griswold's paper, the *International Weekly Miscellany* of August 26, 1850, the advertisement reads, "the late Mr. Poe was accustomed to praise her [Loud's] works very highly, and was to have edited this edition of them." It is difficult to believe that the $100 promised to Poe for producing her poetry (or the balance of it, had he been given an advance in Richmond) would not have kept him in the city until he recovered. If we needed more evidence that he never reached Philadelphia (at least in a coherent state), a letter that Maria Clemm had sent to him there, at his request, was never collected.[47]

Ultimately, none of the sightings of Poe in Baltimore (or on trains bound for Philadelphia) during the week prior to October 3 have ever been corroborated. Moreover, these claims were all put forth after the fact by people who were, for the most part, looking to achieve notoriety. Of course, the occurrence of any of these scenarios is possible, but without supporting evidence, they can be viewed only as conjectural.

Chapter Four

"The Worse for Wear"

During the rainy afternoon of October 3, 1849, Edgar Allan Poe was discovered at a tavern in Baltimore, Maryland, located at what is today 912 East Lombard Street.[1] He was in a conspicuous state of insensibility and wearing soiled clothing that appeared to have been retrieved from the trash. His condition was such that he was unable to answer questions or say what had happened to him; how he came to be there and his movements in the city before his discovery have never been established.

In the years following Poe's death, some confusion arose as to the actual location of his discovery. As discussed in chapter 3, some would spread the story that Poe was seen, passed out, at Lexington Market just north of the downtown area. Dr. John J. Moran, the administrator of the hospital to which Poe would be taken, claimed in one of several versions that Poe was found sleeping (or laying) on a bench at the Light Street wharf on the west side of the harbor.[2] In this version of events, the source of which is unclear, Moran wrote, "He had been found lying upon a bench in front of a large mercantile house on Light Street wharf. He was in a stupor, whether from liquor or opium was not at first known. . . . He had been there since early dawn."[3] Unfortunately, Moran's story would be accepted by the English biographer, John H. Ingram, for inclusion in his 1880 book, *Edgar Allan Poe: His Life, Letters, and Opinions*, and precipitously copied by other writers.[4] In Ingram's defense, it must be observed that conclusive proof of Poe's actual whereabouts only surfaced after his book went to press.

Incredibly, doubt over Poe's place of discovery has been advanced in recent times by the proprietors of a popular nightspot in Baltimore known as "The Horse You Came In On Saloon." Perhaps as a promotional ploy, this Fells Point establishment maintains that it "was the last destination before the mysterious death of the great American writer Edgar Allan Poe," as advertised on their website in 2020.[5] Nevertheless, period directories prove that no saloon or public house of any kind was being operated at their Thames Street address during the time of Poe's death.[6] There can be no question that Poe was found at a tavern, but it was one located on Lombard Street in East Baltimore, not Fell's Point. The first confirmation of this detail came from Edgar's cousin, Neilson Poe, in a letter written to a grief-stricken Maria Clemm on October 11, 1849: "It appears that, on Wednesday, he was seen and recognised [sic] at one of the places of election in old town, and that his condition was such as to render it necessary to send him to the College [hospital]."[7] One of the "places of election" as identified in the letter was Gunners' Hall, a tavern then serving as a polling place for state and congressional elections being held on the day of Poe's discovery. In the letter, Neilson Poe also identifies its location as "old town," a section of Baltimore City east of the Jones Falls River through which Lombard Street passed.

Among those who came to Poe's rescue that day was Dr. Joseph Snodgrass, who would be alerted to the poet's predicament by a handwritten message sent to him by Joseph Walker. Walker was a newspaper compositor, and he had been working in that capacity for the *Baltimore Saturday Visiter*, years earlier when Snodgrass was the literary paper's editor, and Poe a contributor. However, the note summoning Snodgrass to the tavern would not be discovered until 1880, after the doctor had died (by suicide) at his home in Berkeley Springs, West Virginia.[8] This communique, along with a small collection of letters written by Poe to Snodgrass had been found by his widow, Hannah Chandler Snodgrass. Aware of their value, Mrs. Snodgrass had the letters examined by *Baltimore Sun* editor, William H. Carpenter. Carpenter then sent the letters for transcription to his friend, Dr. William Hand Browne, who at the time was assisting John Ingram in his vindicatory memoir of Poe.[9] It was while copying the letters that Browne discovered the note summoning Snodgrass to the tavern and immediately informed Ingram whose book stating that Poe was found on Light Street had already gone to press. Browne then gave press copies of the letters,

Figure 4.1. Poe was found at a tavern that once stood at this location at 912 East Lombard Street. The townhouses now occupying the spot were erected in 2005. *Author (author photograph)*

and note, to Edward Spencer, Carpenter's associate at the *Baltimore Sun*, who edited them for a story in the *New York Herald*—it was in Spencer's newspaper article that Walker's note was first made public.[10] Elements of the short message sent to Snodgrass will be discussed, but it is provided here in its entirety to establish Poe's location:

Baltimore City, Oct. 3d 1849

Dear Sir,—

There is a gentleman, rather the worse for wear, at Ryan's 4th ward polls, who goes under the cognomen of Edgar A. Poe, and who appears in great distress, & he says he is acquainted with you, and I assure you, he is in need of immediate assistance,

Yours, in haste,
Jos. W. Walker

To Dr. J. E. Snodgrass.[11]

After Browne made his transcriptions of the letters, the originals were returned to Carpenter who claimed to have sent them back to Mrs. Snodgrass. Unfortunately, many of the handwritten letters, as well as the note written by Walker, have since disappeared, and only the transcription Browne sent to John Ingram survives in the Ingram Collection at the University of Virginia. This copy now serves as the original text of the note.[12]

How Edgar Poe came to be at the tavern is unknown, a question that is arguably the *true* mystery of his death. Yet his presence and discovery in east Baltimore should not be seen as surprising. The Philadelphia, Wilmington & Baltimore Railroad (PW&B) terminal was just blocks below on President Street, and he would have been, by necessity, in that area to catch his train to Philadelphia. He certainly had intimate knowledge

Figure 4.2. While transcribing a collection of original Poe correspondences in 1880, William Hand Browne discovered the note that was used to summon Dr. Joseph Snodgrass to Gunners' Hall. The original document has since disappeared. *Johns Hopkins University Sheridan Libraries*

106   *Chapter Four*

of the neighborhood, having resided with the Clemms and his older brother on Wilks Street at an address that was only two blocks east of where the train terminal was built.[13] Matthew Pearl also suggests that Poe may have been on Lombard Street intentionally trying to reach Snodgrass's house at 103 North High Street for the same purpose as his *believed* visit to N. C. Brooks earlier.[14] Like Brooks, Snodgrass was well known within Baltimore's literary community, and he could have provided Poe with subscription leads and general insights into the magazine's prospects in the city.

The falling rain may have prevented others from recognizing the poet during the daylight hours, and Walker could have been the first among those who knew him to have a sheltered, unobstructed view, suggesting it took place indoors. However, it is unclear whether Walker was familiar with Poe's appearance or simply overheard him muttering the doctor's name. The two men would have had ample opportunity to encounter each other when at the offices of the *Baltimore Saturday Visiter*, accordingly Walker's recognition of Poe on that October day would present no surprise. But the reason for the printer's presence at Gunners' Hall is unknown. In the autumn of 1849, he was working for the *Baltimore Sun*, their office being on the corner of Baltimore and Gay Streets, almost nine blocks from where he found Poe. If Walker resided within the fourth political ward, he may have come to the tavern to cast his votes. The directories from the period record a "teacher" by the name of Joseph Walker living at 101 South Exeter Street which would have been right around the corner from Gunners' Hall; perhaps he had a second occupation, or was living with relatives at that address.[15]

Regardless of his reason for visiting the tavern, Walker recognized the seriousness of Poe's condition and he sent his note to Snodgrass apparently at the poet's request: "I received a note, stating that a man, answering to the name of Edgar Allan Poe, who claimed to know me, was at a drinking house in Lombard Street, Baltimore."[16] Snodgrass would phrase it differently in a later account: "a man claiming Poe's name, and to be acquainted with me, was at Cooth [Coath] & Sergeant's tavern in Lombard street, near High Street."[17] This would suggest that Poe was still coherent enough to articulate his wishes, lending support to Matthew Pearl's belief that Poe was in that neighborhood to seek out his literary colleague.

If we take a closer look at the note sent to Snodgrass, more information will present itself. In describing Poe's condition, Walker uses the expression, "rather the worse for wear," a phrase that may have been a euphemism for drunkenness. When viewed alongside the seriousness of his other descriptions of "in great distress" and "in need of immediate assistance," Walker's opening phrase does appear to be a consciously softened assessment of the poet's condition.[18] If the phrase was indeed a subtle way of communicating

Poe's over-intoxication, that conclusion would be shared by the other eyewitnesses assisting the poet that day.

In his message, Joseph Walker also refers to Poe's whereabouts by giving the location as "Ryan's 4th ward polls." This detail establishes the tavern's use as a voting place as well as the name of the business's proprietor. However, Cornelius Ryan was not the property owner;[19] the building, at what was then 44–46 East Lombard Street, was actually co-owned by Thomas Coath and William Sargeant (or Sergeant).[20] The arrangement Ryan had with them is not known, but he appears not to have been more than the proprietor of Gunners' Hall, the tavern at the Fourth Ward Hotel.[21]

There are no known photographic images of the original premises but descriptions are afforded by listings in the *Baltimore Sun*. Located on the north side of Lombard Street, the hotel was a three-story brick structure containing fifteen rooms, a tavern, large cellar, an attached stable and carriage house; the rooms for rent were on the upper floors. At the time of Poe's visit, the hotel also had a bowling alley, the advertisement of which extolls the addition of gas lighting.[22]

As the name implies, the Fourth Ward Hotel also had a political purpose and it was a meeting place for members of the local Whig party. In addition to a Whig meeting hall, the tavern, known locally at that time as "Ryan's" or "Ryan's Gunners' Hall," served as the polling place for the Fourth Ward during elections. Located on the bottom floor of the hotel, the tavern had a separate entrance on Lombard Street that would have been shaded by a canvas awning stretching out to the curb.[23] Normally, those coming to the saloon on Election Day would have encountered a gauntlet of "ballot hawkers" and other political operatives on the sidewalk in front, especially near the voting window. Anyone trying to loiter, or lay on the ground there, would not have been welcomed, but on this rainy day, activity would have been largely confined to the area under cover.

We do not know how long it took Snodgrass to respond to Walker's note, but when he arrived he found

Figure 4.3. In this photograph taken in 1949, Richard Hart of the Edgar Allan Poe Society of Baltimore stands at 912 East Lombard Street, the location where the poet was first seen after leaving Richmond. The buildings shown were erected around the turn of the twentieth century and have since been replaced. *Edgar Allan Poe Society of Baltimore*

108   *Chapter Four*

Poe *inside* Gunners' Hall, "sitting in an arm-chair, with his head dropped forward."[24] It has become the tradition that Poe was found outside the tavern, or even in the gutter, but there is no known evidence supporting this belief. Walker's message stated only that Poe was "at" the Fourth Ward Polls, not outside of it, nor in front. It is possible that during the interim before Snodgrass's arrival, Walker could have moved Poe inside, but there is no indication of this in subsequent testimony. Furthermore, in his detailed description of Poe's clothing,[25] Snodgrass gave no indication of it being soaked, or even wet, suggesting that if he had been lying outside, the ground had dried, or that Poe had been indoors for some time.

Snodgrass was positive that Poe's condition was the result of an overindulgence of alcohol; years later when he read in the *Women's Temperance Paper* that someone was saying the poet had died by his own hand, the doctor wrote a rebuttal that included a detailed account of what he saw that day:

> When I entered the bar-room of the house, I instantly recognized the face of one that I had often seen, and knew well, although it [his face] wore an aspect of vacant stupidity that made me shudder. The intellectual flash of his eye had vanished, or rather had been quenched in the bowl; but the broad, capacious forehead of the author of "The Raven," as you have appropriately designated him, was still there, with a width, in the region of ideality, such as few men have ever possessed.[26]

It is clear that Joseph Snodgrass was writing for an audience here. Perhaps to reinforce his portrait of an over-intoxicated Poe, Snodgrass next volunteered a description of the man's clothing:

> But perhaps I would not so readily have recognized him, had I not been notified of his apparel. His hat, or rather the hat of somebody else, for he had evidently been robbed of his clothing, or cheated in an exchange, was a cheap palm-leaf one, without a band, and soiled; his coat, of commonest alpacca [*sic*], and evidently second-hand; and his pants of grey mixed cassimere, dingy, and badly fitting. He wore neither vest nor neck-cloth, if I remember aright, while his shirt was sadly crumpled and soiled. He was so utterly stupefied with liquor, that I thought it best not to seek recognition or conversation, especially as he was surrounded by a crowd of drinking men, actuated by idle curiosity rather than sympathy.

Joseph Snodgrass's written records provide the only surviving eyewitness accounts of Poe's condition when he was found at Gunners' Hall. It must be said, however, that the doctor was a temperance advocate and may have seen in Poe's death, as Poe scholar Jeffrey Savoye has suggested, "an opportunity to spread the faith." For example, the phrases, "worse for wear, and in great distress" in Walker's note became "a state of deep intoxication and great destitution" in Snodgrass's first article; later he would heighten the descriptions to "a state of beastly intoxication and evident destitution."[27] In the doctor's second account, written in 1867 for *Beadle's Monthly*, he was responding (once again) to an earlier article, this time written by Mrs. Elizabeth Oakes Smith, stating that Poe had not died as a "consequence of a drunken debauch," but rather "was cruelly beaten, blow upon blow, by a ruffian" and died from the injuries.[28] Snodgrass rebutted this account, emphatically insisting, "I am positive that there was no evidence whatever of any such violence having been used upon his person, when I went to his rescue at the tavern. Nor was there any given at the hospital, where its detection would have been certain, if external violence had really been the cause of his insanity, for there would have been some physical traces of it on the patient's person."[29]

Figure 4.4. Richard Hart of the Edgar Allan Poe Society of Baltimore is shown here on October 3, 1949, pointing to what was believed to be the approximate spot of Poe's discovery. There is no firm evidence to support the widely held belief that the poet was found outdoors. *Edgar Allan Poe Society of Baltimore*

In the same article, Snodgrass adds even more particulars of what he observed that day:

> His [Poe's] face was haggard, not to say bloated, and unwashed, his hair unkempt, and his whole physique repulsive . . . and that full-orbed and mellow, yet soulful eye, for which he was so noticeable when himself, now lusterless and vacant.

The doctor then offers another, detailed description of Poe's clothing:

> a rusty, almost brimless, tattered and ribbon less palmleaf hat. His clothing consisted of a sack-coat of thin and sleezy [*sic*] black alpaca, ripped more or less at several of its seams, and faded and soiled, and pants of a steel-mixed pattern of cassinette, half-worn and badly-fitting, if they could be said to fit at all. He wore neither vest nor neck-cloth, while the bosom of his shirt was both crumpled and

badly soiled. On his feet were boots of coarse material, and giving no sign of having been blacked for a long time, if at all.[30]

Because of his fanaticism, many scholars have disqualified or voiced skepticism about Joseph Snodgrass's testimony.[31] Indeed, his version of events would be reprinted in several temperance journals across the country. And yet, although he was not practicing medicine at the time, it should be observed that Snodgrass did have a medical credential and the analytical eye of a physician.[32] It should also be said that Snodgrass was one of those who had, outwardly at least, maintained Poe's friendship. It was as a devotee of the poet that Snodgrass thought an honest account of Poe's last moments was required: "Glad should I be, as a sincere friend as well as an enthusiastic admirer of the writings of Edgar Allan Poe, could the assignment of such an agency as the actual cause of his death be made with truthfulness."[33] That he remains one of the only eyewitnesses to events that day cannot be dismissed.

It is not clear whether Joseph Walker remained at the tavern until Snodgrass's arrival, but seeing that Poe needed to be removed from his boisterous surroundings, the doctor began making arrangements to place Poe in one of the rooms of the hotel, "where he could be comfortable until I got word to his relatives."[34] A waiter accompanied Snodgrass upstairs and on their way back down to the bar, they were intercepted by Henry Herring, Poe's uncle (through marriage).[35] How Henry was informed of Poe's situation is not clear, but as an active member of the Whig party, and a nearby resident, he was well known at Gunner's Hall, and could have been contacted by anyone there who was aware of his relation to Poe.[36] Author Matthew Pearl wrote that Henry may have even been alerted by his uncle, George Herring, who was president of the local Whigs; the elder Herring may have been concerned about the disruption that Poe could potentially cause to the electoral proceedings at the tavern.[37]

Figure 4.5. Henry Herring was Poe's uncle through a marriage to his father's sister, Elizabeth. He was among those assisting Poe at Gunners' Hall and it was his decision to send the poet to a hospital. This portrait of him was made many years later. *Edgar Allan Poe Museum, Richmond, VA*

Nevertheless, Henry Herring took charge of the situation and decided against the hotel room, ordering that Poe should be taken to a hospital instead. Snodgrass would write that he was at first surprised by Herring's suggestion, asking "his [Poe's] relative to explain why he had not suggested a still better place—his own dwelling." (Home care for the ill and infirmed was the norm during this time, with hospitals being reserved for serious cases and for those with no family to take them in.) Herring replied, "that Mr. Poe had so frequently abused his hospitality by the rudeness as well as vulgarity of his bearing while drunk, toward the ladies of his household, that he couldn't think, for a moment, of taking him to his house in his present besotted condition."[38] This reply from Herring is somewhat harsher than Snodgrass's earlier version of it, and he may have again embellished the language to appeal to his temperance readers.

Apparently, both Snodgrass and Henry Herring had come to Gunners' Hall on foot, and a hack cab was needed to convey the stricken poet to the hospital.[39] While they awaited its arrival, Snodgrass made another survey of Poe, his appearance and his ill-fitting ensemble. As shown, his depiction of Poe's appearance is detailed, if not graphic, but just as important, is what Snodgrass did not describe. He makes no mention of money, or anything else in Poe's pockets, if indeed he had pockets; Snodgrass's initial evaluation of Poe as being in a state of "evident destitution" would appear to confirm his penniless condition.

There has been some debate as to whether Poe had the key to his trunk, on his person. As discussed in chapter 2, it appears he left his trunk in Richmond, either with the Mackenzies or at the hotel where he had been staying. Bringing along its iron key on the journey north, especially if there was not a duplicate, would have been a reckless exercise, and it is more likely that he left it in Richmond, perhaps with the Mackenzie family. In any event, Snodgrass, and later Moran, made no remark about a key in Poe's pocket. The first mention of the key seems to be by Mary Newton Stanard (in 1925) in her edited collection of Poe letters in the Valentine Museum. Stanard states without any attribution, "the trunk and its key (which was found in the dead poet's pocket) were turned over to Neilson Poe, who sent them to Edgar's sister, Rosalie, at Duncan Lodge."[40] Evidence seems to indicate, however, that Mrs. Stanard has the sequence of custody reversed, with the trunk being taken from Rosalie (at Neilson Poe's request) immediately following Poe's death and returned to her, empty of its literary contents, much later. Stanard's claim of the key being found "in the dead poet's pocket" appears equally as unreliable; nevertheless, it was reiterated by subsequent biographers.[41]

Snodgrass mentions no valise or baggage of any kind in Poe's possession when he was found at Gunners' Hall. Neilson Poe suggested that he may have given a piece of luggage to a porter when he landed, which, at the time of Poe's discovery on October 3, could have still been waiting for him at the ticket depot on Pratt Street, assuming no one had retrieved it by then.[42]

Perhaps most significant is the absence of any remark by Snodgrass or by Moran concerning Dr. John Carter's expensive walking stick that Poe reportedly had with him before leaving Richmond. Several of Poe's biographers, including Arthur Hobson Quinn and George Woodberry, state that Poe was clutching the cane when he was found at the tavern. However, Woodberry qualified his statement about the cane by observing, "had he been drugged and made to vote in any violent manner, as was represented, it [the cane] could hardly have failed to be separated from him."[43] The incompatibility of Poe's circumstances and his attire with an expensive malacca walking stick was not lost on Professor Woodberry.

Although Carter himself would write in 1902 about Poe taking the cane, the first person to propose that he had it with him in Baltimore appears to be Susan Talley Weiss. Written five years later, her book, *The Home Life of Poe* (1907), apparently expands on Carter's story: "the handsome malacca cane . . . was in his grasp when he reached the hospital. This cane was, at Dr. Carter's request, returned to him by Mrs. Clemm, to whom Dr. Moran sent it."[44] Succeeding biographers would mistake Mrs. Weiss's invention for fact.[45] As previously noted, Carter recovered his cane from the same people in Richmond who were caring for Poe's other belongings. It is therefore not probable that Poe had the doctor's walking stick when he was found at Gunners' Hall; nor is it likely that Snodgrass and Moran would have omitted such an incongruity from their detailed descriptions of his attire.

When the cab pulled up in front of Gunners' Hall, Snodgrass and Herring tried to coax Poe to his feet, but apparently, they were unable to revive him. Snodgrass would later recall: "The carriage having arrived, we tried to get the object of our care upon his feet, so that he might the more easily be taken to it. But he was past locomotion. We therefore carried him to the coach as if he were a corpse, and lifted him into it in the same manner." Snodgrass added that while they were doing this Poe was "utterly voiceless

READY COACH COMPANY

George Reilly proprietor

LIVERY – CARRIAGES – HACKS for HIRE

25 Lombard Street

Figure 4.6. From surviving testimony it appears that Poe was sent unaccompanied to the hospital in a hired hack. Because he was still unconscious when he arrived, his identity there may not have been immediately established. *Author (original art in the author's collection)*

as to be capable of only muttering some scarcely-intelligible oaths, and other forms of imprecation, upon those who were trying to rescue him from destitution and disgrace."[46]

From remarks that would later be made by Moran and others, it appears that neither Snodgrass nor Herring accompanied Poe to the hospital.[47] These were busy men who had already suffered a significant disruption to their daily occupations by coming to Poe's aid. Herring was a successful Baltimore lumber dealer and employer while Snodgrass, after closing his paper, the *Saturday Visiter*, became a temperance and abolition advocate, writing and lecturing on these causes. During the day that he was called to Poe's side, Snodgrass could have been involved in the state political elections taking place and working to defeat a disgraced temperance candidate.[48]

Busy though they may have been, neither Herring nor Snodgrass could have been called poverty-stricken, yet payment of the 50-cent cab fare would be left to those at the hospital.[49] Had one or both men been with Poe when he reached the infirmary, his identification to members of the medical staff would have been assured, as would have an enhanced level of care. However, arriving there alone in what appeared to be an alcohol-fueled stupor, wearing the odious attire of a beggar, and in a hack driven by someone who may not have understood his instructions or been believed when relaying the name of his passenger, Poe could have been easily mistaken for just another indigent street-case; the outstanding cab fare only punctuating the effect. A decision by Henry Herring and Joseph Snodgrass to send Poe to the hospital unescorted that day may have ultimately sealed the poet's fate.

Chapter Five

Beware the Ward Heelers

The unexplained death of Edgar Allan Poe on October 7, 1849, should really be viewed as a two-part mystery, each requiring a separate resolution. The first question, and perhaps the most often asked, is what actually caused his death after he was admitted to a public hospital in East Baltimore, possible answers to which will be discussed later in this book. Yet how he came to be found at the Fourth Ward Hotel four days earlier is no less a mystery. There are several viable theories with regard to this, including one by author Matthew Pearl who suggests that Poe was on his way to visit his old friend, Dr. Joseph Snodgrass, who lived at 103 North High Street, only a couple of blocks from where he ended up.[1] Pearl submits that Poe could have been seeking Snodgrass's help with his magazine project and that he intended to call on his friend in the same manner as his *believed* visit to Nathan Brooks.[2] However, if Poe had tried to reach Snodgrass in an impaired condition, it is more likely that he was in search of a bed or financial assistance, not a list of potential subscribers. That he could not appeal to any of his Baltimore relatives for help at the time demonstrates how poor his relationship with them had become.[3]

Others have pointed out that Poe logically would have gravitated to the Old Town section of the city. The Philadelphia, Wilmington & Baltimore Railroad (PW&B) terminal, his point of departure, was just six blocks below the tavern where he was found, and after missing his train, Poe may have remained in the area, perhaps to pass time until the next one left. Writer Michael Powell suggests that Poe was able to walk earlier in the day and that he headed north on High Street, being "intermittently conscious as he approached Ryans' (near the corner of Lombard and High Streets), availing himself there of an opportunity to be heard by someone who might help him."[4] Or he may have

116   *Chapter Five*

simply decided that he had been out in the bone-chilling rain long enough and found the tavern an expedient shelter.

The most persistent theory explaining his discovery at Gunners' Hall is a scenario of kidnapping, confinement, and compelled drinking. In this version of his final days, Poe was the victim of political operatives who abducted him on a Baltimore Street, stupefied him with alcohol (or drug-laced alcohol), and then held him captive until he could be employed as a repeat voter in the state and congressional elections taking place in the city on October 3. Indeed, the tavern where he was found had been designated as the official poll for the fourth political ward of Baltimore City, and the description of Poe's state of deep intoxication while wearing the clothes of another man also conforms nicely to the plot. However, before considering the theory's plausibility, a brief look at Baltimore's political landscape, as well as 1849 voting procedures, should help to explain Poe's circumstances and the city through which he was trying to pass.

By the mid-nineteenth century, Baltimore had earned a reputation as a notoriously lawless municipality, and the political fanaticism of its citizenry was a significant cause of the criminality that pervaded the city. As writer, Richard Bensel, explains, "Before the Civil War, the most violent precincts in the United States were probably located in Baltimore City. . . . Between 1828 and 1861 it is estimated that in Baltimore alone, 28 men died from election-related riots or individual acts of political violence, apparently the highest death toll in the nation."[5] The city's police department had been, since its formation, underfunded and undermanned. Their role in 1849 was still largely that of watchmen stationed at posts throughout the city. These "officers" were not yet uniformed, carried no firearms and often seemed reluctant to respond to incidents of gang or political misbehavior.[6]

At the time of Poe's death there were two (national) political parties in America of which the citizens of Baltimore were almost evenly split. The first, the (Jacksonian) Democrats, supported a general hands-off approach to individual and state's rights, commerce, immigration, and suffrage (albeit only for white males over the age of twenty-one). This party was largely the contingent of the working class. The opposition was the Whig party that had risen from the ashes of the Federalists. Theirs was a more conservative platform favoring stronger central government, trade controls, a central bank, industrialization, and infrastructure improvements. This faction was generally that of entrepreneurs, professionals, and the aristocracy. The importance of the issues at stake—such as slavery, state's rights, tariff protections, Manifest Destiny (and wars of expansion), temperance, and immigration—was recognized by all and stirred deep passions everywhere, especially among the working class who read newspapers.[7] As writer Daniel Walker Howe observed of the time, "party politics was our first national sport, and the public played, and watched, the great game with enthusiasm."[8]

And this "sport" had no more radical fan-base than that found in the Monumental City. A notice in the May 17, 1841, edition of the *Baltimore Sun* attests to the political fervor at the time:

> TO THE POLLS – TO THE POLLS! We imagine there are few who will not remember that this is election day. . . . Choose ye between them [congressional candidates] and remember the axiom, "the man who will not vote, does not deserve the privilege."

To further assist the would-be voter, the notice above also contained a list of the polling locations that included the Fourth Ward polls at Coath and Sargeant's (a tavern on their property) on Lombard Street. At the time, in most municipal voting districts, or wards, there was a shortage of civic buildings such as court houses, schools, post offices, etc., and instead, popular meeting spots were assigned as polling places on Election Day. The most commonly used venues were liquor establishments. As Richard Bensel points

Figure 5.1. The practice of political intimidation and kidnapping was well established by the time of Poe's death. This image depicts two "ward agents," perhaps from opposing parties, accosting an inebriated man on Election Day. *Author (printed engraving from author's collection)*

out: "Saloons were the most important gathering places for immigrants in the mid-nineteenth century and thus were primary centers for their political mobilization as voters . . . and, at least in New York, almost nine of every ten polling places in immigrant neighborhoods were saloons."[9]

When explaining all this to John Ingram, Poe's English biographer, William Hand Browne would write: "At that time the polls were usually held at public houses, and the candidates saw that every voter had all the whiskey he wanted."[10] The systemic use of taverns as voting venues guaranteed that alcohol became a lubricant for the electoral process. "Liquor was both freely available and consumed to excess," according to Bensel. "The parties often provided, either as a courtesy or as a bribe, free drinks to prospective voters . . . and election officials. As a result the street or square outside the voting window frequently became a kind of alcoholic festival in which many men were clearly and spectacularly drunk."[11]

However, it was the simplistic voting procedure, with its almost complete absence of safeguards and regulation that facilitated widespread abuse, and no more so than in the lawless streets of Baltimore. Voting then was accomplished through pre-printed paper ballots showing the names of the candidates; these were deposited into a wooden or iron box, to be retrieved and tabulated later in the day. The ballots were often printed in newspapers for the purpose of their removal but they could also be acquired at the polls by hawkers or indigents hired for the job and often paid in free drinks. In most instances, there was no voter registration mechanism, a situation that left the determination of voter eligibility up to election judges, as their title suggests. It was also the responsibility of these appointed officials to deposit each ballot into the box within full view of the voter, who usually had to step on a raised platform to present his ticket to the judge through a building's exterior window. In this way, the ballot box and judge were given some measure of protection from those who would interfere.[12]

The voting process allowed no privacy, and with many of the party-generated ballots often printed in color, those crowding around the window could easily determine a voter's choice before he was able to submit it. When alcohol was added to the equation, it should come as no surprise that violence became part and parcel of the procedure, and as previously discussed, such behavior would have gone unchecked by the police in Baltimore, where there were no organized daylight patrols until 1857, eight years after Poe's death.[13] And when the undermanned authorities *were* alerted to these Election Day offenses, they usually refused to take any action.[14] The immediate area around the polls was often a scene of vocal (and physical) bedlam, and without making prior arrangements, anyone attempting to vote during the usual hours had to endure an ordeal. Before a prospective voter could climb to the window and be quizzed by an election judge, his eligibility was often challenged by enlistees stationed in the crowd, some of whom were appointed by local clubs for that very purpose. In addition, these political agents, or "ward heelers" as they were called, often conspired with or intimidated judges into accepting ballots from those whom *they* had already certified. It was this practice that exploited one of the principal weaknesses of the antebellum electoral system: ineligible voting.[15]

It quickly became apparent that cooperative or inexperienced judges could be persuaded to accept groups of these "certified" voters whose ballots would then be added to the favored contestant's tally. At first, prospective voters were offered the bribe of "refreshments" in houses or rooms near the polls just before they opened. These clients often drank to excess after which, in "certified" condition, they were marched (under supervision) to the polls to complete the bargain. As elections became more competitive, these refreshment rooms evolved into private holding cells or "coops," where liquor and food were still used to secure votes, but from men who were no longer, in any sense, voluntary participants.[16]

Foreigners, vagrants, and the already inebriated were favorite targets of the ward heelers who, in the absence of law enforcement, would seize any tactic or device that could lure men to their coops. The most often used tricks included offers of employment, lodging, and of course, free drinks. One particularly successful ruse involved approaching a person that was looking for work and then asking that individual for help in carrying a crate or trunk to the train depot. Upon entering the house to pick up the case, the victim would be kidnapped, often at gunpoint and with the aid of accomplices. The person would then be robbed and removed to the holding pen if not at that location. Ultimately, the practice of "cooping" degenerated into overt kidnapping and robbery, with victims often being corralled in rooms that were devoid of any accommodations, including bedding and sanitation, sometimes for days prior to an election. As reported by Edward Spencer in a lengthy article for the *New York Herald*, the prisoners in these coops "were thrust into cellars and backyards, and kept under lock and key, without light, without beds, without provisions for decency, without food. Only one thing they were supplied with, and that was a sufficient deluge of whiskey to keep their brains all the time sodden, and prevent them from imparting intelligibility to their complaints."[17]

According to Spencer, the coop in the rear of the firehouse on High Street (the nearest to Gunners' Hall) held as many as 140 men, the votes from whom could be multiplied by their repeated applications through changes in appearance; 140 captives could possibly yield 600 or more votes at a single location during the course of a day.[18] In addition, these poor wretches were often herded onto omnibuses and transported to different polls across the

120   *Chapter Five*

city to "exercise their franchise," before returning to the coop to change their wardrobe (at gunpoint) and commence another tour.

Nowhere was this tactic embraced more enthusiastically by its practitioners than in "Mobtown," where an op-ed writer for the *Baltimore Sun* asked "whether there is any other [US city] which equals us in the audacity of one of the practices common to our city . . . we speak of the practice of 'cooping?'" The writer then points out that there was no law in place to punish the offenders and that the "citizens should take care to provide for it at the next legislature."[19] Even greater abuses were to occur in subsequent Baltimore City elections, and it would be another eight years before those in the city conceived a Reform Committee that would "secure quiet and fairness at the polls" as well as proffer legislation to make the practice of cooping illegal.[20]

October 3, 1849, was a rain-soaked day in Baltimore, and all the unscrupulous arrangements made by Whig and Democratic partisans would have literally gone down the drain. A writer for the *Baltimore Sun* the following day wondered if the small voter turnout that occurred was the result of soggy weather, adding "we heard of no disturbances at the polls or elsewhere."[21] That Whig operatives had at least planned a day of manufactured voting was certainly anticipated by their opposition as this notice appearing in a Baltimore newspaper indicates: "Democrats of the Fourth Ward protect your rights—yours is the ward that will receive the great mass of foreign Whigs. It is in your ward that they expect to swell the vote."[22] Another alert followed later on Election Day: "Beware of the Whig tricks. Our opponents are at their old game again. Tickets are out with their candidates and the hickory emblem. Colonization on a large scale is to be resorted to. Illegal votes will be polled from a distance and otherwise. Coops have been started by them. All this and more the Whigs are doing."[23] However, the miserable, daylong downpour would have tested the resolve of even the most devoted of political hoodlums in each party. Perhaps the Democrats had succeeded in providing better weather protection for their operatives and kidnapping victims, for the bonfires (and celebratory gunfire) at the end of the day would be for *their* victories at the polls.[24]

The theory that Edgar Poe could have been one of these victims was not proposed until many years after his death, and as Poe scholar Jeffrey Savoye points out, the lack of attention given to the idea during the interim is somewhat troubling.[25] Of course, this lapse may have been the result of those involved covering their tracks. Although the practice of cooping was not illegal in Maryland in 1849, the attendant acts of kidnapping and robbery *were* against the law, and those complicit in such schemes would not have been eager to come forward, especially if a fatality had resulted. In the immediate period following Poe's death, it was the common belief that he had died as a result of a drunken debauch, an explanation no doubt accelerated by its depiction in a poisonous memoir of the poet that was written by Rufus Griswold and attached to Poe's collected works in 1850.[26]

There were some who began looking for exculpatory explanations, wanting to rescue his reputation. For example, as previously discussed, when temperance advocate Snodgrass came across the theory in 1855 that Poe's death was a suicide, and not the result of alcohol, he immediately jumped to snuff out the exonerating flames. Two years later, Mrs. Elizabeth Oakes Smith would state in a magazine feature on Poe that he was "cruelly beaten by a ruffian who knew of no better mode of avenging supposed injuries. It is well known that a brain fever followed."[27] She would use a different publication in 1867 to repeat the story which brought forth another written extinguishment from Snodgrass.[28]

The cooping theory must also be seen as an exonerative explanation of Poe's death. The first recorded mention of it can be found in John R. Thompson lecture series titled, "The Genius and Character of Edgar A. Poe." While it is not clear how or when Thompson came upon the idea, it is probably no coincidence that he delivered his first lecture in Baltimore, in the summer of 1860.[29] A notice in the November edition of the *Southern Literary Messenger* of that year reads, "We learn that John R. Thompson, Esq. . . . intends delivering his Lecture on Edgar A. Poe in the Southern cities during the coming winter. Delivered first in Baltimore, and subsequently in Richmond and other cities of Virginia, this Lecture excited the highest encomiums."[30] It is possible that the cooping story had been circulating before Thompson began his talks, but he did not cite any authority or witnesses to support his theory:

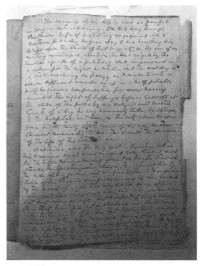

Figure 5.2. The story that Edgar Poe had been a "cooping" victim was first presented in a lecture during the summer of 1860 by writer and publisher, John R. Thompson. The original manuscript of the lecture, shown here, is held at the Edgar Allan Poe Museum in Richmond, Virginia. *Edgar Allan Poe Museum, Richmond, VA*

On his way through Baltimore . . . he either, as some say, gave way to his besetting sin, or he was drugged. Adrift on the streets of that large city, on the eve of an exciting municipal election, he was seized by the lawless agents of a political club, imprisoned in a cellar for the night, and taken out the next day in a state bordering on frenzy and made to vote in eleven different wards .... Cast off at the close of the polls by his vulgar and brutal tyrants of a day, he was humanely taken by strangers to the hospital, and there ... he chanced miserably to die.[31]

The detail of "eleven different wards" would suggest that Thompson had a source from which he derived the story. Nevertheless, it should be pointed out that with this account, Thompson had departed significantly from his first version of how Edgar Poe died. In a letter to Edwin Patterson, written only weeks after Poe's burial, Thompson describes the poet's alcoholic habits saying, "no influence was adequate to keep him from the damnable propensity to drink, and his entire residence in Richmond of late was but a succession of disgraceful follies." He finishes his note with an equally unattractive explanation of which he had no firsthand knowledge: "He died, indeed, in delirium from drunkenness; the shadow of infamy beclouded his last moments."[32] In this communique to Patterson, Thompson made no suggestion that Poe may have been abducted.

John Reuben Thompson had taken over the editorship of the *Southern Literary Messenger* from Benjamin B. Minor in 1847. He pursued the life of litterateur and journalist even though he was a member of the Richmond Bar. (His legal degree from the University of Virginia would come in handy when he represented Poe's sister Rosalie in the contest over her brother's "estate.") Thompson first met Poe during the poet's brief visit to Richmond in the summer of 1848. Thompson claimed that after recovering from a two-week spree, "in one of the lowest haunts of vice upon the wharves of this City," Poe, in the company of John Mackenzie, called on him at the magazine office. In response, Thompson offered Poe a desk and a base of operations while he was in town.[33] Because of his association with Poe (which was probably overstated by Thompson), many saw

Figure 5.3. John Reuben Thompson was editor of the Southern Literary Messenger and became acquainted with Poe during his final visits to Richmond. Following the trend, Thompson would later grow a full beard but this is how Poe would have known him. *University of Virginia Library*

the editor as a reliable authority on Poe's death and gave his "cooping theory" a greater measure of credibility. In time, some would take the story and spin it into detailed accounts.[34] However, it is important to understand that all the so-called eyewitnesses to Poe's kidnapping came forward only after the cooping idea had been well publicized and in circulation for many years, and when any association with Edgar Allan Poe would bring someone notoriety.[35]

Some of these included relatives of the poet, their family connection conferring additional authority to the stories. Edgar's cousin, Neilson Poe, was one of the first to sign on to the cooping theory, describing his version of the idea during an interview with photographer George B. Coale in 1871: "He was insensible from intoxication and probable drugging. (There was a horrible suspicion that some political 'ward managers' had voted him over the city the day before—he was found in the backroom of a 'headquarters' and had probably been 'cooped'—it is not necessary to say this)."[36] Neilson Poe also related the story to Poe's early biographer, Eugene L. Didier, who would include it in his 1876 *Life and Poems of Edgar Allan Poe*.[37]

Another family member who gave the story some gravity was Elisabeth Ellicott Poe, a third-generation cousin to the poet. In the February 1909 issue of *Cosmopolitan Magazine*, she wrote that, "His drink was drugged under the direction of a gang of plug-uglies [Whigs or Democrats] and he was voted about the city next day in the elections as a repeater while still drugged. . . . A certain Passano of that [political] society, in after years said that Edgar Poe was kept in his coop that night. After *they* had finished with the unfortunate man, he was thrown carelessly into the street, left to die if he willed."[38] She repeated the story in an *imaginative* biography of Poe printed more than twenty years later, adding that the man, "Passano," admitted his involvement to relatives (of Poe) but that no formal record was made.[39] Although Elisabeth's anecdote has never been documented, a search through the city directories and archives of the *Baltimore Sun* revealed the existence of a Lewis (or Louis) Passano as a political operative for the Whigs during the time of Poe's death.[40] That Mr. Passano would have later confessed is not too farfetched, given that he was apparently penitent enough to become an officer in the Reform Committee of 1859, a Baltimore organization dedicated to ensure peace and fair voting at the polls.[41] Of course, Passano's tale could have also been a boast, or a contrived rationale for joining the committee.

Perhaps the most detailed version of the cooping story was given by Edward Spencer in his lengthy feature for the *New York Herald* in which he describes the practice and location of the different holding cells being used:

> The Whig "coop" in the Fourth Ward, on High Street, was within two squares of the place where Poe was "found." It is altogether possible . . . that Poe was "cooped" and that his outlaw custodians, discovering too late the disastrous

> ☞ *FOURTH WARD.—RELIEF OF THE POOR.*—The Purchasing and Distributing Committee of the Fourth Ward will meet at the new VIGILANT ENGINE HOUSE, Lombard street, between Exeter and High streets, EVERY DAY, from 11, A. M. until 4 o'clock, P. M., until the funds *are distributed,* for the purpose of receiving applications for relief.
>
>   WM. H. COLE, Jr., ⎱
>   HARRY R. REYNOLDS, ⎰ Committee.
>   EDW'D. J. SANDERS,
>
> The Committee appointed for the following districts are *earnestly requested* to *complete* their collections forthwith, and return the same to Capt. RICH'D LILLY, Treasurer.
>
> Second District—East side of Exeter, north side of Baltimore, south side of Pitt street to Harford Run—Col. Wm. Chesnut, Capt. Jos. Trippe, Jas. S. Suter, Collecting Committee.
>
> Fourth District—North side of Lombard street, from east side Exeter, south side of Baltimore st., to Harford Run—Wm. Reany, Thos. Moore, Lewis Passano, Collecting Committee.
>
>   EDW'D G. STARR, President.
> RICHARD LILLY, Secretary.   1t*

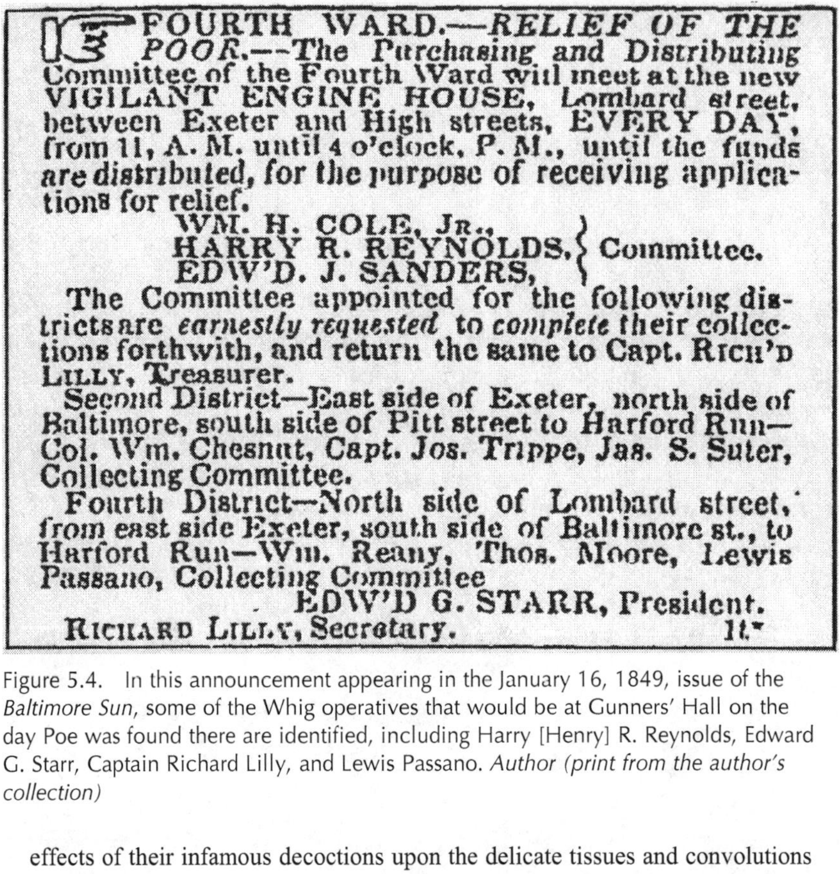

Figure 5.4. In this announcement appearing in the January 16, 1849, issue of the *Baltimore Sun*, some of the Whig operatives that would be at Gunners' Hall on the day Poe was found there are identified, including Harry [Henry] R. Reynolds, Edward G. Starr, Captain Richard Lilly, and Lewis Passano. *Author (print from the author's collection)*

effects of their infamous decoctions upon the delicate tissues and convolutions of his finely organized brain, sought to repair some of the damage they had done, and caused inquiry to be made for the friends of the man they had murdered. Too late![42]

From its emergence, Thompson's theory was immediately embraced by Poe enthusiasts who did not believe that the poet was a man with any weaknesses. The idea was also appealing to those who found it more lucrative to paint Poe in a better light, including those who would write and lecture on him. One exception was Dr. John J. Moran, who ultimately decided that it would be better to disavow any mention of Poe's intoxication, compelled or otherwise. In a feature article for the *New York Herald* in 1875, Moran would state unequivocally that when he treated Poe at the hospital, "There was no smell of liquor upon his person or breath."[43] Moran would reinforce this position in a book he penned ten years later: "I have stated to you the fact that Edgar Allan Poe did not die under the effect of any intoxicant. . . . It has been charged that POE was made drunk and then 'cooped,' and voted a number of times at an election held in Baltimore about that time. This charge I unhesitatingly deny."[44] However, this disavowal marks a complete reversal of his original diagnosis made when the dying poet was in front of him. Moran produced a catalog of contradictory statements, all of which will be examined in chapter 7 of this book.

William Hand Browne was also among the early adherents to the cooping theory. He wrote to biographer John Ingram in 1875 that his friend, Dr. James W. Alnutt, knew details of Poe's cooping.[45] Browne believed that the discovery of Joseph Walker's note in 1880 establishing Poe's location at the Fourth Ward polls provided indisputable proof of his being "cooped" and he wrote again to Ingram that Edward Spencer was "hunting up all about Ryan's place and will try to see if any of Poe's fellow prisoners in that den can now be found."[46] Professor Browne would eventually come to reject the idea, but most of Poe's subsequent biographers would accept or record different versions of the cooping story. These included John Ingram, Susan Talley Weiss, George Woodberry, Hervey Allen, Mary Phillips, and Arthur Quinn, all of whom added no new evidence.

While Poe's condition and circumstances on that Election Day would seem to validate the cooping theory, the idea that he was kidnapped and used as a repeat voter is not without some difficulties. One significant factor is the location itself. It was the usual practice of the political "coyotes" to discard their prisoners away from their base of operations in order to reduce the chance of detection—in many cases it would be the last voting venue to which the victims were taken. Once they were finally free of their captors, these unfortunates could potentially communicate their mistreatment, and any *coherent* complaints might find sympathetic and even believing ears, but with their fraudulent ballots mingled in with legitimate votes, nothing could be used to prove (or undo) the scheme. Yet when considering the place of Poe's discovery, it is just as probable that he could have been abused by the Democrats instead of the Whigs. In this scenario, he would have been abandoned afterward at the latter's stronghold on Lombard Street.

If, however, Poe was taken and exploited by the Whigs as most adherents of the theory believe, his discovery around the corner from their headquarters on High Street would require further explanation.[47] For example, instead of being shanghaied by ward agents, Poe could have volunteered for the voting duty that day, possibly motivated by the reward of free drinks. What we know of his political thinking seems to agree with Whig ideology. He had been raised among the Virginia aristocracy, where the subjugation of other human beings and elitist thinking was part of the landscape. Poe gave subtle confirmation of this perspective in works such as "Some Words with a Mummy"

Figure 5.5. This conception of Poe's "cooping" made by artist E. H. Gunder depicts his confinement in a basement with other victims. The walking stick he is shown holding was most likely not in his possession at the time. *Author (printed photo from the author's collection)*

(1845) and "Mellonta Tauta" (1849), where he intimated an unfavorable view of democratic government, equating it with mob rule: "As for republicanism [democracy], no anthology could be found for it upon the face of the earth—unless we except the case of the prairie dogs, an exception which seems to demonstrate, if anything, that democracy is a very admirable form of government—for dogs."[48] And when trying to win a government job during the administration of John Tyler, he expressed Whig sympathies to his friend, Frederick Thomas, a political appointee who was working on Poe's behalf through Tyler's son: "My political principles have always been as nearly as may be, with the existing administration, and I battled with right good will for Harrison, when opportunity offered."[49] With someone who genuinely held these views, coercive measures may not have been necessary to secure their participation on Election Day.

Another possible difficulty with the cooping theory is the notoriety of Edgar Allan Poe. By 1849, he had achieved international fame, and after years of residence in and visitations to the city, Poe's face would have been familiar to many in Baltimore. Furthermore, he had the reputation of being effusive, even boastful when intoxicated, and would have been eager to enlighten those around him as to his celebrity. Had political operatives trotted *him* around town to be used as a repeat voter, it is probable that Poe would have called attention to himself, and sparked recognition. Certainly, any acquaintance having such an encounter with the poet would have remembered it, especially after his death became public. Yet there remains no credible testimony by anyone crossing paths with him that day.

Of course, Poe could have remained in that one location having been put to work as a ballot hawker at the Fourth Ward polls, although the inclement weather would have made that an especially miserable task. That Poe had some interaction with the people at Gunners' Hall before his discovery there is implied by his relentless shouting of the name "Reynolds" while he was in the hospital; Henry R. Reynolds had served as one of the Fourth Ward election judges. A resident of the Old Town section of the city, Reynolds was a professional builder who, with his brother Josiah, operated a well-known construction company out of an office on Front Street.[50] Along with Captain Richard Lilly and Edward G. Starr, both of whom were also Whig party officers, Reynolds had been appointed as an election judge at Ryan's Gunners' Hall and in this role, he could have eventually disqualified Poe as a voter, severing his supply of free alcohol.[51] Novelist Matthew Pearl offers a different interpretation of the scene in suggesting that Poe's delirious beckoning of Reynolds in the hospital could have been a plea to the man. In this view, Poe appealed to Reynolds for rescue from political thugs, which would have also been the election judge's responsibility.[52]

128   *Chapter Five*

Edgar Poe's proximity, when at the tavern, to a man named Reynolds is too much a coincidence to dismiss, although another writer has suggested that when Poe was in the hospital, he actually cried out the word "Herring," the last name of his uncle, Henry Herring. In his paper, "Dr. Moran and the Poe-Reynolds Myth," William Bandy presumes that John Moran, in his 1875 article for the *New York Herald*, mistakenly confused the Reynolds Family with the Herrings. He must therefore have also mixed up the families when writing to Maria Clemm five weeks after Edgar Poe's death and made the first mention of Poe shouting the name.[53] However, in that part of Moran's letter to Clemm (appendix D), he appears to be transcribing from a case-record, perhaps compiled by others, and it is possible that Moran never heard the shouts himself. How much time (if any) Moran spent with Poe during his last days in the hospital will be discussed in chapters 6 and 7.

Perhaps the strongest evidence for the cooping story is the clothing that Edgar Poe was found in that day, attire that would seem to cement the premise that he was used as a repeat voter. As discussed, by changing the appearance of their captives, political agents could harvest more votes with recurring visits to the same polls. When discovered by Joseph Walker, Poe was wearing an outfit that can best be described as retrieved from a trashcan; certainly not the clothes he was in when leaving Richmond. By distilling the varied descriptions of Poe's apparel provided by Snodgrass and Moran, a somewhat clearer image of Poe's outfit emerges. When discovered at the Fourth Ward Hotel he was wearing a badly fitting pair of pants that were stained and faded. He wore a crumbled, dingy shirt with no vest or neck cloth, and had on a topcoat of cheap alpaca wool (Moran would later call the material bombazine) that was soiled, faded, and ripped at several of the seams. On his feet were a pair of ruined shoes (or boots) with heels that were completely worn down, and on his head, he wore a cheap palm-leaf hat that was tattered, and without a ribbon or adequate brim. Poe had been wearing a broad-brimmed planter's hat during his time in Virginia, but both descriptions of his clothing, after his discovery, mention an older, rust-colored hat and probably not the one he had in Richmond.

The secondhand or discarded clothing of the type described would certainly have been the wardrobe of repeat voters. Nonetheless, Poe's odious apparel can also be explained in ways that have nothing to do with "cooping," explanations that are not very attractive, but just as plausible. For instance, at some point he could have soiled his original outfit especially if he were in an insensible state, similar to his disastrous trip to Washington, DC, in 1843, where he was compelled to wear his coat inside out. Or perhaps after spending a couple of days in the cold rain he sought whatever dry clothes he

Beware the Ward Heelers 129

could find. Having misplaced his luggage, the filthy suit he was wearing was perhaps the best that could be found at the spur of the moment.[54]

It is also possible that Poe had become delusional and, thinking that he was being pursued by assassins, looked for a change of clothes as a disguise. As we have seen, this same scenario is believed to have occurred during the first leg of Poe's trip down to Richmond. On that part of the journey, when passing through Philadelphia, Poe turned up on the doorstep of his friend John Sartain after having been on the streets there for days, probably even after spending some time in jail for public drunkenness. Poe was out of his mind and told Sartain of pursuers out to kill him. Looking to change his appearance, he begged for a razor so that he could remove his mustache.[55] Perhaps this time he decided that a change in outfit would work better.

By attributing the clothes Edgar Allan Poe was wearing that October afternoon to causes other than cooping, the theory ultimately loses some of its potency. In the final analysis, the evidence for Thompson's idea, compelling as it may be, is only circumstantial and there remains no document, official report or credible eyewitness testimony that directly supports the theory of Poe's kidnapping. When considering the totality of the facts before us, it seems probable that Edgar Poe had some interaction with the people at Gunners' Hall before he was taken away to the hospital—one has to ask why Poe was not ejected from Ryan's tavern if he had no money.[56] However, until further, *irrefutable* evidence can be presented, the cooping theory must remain just that: another theory.

Chapter Six

Hospital on the Hill

Sometime in the late afternoon of October 3, 1849, Edgar Allan Poe was transported to the Baltimore City and Marine Hospital, which stood approximately twelve blocks from the tavern at the Fourth Ward Hotel where he was found. Of the city's infirmaries, the one located on North Broadway was the nearest, for *perceived* cases such as Poe's.[1] With Baltimore Street not yet completed that far away, the most expeditious route would have been via Fayette Street.[2] If Poe's hack driver was unacquainted with the facility and had stopped at the hospital's main entrance (on Broadway), the attendant there would have directed him to the ambulance entrance on the north side of the building which was at ground level and had no staircase to impede arriving patients or those handling them. From there Poe would have been placed on a gurney and after evaluation, perhaps conducted by Resident Physician, Dr. John J. Moran, taken to an upper level on a mechanical hoist through an enclosed chute that was originally intended to handle cadavers for the university.[3] Moran would maintain that Poe was placed in a private room, later identifying the location as on the second floor (not counting the basement level) in the southwest turret; however, as we shall see, subsequent remarks made by the doctor and others conflict with this account.

When he came to the hospital, it is believed that Poe was still unresponsive and unable to speak, coherently at least.[4] That he arrived unaccompanied is very likely, and there has been much discussion over whether anyone there knew (or was given) the identity of the newly arrived patient. Moran, who had assumed management of the facility only six months prior, would later claim that the hack driver had been given a handwritten card (by the *man* who found Poe) stating "my address, and on the lower right-hand corner the name of POE."[5] Had such a card indeed been given to Moran, it is not hard to imagine his incredulity when looking at the human wreckage before him:

Figure 6.1. This 1845 advertisement for Washington University in Baltimore depicts the design of the school and hospital as originally planned but the western wing would not be added until 1891. *Author (print from the author's collection)*

surely the man had only *claimed* to be Edgar Allan Poe. On the other hand, the note could have been a fabrication by Moran in response to those later questioning his assiduous care for the poet. Indeed, any cab driver with even a brief amount of experience in the city would know the location of its hospitals.

The establishment of Poe's identity would have been a determining factor in the quality of his medical care. If recognized as someone of social standing with concerned family members (who could also pay his bill), Poe would have been assigned private quarters and afforded better attention. However, if he were deemed just another drunken derelict, a charity case without means to compensate the facility for his care, it is more likely that Poe would have been deposited in the public ward where such cases were left to "sleep it off."[6] If it can be demonstrated that Poe was taken to a ward and not *initially* given a private room as Moran would later claim, it would seem to follow that his identity was not known to (or at least accepted by) those at the hospital when he first arrived.[7] Certainly, a celebrity of Poe's caliber would have warranted special treatment in a fledgling medical facility trying to establish itself; the hospital would risk negative attention if it became known that not all was done for the world-famous poet. In his 2009 book, *Too Much Moran: Respecting the Death of Edgar Poe*, writer Michael A. Powell suggests that Poe's identity was never discovered at the hospital and that he lay unattended, and untreated, until he was found dead on October 7.[8] As will be demonstrated, this is not likely, but Powell is probably correct in asserting that Poe's identity was not established when he first landed in Moran's care.

THE HOSPITAL ON THE HILL

The story of the hospital building, and those who first occupied it, is almost as troubled as that of Edgar Allan Poe. In 1826, after being denied by the Maryland state legislature for a charter to establish a medical college in Baltimore, a group of physicians, led by Dr. Horatio Gates Jameson, received approval to start the school under the charter of Washington College, a small liberal arts institution in Washington, Pennsylvania. The following year, the Washington Medical College opened its doors in a purpose-built structure on Holliday Street, directly across from the old City Hall (today the Peale Museum). In 1833, after establishing a solid record and conferring many medical degrees, the school again applied for an independent Maryland charter which was finally approved. With their growing success and the city's need for another medical facility, the school began construction on a much larger complex that could house medical students and also serve as a functioning hospital. The new structure was completed around 1836, and it sat on an elevated piece of ground at 100 North Broadway, giving the building an unobstructed view of the city and Patapsco River at the time. The construction cost of the new facility was given as $40,000, a price that did not include the property on which the building sat. The land rent agreement was ultimately signed by the college president, Dr. James H. Miller, who had also served on the three-member panel that awarded Poe his first literary prize three years earlier.[9]

Only half of the planned facility was completed at the time. Featuring a circular main section approximately forty feet in diameter, the six-story building was surrounded at four equidistant points by tower-like structures (with a corresponding number of floors) that incorporated the student dormitories. This segment served as the medical college and on different levels included the kitchen, dining room or refectory, operating rooms, lecture halls, and dissecting theater. The south-facing main entrance was on the first floor (not counting the basement level) requiring visitors to ascend to a small porch nestled between two of the towers. Attached to this section on the east side was the five-story hospital wing that was approximately sixty feet in length; it housed individual rooms (for patients and staff) beneath wards, the latter occupying the top two floors.[10] Two elevated entrances to the hospital section are shown in early images, one just to the right of the school's front doors, and a second porch attached to the eastern face of the building. A western hospital wing with matching dimensions was also intended but would not materialize while the college occupied the building; it would not be added until 1891, and then in a much modified design.[11]

After a year in the new facility, the college was granted a new charter as a university and the name was changed to Washington University of Baltimore,

Figure 6.2. The building depicted in the center of this 1852 lithograph by Edward Sachse is the Baltimore City and Marine Hospital, to which Poe was taken. The Fair Mount resort hotel originally built and owned by Poe's uncle, Henry Herring, is shown in the lower right. *Author (print from the author's collection)*

although many in the city would continue referring to the facility as Washington College Hospital out of habit, even after the school had later moved to a new location. In addition to serving as a medical school, Washington University also received federal funding as a marine hospital to treat sick and injured sailors landing in Baltimore, who were often unable to pay for their own care. This arrangement would be continued with the succeeding operator of the hospital until they closed in 1855. These seamen were often brought to the facility after suffering for prolonged periods and, in many cases, after it was too late for them to benefit from any medical care. Indeed, the hospital became a depository for dead sailors, a state of affairs that was welcomed by a college that emphasized instruction on anatomy and advertised an inexhaustible supply of "material" for dissection. A pamphlet sent to prospective students describes this distinct feature of the college: "A special advantage is the ease with which subjects for anatomical investigation and preparation may be obtained here." The brochure also claimed that the shortage of "subjects" in northern schools was often alleviated by shipments from Baltimore's surplus.[12]

According to William N. Batchelor, who lived with his family as caretakers in the hospital building after the facility closed down, doctors who originally worked there periodically arranged for the acquisition of dead bodies from the nearby Presbyterian Cemetery that had existed between Wolfe and Chester Streets at the time. On the first night of the Batchelor family's stay as watchmen in the building, a man appeared at the front gate with a large bag containing a corpse that had to be stood against the fence. The family ultimately refused entry to the grave robber, explaining "that there were no more doctors at the Washington College [and that] the only thing he could do was to carry the corpse to the home of the doctor that ordered it." In his memoir of the hospital, Batchelor wrote that doctors paid these "resurrectionists" about ten dollars for a cadaver and that many were brought to the facility, adding that dead bodies "was about all they could get to operate on."[13] This morbid aspect of the hospital's history also suggests Poe's eventual recognition there: had he died as an unknown, his body certainly could have been added to the university's stock of "material" for dissection.

Although brilliant surgeons and teachers they may have been, the lack of business acumen among the directors of the university was reflected in the school's apparent difficulty in paying its bills.[14] In 1848, it was decided to move the university to a smaller facility and surrender the building on Broadway to creditors, the public explanation for this decision being that the east Baltimore venue was too remote from the city to be practical. A new, three-story structure was started at the corner of Hanover and Lombard Streets with classes scheduled to begin there in March 1849. Funding for the new building ultimately proved inadequate, and it is not clear if the school held any sessions there. Period advertisements in the *Baltimore Sun* show a struggling institution, bereft of adequate enrollment and searching for a viable location for holding classes. By the fall of 1849, the Lombard Street building, still not completed, was being sold by the university's creditors.[15] The medical school itself managed to soldier on for another year after which its debts became too great, and the institution was forced to close in 1851.[16]

The hospital established at the Broadway location after the college's departure was named "Baltimore City and Marine Hospital," a title that reflected the facility's mission, and clientele.[17] The new enterprise had taken over operation of the hospital during the spring of 1849 with newspaper advertisements beginning to appear in July.[18] Although the Washington University students then had to take their classes in the city, they continued to lodge at the building on Broadway, also serving there as stewards, nurses, and "apprentices." However, even with federal subsidies for the marine and indigent cases, the new hospital also struggled to be profitable.[19] The facility's administrator, John Moran, tried to find money wherever he could and offered empty hospital rooms for rent as apartments to the general public. Incredibly, he found some who did not mind rooming with the moans of the sick and injured.[20]

136   *Chapter Six*

In the spring of 1855, the Baltimore City and Marine Hospital also went bankrupt, and the building was taken over by its owner, identified as the Fells Point Savings Institution. It was during this time that William Batchelor, who had been employed as watchman for the bank, installed his extended family as live-in caretakers at the empty hospital. After being closed for almost two years, the building was purchased in 1857 by an Episcopalian group and reopened as the Church Home and Infirmary to provide charity hospitalization, as well as long-term care, for the poor and elderly. It would generally function in this capacity until the end of the twentieth century.[21]

MORAN'S FIRST DIAGNOSIS

This was the place to which Edgar Allan Poe was taken, unconscious and probably unrecognized. It was a facility in transition with evolving (if not revolving) policies where every penny of expenditure was scrutinized. The treatment Poe received there would of course have depended on his diagnosis or perceived condition when he arrived, but as writer Charles Rosenberg points out, alcohol cases during Poe's time were treated disdainfully, with "attending physicians often slighting the hospital wards."[22] Alcoholism, or intemperance as it was known then, was not universally accepted as a disease in Poe's time. Patient's suffering from the condition who were dropped at the hospital's doorstep would not have been candidates for the best medical care the facility had to offer, especially if those patients were also perceived as charity cases.

It must be said that no record survives in which Dr. Moran specifically states that Poe's condition was the result of over-intoxication, yet there is sufficient evidence that points to it as his original diagnosis. The first indication of this can be found in the doctor's response to an inquiry dated November 9, 1849, from Maria Clemm in which she asked for the details of Poe's final days. Replying only five weeks after Poe's death, Moran's handwritten letter opens with extravagant praise of the poet and his reputation, perhaps preparing her for the explicit account that followed (appendix D). He then gives the only intimation in the letter as to the actual cause of death when he begins a sentence by telling Clemm: "Presuming you are already aware of the malady of which Mr. Poe died," a phrase that appears to be a delicate way of conveying an unmentionable cause to Poe's bereaved aunt. Moran followed this statement with what reads like a transcription from a case record in which he depicts, among other things, manifestations of delirium tremens, an image that would not have brought much comfort to Maria Clemm, especially if she had seen such symptoms in Poe before:

When brought to the Hospital he was unconscious of his Condition—who brought him or with whom he had been associating. He remained in this Condition from 5. Ock [o'clock] in the afternoon—the hour of his admission—until 3 next morning. This was on the 3rd Oct.

To this state succeeded tremor of the limbs, and at first a busy, but not violent or active delirium—constant talking—and vacant converse with spectral and imaginary objects on the walls. His face was pale and his whole person drenched in perspiration—We were unable to induce tranquility before the second day after his admission.

Figure 6.3. Church Home and Infirmary was the third occupant of the building in which Poe died, after Washington University and the Baltimore City and Marine Hospital. This photograph, taken during the 1870s, shows the exterior materially unchanged from its original construction in 1836. *Author (print from the author's collection)*

138   *Chapter Six*

> . . . .When I returned I found him in a violent delirium, resisting the efforts of
> two Nurses to keep him in bed. This state continued until Saturday evening (he
> was admitted on Wednesday) when he Commenced Calling for one "Reynolds,"
> which he did through the night up to three on Sunday Morning. At this time a
> very decided change began to affect him. Having become enfeebled from exer-
> tion he became quiet and seemed to rest for a short time, then, gently moving
> his head he said "Lord help my poor Soul" and expired!

Dr. Moran concludes the note by writing, "This, Madam, is as faithful
an account as I am able to furnish from the Record of his Case. . . . Your
imperative request urges me to be candid, else I should not have been thus
plain." Moran then describes Poe's funeral and those who attended.[23] In light
of John Moran's subsequent career of disseminating falsehoods about Poe,
many have questioned the veracity of these first statements about the poet's
death.[24] While parts of the document appear to be embellishments, and even
outright fabrications, it would be a mistake to reject his detailed, clinical
description of Poe's symptoms. After all, Moran oversaw a public hospital
which required delegation of patient care to surrogates, and the "Record of
his Case" which he cited in the letter to Clemm was undoubtedly compiled,
or at least supplemented, by others.[25]

Another indication of Moran's belief that Poe's condition was indeed the
result of a "terrible debauch" was provided by the Reverend William T. D.
Clemm, Poe's uncle by marriage and the presiding clergyman at Poe's viewing and burial. With the apparent approval of Neilson Poe, Moran called on
the reverend at the parsonage of the Methodist-Episcopal Church on Caroline Street during the day of October 7.[26] During the visit, when arranging
for Poe's funeral service the following day, Moran confided to Clemm the
details of the poet's death. Years later, when anthropologist and Poe enthusiast, Dr. Elmer R. Reynolds, read that Moran had claimed Poe "did not die
under the influence of any kind of intoxicating drink,"[27] he contacted then
Pastor Clemm to confirm the story. Recalling his conversation with Moran
on the day of Poe's death, Clemm replied to Reynolds with the following
assessment:

> Allow me to say that this remarkable statement of Dr. Moran* both confuses and
> surprises me because it positively contradicts the statement made to me person-
> ally by the Doctor; and surprises me because he did not years ago give to the
> public what he now avers to be the true cause of Mr. Poe's death.
>
> I think it due, therefore, to the truth of history, to give the Doctor's statement
> made to me by himself immediately upon the death of the poet and while, as yet,
> he lay a corpse in the hospital.
>
> "Mr. Poe", said the Doctor, "came to Baltimore on his way to Philadelphia
> to be married. . . . Upon landing on the wharf from the Norfolk steamer, Mr.

Hospital on the Hill 139

Poe was greeted by some of his old and former associates, who insisted that they should take a sociable glass of ardent spirits together for old acquaintance sake. To these persuasions the unfortunate poet yielded. . . . Sad enough for Poe; it revived his latent appetite for drink, and the result was a terrible debauch which ended in his death. . . . His appearance and condition were pitiable in the extreme, and in that drunken and stupid state he was brought to my hospital. . . ."

The preceding is in substance a truthful account of the statement made to me by Dr. Moran, and if he has proof that Mr. Poe died from other causes, by all means it should be produced.

W. T. D. Clemm,
Pastor Catonsville Methodist Episcopal Church Baltimore Conference.[28]

We cannot be sure why John Moran later reversed his verdict on Poe's condition. He may have been "persuaded" during a visit from a Richmond temperance advocate who sought to establish, following Poe's death, that the poet had not broken his pledge of abstinence.[29] As will be shown, Moran was not above placing a premium on his findings, and indeed he would later enroll in a Virginia chapter of the Independent Order of Good Templars, a temperance organization. Or perhaps the doctor thought his story of meticulous medical care would be better believed if Edgar Poe had not been seen (and treated) as an alcohol case when admitted to his hospital.

Poe's room assignment, or the section of the hospital in which he was placed, would also be an indication of how Moran viewed his patient's ailment at the time. If, upon his arrival, Poe's malady was perceived to be the result of drink but was not then indicative of the explosive and disruptive symptoms of delirium tremens, the severity of his condition would not have been apparent, as would any need to isolate him from other patients.[30] Although Moran would later be emphatic in his insistence that Poe was given a private room, eventually identifying its location as on the second floor in the southwest turret, there is ample evidence to indicate that he was instead placed in one the public wards on the upper floors. In his 1885 book, *A Defense of Edgar Allan Poe*, Moran recreates a "conversation" he had with the dying poet in which "he [Poe] was looking the room over with his large dark eyes, and I feared he would think he was unkindly dealt with, by being put in this prison-like room, with its wired inside windows, and iron grating outside." Here Moran, perhaps inadvertently, is recalling a room with "iron grating" over the windows, which does not sound like a feature of one of the private "apartments" that framed the medical school's front entrance.[31] Unfortunately, there are no known *close-up* photographic images of the building's exterior (during Poe's time) that conclusively reveal rooms fitted with bars over the windows. The

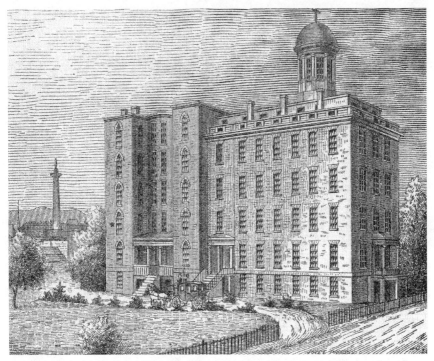

Figure 6.4. In his book on Poe's final days, Dr. John Moran used this engraving of the hospital to show the location of Poe's room by placing a star at its window on the far left. New information and analysis seem to disprove his claim. *Author (printed engraving from author's collection)*

earliest renderings of the hospital are only drawings or engravings of an idealized structure with such unsightly features eliminated.[32]

In the same "conversation" when replying to Poe's question, "Where am I?" Moran claimed to give the following answer: "You are in the hands of your friends . . . and as soon as you are better, I will have you moved to another part of the house, where you can receive them." This statement appears to be another mental slip on the doctor's part revealing his true recollection of Poe's environs in the hospital. If Poe had already been placed in a private room, why would he have to be moved to receive visitors?

John Moran would throw even more doubt on the location of Poe's room when returning to the hospital building in 1869. Unfortunately for Moran, he was accompanied by writer John Joyce, who would record the incident for posterity.[33] Moran was there to pay a call on Maria Clemm who had been staying at the Episcopal Church Home and Infirmary since her acceptance there in April 1863.[34] Upon their arrival, the pair was escorted to her room by "Sister Margaret," an administrator at the facility whom Moran had met before, according to Joyce. Clemm's third-floor apartment was in the extreme northeast corner of the building and when they reached it they found her sewing on a garment. Clemm was still in good health and rose from her rocking chair as they entered the room. After making the introductions and listening to a few reminiscences of the old woman, the conversation turned to the room where Poe died, and Clemm asked Moran to show it to her. Undoubtedly, during the six years of her residence in the building, she had asked others this same question and she may well have had her own idea of where the room was.[35] But here at last was Poe's "attending physician" who would put the matter to rest. John Joyce wrote what happened next:

> The doctor led us down the hall, several doors from that of Mrs. Clemm's, and pointed out the corner where Poe passed out to eternity. "Sister Margaret" was not certain as to the exact location, and I could see that even Dr. Moran had lost his bearings; for twenty years had then passed.[36]

This account reveals that either Moran did not want to commit to the room's location, or simply did not know it. Not only does Sister Margaret's statement indicate a lack of confidence in Moran's room choice, but John Joyce notes the doctor's uncertainty as well, implying that he should be pardoned for understandably losing his bearings after twenty years. In any event, "several doors" from the building's northeast corner does not describe a room in the southwest tower that Moran would later declare as the one he assigned to Poe.[37]

The doctor would pay a later visit to the hospital building during the time of his lectures, perhaps in a final attempt to devise an actual location for Poe's "room." In this account given by Clara Dargan Maclean in 1891, as recalled by the then presiding matron of Church Home and Infirmary, Moran "came to the newly habilitated Home . . . for the express purpose of locating the apartment where the tragedy occurred. . . . He ran up several flights of the old [main] stairs to the third story, crossed the gallery (formerly a lecture-room) which now surrounds the chapel, and opened a door. 'This is the place,' he said, and stood a few minutes looking around and pondering deeply." Maclean then relates that the door in question opened into a private stairway that she was told had replaced the tower rooms during a renovation of the building.[38] After circulating for many years among those who worked at Church Home and Infirmary, the story was accepted as authentic, and a bronze plaque was hung in the stairway in 1949 to mark the spot of Poe's supposed hospital room.

Yet there is reason to believe that the staircase in question was part of the building's original design and that it was in use at the time of Poe's death. When describing one of the floors in the rotunda during the time of

Figure 6.5. This daguerreotype of East Baltimore, taken in the weeks before Poe died in 1849, shows his hospital at the very top. Close examination of the building reveals the southwest turret without windows on its western wall indicating it then housed a staircase and not individual rooms. *Author (Printed photo from the author's collection)*

his residence there in 1855, William Batchelor recalled the following details about the layout, "On each corner of the room there was a small room, except in the southwest corner which was a stairway that led from the yard to the top floor and was used by the students after they came in through the gate on the southwest corner of the yard."[39] When added to other contemporaneous descriptions of the interior, Batchelor's account affirms that the building, as constructed in 1836, apparently had two separate staircases.[40] The main stairway that serviced the hospital was to the right of the *school's* entrance, and was accessed from the corridor separating the rotunda from the hospital wing.[41] For the students of the college, a narrower set of stairs was provided to the left of the school's entrance, allowing their passage without interfering with, or being encumbered by, hospital business. This is the stairwell that Moran, and those at the facility, believed had displaced Poe's room. If the staircase had instead been an original feature of the building, the poet could not have died in a private room in the southwest turret.[42] Of course, it is possible that Moran eventually moved Poe from the public ward to a single room

Hospital on the Hill   143

somewhere else in the building, but the doctor's inability to recall a location would suggest how little time, if at all, he spent with the dying poet.

Then there is this recollection from Mary Moran, wife of Dr. Moran, as relayed to Professor James A. Harrison by her nephew: "When the young man was brought into the hospital in a stupor, it was supposed he was overcome by drink. . . . We soon saw he was a gentleman; and as our family lived in a wing of the college building, the doctor had him taken to a room easily reached by a passage from our wing."[43] Here Mrs. Moran appears only to be supporting her husband's version of events; and how Poe was deduced a "gentleman" while he was in a stupor and wearing the clothes of a beggar is equally difficult to accept.

In his feature article printed in the October 28, 1875, edition of the *New York Herald*, Moran claimed that after being placed in a separate room, Poe was given tender care: "He was immediately placed in a private room, carefully undressed and critically examined. . . . He was sponged with lukewarm water, sinapisms applied to the feet, thighs and abdomen, and cold applied to the head." However, in what appears to be yet another mental lapse, Moran would later indicate that Poe was left in the clothes he was wearing: "He was clad in the shabby suit I have described, and being unconscious I had him put in the place indicated, not knowing at that moment the cause of his distress," a description that seems to depict abandonment, if not less-then-meticulous care.[44] Without the original hospital record of Poe's case, there is no way to gauge the level of attention that he actually received, but Moran's title as "Resident Physician and Surgeon" would suggest that he was the only doctor-on-call at a facility with two hundred beds,[45] a state of affairs that better describes a modern nursing home than a public hospital.

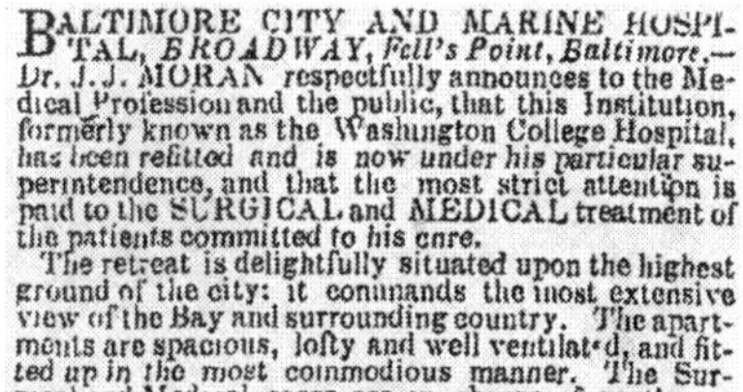

Yet Moran's *claim* of assiduous care for Poe would have been expected for many obvious reasons, not the least of which was consistency with the spa-like experience that he promised to those considering his facility. In a newspaper advertisement

BALTIMORE CITY AND MARINE HOSPITAL, *BROADWAY, Fell's Point, Baltimore.*—Dr. J. J. MORAN respectfully announces to the Medical Profession and the public, that this Institution, formerly known as the Washington College Hospital, has been refitted and is now under his particular superintendence, and that the most strict attention is paid to the SURGICAL and MEDICAL treatment of the patients committed to his care.

The retreat is delightfully situated upon the highest ground of the city; it commands the most extensive view of the Bay and surrounding country. The apartments are spacious, lofty and well ventilated, and fitted up in the most commodious manner. The Surgical and Medical cases are in charge of gentlemen well known for their experience and judgment in both departments, and are regularly visited by them. The nurses are prompt and efficient in the discharge of their duties, and there is nothing spared that would contribute in the slightest to the comfort and recovery of the patients.

☞ Students of Medicine boarding in the Institution, will have the advantages of Clinical instruction.

BATHING ROOMS, with shower, &c., are available to all the inmates, and a Resident Physician always in the house. Patients desiring PRIVATE APARTMENTS, can be accommodated on the most liberal terms.

Terms, payable in advance:
To Public Ward, including board, nursing, medicine, &c.....................$3 per week
To Private Rooms, do. do. do., from 5 to 7 " "

JOHN J. MORAN,
s12-law4w   Resident Physician.

Figure 6.6. This newspaper ad appearing in the *Baltimore Sun* for October 5, 1849, promises a spa-like experience for those admitted to Moran's hospital on Broadway. Poe's short residency there would not be so luxurious. *Author (print from the author's collection)*

that appeared while Poe was his patient, the resident physician declared (in third person) that Baltimore City and Marine Hospital, "is now under his particular superintendence, and that the most strict attention is paid to the SURGICAL and MEDICAL treatment of the patients committed to his care." Moran then adds, "The Surgical and Medical cases are in charge of gentlemen well known for their experience and judgment in both departments, and are regularly visited by them. The nurses are prompt and efficient in the discharge of their duties, and there is nothing spared that would contribute in the slightest to the comfort and recovery of the patients."[46] Notwithstanding the financial economies that encumbered him, Moran portrayed an institution where there was no compromise in quality.

It is apparent that at some point the identity of his patient became known to Moran. If Neilson Poe had, as he claimed, paid a visit (or visits) to the hospital, even if only to offer linens in lieu of paying his cousin's bill,[47] Moran would then have been compelled to investigate his patient's location, status, *and* identity. Neilson's version is that he was refused visitation to prevent over-stimulating the excitable patient: "As soon as I heard that he was at the College, I went over, but his physicians did not think it advisable that I should see him, as he was very excitable. The next day I called and sent him changes of linen etc. and was very grateful to learn that he was much better, and I was never so much shocked, in my life, as when on Friday [Sunday] morning, notice was sent to me that he was dead."[48]

Figure 6.7. Edgar's first cousin, Neilson Poe, claimed to have made a visit to the hospital on Broadway just prior to the poet's death there. This previously unpublished tintype shows him in his later years. *The Collection of Brian Shipley*

How Neilson learned of his cousin's predicament is not clear; at least one biographer believed Moran's story that he contacted the lawyer directly.[49] It is more

Hospital on the Hill   145

likely that Henry Herring or someone in his family sent word to Neilson Poe.[50] In this case, Neilson's arrival at the hospital could have been the actual moment when Poe's identity was confirmed, and perhaps realizing the mistake of designating him a derelict, Moran exploited the "excitable patient" excuse in order to buy time and form a course of action. Yet given his symptoms, Poe was probably in no condition to receive visitors.

Whether any visits to the hospital were indeed made by Neilson Poe has been a matter of question; we only have his testimony that he tried to see his cousin, a story that even his family would later (seem to) question. After Neilson's death, Moran would also deny that Poe's cousin "called to see him."[51] Writer Michael Powell discovered that Neilson was inextricably involved with a criminal court case during the week of Poe's collapse in Baltimore, perhaps too absorbed to be bothered with another episode of his cousin's "drink-sickened self."[52] Neilson had been defending a man on several charges (one of which implies a sexual assault) but apparently his presentation was not successful. On Thursday, October 4, after the case had gone to the jury, he asked for a new trial "on the grounds that new and important evidence had been communicated to him."[53] If the jury still had the case on Friday, he would have had to remain at the court's disposal making a daytime hospital visit before Saturday difficult to manage.[54] Yet, even if Neilson Poe had spun a single visit into two attempts, the detail of the "linens" adds a degree of believability to his claim.

Perhaps the best evidence that Edgar Allan Poe's identity was known to those at the hospital before he died is provided by Dr. William M. Cullen (or Cullin), who is listed among the graduates of the Washington University School of Medicine for 1851, and at twenty-two years old,[55] was serving an internship at the facility during the time of Poe's death two years earlier.[56] Charles Scarlett Jr., in a magazine article for the Maryland Historical Society, claimed that Cullen ministered to Poe under the guidance of Dr. John C. S. Monkur, then a professor at Washington University.[57] But it was only after Moran's article appeared in the *New York Herald* (1875), a piece that included Poe's fantastic deathbed soliloquies, that Cullen came forward to confirm his role in caring for the dying poet and to refute the claims made by Moran. Sometime after he published his biography of Poe,[58] Eugene Didier was introduced to Cullen who apparently gave him a truer version of Poe's final hours. In 1880, Didier would write, "Dr. Moran was the resident physician of the hospital; but Poe died in the arms of Dr. William M. Cullen, the physician whose duty it was to attend to the patients; and we have his authority for saying that the wild and incoherent words attributed to the poet [by Moran] were never uttered by him on his death-bed."[59] As the administrator of a hospital, it would have been difficult for John Moran to spend much time

Figure 6.8. Dr. William M. Cullen, who as a student at the Washington University School of Medicine, served his "apprenticeship" at Baltimore City and Marine hospital in the fall of 1849. Cullen asserted that it was he, and not Dr. Moran, who provided care for Edgar Allan Poe during his final days. *Courtesy of the Enoch Pratt Free Library, Special Collections*

Hospital on the Hill 147

with individual patients, and his reliance on "stewards" to render treatment would have been the normal practice. Of course, it is possible that after learning the identity of his famous resident, Moran paid more attention to Poe and even assumed a disproportionate role in his care.

Yet in his 1885 publication, *A Defense of Edgar Allan Poe*, Moran would perhaps begrudgingly acknowledge his association with Cullen by including him on an absurd list of those in attendance at Poe's burial.[60] Cullen's appearance on the list, after thirty-five years had passed, would suggest that he was still around to contest Moran's story. In any event, this wrestling match over who actually attended to the dying man in the hospital would seem to establish awareness among the staff of Poe's identity before he passed away. How great a role Moran played in the custody of his most famous patient may never be known, but as will be shown, that inconvenient *detail* would not prevent the unabashed self-promoter from portraying himself as Edgar Allan Poe's principal caregiver.

Chapter Seven

The Island of Dr. Moran

After the Washington University School of Medicine left the Broadway premises in early 1849, a new medical center, the Baltimore City and Marine Hospital, immediately opened for business in the same building. To manage the daily operation of the new enterprise, the owners installed John J. Moran, a practicing physician and surgeon who had little business and administrative experience.[1] He would later describe his job as follows: "I conducted and controlled this institution for six years as resident physician, living with my family on the premises. I had the entire charge and responsibility of house and patients, including United States sailors, a portion of the hospital being set apart for this class of patients, who were sent there by order of the Government."[2]

As the doctor overseeing the hospital in which Edgar Allan Poe perished, John Moran should have become one of the most reliable and important informational resources on the poet's death. However, his testimony has proven to be anything but trustworthy; indeed no one has done more to mislead those seeking the facts of Poe's final days. Moran would exploit his proximity to the affair as a license for written articles, a book, and lectures.[3] His talks included dreamed-up details of Poe's final days, as well as deathbed speeches that seemed to grow in length and splendor with each recital, even though Moran may have spent little time at the dying man's side. The doctor would also give varying causes of death for Poe, as well as inconsistent explanations of his whereabouts in Baltimore before being brought to the hospital. When Moran did not know the facts, he appears to have often fabricated them, giving no thought to posterity. Nevertheless, his role in Poe's story remains a significant one if only to establish what did not take place, and his testimony, although seeming to have been in a state of constant flux, is not completely without value. To better explain Moran's manifest irresponsibility in

150   *Chapter Seven*

fictionalizing the final days of Edgar Allan Poe, a brief look at his life should provide some context as to his character and motivations.

Little is currently known of John Moran's early life; he was born in 1820, in Maryland, as were both of his parents.[4] Within a year of getting his medical degree from the University of Maryland, School of Medicine in 1845,[5] Moran married Mary Jane Green of Baltimore, a girl eight years his junior. Reports that he began his practice in Bladensburg seem to have no foundation, by all appearances Moran remained in the Baltimore area following his graduation.[6] That he was practicing surgery during this time is indicated by an item in the *Baltimore Sun* stating that he assisted Dr. Dunbar, his old college professor, in the amputation of a man's arm after the patient was injured by an explosion.[7]

How he came to the notice of those organizing the new Baltimore City and Marine Hospital in 1949 is unclear, but John Moran was apparently very articulate and adept at selling himself. When interviewed later in his career by a correspondent for the *New York Times*, the doctor was found to be "a polished and agreeable gentleman, of hitherto good character."[8] Moran was put in charge of the new facility in East Baltimore and a notice in the *Baltimore Sun* establishes his employment there as early as March 1849; however, his later claim of having been on the university's staff at that time is doubtful as he appears to have been only assisting with information on the school's lectures.[9] As the resident physician, Moran and his growing family lived on the premises and he was on call twenty-four hours a day to oversee the hospital and its patients. In this capacity, the twenty-nine-year-old doctor was handling the facility when Edgar Allan Poe was brought to its doors in October 1849, and he would remain its superintendent until its closure in 1855.[10] He was also socially and politically active during this time, becoming a member of the Independent Order of Odd Fellows and even traveling to Shrewsbury, Pennsylvania, for the dedication of the organization's new facility there.[11]

After Baltimore City and Marine Hospital closed, Dr. Moran moved to Frederick, Maryland, for a position as the attending physician at the county jail—a role that would prove a rehearsal for what was in store for him.[12] He was then residing on a small, 130-acre farm just outside of town,[13] and at the start of the Civil War, his relationship with the local government put him in line for a gubernatorial appointment as Frederick County's Examining Surgeon (for the draft).[14] His task was to evaluate and approve those applying for a medical exclusion from military service. But after only two months in that position, Moran was arrested by an agent of the federal government and charged with malfeasance in office; more precisely he was accused of "receiving illegal fees for the granting of certificates of exemption."[15] He was at first placed under guard at his house but later removed to the Old Capitol Prison in Washington, DC, for trial, all while proclaiming his innocence.[16] During the course of the proceedings, it was revealed that in addition to making the medical exemptions available for a price, Moran also refused to issue the disability certificates to qualifying applicants who would not pay. He was duly convicted and subsequently confined at Old Capitol Prison. His scheme threw the Frederick County draft into chaos and caused the Adjutant General to vacate all medical exemptions, forcing the applicants to reapply. As a result, the draft there was delayed for months.[17]

By the time of Moran's incarceration, during the early part of the Civil War, Old Capitol Prison had become a warehouse largely for political prisoners and enemies of the federal (Northern) government, with many of its inmates having never seen a courtroom. Moran was one of the few who *had* been tried, but his conviction was for criminal activity. To his good fortune, he was lumped in with political detainees who were offered early release by taking and signing an oath of allegiance to the United States, and by January 1863, he appears to have been given his freedom.[18] Whether he had been ordered to make restitution of any part of the funds he extorted in his scheme

Figure 7.1. During the Civil War Dr. John Moran was convicted of malfeasance by the federal government and for a time incarcerated at the old Capitol Prison in Washington, DC. His confinement was short-lived. *Library of Congress*

is unknown, but immediately after his release, he had the means to purchase (and skedaddle to) a farm in Bladensburg, Maryland, even before disposing of his property in Frederick.[19]

With the end of the war he returned to Baltimore, presumably setting up a medical practice at his residence on North Stricker Street.[20] A notice in the paper about this time mentions Moran attending to a man that died at 53 Raborg Street. It was thought newsworthy in that Moran had overturned the original finding of cholera to say that the death was the result of an inflammation of the stomach caused by excessive drinking.[21] Like his contemporary, Dr. Joseph Snodgrass, Moran had become a temperance advocate.

Perhaps in an effort to scrub his past and restore his standing within the community, Moran became politically active again, involving himself with the Democratic Party. On September 26, 1867, he was elected as a delegate to represent the Nineteenth Ward at the Mayoralty Convention being held at the Front Street Theatre the following evening. There he made several motions including one that asked for Robert T. Banks to be declared the unanimous mayoral candidate.[22] He would later be elected as an officer in the local democratic conservative party (along with George W. Herring, Henry Herring's uncle). These activities were not those of a man trying to observe an inconspicuous life.[23]

Moran began to disengage from his medical practice, and he seems to have become more involved in real estate deals.[24] He also began an association with Henry R. Robbins, perhaps as a financial backer. Robbins was involved in the manufacture and marketing of stoves, and along with another man, the trio was granted a patent in 1868 for the design of a steam pipe coupler for railroad car heaters. Three more patents were granted to Robbins and Moran the following year for designs of stove accessories that included a tobacco and grain curer.[25] Moran became Robbins' partner in what today would

Figure 7.2. This is the only known image of Dr. John J. Moran, administrator and resident physician of the Baltimore City and Marine Hospital. Its date and how it came to be in this condition is unknown. *Mary Riley Styles Public Library, Falls Church, VA*

be called a chain of stores, in the city and county, that offered stoves and tinware (duct and smoke pipe fittings).[26]

By 1873, there is no mention of John Moran in the Baltimore City directories. It appears that he had by then divested his interest in the stove business and moved to an area of Virginia, just across the Potomac River from Washington, DC. Now financially independent, he also seems to have left his medical practice behind in Baltimore.[27] Moran also became active in the local Methodist Episcopal Church, and he focused on growing a relationship with his new Virginia neighbors. By the spring of 1875, his standing in the community there had become such that members of the town council of the newly incorporated village of Falls Church selected Moran as its first mayor. The office, however, seems to have been largely ceremonial at that time with the council retaining all the decision-making and governing power.[28] Yet with this political appointment, Moran had finally "arrived." He had not only become an influential citizen of his new community, but was also a financial *player* as well. His political and civic activism included membership in the temperance organization, Independent Order of Good Templars, as well as affiliation with the Conservative Democrats.[29]

In 1880, Moran received another appointment, this time from Virginia Governor Frederick Holladay, as "Special Agent" tasked with collecting revenue owed to the state by the federal government. In Moran's words, his assignment was "to settle, adjust and determine all debts or claims due the state of Virginia by the United States."[30] His commission, authorized by an act of the General Assembly on March 3, 1880, was that of a private contractor with his compensation being a portion (25 percent) of the realized revenue. Although it is not clear who proposed the arrangement, Moran's work, which was considerable, was undertaken on a contingency basis and did not burden

Figure 7.3. At the time of his death, Dr. Moran was living in Falls Church, Virginia. His subsequent burial at Green Mount Cemetery in Baltimore confirms his Maryland nativity. Mary Jane Moran, his wife, survived him by only four months. *Author (author photograph)*

154   *Chapter Seven*

Virginia with upfront costs. Moran would ultimately retrieve for Virginia a bonanza from the US government that today would be the equivalent of $12 million, but the enormous amount owed to the doctor as payment for his work was apparently balked at by the state legislature.[31] Ten years after Moran's death, it was discovered by his family that the Commonwealth of Virginia had never settled with the doctor for the work he did and the *Baltimore Sun* reported that his son, (Washington) Ellis Moran, had filed suit to collect the unpaid monies.[32] The retired Governor Holladay, who had originally appointed Moran, denied having any knowledge of the arrangement; however, documents were ultimately discovered to support the family's claim. Yet it was not until 1903 that the Virginia General Assembly approved a payment of $10,000 to Moran's heirs, far below the amount of $45,000 they sought.[33] Moran continued to reside in the Virginia village of Falls Church until his death on December 13, 1888.[34] His gentle and soft-spoken wife, Mary J. Moran, died less than four months later, on March 30, 1889.[35] Both were returned to Maryland and interred at the prestigious Green Mount Cemetery in Baltimore.

MORAN THE POE SCHOLAR

From the very beginning of John Moran's association with Edgar Allan Poe, he seems to have had difficulty relating any part of the poet's story without embellishments. Moran's propensity for grandiloquence is evident in the opening words of his response to Maria Clemm, who in writing to the doctor five weeks after Poe's death had only inquired as to the circumstances:

> It falls to the lot of but few, to enjoy the extensive popularity that was unquestionably his. Wherever talent—mental worth, nay Genius, was prized there "E. A. Poe" had warm friends. To his rarely gifted mind are we indebted for many of the brightest thoughts that adorn our literature to him is Belles Lettres indebted for the purest gems her Casket Contains. "Poe is gone!" How many hearts have heaved a sigh in uttering these three words![36]

How much of the information in his letter to Clemm was contrived has become a matter of much debate (see appendix D). His description of Poe's condition and symptoms (along with the dates and times given) appears to have been transcribed from a prepared report; yet there is reason to suspect that most, if not all, of the dialogue between Moran and Poe was invented by the doctor, perhaps first as a ham-fisted attempt to soothe the grieving aunt. There are details here that may indeed have come from an incoherent Poe such as having a wife in Richmond and not knowing when he left that city. But Moran's claim that he discussed with Poe the disposition of his trunk of clothing appears artificial: unless Poe had the presence of mind to raise the subject himself, the doctor's inquiry, as stated, would presume prior knowledge (of the luggage). Moran had also, by this time, been approached by Neilson Poe who was looking for his cousin's belongings at the behest of Maria Clemm and Rufus Griswold. Moran apparently thought this detail an important one, and he would later alter the wording in another letter he received from Clemm to make it look as though he had been instrumental in the trunk's recovery—an act that expands the definition of embellishment.[37]

In his response to Clemm, when recounting his supposed conversation with the dying poet, Moran described his effort to comfort her nephew:

> Wishing to rally and sustain his now fast sinking hopes I told him I hoped, that in a few days he would be able to enjoy the Society of his friends here,

Figure 7.4. During his last visit to Richmond, Edgar Allan Poe acquired a steamer trunk for his accumulating possessions. After the poet's death Dr. Moran would claim that he was instrumental in its recovery and even altered a handwritten letter from Poe's aunt to provide "proof." *Author (author photograph)*

156   *Chapter Seven*

and I would be most happy to Contribute in every possible way to his Ease & Comfort. At this he broke out with much energy, and said the best thing his best friend could do would be to blow out his brains with a pistol. [appendix D]

It is possible that Moran may have heard these words from Poe directly, but it is just as likely that someone else recorded (or invented) them. When contesting Moran's version of events in 1889, the Reverend William Clemm would recall meeting the doctor, on the day of Poe's death, and claim that he heard from him the very same remark.

But it was in 1875, at the age of fifty-five years, that Moran began his role as an *authority* on Edgar Allan Poe. It is not clear what motivated him to come forward, seemingly out of nowhere, to tell his story about Poe after so much time had elapsed. It may have been to exploit the opportunity that arose from John R. Thompson's death in 1873, an event that cleared the course for Moran to offer his version of events unchallenged. Or perhaps it was the appearance of Richard Stoddard's memoir of Edgar Allan Poe that had prefaced a collection of his poems the following year.[38] Stoddard's biography of Poe, which was first published in the September 1872 edition of *Harper's Monthly Magazine*, incorporated Thompson's "cooping theory" as well as a conversation between Poe and his unidentified doctor, the source of which had to be Moran himself, perhaps as related to the writer secondhand through Neilson Poe.[39]

Stoddard, who was an acquaintance of both John Thompson and Edgar Poe, would later peg the launch of Moran's "Poe" career to the announcement of the poet's monument in 1875 and dedication ceremonies scheduled for later that year at Baltimore. He stated that Moran had written to the New York newspaper, *The World*, on January 17, 1875, claiming to have "ten single pages already of facts in detail, as committed to me by the dying Poe" as well as his correspondence with Maria Clemm.[40] Perhaps on Stoddard's word, *The World* passed on Moran's feature and it would not be until October 28, three weeks before the monument's dedication, that his essay was eventually published, but then by the *New York Herald*.[41]

This account differed significantly not only from what others were telling, but also from the story Moran himself originally gave immediately following Poe's death. In the November 15 letter sent to Maria Clemm (see appendix D), the doctor graphically describes Poe's death with symptoms consistent with delirium tremens; however, in this retelling, Moran states, "There was no smell of liquor upon his person or breath. There was no delirium or tremor." He originally informed Clemm that Poe was brought to the hospital on the afternoon of October 3, but now he had the poet arriving on the morning October 7 and dying sixteen hours later at the stroke of midnight. And the funeral first described to Clemm as a dignified affair, was now depicted as a lavish production attended by the city's luminaries, with at least fifty women acquiring a lock of his hair while his body was displayed in the hospital's rotunda "for one whole day." To account for the amount of time needed for such rituals, Moran shifted Poe's interment to October 9, apparently giving no thought to any record that might exist in the newspapers.

For all that, it was Edgar Allan Poe's dying words, now recalled by Moran in detail after more than two decades, that elicited the most reaction, and disbelief. In the article, Moran claimed a prolonged and measured exchange with a composed Poe, after which he provided a precise reconstruction of his final remarks:

> Oh; wretch that I am! Sir, when I behold my degradation and ruin, what I have suffered and lost, and the sorrow and misery I have brought upon others, I feel that I could sink through this bed into the lowermost abyss below, forsaken by God and man, an outcast from society. Oh, God, the terrible strait I am in! Is there no ransom for the deathless spirit?

And then:

> Death's dark angel has done his work. I am so rudely clashed upon the storm without compass or helm. Language cannot tell the gushing wave that swells, sways and sweeps, tempest-like, over me, signaling the 'larum of death.

Skepticism about Moran's published recollection of events appeared simultaneously, in the same periodical: "We cannot imagine Poe, even if delirious, constructing such a sentence as that beginning, 'Language cannot tell the gushing wave,' &c.; or uttering in the hour of his death the abstraction about 'the arched heavens.'"[42] Stoddard and Dr. William Cullen were among others who would publicly reject the account of Poe's deathbed oration, the former saying of Moran's reconstructions, "I do not believe that he, or any other man under the circumstances, could have reproduced [Poe's words] verbatim, after a lapse of twenty-five or twenty-six years."[43] The *Baltimore Sun*, when reprinting Moran's "official record" the day following its appearance in the *New York Herald*, did not challenge the ludicrous conversation with Poe that the doctor was claiming. Instead, the editor was incredulous that Moran was denying that Poe had died in an alcoholic stupor, saying "there is such evidence corroborative of its truth in Baltimore that many will still entertain doubts on that point."[44]

Still another who openly voiced disbelief in Moran's official story was fellow Baltimorean, Eugene Didier: "Dr. Moran gives a detailed account of Poe's 'last words.' Here is a specimen 'The arched heavens encompass me, and God has His decrees legibly written upon the frontlets of every created

Figure 7.5. The Merchants Exchange Building on Gay Street in Baltimore (today the site of the US Custom House) also served as the city archives. In 1881, Dr. Moran came here to find records that would prove his employment at Baltimore City and Marine Hospital. *Author (Printed photo from the author's collection)*

human being, and demons incarnate; their goal will be the seething waves of black despair. Where is the buoy, life-boat, ship of fire, sea of brass? Rest, shore no more' ... wild and incoherent words attributed to the poet were never uttered by him on his death-bed."[45]

Perhaps not remembering what he originally communicated to Maria Clemm and not realizing that his first letter to her would be preserved, Moran thoughtlessly committed this wildly expanded version to print. That he had not retained any records or documents from Poe's death at Baltimore City and Marine Hospital is made clear by his appearance in December 1881 at the Baltimore Custom House which at the time held the city's records. Some were openly questioning not only Moran's veracity but also his role at the hospital where Poe had died, and the doctor went to the Custom House to find documents that would prove his six-year term as resident physician at the medical facility. He apparently succeeded in finding some of his employment records; what else if anything Moran may have found he never divulged.[46] Nevertheless, the lack of original documents about Poe's death did not deter Moran from claiming to have such material, as the preface to his *New York Herald* article makes clear: "The record of this closing period of the poet's life is now preserved to history, finding light for the first time in the columns of the HERALD through the following *transcript* of memoranda which were made by the physician in charge of the hospital at the time the unfortunate man was under his care."[47] The only truth found in Moran's "Official Memoranda" was his claim of cohabitation in the same building where Poe died; the rest was a product of the doctor's imagination.

In addition to publishing his feature in the *Herald*, Moran seemed eager to tell his new version of Poe's final hours to anyone who would listen. While representing his lodge, Good Templars, at a state meeting held in Richmond, Virginia, Moran gave an interview to a temperance reporter from an area newspaper: "He [Moran] denied the statement which had been current for so long, that Poe died in a delirium. He states that he was with him during his last hours, and that he was perfectly rational.... His description, however, was a terrible warning to the devotee of the wine cup."[48] Moran may have been surprised by the writer's concluding remark, which was not in synch with the story he was then peddling.

It appears that Moran did not launch his lecture "career" until 1882, which seems to have been in preparation for some time as his earlier visit to Baltimore in the pursuit of documents suggests. By then, Moran had also committed many of Edgar Allan Poe's poems to memory and it would be fair to say that he had become conversant with Poe's history and body of work.[49] On February 1, Moran delivered his lecture titled "Life, Character, Dying Declarations and Death of Edgar Allan Poe" at the Congressional Church in Washington, DC, under the auspices of the Literary Society.[50] Moran was given a written invitation to speak before this group, one of the signatories being President Garfield who was a Poe enthusiast and the club's president at the time of his assassination. Some extracts from Moran's presentation later appeared in the *Baltimore Sun*; for the first time, there were details reporting that Poe's cab driver was an Irishman; that Maria Clemm and Sarah [Elmira] Shelton asked the doctor to inquire about Poe's movements before his arrival at the hospital; and that Poe made his train connection but returned to Baltimore after declining the ferry ride across an angry Susquehanna River—all of which are unsupported. Moran also restored the date of Poe's burial to October 8,[51] but he insisted that it was impossible for the poet to have been "cooped," giving his Baltimore arrival as October 4, the day after the election.[52]

Sometime before February 27 of that year, Moran gave his talk in Richmond, Virginia, and, according to the doctor, sitting in the audience was

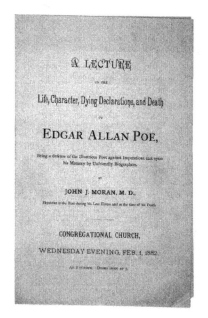

Figure 7.6. This original four-page brochure for Dr. John Moran's Washington, DC, lecture describes the evening's program which included recitals of Poe's "The Raven" and "Annabel Lee" that were set to music composed by John H. Hewitt. *Library of Congress, Rare Book and Special Collections Division*

Figure 7.7. In April 1882, Dr. John Moran delivered a lecture on Poe's final hours at the YMCA Hall in Baltimore City, still standing at 300 North Charles Street. It was Moran's third, and perhaps last, public address on the topic. *Author (Printed photo from the author's collection)*

seventy-two-year-old Elmira Shelton. After his lecture concluded, the two were introduced, and Moran claimed that he then spoke with her at length: "she and I, met for the first time . . . it was a meeting I shall never forget—so deeply were we impressed, that our tears could not be restrained."[53] Whether Shelton believed any part of the speaker's portrayal of Poe's final hours is unknown, but if indeed she could still weep after more than thirty years, Moran must have reawakened something in her.

That spring, he returned to Baltimore to deliver his lecture at the YMCA Hall. Now titled, "Edgar Allan Poe's Character Vindicated," the talk was scheduled for the evening of April 11, but Moran came a few days earlier to visit Church Home and Infirmary (as discussed in chapter 6) in order to establish a location for Poe's room and weave the new information into his speech. The doctor declared, "He [Poe] was placed in the third-story room of the turret, at the southwest corner of the building, about 7 by 10 feet in size," giving for the very first time this part of the building as the scene of the poet's death.[54] In his talk, Moran also stated that his patient "was very weak, but there was no tremor of the limbs, no agitation of the body, no smell of liquor on the breath or person, nor any symptom of intoxication." When the doctor informed Poe that he wanted to administer a stimulant, the poet replied, "If I thought its potency would transport me to the elysian [sic] bowers of the undiscovered spirit-world I would not touch it." And when Moran asked if he wanted a pain killer instead, Poe answered, "Twin sisters of the doomed and crazed in perdition." To the followers of Edgar Allan Poe in attendance at J. J. Moran's performances, this account would have been exactly what they wanted to hear: Poe was not intoxicated after all, and he spoke lyrically even in casual conversation.

But some were not so impressed with Moran's sermon; among these was a writer for the Washington, DC, publication, the *Evening Critic*, who offered the following critique:

Dr. John J. Moran, of Falls Church, Fairfax County, Virginia, is a very slow and deliberate person. After a silence of some thirty years, he now comes boldly forward and declares, as the attending physician, that Edgar Allan Poe did not die of "jim-jams" [a nineteenth-century expression for the jitters or delirium tremens]. Moran's deliberate silence during all the years of detraction of the dead poet's memory is something singular, when compared with his present fiery zeal. Who is left to dispute Moran? Nobody. Everybody else who knew anything about the attendant circumstances of Poe's melancholy death, is dead. Only Moran and his tale are left.[55]

It is not clear how many talks Moran ultimately gave; he claimed that he had also been invited to speak in Boston and Philadelphia but no record of his lectures in those cities has been found.[56] As previously discussed, Moran was also working at the time to recover money owed to the state of Virginia, an endeavor that *promised* a more tangible reward than presenting himself as an authority on Edgar Allan Poe.

In 1885, perhaps in answer to those who were publicly challenging the doctor and his story, Moran published an eighty-eight-page booklet that included much of the material he espoused in his lectures.[57] Titled *A Defense of Edgar Alan Poe: Life, Character and Dying Declarations of the Poet*, this work also contained a purposed (and comically inaccurate) memoir of Poe, replete with cherry-picked testimonials of his character, as well as rationalizations for but a few occurrences of inebriety "in his earlier manhood," all of which was only window dressing for Moran's lengthened version of the poet's final moments. In the foreword of the booklet, which also appears to have been written by the doctor, the rationale for the publication is declared:

> The following pages have been received from his learned physician, Dr [sic] John J. Moran, who attended him in his last hours and who received from the expiring poet his dying declarations, with a brief history of his life. This full and complete statement will, for the first time, be given with the hope and belief of the publisher

Figure 7.8. In 1885, John Moran published a largely fictional account of Poe's final hours; the only thing missing from this "dime novel" was a Pratt Street shootout between Poe and a pursuing posse. *Author (author photograph)*

162   *Chapter Seven*

that the truth, so long delayed, will meet with sympathy and kindness from an impartial and discerning public, will dismiss the false impressions that have been made upon the mind of his friends, will triumph over envy, error and falsehood, and the pure stream of POE'S genius will flow on and on forever.[58]

Moran portrayed himself as the final authority and single most important figure in Poe's death. He described his heroic attempts to save the poet, his efforts in making *all* the arrangements for his funeral and burial, and his personal communications with Poe's family members and loved ones:

> He was in my care and under my charge for sixteen hours. He was sensible and rational fifteen hours out of the sixteen. He answered promptly and correctly all questions asked, spoke freely, and made certain statements, and gave certain directions to whom I should write . . . He told me, in answer to my questions, where he had been, from whence he came, and for which place he started when he left Richmond, when he arrived in Baltimore, and the name of the hotel where he registered, from which I received his trunk before his death. The names of the ladies to whom he requested me to write were given, and their answers to my letters after his death came speedily and are with me now.[59]
>
> It has been charged that POE was made drunk and then "cooped," and voted a number of times at an election held in Baltimore about that time. This charge I unhesitatingly deny. One word will demonstrate its falsity. That election was held October 3d, the day before POE, left Richmond, and he was not in Baltimore until October 5th.[60]

The doctor then provided his account of Poe's whereabouts before being brought to the hospital which included the story of his aborted train ride north, the details of which he claimed to have gotten directly from the train conductor:

> The following testimony was given to me by the conductor a few days after the poet's death: . . . "I saw in the papers the death of the gentleman I had on my train the other day . . . I was attracted to him from his appearance." I said, "Captain, how was he dressed?" He replied, "In black clothes; his coat was buttoned up close to his throat" . . . I asked the conductor if POE was in liquor. "Why," said he, "I would as soon have suspected my own father . . ."
>
> A similar statement was given by this conductor to Judge Nielson Poe sometime during the same month, of the year 1849, and was repeated to me by Judge Poe last April two years ago. . . . We spent more than an hour discussing the poet's life and death.[61]

Moran's claimed interviews with the train attendant, Neilson Poe and the Irish cab driver all remain unsupported.

But it was *his* time and care given to the dying poet that Moran wanted to emphasize with this publication. As the doctor now recalled, Poe awoke after only a few minutes of being placed in his room upon which Moran was summoned to his bedside by the attending nurse. What followed, according to the book, was a long and detailed exchange between Moran and his "perfectly conscious" patient, during which the doctor tried to ascertain from Poe how he came to be in his condition, the level of his discomfort, and the whereabouts of his belongings. Moran then endeavored to establish the nature of Poe's illness, claiming that his patient's condition was not alcohol related. This conclusion apparently rested on Poe's *coherency* and his refusal to take liquor when offered;[62] for Moran, the normal response would have been, "Yes, Doctor, give me a little to strengthen my nerves." Yet Moran exposes the infirmity of his own rationale a few sentences later when he writes that he "administered a stimulating cordial" before allowing Poe to sleep.[63]

According to Moran, Poe was in and out of consciousness during the day, but later the doctor returned to find him dangerously close to death. Another exchange ensued between him and a barely audible Poe, although Moran claimed to have recorded every syllable. In this version, Poe's last words of "Lord help my poor soul," as recorded in the letter to Maria Clemm, were changed to a quote from the 1875 *New York Herald* piece, "O God! is there no ransom for the deathless spirit?" This was followed by another borrowed passage, "He who arched the heavens and upholds the universe, has His decrees legibly written upon the frontlet of every human being, and upon demons incarnate," after which Moran observed, "The glassy eyes rolled back; there was a sudden tremor, and the immortal soul of EDGAR ALLAN POE, was borne swiftly away to the spirit world."[64]

Unfortunately, segments and ideas appearing in Moran's publication would find their way into later histories of Poe. Mary E. Phillips, in her exhaustive record of the poet's life, would credit Professor John C. S. Monkur's deathbed examination and subsequent diagnosis of Poe,[65] an uncorroborated claim that was made in the doctor's book. Professor James A. Harrison also accepted as truth Moran's written and oral exchanges with Elmira Shelton, seemingly on the strength of his 1885 written account.[66] And then there is the testimony by "well known" train conductor *Captain* George W. Rollins [Rawlings] that was, according to Moran, taken in person. This story of Poe's abbreviated trip north from Baltimore was taken up by writers John Walsh and Michael Powell.[67]

Yet among the many difficulties with Moran's book is the probability that some of his stories may have been *tainted* with validity. One example can be found in the intriguing claim that he arranged and paid for Poe's coffin out of his own pocket, the doctor volunteering a corroborating statement

164   *Chapter Seven*

from Frederick T. Nemuth [Namuth] who was trading as a cabinet maker and undertaker at the time of Poe's death.[68] In matters of money, especially his own, Moran's memory seemed less tenuous, and if the doctor's story is true, it would not be too difficult to accept that he would also have arranged to exhibit his famous patient (at the hospital) in the coffin he had procured, a potentiality that would check Henry Herring's claim of being its provider.[69] The descriptions of the coffin's faux walnut finish, and of Moran's wife producing a linen (muslin) sheet to hide it, are also compelling details.[70]

John Moran's claim that he organized a viewing and service for Poe at the hospital also seems to be true. It has long been thought by Poe's biographers that this was just another of Moran's fabrications, made more difficult to swallow by his description of a lavish, three-day affair attended by "hundreds of his acquaintances and friends," and during which "at least fifty ladies received a lock of his hair."[71] However, before he died, the Reverend W. T. D. Clemm gave his recollections of Moran's service in an 1894 newspaper article: "I truly expected to see a large gathering at the obsequies. I was amazed when I walked into the hospital the afternoon of the funeral to see the large hall where the coffin was placed almost deserted. There were only the inmates of the hospital present and five or six other persons." Clemm gave the sparse attendance as the reason for not delivering the address that he had expected to give there.[72]

Likewise, Moran's claim that he personally settled with Poe's hack driver is plausible; keeping in mind the parsimonious policies of the facility, no one else may have had the authority let alone the means to pay the driver, unless deputed by the doctor, although the recalled conversation between the two men was most likely another of Moran's inventions.[73]

Notwithstanding the few possible granules of truth that Moran's publication contains, the booklet survives largely as a work of fiction. As Poe's attending physician, Moran should have offered an unimpeachable record on the poet's death; instead he authored a "dime novel" that provides little informative value—the only thing missing from his romance is a shootout between Poe and the Shelton brothers on Pratt Street. If it had been the doctor's purpose to produce a popular publication, uncontaminated by scholarship, it could be said that he succeeded spectacularly. Perhaps the work's sole redeeming aspect, especially among the increasing number of Poe's followers at the time, was that it was undertaken in the poet's defense.

With the release of his book, Moran's identification with the great American writer increased considerably. He was among the public figures invited to the grand ceremonies on May 4, 1885, at the Metropolitan Museum of Art in New York City for the unveiling of the Actors' Memorial to Edgar Allan Poe. The gala event, said to have been attended by more than 3,000 people, featured an address by actor Edwin Booth (who was instrumental in the monument's creation), an orchestra, and a large choir. In attendance were other notable figures including Professor William Elliott Jr., E. C. Stedman, Sara Sigourney Rice, and John Prentiss Poe, whose father, Neilson Poe, had died the previous year.[74] To be announced at such a prestigious event in honor of the poet was to have one's bona fides validated at last—this would arguably be John J. Moran's high watermark.

When tallying his life and legacy, it should be stated that Moran was perhaps not quite the villain that posterity has painted him.[75] By any standard, some of his deeds were certainly inexcusable, especially when viewed in a modern context; nevertheless, it would be unfair to conduct an estimate of him without also examining the times in which he lived. His blatant fictionalization of Poe's final hours seems comical now, but journalistic sensationalism was nothing if not proliferous in the nineteenth century. At a time when American newspapers were, in the words of Oscar Wilde, "somewhat imaginative," presentation was prized as much as accuracy.[76] How much historical harm, if any, resulted from Moran's monkey business is a matter of debate; however, it must be remembered that his fiction was generated only in *defense* of Edgar Allan Poe—unlike Rufus Griswold who endeavored as much mythology in his effort to maim the poet's reputation.[77]

Figure 7.9. After the publication of his book, Dr. Moran was among those invited to attend the public unveiling of this monument to Poe commissioned by a group of New York actors. The sculpture is currently on display at the Edgar Allan Poe Museum in Richmond, Virginia. *Author (Printed photo from the author's collection)*

Moran's scheme of extorting money from those who sought a medical exclusion from service during the Civil War would inform a corrupt character and lack of integrity. Yet in modern (peaceful) times, his arrest and trial may have had a different outcome. His purely criminal offense was appropriated as a crime against the federal government, when in fact it was perpetrated

166   *Chapter Seven*

against the state of Maryland, and the trial was held in, what was essentially, a military court of questionable authority.[78] But the consequences of his actions in disrupting the draft, and the subsequent delay in the acquisition of union soldiers, could have been interpreted in some quarters as an effort for the southern cause.

With all the faults of John Moran of which we are now aware, it would nevertheless be a dereliction to ignore the positive things he accomplished. He was, of course, the recipient of a degree in medicine from the University of Maryland, no small achievement even in 1845. During his life, Moran was awarded at least four patents in his name, and he was chosen to be the first mayor of Falls Church, Virginia. By all accounts he had a loving family and a devoted wife, one who even proved willing to fib on his behalf. And in 1886, notwithstanding his potential dividend from the transactions, Moran retrieved for the Commonwealth of Virginia an enormous amount of money (from the federal government); funds that appear to have been used primarily for road and infrastructure improvements across the state. Even if he ultimately became the bane of Poe biographers, it must be observed that the people of Virginia, at least, remain indebted to Dr. John J. Moran.

Chapter 8

"Congestion of the Brain"

Sometime during the morning of October 7, 1849, Edgar Allan Poe died at Baltimore City and Marine Hospital from a cause or causes that remain to be established; a death certificate or hospital case record has never been discovered.[1] Poe's brief obituary in the *Baltimore Sun* for October 8 included no cause of death, saying only that he died "after an illness of four or five days." The following day, the *Baltimore Clipper* gave the cause as "congestion of the brain," an inexact and often euphemistic explanation that was used during the time to describe several conditions.[2] Medically, it was then a term that referred to restricted cerebral blood flow causing headaches and coma, but also as a cause of manic outbursts and seizures. It was in the latter context that it was employed as a softened description of delirium tremens.

The absence of a record or document containing the cause of his death was not unusual for the period. The registration of deaths was not then required by the state of Maryland, but was instead undertaken by the respective churches that recorded the births and burials of their congregation members. However, these records were inconsistently maintained,[3] and they included only the name and burial date of the deceased, rarely indicating anything about the cause. It was not until 1865 that the state legislature passed an act requiring all deaths to be recorded at the county circuit courts, but as there were no penalties for noncompliance, initial observance of the law was very poor. Finally, in 1874, a law was passed in Baltimore requiring deaths to be registered in the city.[4] Enactment of the regulation fell to the Commissioner of Health who was then required to record all relevant facts including the cause of death.

Hospitals, of course, created case records on their patients even during Poe's time, but a protocol for the length of their retention, if any, is unknown. In Baltimore City, when a hospital patient died, a copy of his or her case record was immediately turned over to the Commissioner of Health

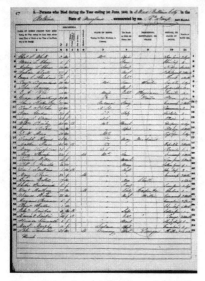

Figure 8.1. For the first time, in 1850, mortality schedules were added to federal census records and Poe's death appears to have been recorded in an official ledger. The entry is eighth from the top on the page shown; the cause of death is listed as "phrenitis." *Edgar Allan Poe Society of Baltimore*

who collated them (by causation) as an annual Report of Interments presented to the city council.[5] As a public service, weekly totals were also printed in the newspapers. On October 9, 1849, a list of the previous week's interments (ending on Monday, October 8) appeared in the *Baltimore Sun*, that included only one death by "Congestion of the Brain."[6] Unfortunately the respective names of the deceased were not given in these reports and it is not known whether the single listing was indeed for Edgar Allan Poe.

His death, however, appears to have been recorded in a federal census ledger. For the first time, in 1850, mortality schedules were added to the general census records that are compiled every ten years by the federal government. The new schedules listed information about the deceased including the name, age, sex, color, occupation, birthplace, and month and cause of death. For individuals who perished within the prior year, the documentation also recorded the number of days they were ill; Census-takers, or marshals as they were called, conducted interviews where they were instructed to inquire about any deaths occurring in the subject's family during the previous twelve months.[7] Appearing in an official state ledger under the heading, "Persons who Died during the Year ending 1st June, 1850, in 3rd Ward Baltimore City," is an entry for "E. A. Poe," for which the month of death is shown as October, and the cause named as "phrenitis."[8] As defined in appendix A of this book, phrenitis was an archaic term (even in 1849) that referred to frenzy or a fevered delirium that was *caused by* an inflammation of the brain or its lining. It is possible the person interviewed may have been trying to describe encephalitis; but use of the term would have normally been a description only of the delirium and not its cause.[9]

The source of the census information on Mr. "E. A. Poe" has not been established but some of the particulars shown, such as his forty years of age, and place of birth given as Massachusetts, would not have been widely known outside the family, especially in light of Poe's public insistence that he was thirty-eight years old and born in Baltimore. Yet this personal information may not have come from the Poe, Clemm, or Herring families, none of which then resided within the city's Third Ward.[10] The site of Poe's death, Baltimore City and Marine Hospital, however, *was* located within this political district and an indication that the information may have been collected there is suggested by the erroneous entry for Poe's occupation which is shown as "physician." When a subsequent discovery of this error (and other mistaken entries for "Occupation") was apparently made, the entire category on the page was at some point annulled.[11]

MINISTERS OF REVISION

Without a surviving hospital record or formal document establishing the cause of death, the way was clear for those looking to propose exculpatory explanations. There would be many who wanted to discredit the accepted idea that Poe had perished from an alcoholic binge, and the search for mitigating circumstances began almost immediately. In the weeks following Edgar's death his cousin, Neilson Poe, who had been sucked into the search for the poet's belongings as well as information on his death, wrote in a letter to Rufus Griswold, "I think I can demonstrate that he [Poe] passed, by a *single indulgence*, from a condition of perfect sobriety to one bordering upon the madness usually occasioned only by long continued intoxication, and that he is entitled to a far more favorable judgment upon his last hours than he has received."[12] Considering that Griswold's defamatory biography portraying Poe's debauched ending had yet to published,[13] Neilson's implication that Poe would be unfavorably judged based on his last hours

Figure 8.2. Neilson Poe was among the first to offer an exculpatory explanation of his cousin's condition after he was found at a tavern in East Baltimore, inferring that it was the result of a "single indulgence" and not a prolonged drinking spree. *The Collection of Brian Shipley*

could have only come from those who found him at the tavern, or perhaps from Dr. Moran.

As discussed, the doctor at some point changed his initial finding that Poe was brought to the hospital in an alcohol-fueled stupor. His reversal may have been the result of a visit from a Richmond temperance advocate who, it is believed, came to Baltimore ostensibly to determine whether Poe had gone back on his pledge of abstinence; this meeting with a "Mr. Benson" may have fomented Moran's revised diagnosis.[14] There is no indication of when this visit may have occurred, but it could have been prompted by the following statement in Rufus Griswold's 1850 memoir: "he met acquaintances who invited him to drink; all his resolutions and duties were soon forgotten."[15] If the advocate's interview with Moran indeed took place, it probably was not during the days immediately following Poe's death; in the doctor's letter to Maria Clemm, five weeks later, Moran still implied that Poe had died disgracefully.[16] The claim, however, was that Benson visited with Moran while he was still working at the hospital, which would have made their meeting no later than 1855.

Moran's explanation (to the temperance man) that Poe had not been drinking but was instead drugged would have represented his earliest version of an exonerating cause of death.[17] Yet by the time of his 1875 feature article in the *New York Herald*, Moran had settled on a completely different conclusion that, he said, had been put forth by Professor John C. S. Monkur, who had assisted him at the hospital. Monkur's finding was that Poe had succumbed to an "excessive nervous excitement from exposure, followed by loss of nervous power. The most appropriate name for his disease is encephalitis."[18] When lecturing years later, Moran would change the wording to a less scientific description: "The cause of death was exhaustion of the nervous fluid, the result of exposure, hunger and other causes acting upon a sensitive

Figure 8.3. In a malicious memoir of the poet that Rufus Wilmot Griswold (shown) appended to Poe's collected works, he claimed that Poe abandoned all his "resolutions and duties" made when he joined the Sons of Temperance. The declaration may have indirectly caused Dr. Moran to change his initial diagnosis. *Author (printed engraving from author's collection)*

"*Congestion of the Brain*" 171

organization."[19] But Moran would not shift significantly from Monkur's diagnosis of encephalitis for the rest of his career.[20]

MURDER

There were others who wanted to put forth the idea that Poe had died as a consequence of murder, and not drug or alcohol abuse. Within only a few years following his death, Mrs. Elizabeth Oakes Smith penned a vindicatory view of the poet's life in which she stated that after being cruelly beaten by a ruffian, Poe fled to Baltimore where he died of a resulting "brain fever."[21] Here, Smith apparently referred to the episode in New York when Poe was threatened by the brother of Elizabeth Ellet in response to the poet's exposure of her to romantic embarrassment.[22] Somehow Smith came to believe that the episode took place in 1849, more than three years after the actual occurrence; and any beating Poe received would have actually been the result of an argument with Thomas Dunn English (in January 1846), not the enraged girl's brother. There is no evidence to indicate that he fled south after this *interview* with Mr. English.

Another who believed that Poe was murdered by relatives of an exploited woman was writer John Walsh. In his book, *Midnight Dreary: The Mysterious Death of Edgar Allan Poe*, Walsh claimed that the poet was assailed by the brothers of Elmira Shelton, who wanted to prevent her marriage to someone they thought to be a fortune hunter.[23] The story goes that after being beaten, the poet was physically forced to drink a quantity of alcohol, the combined effect of which resulted in his condition when found, and ultimately his death. But as previously discussed, one of those finding Poe at the tavern was Dr. Joseph Snodgrass who would specifically state that he saw no evidence on "his person" of a physical assault.[24]

It is difficult to assign murder as a cause of Poe's death given that hospitals were required to report all suspicious physical injuries to authorities. Poe would have, at some point, been examined at the medical facility and had any such wounds or irregularities been discovered on his body, Moran would have been obliged to report them. And had his death been thought the result of those injuries, the doctor would have notified the coroner (medical examiner) in order to convene an inquest.[25] An examination conducted by the author in 2019, of all coroner inquest reports extant issued within Baltimore City during 1849 produced no document on Poe.

Because no external physical injuries were noted at the tavern or hospital, others have suggested that Edgar Allan Poe was poisoned. During the nineteenth century, toxins such as arsenic, cyanide, and strychnine had practical

172 *Chapter 8*

uses, most often as euthanizing agents to kill sick or injured animals. Readily available in several forms and strengths, poisons were also commonly used as pesticides and insecticides, as well as in color pigmentations for candles, textiles, and wallpaper. Arsenic was even used medicinally to treat cholera, malaria, and skin disorders, among other conditions.[26] Then, as today, poisoning, whether accidental or deliberate, was not an uncommon ailment that sent people to the hospital, and the largely gastrointestinal symptoms of a quantity-ingestion such as abdominal pain, stomach cramps, nausea, and vomiting were recognized.[27] And when it was believed to have been a cause of death, there was, by 1836, already a fairly reliable way to check for the presence of arsenic in tissue.[28] In Poe's case, there is no indication that such a forensic test was discussed.

In modern times, an analysis of surviving hair samples belonging to Edgar Poe and his wife was conducted to determine the levels of various heavy metals and toxins, including arsenic, that the pair may have had in their system at the time of their death.[29] The study was organized in 2003 by Albert Donnay, an environmental health engineer in Baltimore who believed that Poe suffered from a form of neurasthemia caused by the effects of exposure to carbon monoxide emitted from the gas lamps that were used for interior lighting during his time.[30] Since the accrual of metals in hair varies with exposure and over time, the researchers analyzed the two ends of each sample separately; the longer length of Virginia's hair sample permitted a test of a third, middle section. Although the quantities of arsenic, lead, mercury, and nickel detected in each sample were at elevated levels by modern standards, they were not found to be in lethally high amounts. In addition, the level of uranium, sourced from coal gas, measured in Poe's small sample was below the detection limit of the spectrometer used, suggesting that he had not been suffering from exposure to gas or carbon monoxide at the time of his death.[31]

While a metals hair-test can be useful in detecting physiological abnormalities occurring over a period of time, it should be observed that a deadly quantity of poison swallowed by Poe during his final days may not have had time to infiltrate enough of the hair to provide an adequate sample for analysis. To establish that Poe had ingested a toxin, tests of blood, urine, and stomach contents would provide better grounds. Nevertheless, it is reasonable to disqualify poisoning as a cause of Poe's death given that Moran neither mentions this possibility nor gives an *implied* recognition of it in any of his statements.

DRUG OVERDOSE

It has been another popular belief that Edgar Allan Poe's death was the result of a drug overdose, whether accidental or deliberately perpetrated by political kidnappers who used opium to suppress the resistance of their victims. Some telling *this* story, of which they had no firsthand knowledge, would claim that Poe was put under the influence of a drug by these operatives and made to vote repeatedly about the city; although in his lecture on the cooping theory, John Thompson deviated slightly by suggesting that Poe was seized by the "lawless agents of a political club" only *after* he had been drugged.[32]

In his 1909 book, *The Poe Cult and Other Poe Papers*, Eugene L. Didier claimed that a so-called acquaintance of Poe informed him that the poet had been dosed with laudanum (a commonly used anodyne consisting of opium-laced whiskey) by political thugs wanting to use him as a repeat voter on Election Day.[33] The alleged acquaintance, a California man, was never identified by Didier, and the story is dismissed by most scholars as an attempt to sponge some of Poe's fame. *Baltimore Sun* reporter, Edward Spencer was another who claimed, without any proof, that Poe was overdosed with infused whiskey, "by his outlaw custodians, discovering too late the disastrous effects of their infamous decoctions upon the delicate tissues and convolutions of his finely organized brain."[34] None of these stories have ever been substantiated.

This is not to say that a frenzied Poe could not have been administered opium as a sedative while in the hospital; then, as today, an opiate is part of the prescribed therapy for delirium tremens and Moran indicates that it was given to Poe.[35] Even if he was at times raving and filling the halls of the hospital with hysterical outbursts, there is no known evidence that the staff dispensed anything more than prescribed dosages to their patient. However, if Poe's identity had not been immediately established, as

Figure 8.4. Elizabeth Rebecca Herring was Edgar Poe's first cousin. According to another relative, she disavowed Poe's weakness for alcohol and instead made the incredible claim that "his periods of excess were occasioned by a free use of opium." *Edgar Allan Poe Society of Baltimore*

discussed in chapter 6, it is not improbable that an irritated nurse could have clandestinely increased the dosage in an effort to silence someone seen as only a disruptive derelict.

Likewise, there is no hard evidence supporting the notion that Poe had a drug habit or was even an occasional user. This remains the case regardless of declarations from relatives and biographers who, many years after the fact, were only voicing their opinions or what they had heard from others.[36] Hervey Allen, in his 1926 examination of the poet's life wrote that "During the stay in Baltimore from 1831 to 1834, there can be no moral doubt that Poe was using opium, at least from time to time. The indubitable evidence of the fact, lies in the work which he produced. The *Tales of the Folio Club* are replete with opiate dreams." Yet Allen would immediately qualify his assertion by saying, "Besides this, there were also secondary manifestations of a decided change in his character through the Baltimore years which tend to confirm the *suspicion*."[37] While it is true that some of Poe's stories are narrated by characters who are familiar with the effects of opium, the experiences of these storytellers were only a device used to confer authenticity. So adept was Poe at employing this trick, that many of his readers, as well as critics, confused Poe with his storytellers, awarding to him the same traits and habits seen in his characters; indeed, this tactic is one of the causes of his fame as a short story writer.[38]

There is sufficient reason to trust that Edgar Allan Poe was not a drug user. One of several of his contemporaries that would testify to this was Dr. John F. Carter, a physician who treated the poet during his last weeks in Richmond and who did not shrink from describing his drinking habits. When asked in 1884 by Poe biographer, Professor George E. Woodberry, about Poe's drug use, Carter shot it down: "Poe never used opium in any instance that I am aware of, and if it had been an habitual practice, we certainly would have detected it, as he numbered amongst his associates half-dozen physicians.... I never

Figure 8.5. Of Edgar Poe's enemies, Thomas Dunn English was arguably the most dedicated, yet he rose to the poet's defense when a biographer wrote of his opium use, stating, "I should, both as a physician and a man of observation, have discovered it during his frequent visits." *Edgar Allan Poe Society of Baltimore*

"Congestion of the Brain" 175

heard it hinted at before, and if he had contracted the habit, it would have accompanied him to Richmond."[39]

Another with the analytical eye of a doctor who knew Poe even more intimately was Thomas Dunn English. As discussed in chapter 1, English became one of Poe's most bitter enemies yet he rose to the poet's defense when Woodberry wrote that he had used drugs: "Had Poe the opium habit when I knew him, I should, both as a physician and a man of observation, have discovered it during his frequent visits to my rooms, my visits at his house and our meetings elsewhere. I saw no signs of it, and believe the charge to have been a baseless slander."[40]

Woodberry himself admitted, "though the direct evidence of the habit is very scanty the indirect evidence is constant, varied, and convincing."[41] Yet even after receiving the written repudiations of two doctors who had actually known Poe, the professor seems to have remained intractably convinced that the poet was a drug user. Based on a single, inaccurate account given by Susan Archer Talley Weiss describing an 1845 visit to Fordham by Poe's sister Rosalie (Poe did not move to Fordham until 1846), Woodberry believed that the poet begged for laudanum after his drinking sprees, "a sign of [his] lapsing into an older habit."[42] It is just as likely that Poe viewed the potion not as a medicine or even a recreational drug but rather as a medium for suicide and the sympathy the threat of it could win. This possibility is suggested by the story of Poe's bid to take his own life in November 1848. In a letter he wrote to Mrs. Nancy Richmond two weeks after a disappearance in Boston, Poe claimed to have attempted suicide by taking an overdose of laudanum:

> Finally I procured two ounces of laudanum & without returning to my Hotel, took the cars back to Boston. When I arrived, I wrote you a letter, in which I opened my whole heart to you . . . I told you how my struggles were more than I could bear . . . I then reminded you of that holy promise, which was the last I exacted from you in parting—the promise that, under all circumstances, you would come to me on my bed of death—I implored you to come then—mentioning the place where I should be found in Boston—Having written this letter, I swallowed about half the laudanum & hurried to the Post-Office—intending not to take the rest until I saw you . . . But I had not calculated on the strength of the laudanum, for, before I reached the Post Office my reason was entirely gone, & the letter was never put in. Let me pass over, my darling sister, the awful horrors which succeeded—A friend was at hand, who aided & (if it can be called saving) saved me—but it is only within the last three days that I have been able to remember what occurred in that dreary interval.[43]

This unconfirmed story came from Poe, and it may have been concocted both to mask another drinking spree (and subsequent period of recovery) while in Boston and to exact sympathy from Mrs. Richmond. The description

176   Chapter 8

of swallowing only half the amount before being sickened is a compelling detail, and considering Poe's capacity for alcohol, his regurgitation of the potion, if true, would seem to suggest an intolerance to (and inexperience with) the opium it contained. However, it must not be overlooked that if anyone knew how to craft a convincing tale it was Edgar Allan Poe.

HEART DISEASE

Heart disease has also been discussed as a cause of Poe's death. The first inference of this condition (as a cause of death) appears to have been made by Hervey Allen in his 1926 biography of Poe. Positing that Poe was excited by the circumstances of his imminent relocation and marriage in the autumn of 1849, Allen wrote that the poet required stimulants for his *failing heart* which would prove disastrous to his brain, and inevitably, fatal.[44] The source of Allen's belief in Poe's heart disease may have been a 1920 magazine article in which a man from "the West" (Cincinnati, Ohio) by the name of E. M. Murdock was reported to have been introduced to Poe in the winter of 1840–1841, while he was working at *Graham's Magazine*, and who claimed that the poet had "heart failure" at the time. But the phrase appearing in quotation marks may have been another wording for "a loss of heart" or "conspicuous depression," which could have been misinterpreted by the biographer as heart disease.[45] Allen wrote that the poet and his wife were then being treated by Poe's friend, Dr. John Kearsley Mitchell, who advised and even arranged a vacation for him (alone) at Saratoga Springs, New York, during the summer of 1843, and that when "Poe returned to Philadelphia, where Virginia had been having hemorrhages about that time . . . [he] almost succumbed to an attack of heart failure himself, the third since 1834–35."[46] However, Allen qualified this statement by writing that Dr. Mitchell "found Poe's condition more perplexing than his wife's, whose complaint, if then incurable, was at least not a puzzle to diagnose,"[47] And the biographer is equally ambiguous about the earlier occurrences of Poe's heart ailment, associating them more with depression and creative paralysis.[48]

After Virginia's death in January 1847, Edgar Poe collapsed and was treated by his wife's nurse, Marie Louise Shew. He eventually recovered, but during another episode in the city the following year Poe was taken in by Shew; when he was examined at her house by Dr. John W. Francis, the physician believed that Poe was suffering from heart disease. In a letter to biographer John Ingram, Mrs. Shew wrote:

> While he slept we studied his pulse, which I so often had noticed . . . . I called in old Dr. Francis who was one of our neighbors[.] [H]e said "he had heart

disease and would die early in life according to the storms or sunshine of his environment", his own words. The old man was odd but very skillful, and a noted man[.] We did not wake him, until he slept it off.[49]

Shew also recalled discovering a scar near Poe's heart: "I have seen the scar of the wound in the left shoulder, when helping Mrs. Clemm change his dress or clothes while ill. She said only Virginia knew about it. She [Mrs. Clemm] did not. I asked him if he had been hurt—in the region of the heart and he told me yes."[50] Yet Poe would later deny the diagnosis of heart disease in a letter to Sarah Helen Whitman,

> And more frequently are we deceived in respect to its actual existence. Long-continued nervous disorder . . . will give rise to all the symptoms of heart-dis[ease an]d so deceive the most skillful physicians—as even in [my o]wn case they were deceived.[51]

Although it is possible that a heart ailment or a previous injury to the organ may have contributed to his death, it has never been *conclusively* established that Poe suffered from any of the various types of heart disease. Other than noting Poe's "feeble" pulse, it must be observed that Moran made no specific mention of cardiac irregularities in any of his accounts. The phenomenon of an abnormal heartbeat after an excessive consumption of alcohol is known today as Holiday Heart Syndrome, and that could have been what Shew, Francis, and ultimately Moran encountered when examining the stricken poet. Of course, his irregular heart rate could have had other causes, as will be discussed.

ENCEPHALITIS/RABIES

Poe's terminal symptoms were consistent with several conditions, including encephalitis. The fever, tremors (or seizures), mental confusion, and hallucinations that he exhibited during his final days could be explained by infected or inflamed brain tissue. Indeed, the cause of "congestion of the brain" as given in the newspaper, *Baltimore Clipper*, could be interpreted as another description of this condition.[52] And then there is Moran's concurring diagnosis of encephalitis coming after Monkur's reported examination of the poet which stated that "POE would die from excessive nervous prostration and loss of nerve power, resulting from exposure, affecting the encephalon, a sensitive and delicate membrane of the brain."[53] It must be remembered, however, that with this pronouncement, Moran was giving a third cause of death: in his letter to Maria Clemm (see appendix D), he had

Figure 8.6. Dr. John C. S. Monkur was a professor on the faculty of the Washington Medical College (Baltimore) during the time of Poe's death. John Moran would claim that he consulted with Monkur who diagnosed encephalitis. *Author (printed engraving from author's collection)*

first indicated traumatic delirium as "the malady of which Mr. Poe died," only to change his opinion to a drug overdose. Furthermore, we only have Moran's word that the professor was assisting him that day; with Monkur's death in 1867, Moran had a free hand afterward to apply the professor's prestige when (and where) needed.[54]

Rabies is a similar neurological infection that has been recently proposed as a possible cause of Poe's death. First presented as a case study by Dr. R. Michael Benitez at the University of Maryland, School of Medicine Historical Clinicopathologic Conference (CPC) in 1995, his theory relies on flawed information (background and stated symptoms) taken from an article written by Charles Scarlett Jr. for the Maryland Historical Society in 1978.[55] Scarlett in turn based much of his essay on the unreliable accounts of Moran who first reported that Poe had difficulty swallowing liquids—the inference being that he suffered from hydrophobia. Scarlett's (and subsequently Benitez's) statements that Poe "vehemently refused to drink," and later "drank water only with great difficulty," were extracted from jumbled, and probably fabricated, recollections by Moran that he later revised.[56]

Furthermore, some of the background information employed by Benitez—namely, that Poe had contracted cholera three months earlier, that he had abstained from drinking (alcohol) for six months prior to his death and that he had no history of delirium tremens—is not supported by the facts. Because some people with encephalitis suffered from intermittent seizures and spasms, Benitez thought that the condition applied to Poe who had experienced a period of recovery before succumbing. But this detail about Poe's brief reversal may have been yet another of Moran's embellishments. Nevertheless, an encephalitic infection remains one of the theories that have some plausibility, but without the presence of hydrophobia, its form as rabies is difficult to apply here.

SUICIDE

According to Weiss, Edgar Poe suffered two attacks (believed to have been delirium tremens) during his final visit to Richmond, the second nearly taking his life. She stated that it was the opinion of the physicians attending him that he would not survive another such attack, and she noted that the doctor's warning was communicated to him.[57] Having this knowledge, it has been suggested that he deliberately undertook a final drinking spree in order to end his life. It would not be hard to imagine that Poe, feeling pressured by the looming, and perhaps unwanted, marriage to Elmira Shelton, and recognizing his inability to quit the bottle, may have just given up, deliberately drinking past the point of no return.

That Poe had at one point welcomed the idea of suicide is suggested by Moran who claimed that when asked on his deathbed about his friends Poe replied, "the best thing his best friend could do would be to blow out his brains with a pistol."[58] Poe also claimed, a year earlier, an attempt to take his own life by overdosing on laudanum; even if this admission was only one of his tales, it nonetheless establishes contemplation.[59] And we must also consider John Sartain's belief that when the two were together in Philadelphia prior to the poet's death, Poe planned to jump from the bridge overlooking the reservoir at the Fairmount Water Works.[60]

Figure 8.7. This iconic photograph of Poe was taken in November 1848 four days after he claimed to have attempted suicide by drinking two ounces of laudanum. However, he wrote that after swallowing only half the amount he became sick and rejected the potion. This remains the only contemporaneous mention of Poe's drug use. *Library of Congress*

Without a written declaration from Poe, verifying suicide as his intent would be difficult at best; yet establishing that he had *no* plan to kill himself would seem to be just as problematic. In their study presented in 2020, Hannah J. Dean and Ryan L. Boyd employed text analysis software (LIWC2015) to identify linguistic markers and patterns in Poe's surviving writings (personal and professional) that would indicate suicidal tendencies as well as phases of severe

180 Chapter 8

depression. Although their study suggested three periods of Poe's life in which he appeared most affected, they found that "the lack of pervasiveness of depressive markers in the years preceding Edgar Allan Poe's death contraindicates the suicide hypothesis."[61] Of course, one obvious issue with such an experiment is that its conclusions are based on the finite amount of Poe's surviving correspondence, material that constitutes only a portion of what Poe generated during his life. There is also the possibility of communicative "whitespace," potentially significant periods when Poe was too depressed to write anything that might bear analysis; these phases could include his final days. Indeed, Dean and Boyd qualified their results by stating, "given the sampling method, it is not possible to establish direct causality; results should be considered informed but tentative."[62]

There can be little doubt that during his life Poe suffered bouts of severe, debilitating depression. Following the death of his wife, his drinking, like his social interactions, seemed to grow more reckless. While his habits during his final years may have become increasingly self-destructive, tangible evidence that his death was the product of suicide remains to be established.

PNEUMONIA

As discussed, the level of care Poe received after his admittance to the hospital has also been called into question, most notably by author Michael A. Powell, who hypothesized that the poet remained unidentified and untreated until the morning of October 7, when his lifeless body was discovered in the hospital's ward for indigent patients.[63] Compounding this neglect was Poe's weakened condition from malnourishment and exposure that Powell believed would have allowed opportunistic infections. The fever, anxiety, restlessness, and disorientation he exhibited in the hospital were therefore likely the result of pneumonia, not delirium tremens.[64] The writer qualified this by claiming that Poe had a hypersensitivity (or pathological reaction) to alcohol which made it impossible for him to have become a heavy drinker thus precluding a death by delirium tremens.[65] Powell resolved that Poe ultimately succumbed from a "cardiopulmonary collapse" when "the heart and lungs, paralyzed by pneumonia," were "no longer able to metabolize oxygen for the brain."[66]

Similarly, it has been theorized that Poe became ill before leaving Richmond and that he was suffering from the flu when he landed in Baltimore. His time outdoors in the raw, rainy October weather then caused his condition to deteriorate, allowing the lung infection. This scenario rests largely on the remark made by Elmira Shelton in her letter to Maria Clemm written two weeks after her last meeting with Poe: "He came up to my house on the evening of the 26th Sept. to take leave of me. He was very sad, and complained of being quite sick. I felt his pulse, and found he had considerable fever, and did not think . . . he would be able to start the next morning."[67] On the other hand, Shelton's description of Poe's condition on the "eve" of his Richmond departure conflicts with the accounts given by Weiss and Thompson, both stating that Poe was well. And there is no indication that Poe was admitted to the hospital in Baltimore as a pneumonia patient.

Pneumonia is a bacterial or viral infection of the lungs that is often fatal if untreated. Symptoms usually include coughing that can produce discolored mucus, shortness of breath, and labored breathing, or fever that is accompanied by sweating and shaking chills; the condition can also cause a confused or delirious mental state, especially in older adults. Although not seen as a microbial infection, pneumonia was recognized as a serious condition in 1849: the report of interments by the Baltimore City's Board of Health for that year records that six individuals had succumbed from the illness.[68] But in Dr. Moran's November 1849 statement to Maria Clemm (see appendix D), parts of which were probably taken from the case report he sent to the health commissioner, there was no mention of coughing, mucal discharges, or chills. It should also be pointed out that for his medical school degree, John Moran presented his thesis on pneumonia.[69] If Poe had displayed the associated symptoms while under the doctor's care, it is difficult to believe that Moran would not have recognized them.

Although Michael Powell's argument of gross medical neglect remains largely unsubstantiated, it still cannot, at present, be eliminated as a possible cause of death. Had a nineteenth-century hospital patient contracted pneumonia during, or prior to, a battle with delirium tremens, the probability of survival would not have been great, especially if the patient went untreated, and the respiratory infection undiscovered.

DELIRIUM TREMENS/*MANIA-A-POTU*

Most of the obituaries published in the days immediately following Edgar Allan Poe's passing implied a disgraceful cause of death. Some of the notices also presented details that could only have come from those involved in his care or rescue. In an October 9 notice provided by a Baltimore correspondent, the *New York Herald* reported the following details about Poe: "On last Wednesday, election day, he was found near the Fourth ward polls laboring under an attack of mania a potu, and in a most shocking condition."[70] In fact, ten weeks before his death, Edgar Poe admitted, in a letter to Maria Clemm, that he had suffered such an episode while he was stranded in Philadelphia.

182   *Chapter 8*

He expressed remorse, but his words were also tinged with genuine fear: "during this interval I imagined the most horrible calamities. . . . All was hallucination, arising from an attack which I had never before experienced—an attack of *mania-a-potu*."[71]

Mania-a-potu was then a well-worn medical term for delirium tremens, an often fatal condition resulting from abrupt alcohol deprivation to those who have developed a chemical dependence. Within twenty-four to forty-eight hours of ceasing alcohol consumption, a sufferer can exhibit confusion, an elevated heart rate, fever, and profuse sweating. If untreated (or unserviced) these symptoms are supplemented by intense paranoia, vivid (often nightmarish) hallucinations, recurring vocal outbursts, frenzied delirium, and ultimately violent, uncontrollable tremors; the combative behavior that results from these symptoms often necessitated the use of restraints to protect the patient as well as caregivers.[72] The disorder is usually progressive, with the first encounters by the sufferer being not as serious. However, repeated occurrences increase in severity and if untreated, the condition can ultimately lead to fatal consequences. In their 1942 study of alcoholism, Howard Wilcox Haggard and E. M. Jellinek claimed that delirium tremens by itself is rarely fatal and that when death occurs, it is usually the result of an underlying or consequential condition, with pneumonia being the most prevalent cause.[73] Regardless of the actual agency, one estimate put the mortality rate among sufferers of acute delirium tremens as high as 37 percent before the advent of modern treatments.[74]

Known as "the horrors" among sailors and the poor, the consequences of sudden alcohol deprivation to heavy drinkers were well known long before the condition attracted new attention in the early nineteenth century.[75] The Latin term then being used to describe the disorder, *mania-a-potu*, roughly translated to "manic reaction to drink" and did not accurately reflect a condition that would have been better explained as a manic reaction to *no more* drink. In 1813, English physician, Thomas Sutton, accurately described the disorder and began referring to it by its chief symptoms of delirium and tremors, but the condition was not identified as a probable consequence of alcohol withdrawal until 1827.[76] Based on his empirical studies Philadelphia doctor, Benjamin H. Coates, argued that the disease was not the result of heavy drinking but rather its "sudden intermission." He further stated "that delirium tremens followed only long-term, 'habitual' drinking. In every instance, it has either occurred from the sudden change of a fixed habit, or at the abrupt termination of a debauch . . . of long continuance."[77]

Although Poe's written confession to his aunt is the first verifiable evidence that he suffered from this condition, it may not have been his first encounter—his daylong panic attack at the Whitman house in Rhode Island comes to mind. As Dr. Coates also pointed out, a single incidence of prolonged alcohol consumption will not bring on the condition in those who do not already have the chemical addiction,[78] so to predicate delirium tremens as Poe's primary cause of death is to assume that he had become *by then* a habitual drinker. And if indeed he had acquired the dependency, sustained drinking would have become a compulsion and not a choice, requiring not continuous binging but rather frequent nips (perhaps a.m. and p.m.) in order to stave off the "shakes." During his last weeks in Richmond, this is what Poe may have been doing in lieu of binge drinking.

It must be observed that Moran never explicitly stated delirium tremens to have been the cause of Poe's death; however, his original description of symptoms as provided to Maria Clemm would have left her with only one conclusion:

> When brought to the Hospital he was unconscious of his Condition—who brought him or with whom he had been associating. He remained in this Condition from 5. Ock in the afternoon—the hour of his admission—until 3 next morning. This was on the 3rd Oct.
>
> To this state succeeded tremor of the limbs, and at first a busy, but not violent or active delirium—constant talking—and vacant converse with spectral and imaginary objects on the walls. His face was pale and his whole person drenched in perspiration—We were unable to induce tranquility before the second day after his admission . . . .
>
> When I returned I found him in a violent delirium, resisting the efforts of two Nurses to keep him in bed. This state continued until Saturday evening (he was admitted on Wednesday) when he Commenced Calling for one "Reynolds," which he did through the night up to three on Sunday Morning.[79]

Considering his escapades in Boston, New York, and Philadelphia during the previous year, it is difficult to believe that Clemm had not already shared the ordeal with Poe, although it *is* possible that he had managed to conceal or recover sufficiently from any occurrences before returning to her house. Nevertheless, there is no record of her being surprised by, or questioning, Moran's description of her "Eddie's" final hours.

Moreover, the lack of *any* statement by Moran assigning delirium tremens as a cause of death would not have been unusual. Although by then the medical community collectively began to recognize alcoholism as a disease, many practicing physicians, as well as the general public, still viewed it as a "manifestation of moral incapacity."[80] Notwithstanding the practical aspects of avoiding the irritation of the family of the deceased, the social stigma of an alcohol-related diagnosis such as delirium tremens often compelled its relabeling to the softer-edged designations of "phrenitis," "brain fever," and

184   Chapter 8

"congestion of the brain." A *Baltimore Sun* article from the period explains the need for these euphemisms.

> Physicians do not like, in the certificates, to write such words as delirium tremens, unless they are writing in hovels at the time. Fortunately for their feelings and those of weeping friends, drunken sprees do not kill men per se, as we may say, but through the intervention of a congestion, in this or that organ . . . or a fatal inflammation in another. The weeping wife knows that the liquor did it. . . . The children know it is no secret that their father died of drunkenness; but there is one consolation—the doctor writes, "died of congestion of the brain." Nobody's feelings are hurt: the family is not disgraced by the necessary record.[81]

This is not to say that deaths were never officially attributed to the condition. Reports of interments printed in newspapers did list mortalities under the category of delirium tremens; however, these were only numerical totals that did not reveal the respective identities of the deceased.[82] And in Baltimore City, there seemed to be an unwillingness at the time to use the term at all, labeling these deaths with alternative designations as late as 1858.[83] This could have been a deliberate policy put in place to blunt Baltimore's notorious reputation: in the annual report presented to the city council for 1849, the year of Poe's death, only five fatalities are attributed to *mania-a-potu*, and nine for Congestion of the Brain. Even with thirty-three deaths falling under the broader category of Intemperance,[84] these seem to be artificially low numbers for alcohol-related fatalities in a city with a population of 170,000.[85]

During his final days in the hospital, Poe demonstrated most if not all of the recognized symptoms of delirium tremens: sweating, fever, abnormal heart rate, hysterical outbursts, combative behavior, hallucinations, and convulsive tremors. The initial delay in the emergence of symptoms, as well as their four-day duration prior to death, are also prototypical indicators of the disorder. As stated, some of these can be descriptive of other conditions, but when supplemented by the catalogue of his known drinking episodes and prior bouts of alcohol withdrawal, there is a preponderance of evidence identifying delirium tremens as the most *probable* cause of Edgar Poe's death.

WHY NO AUTOPSY?

It has been often asked why an autopsy was not ordered by Moran after Edgar Allan Poe had died; the facility was, after all, originally established for the purposes of anatomical examination. Although Washington Medical College had by then quit the premises and relocated to the inner city, it is suggested that the dissection theater in the building continued to be used by the school.[86]

But it must be understood that if those at the hospital were satisfied with the determination of Poe's death, and if they found no reliable evidence to indicate another possible cause, they would have had little incentive to investigate further, especially at the facility's expense. In any event, an autopsy had to be requested (or acceded to) by the family of the deceased, and in this case, Poe's relatives were probably equally convinced of the cause and not receptive to further disclosures.[87]

Yet even had a postmortem examination been conducted, the results may not have been satisfactory. As writers Lester S. King and Marjorie C. Meehan explain in their work on the subject, forensic medicine was then in a primitive state: "The autopsy had in large part been only a capricious dissection that came to an end when some antecedent questions seemed answered . . . [and] performed principally by young and untrained surgical assistants . . . with no regular method, so that it was a matter of difficulty to make any discoveries."[88] Efforts during the early nineteenth century were made at procedural standardization, especially in Europe, but in America it would not be until 1872 that pathologist Francis Delafield published *A Handbook of Postmortem Examination and Morbid Anatomy* to establish protocols and give some uniformity to the process.[89]

Had any suspicions regarding the manner of Poe's death lingered after his burial, the Baltimore City coroner's office would have been eager to conduct an inquest.[90] Furthermore, it is difficult to believe that Dr. Moran would have hesitated to suggest foul play if he thought he could deflect the responsibility (of Poe's death) away from the hospital. But, as previously indicated, a search of coroner reports issued within Baltimore City during 1849 failed to identify a document pertaining to Poe, or anyone else sharing the same last name. An autopsy or coroner's inquest would have been thought unnecessary when those attending a hospital patient were satisfied with their diagnosis—the *mystery* of Edgar Allan Poe's cause of death would come later, and it would be generated mostly by those who were not there.

Chapter 9

Premature Burials, an Epilogue

When Edgar Allan Poe died in the early hours of October 7, 1849, there can be no question that Dr. John J. Moran, the physician in charge of the hospital, had by then learned the identity of his patient, evidenced by his ensuing actions. Sometime during that day he called on Poe's relative, Reverend William T. D. Clemm, at the parsonage of the Caroline Street Methodist Episcopal Church to secure his services for the poet's funeral.[1] The church was then only a few blocks west of the medical facility and Moran may have been acting at the request (or at least with the approval) of the poet's cousin, Neilson Poe, who lived more than a mile away on Hollins Street at the time. Edgar's grandfather, David Poe Sr., had been among the first to purchase a family burial site at the First Presbyterian Cemetery in West Baltimore in 1787,[2] but arrangements for Edgar Poe's interment there probably would have been allowed only by a family member, in this case Neilson Poe.

Rather than being sent to a mortuary, Poe's body was prepared at the hospital for a funeral and burial, according to Moran and his wife.[3] Students still residing at the facility donated various articles of clothing to comprise an all-black ensemble, with the doctor himself contributing a white cravat and collar. There is, however, some uncertainty as to who provided Poe's coffin. Henry Herring stated that he arranged to have one made by Charles Suter who was a cabinet maker; as a lumber dealer, Herring certainly would have known those in the trade who built and sold coffins.[4] Yet Suter's grandson, Oscar S. Benson DDS, later informed Poe scholar Thomas Ollive Mabbott that Poe's coffin was the only one that his grandfather would have ever made in his profession as a cabinet builder.[5] Conflicting with this account is Moran's declaration that he furnished the casket through the efforts of Frederick Namuth who was indeed trading as an undertaker at the time; Namuth later stepped forward to corroborate the doctor's claim.[6]

Final arrangements such as these would normally have been made by the family of the deceased and Moran's involvement must be seen as curious, especially since he later claimed that he never received a dime from Poe's relatives.[7] Of course, he may have been acting on behalf of the hospital for purposes of public relations, or perhaps Moran simply wanted to exploit his proximity to the famous man. Either way, the death of Edgar Allan Poe was bound to attract public notice, and it would not hurt the doctor's reputation to be seen taking such measures in preparation for the funeral. It is also possible that Moran's extraordinary accommodations were extended simply out of a *felt* responsibility for the poet's death.

It now appears probable that Moran was as deeply invested in Edgar Allan Poe's funeral as he later claimed to be. As previously discussed, Moran had the body prepared and clothed immediately following Poe's death on October 7, perhaps even acquiring the coffin—like Henry Herring, the doctor would have had relationships with those in the trade. Following this, he made arrangements for a viewing and service to take place at the hospital the next day. Evidence that the funeral took place as Moran described was provided

Figure 9.1. Before his burial at Westminster Presbyterian Cemetery, it appears that a viewing and funeral service was held for Poe in the rotunda section of the hospital. According to one account, the coffin was removed from the building through the eastern entrance, visible in this photograph taken in 1876. *Author (Printed photo from the author's collection)*

Premature Burials, an Epilogue

by the statements of Reverend Clemm, the officiating clergyman. When Clemm recalled his astonishment at the poorly attended viewing staged in the hospital's "large hall," he also gave a description of the deceased: "Poe was decently clad in black and placed in a mahogany casket. His countenance was expressive of perfect peace, there being no evidence of the awful death he had died."[8] Yet Moran's over-the-top depiction of Poe's body "lying in state" at the hospital, like a fallen president, where "hundreds of friends and admirers came in crowds to pay their last tribute" could not have escaped some notice in the newspapers, a mention of which has yet to be discovered.[9]

Both Moran and Reverend Clemm asserted that the funeral cortege departed for the cemetery directly from the hospital.[10] William Hubner, a fourteen-year-old Baltimore art student, seemed to corroborate this claim. According to Hubner, he was passing by the hospital just as Poe's coffin was being carried to an awaiting hearse parked at the curb. Hubner stated that he quizzed one of two bare-headed men standing near the vehicle about the identity of the deceased, and the man reportedly answered by saying, "My son, that is the body of a great poet, Edgar Allan Poe." The teenager, unable to follow the coaches, could only watch as they rolled away from the hospital. Yet it must be observed that Hubner offered this recollection only after many years had passed; and during his long career as a journalist and book author, he never published a full report of his encounter.[11]

A conflicting portrayal of Poe's obsequies was given by Henry Herring's granddaughter, Miss Ella L. Warden, who stated in 1936 that the viewing for Poe was held at her grandfather's house and not the hospital.[12] She bolstered this claim by presenting a lock of Poe's hair to the Edgar Allan Poe Society of Baltimore. As Warden explained, her mother clipped the hair from Poe "when the body of the poet lay at the home of Mr. Herring."[13] While there is no reason to suspect that the donated lock of hair was not genuine, Miss Warden did not witness the service, and it appears that she was only repeating a family tradition. Moreover, the statements given by Reverend Clemm, that a viewing was held only at the hospital, were sequentially much nearer to the event, and as an eyewitness his account must be given greater weight.

Sometime after 3 p.m., the small entourage comprised of a hearse and one hackney coach, both apparently arranged by Neilson Poe, arrived at the Presbyterian Cemetery in West Baltimore for Poe's burial. There were no more than five people in the arriving party, and no more than eight at the interment. The most reliable accounting of those in attendance was provided by Neilson Poe in a letter written to Maria Clemm just three days after the event:

> The body was followed to the grave by Mr [Henry] Herring, Dr [Joseph] Snodgrass, Mr. Z. Collins Lee, (an old classmate) and myself. The service was performed by the Rev Wm T. D. Clemm.[14]

In addition to these five men present at Poe's burial was George Spence, the church and cemetery sexton, and a grave digger named Andrew Jackson Davis (and perhaps a second laborer). The drivers would have remained with their carriages, whether on Greene Street or in the cemetery.[15] As part of his instructions as the cemetery caretaker, Spence may have been advised to prepare for a crowd and a quantity of floral arrangements; after all, the man they would be burying that day was Edgar Allan Poe, the famous poet. If so, Spence was seemingly disappointed by the small contingent that arrived, an incongruity that apparently never left his memory:

> You would have been surprised to see that funeral procession as it came up to the burial ground. Nobody would have thought that it was anybody famous-like. There was only just the hearse with one hack coming after it. There wasn't any flowers, not one.[16]

Much has been made of the small number of those in attendance but, as in modern times, there were probably some who found it more convenient to pay their respects at the viewing rather than becoming more invested with travel to the cemetery, which was then certainly more of an ordeal. Other

Figure 9.2. As church sexton in 1849, George Spence (shown here in 1893) oversaw Poe's burial at the Presbyterian cemetery in Baltimore. In preparation for the monument's dedication in 1875, he also supervised the relocation of Poe's remains. *Edgar Allan Poe Society of Baltimore*

Premature Burials, an Epilogue　　191

factors that may have contributed to the poor turnout include the day of the week (Monday), and the weather, which was unseasonably cold and threatening to rain. There was also the short notice: the first public announcement of Poe's death did not appear in the paper until the day of his burial; because embalming was not yet a widespread practice, expeditious interments were customary.

In the following years, the number of those said to be in attendance would be expanded. While these inflated numbers sometimes resulted from a mistake, they were also likely invented by those who wanted to borrow from the poet's fame.[17] One who later claimed to have clandestinely attended the burial was Colonel (CSA) J. Alden Weston. Weston stated that he encountered Poe's cortege en route and followed it to the cemetery where he "remained somewhat in the rear." However, he presented this account in 1909 when he was eighty-three years old—sixty years after Poe's death. Weston also included his recollection of multiple vehicles following the hearse which does not agree with other descriptions of a single carriage.[18]

Incredibly, there was for a time some confusion as to the actual day of Poe's burial. Biographers Mary Phillips and William Gill assigned the date of October 8, while Arthur Quinn and John Ingram gave it as the following day. Even George Spence indicated the date to be October 9 when quizzed by *Baltimore Sun* reporter, May Garrettson Evans, in 1893. Spence was just as certain when recalling the weather, saying that the burial took place "on a gloomy day, not raining but just raw and threatening."[19] Although not among those attending, Moran would also assert that, "The day was most unpleasant; a cold, cheerless one, accompanied by a cold, drizzly rain."[20] To settle the matter, Evans thought to consult meteorological records in the hope that the weather on each of these days differed significantly. According to John C. French of the Poe Society, area weather records, then housed at the National Archives in Washington, DC, confirmed to Evans that "October 9 was clear, whereas October 8 was cloudy."[21] This information, along with Neilson Poe's statement to Maria Clemm only three days after the event in question, informing her that the burial "took place on Monday afternoon at four o clock,"[22] would seem to spoil the schemes of the mystery-mongers, on this matter at least: Poe was indeed buried on October 8, 1849.

After a brief (some would recall it lasting only three minutes) Methodist-Episcopal ritual for the dead delivered by the Reverend Clemm, Poe's body was interred in the family lot of David Poe Sr.[23] The Poe lot was in the southeastern quadrant of the cemetery, just below the carriage-path, and unobscured by any structures or large vaults. Edgar Poe was placed at the north end of the family plot between his grandfather and the Reverend Patrick

192 *Chapter 9*

Allison, a founder and the first pastor of the First Presbyterian Church of Baltimore; this was certainly not an unfavorable location.[24] It is a persistently held belief that Poe's original grave site was a hidden, undesirable spot, but on the day he was buried, the Westminster Presbyterian Church had not yet been constructed, and the cemetery then was still an open field only partially obscured from view by its surrounding brick wall.

There is no indication that a marker or headstone to designate Edgar Poe's grave was originally planned by his Baltimore relatives who may have thought it the responsibility of someone closer to the poet, such as Maria Clemm. Yet her remoteness from the city and utter lack of means may have had her thinking just the opposite. Nevertheless, his grave, like all the others in the family lot of David Poe, went without a marker, and as it happens, the original location remains unmarked to this day.[25] But even without a headstone, Spence and Neilson Poe were often called upon to conduct people to Poe's gravesite after his burial, so the location was well known and never mistaken for another. To assist the growing number of people searching for the spot when he was not available, Spence placed a portion of a small sandstone block inscribed with the number "80" at the head of the grave.[26] As will be discussed, the precise location of Poe's original gravesite would later become an issue.

Shortly after Edgar Poe's interment, leaders of the Presbyterian Church began to express concern about the future of their western burial ground. The secular cemeteries of Green Mount and Baltimore City were more picturesque and attracted newer congregation members, some who actually removed the remains of deceased relatives from the Greene Street graveyard to family lots purchased in the newer cemeteries.[27] In addition, the city's business district had swallowed the once rural location of the graveyard and fears of it becoming an "obstruction to municipal growth," as one newspaper later reported,[28] prompted a plan to form a western branch of the Presbyterian Church and construct its place of worship on the cemetery grounds. The elders were equally worried about the upkeep of their aging cemetery, as recorded in the minutes of a committee meeting held just a year after Poe's burial, "it is thought that the erection of a church on the lot will tend to preserve and secure proper care to the ground and the monuments there."[29] The unanimous permission of those with loved ones buried at the site was secured when it was explained that the church's design would not disturb any of the existing burial sites; this was accomplished by supporting the structure on carefully placed piers that straddled the existing graves. Construction of the newly named Westminster Presbyterian Church began in July 1851, and the project was completed in just one year, with the first services held inside on July 4, 1852.

The church and parsonage covered almost 40 percent of the graves in the one-acre cemetery; however, the family plot of David Poe was not among these.[30] Edgar Poe's grave, although not under the church, was now hidden behind it; the structure's imposing presence conferred even more anonymity to the unmarked patch of ground. Some who trekked to Baltimore in order to visit the grave needed help to identify it and were disappointed by what they were shown. After one such visit by a correspondent of a St. Louis newspaper, the reporter wrote, "the remains of to the late Edgar Allan Poe are still reposing in an obscure corner of the Potter's Field of Baltimore ... It seems as if, in the 'Monumental City,' a little slab, at least, might be raised, inscribed with the poet's name."[31] Others would propose a more substantial marker befitting the poet's genius. Among these were C. L. Derby, editor of New York's *Cosmopolitan Art Journal*, and Mrs. Sarah Anna Lewis, who first sought to remove Poe's remains to a cemetery near her home in Brooklyn, New York, after which a suitable memorial would be erected over the grave. At some point, she contacted Neilson Poe who gave his consent to the proposal on the condition that Maria Clemm "desired it"; apparently Poe's aunt no longer looked upon the Lewises with favor and did not approve the idea.[32]

Figure 9.3. At the time of his death in October 1849, the church at the Eastern Presbyterian cemetery did not exist; the graveyard in which Poe was buried was an open lot dotted with various headstones and vaults. It was only after the church's construction there in 1852 that his original gravesite became obscured. *Author (printed engraving from author's collection)*

Burials continued at the West Baltimore graveyard but grew increasingly sporadic. Despite the presence of a new church on the premises, the urban location fell out of fashion, and with the number of those coming to maintain the graves of their relatives dwindling, the cemetery eventually fell into neglect. Yet those making the pilgrimage to view Poe's gravesite continued to grow in number, with many appalled by the condition of the overgrown and often vandalized yard. An exaggerated report of Poe's neglected grave

194 *Chapter 9*

reached Maria Clemm, then living in Alexandria, Virginia. In response, she immediately wrote to Neilson Poe:

> A lady called on me a short time ago from Baltimore. She said she had visited my darling Eddie's grave. She said it was in the basement of the church, covered with rubbish and coal. Is this true? Please let me know. I am certain both he and I have still friends left to rescue his loved remains from degradation.[33]

Of course, Poe's burial site was out in the open, not in the church basement, and since it was directly adjacent to that of the Reverend Allison, the grave was not likely to have been covered in rubbish. It is possible that Maria Clemm's informant was shown the grave of the poet's cousin, George Poe, who *was* buried under the church.

Whether or not he wanted the role, Neilson Poe had become the point-man for the Poe family in Baltimore. However, he often seemed a reluctant resource for those with questions about the poet, as reported by the *Baltimore Sun*, "since 1849 scarcely a week has elapsed but one or more persons have come to see him in relation to Edgar A. Poe."[34] Tired of receiving complaints about a neglected, unmarked grave—complaints that were now also coming from family members—he finally arranged for a modest headstone.[35] It was described as a "perhaps" three-foot high tablet of white Italian marble inscribed with the Latin epitaph, "HIC TANDEM FELICIS CONDUNTUR RELIQUAE. EDGAR ALLAN POE, OBIIT OCT. VII 1849." In translation, the inscription reads: "Here, at last, he is happy. Edgar Allan Poe, died Oct. 7, 1849." A matching footstone carved with the initials "E. A. P." was also planned.[36] Yet according to Hugh Sisson, the appointed monument maker, a stone was produced but never delivered:

> That tablet was finished and standing in my yard. It was to be erected in the cemetery the following week, and would have been but [for] a most extraordinary accident on the Friday or Saturday preceding. My yard adjoins the tracks of the Northern Central Railroad. A freight-train ran off the track, broke down the fence, and did more or less damage to other work; but the only irreparable damage was done to Poe's tablet. That was smashed to pieces, beyond all power of restoration.[37]

It was stated that because Neilson Poe was not a wealthy man, a second stone was not ordered. Yet some have questioned this story of Neilson's attempted marker. Supposing that orders for custom gravestones, such as the one described, were usually paid in advance, the stonecutter should have been responsible for anything in his care and thus obliged to produce a replacement if ruined; the client in this case was, after all, one of Baltimore's better-known lawyers, even if he was of limited means. Furthermore, the explanation that

Poe's headstone was the only one in the yard completely destroyed by the invading locomotive is difficult to accept without having additional facts. Of course, if the finished tablet had been at the stonecutter's awaiting payment at the time of its destruction, Sisson's disinclination to make a second example would be better understood. In any event, he would later get another chance to create a marker for Edgar Allan Poe, an effort that would have a much better outcome.

TWO MORE BURIALS

Neilson Poe's ill-fated attempt to place a headstone at his cousin's grave did not stop people from publicly commenting on the condition of the burial site and making proposals for erecting a marker or monument there. Perhaps no group was more sensitive to the lack of attention given to the poet's grave than those in Baltimore who were tasked with teaching American literature. On October 7, 1865, during a scheduled meeting of the Baltimore City Public School Teachers' Association, the school principal, John Basil Jr., proposed that a committee be formed to "devise some means best adapted in their judgement to perpetuate the memory of one who has contributed so largely

Figure 9.4. Miss Sara Sigourney Rice was a teacher at the Western Female High School in Baltimore and led the effort to create a memorial to mark Poe's burial place in the Westminster Presbyterian Cemetery. *Edgar Allan Poe Society of Baltimore*

Figure 9.5. Sara S. Rice initiated the funding for Poe's monument by arranging literary readings and musical performances by Baltimore school students. One of the recitals was held at the prestigious Concordia Hall on Eutaw Street. *Author (Printed photo from the author's collection)*

196   *Chapter 9*

to American literature."[38] The proposal was unanimously adopted, and a five-member committee was appointed; they subsequently recommended that a suitable monument be created (the location of which was to be determined) and that financing for the project should be immediately pursued.

To kick off the fund-drive, literary readings and musical performances by school students were organized by Sara Sigourney Rice, a teacher at the Western Female High School that adjoined the cemetery's property at the time.[39] Two performances generated $455.92, an astonishing amount for those economically depressed times for the city. There were additional contributions from New York Poe enthusiasts that increased the fund (after interest) to $587.02.[40] It is also widely believed that a "Pennies for Poe" campaign, in which Baltimore City school students donated their spare change, was responsible for raising a significant amount of the monument's cost; however, the only suggestion that any of the memorial's expense was provided for by school children appeared in the *Baltimore Sun*'s coverage of the dedication ceremonies: "Miss S. S. Rice, a member of the committee, collected in small sums $52 more," hardly the $600 figure that has become the tradition.[41]

After six years, the enthusiasm that fueled the project's launch had largely dried up, and proposals for its abandonment were being considered. Since the program began in 1871, the roughly $600 amount that had been raised was seen as inadequate for a substantial monument, the design and location of which had still to be settled. Ultimately, though, the five-member committee was reappointed, and a plan emerged at last to place the finished memorial over Poe's grave which had remained unmarked.[42] A target amount of $1,000 was then believed obtainable and sufficient for procuring a dignified marker of appropriate dimensions. To that end, members of the new committee began appealing to "fellow citizens who favored the project" for contributions that would eliminate the shortfall.[43] With confidence that the deficit could be met, the group then contracted the services of the new city hall's architect, George A. Frederick, for the monument's design. But when his plan for the memorial was submitted to stone-cutter Hugh Sisson, the cost was found to be far above the anticipated funds. As a consequence, the group began to pursue benefactors outside the city, and after being contacted by the committee's chairman, Philadelphia publisher George W. Childs stepped forward and pledged to fill the financial gap; by that time (1874), the cost of the monument and its installation had risen to $1,500, and Child's contribution would ultimately amount to $650.[44] With the funding finally in place, planning then began for an elaborate dedication ceremony to be held in early September of the following year.

The design chosen by the Public School Teacher's Association of Baltimore was "simple, chaste and dignified,"[45] and it is best described by the woman who saw the project through. In the following depiction, Sara

Premature Burials, an Epilogue 197

Sigourney Rice provides details about the monument that often escape the casual observer:

> The monument is of the pedestal or cippus form, eight feet high; the surbase is of Woodstock [Maryland] granite, six feet square and one foot thick; the rest being of fine, white-veined Italian marble. The pedestal has an Attic base three feet ten inches square; the die-block is a cube three feet square and three feet two inches high, relieved on each face by a square projecting and polished panel, the upper angles [corners] of which are broken and filled with a carved rosette. On the front panel is the bass-relief bust of the poet, modelled by Frederick Volck from a photograph, and executed in the finest statuary marble. On the opposite panel is inscribed the dates of the poet's birth and death. On the Attic base below the front panel is the name of Edgar Allan Poe, in large raised letters. The die-block is crowned by a bold and graceful frieze and cornice four feet square, broken on each face in the centre by the segment of a circle. The frieze is ornamented at the angles [corners] by richly-carved acanthus leaves, and in the circled centres by a lyre crowned with laurel. The whole is capped by a blocking three feet square, cut to a low pyramidal form.[46]

It is not clear if those who had approved the monument's design were acquainted with the actual location of Poe's burial site. The niche between the graves of his grandfather and the Reverend Allison was too narrow to accommodate the grand marker's six-foot base, and it may have been the organizers' intent from the beginning to shift Poe's remains to the less restricted area alongside Maria Clemm at the south end of the family plot; according to Spence, it had been Mrs. Clemm's wish to be buried next to her "Eddie." Whether planned or not, the October 1 edition of the *Baltimore Sun* reported that "it was found necessary, in order to get space required for the foundation of the monument, to remove the remains of Poe to the grave of Mrs. Clemm ... buried nearby."[47] The following day, the paper revealed that the monument had been successfully placed over the new grave located approximately twelve feet to the south;[48] the dedication ceremony, originally planned for September, was then rescheduled for October 27.[49]

It was at this point that a political battle erupted between the committee's chairman, Professor William Elliot Jr., and individuals "whose opinions he [was] disposed to regard," over the location of the monument.[50] Apparently it had been assumed, by many who had long thought the original site behind the church too obscure, that the monument (and Poe's remains) would be given a more auspicious location, some even arguing for Green Mount Cemetery or a public park. Before the installation of the monument behind the church on October 1, the committee had indeed considered the northwest corner of the cemetery as a possible location, but after consulting with Neilson Poe, who preferred that Poe's remains not be disturbed, they decided to place

198   *Chapter 9*

the marker where it had been originally intended.[51] When some pointed out that the high masonry walls surrounding the cemetery would block any view of the monument from the street, the committee proposed an iron fence to replace the brick barrier; but even this solution was not enough to quell the rising chorus for a better location. In the end, the unveiling ceremonies were postponed yet again to allow time for the monument's removal, along with the buried remains of both Poe and Maria Clemm, to the more "conspicuous locality" in the northwest corner where it now rests.[52] This indecision ultimately resulted in three burials for Edgar Allan Poe, in disregard to the wishes of his cousin.

However, the corner site at the top of the cemetery was already occupied, and before Poe's monument, and his bones, could assume the new location, it was necessary to secure permission from relatives of the two individuals already buried there. After discussions, the families of Robert Wilson and Alexander Fridge gave their consent, and their relatives' remains were transferred to other spots within the Westminster Cemetery. Wilson was moved to a lot under the church and Fridge to a vault just south of Poe's memorial.[53] It was during this graveyard game of "musical chairs" that a myth arose claiming that the remains of a soldier from the War of 1812 by the name of Phillip Mosher Jr. were actually moved to the new site instead of Poe's.[54] The legend *largely* derived from the fact that most knew where Poe had been originally buried, but were not aware that he had first been moved twelve feet away to accommodate the girth of new monument. As a result, when Poe's relics were extracted from this other location, some assumed that the wrong remains had been taken. But overseeing the entire relocation project was Spence, then acting in a professional capacity as undertaker, and who, as the church's sexton in 1849, had also supervised Poe's original interment. Although some of Spence's later testimony would prove unreliable, it is unlikely that he forgot the location of Poe's first grave, or that he bungled these important burials while *the world* was watching.

Yet, like Poe, the rumor would not stay buried, with additional "support" for it being taken from the description of Poe's original coffin which was said by different people to have been of poplar wood, walnut, or mahogany. There was also some ambiguity as to who actually made the casket, whether an outer coffin liner had been used and of what type of wood the liner may have consisted.[55] And then there was Spence's changing statements. Initially, he said that he burned *all* the leftover debris from Poe's first coffin,[56] but he later claimed to have placed the remaining bits in the new grave, saving a few mahogany slivers for souvenirs;[57] the implication here is that if Poe's coffin had indeed been made of anything other than mahogany, then the box they moved was not his.

Another legend that sprang from Poe's disinterment contended that he had died as a result of a brain tumor. In this story, a Poe admirer from St. Louis, Missouri, was visiting the poet's monument in 1878 and supposedly spoke with the cemetery caretaker who related details about the reinterment three years earlier, describing the condition of the remains as found in the original grave. The man stated that he saw a "tolerably well preserved skeleton" but that when the skull was lifted, "His brain rattled around inside just like a lump of mud," the inference being that the brain had petrified over time.[58] More recently (in 2006), writer Matthew Pearl used this story as the basis for his theory that the mass was not calcified brain tissue but rather the remains of a tumor which had caused the poet's death (see appendix A). However, George Spence offered a lengthy denial of the theory in the *Baltimore Sun* only a week after the claim of Poe's "rattling brain" was printed.[59] He pointed out that the man who was interviewed by the visitor from St. Louis was Robert Davidson, an unofficial watchman for the cemetery. Spence stated that although Davidson was permitted to live under the church, he had no official connection with it, and was certainly not the sexton who, during the time of Poe's relocation, was Spence's son, John.[60] Furthermore, it was indicated that Davidson was not around when the exhumation occurred and was known as someone who "dreads to touch a coffin, and could not be prevailed upon to lend a helping hand in raising the remains of Poe."[61] The *Baltimore Sun* article dismissed the idea of a petrified brain as a "sensational yarn," further quoting Spence that "no interference with or handling of the poet's remains were allowed." Of course, it is possible that the undertaker was only trying to cover up his own culpability. As shown, Spence's testimony could be untrustworthy—his claim of multiple encounters with Poe in the cemetery before his death

Figure 9.6. The ceremonies preceding the unveiling of Poe's monument were held in the Western Female High School building that adjoined the cemetery's property on Fayette Street, just to the east. *Author (Printed photo from the author's collection)*

is more than a little difficult to believe. However, in this case, his rebuttal is better trusted.

The dedication and unveiling of Poe's monument finally took place on November 17, 1875, the ceremonies for which were held in the Western Female High School that directly adjoined the grounds of the Westminster Presbyterian Church and cemetery. The 2 p.m. start time allowed city teachers to attend the function after their school day, which was shortened for the event.[62] The number of those in attendance was certainly swelled by their presence, and by one estimate, there were as many as 1,000 people cramming the high school's main study hall.[63] Among the "some seventy-five" notables that occupied the speakers' platform were Neilson Poe and his extended family; John H. B. Latrobe—the last surviving member of the panel that awarded Poe his first literary recognition; writer and music composer John H. Hewitt—Poe's nemesis in that first literary contest; Nathan Covington Brooks—Poe's Baltimore literary colleague; Dr. Joseph Snodgrass—who along with Neilson Poe and George Spence, had attended the original burial;[64] Professor Joseph H. Clark—a Richmond schoolteacher from Poe's childhood; William F. Gill—author of an early biography of the poet; and of course, Miss Sara Sigourney Rice, who, along with William Elliott, had engineered the dedication ceremony after she had almost singlehandedly kept the monument project alive when the enthusiasm of the other committee members' had waned.

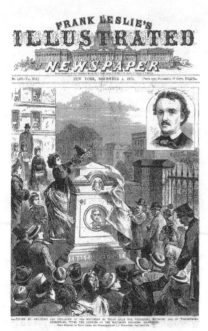

Figure 9.7. The massive crowd—by one estimate to be around a thousand in number—that attended the lengthy dedication of Poe's monument in 1875 was in stark contrast to the somber, three-minute ritual at his original burial that was witnessed by six people and two gravediggers. *Author (printed engraving from author's collection)*

During the year-long run up to the event, Rice had extended invitations to many of the more well-known poets and authors in the United States and abroad, but ultimately, most of the writers sent their regrets. Instead, she read aloud their letters of tribute to Poe during the exercises, included among these were communiqués from William Cullen Bryant, Henry

Longfellow, Alfred Tennyson, Oliver Wendell Holmes, James Lowell, and Sarah Helen Whitman.[65] Walt Whitman, no relation to the poetess from Providence, who had met Poe while he was editing the *Broadway Journal* in New York, was the only one of her invited literary celebrities to attend. At the time of the dedication, Whitman was still recovering from a stroke and although he was given a prominent place on the dais, he declined to make a speech, offering only informal remarks after the ceremonies.[66]

Not surprisingly, the program included *much* oratory. The history of the monument project was described by Professor William Elliott Jr., president of the Baltimore City College and chairman of the monument committee. His speech was followed by the main and ponderous address on "The Genius and Literary Character of Edgar Allan Poe" given by Professor Henry E. Sheppard, the superintendent of Baltimore City schools. John H. B. Latrobe then provided a somewhat shorter account of Poe's first literary award by the *Baltimore Saturday Visiter* after which Neilson Poe rose to offer a brief appreciation for the monument on behalf of the Poe family. The speeches were capped by choral renditions from the one-hundred-member Philharmonic Society perched on raised seats at the rear of the room.[67]

After all the poems were recited and the dissertations delivered, the assembled audience and dignitaries poured out into the small cemetery for the unveiling ceremony, overwhelming it entirely: "The large number ... filled the surrounding streets, and every available position in windows and on door-steps of the houses in the vicinity."[68] As there was then no cemetery gate by the monument (its installation by Orrin Painter would not take place until 1912), the brick and wrought-iron palisade surrounding it became a precarious "grandstand" for those who could not gain admission. There, to the accompaniment of choral music by the Philharmonic Society that floated through a part of town not accustomed to it, William Elliott removed the memorial's muslin

Figure 9.8. Edgar Allan Poe's remains have undergone three separate burials, their final resting place being beneath the monument of 1875. Today it has become one of the most visited sites in Baltimore. *Author (printed engraving from author's collection)*

202 *Chapter 9*

cover, revealing it to public gaze for the first time—the resulting eruption of applause completely eclipsing the voices of the choir. The quake of clapping hands continued while Rice, standing on a small set of steps, crowned the marble pedestal with two floral wreaths, the second of which was made of black immortelles and fashioned into a raven. The massive crowd punctuating each segment of the ceremony with their applause was in stark contrast to the somber, three-minute ritual at Poe's original burial that was attended by six people and two gravediggers. Apparently photographs of the event were taken but none are known to have survived, the only contemporaneous depiction being an engraving (perhaps derived from a sketch) made for the cover of *Leslie's Popular Magazine* of December 4, 1875.

Although other poets and authors had been given elaborate headstones by 1875, as reported by the *Baltimore Sun*, this monument was "the first memorial expression of the kind ever given to an *American* on account of literary excellence."[69] The *Sun* also added that the national attention given to the creation and presentation of Poe's obelisk "marked the turning of the tide in his favor." Indeed, it was Poe's notorious personal reputation at the time that still mitigated a wider appreciation of his writing—in the year after the poet's death, the editor of his collected works, Rufus Griswold, had crafted and appended to the collection a malicious "memoir" in an effort to validate the apparent hatred he still held for the man.[70] As it would happen, his poisonous profile, replete with descriptions of treachery and plagiarism, as well as exaggerations of his drinking, remained the only *readily available* biography of Poe for the next twenty-five years. According to Poe scholar, Jeffrey Savoye, by the time of the monument's dedication, Griswold's memoir "had worked itself deeply into the public consciousness, [and] what strength his accusations lacked in truth they gained in repetition."[71] Yet at the time that the people in Maryland were gathering to celebrate Poe's memorial, new biographies from John H. Ingram, Eugene L. Didier, and William Fearing Gill were being written that would describe Poe's life without vindictiveness. The release of these new accounts at the very moment that Poe's monument was being unveiled to the public proved to be a fortunate confluence of events for the poet's reputation, ultimately serving to marginalize Griswold's mendacities and launch a greater acceptance of Edgar Allan Poe's genius. This reassessment of Poe enabled many others in cities and villages in the land of his birth to hear the poet's words; however, after those fateful days in 1849, he would be seen again . . . *nevermore* in Baltimore.

Appendix A

Proposed and Popular Causes of Poe's Death

The following is a list of proposed and popular theories on Edgar Allan Poe's cause of death, as known at the time of publication. The symptoms Poe displayed at his death are consistent with many of these; however as compelling as they may be, symptoms by themselves must not be mistaken as confirmation. Although some of the theories listed here cannot be disqualified, without irrefutable evidence for support (such as a case record or death certificate) they must been seen only as speculative.

To assist the user, the list has been compiled alphabetically with each entry containing an attribution (when known), a brief description of the condition and remarks, as relating to Poe. The order of their appearance confers no rank of viability.

It is very possible that Poe suffered from a comorbidity of conditions appearing on this list. In an age of primitive medicine, a simple combination of the maladies shown below could have been fatal.

ALCOHOL DEHYDROGENASE (1984)

(Arno Karlen. *"Napoleon's Glands . . ."* [Little Brown, 1984], 92.) Symptoms include alcohol intolerance, facial flushing, nausea, elevated heart rate, headache and fatigue. Dr. Arno Karlen theorized that Poe had a genetic enzyme deficiency (Alcohol Dehydrogenase Syndrome) as well as a brain disorder which produced an acute sensitivity or intolerance to alcohol, explaining his fits of "insanity" and sudden death. However it is difficult to see how such a devastating reaction to small quantities of alcohol would not deter the sufferer from heavy drinking, a limitation Poe did not seem to have.

ALCOHOL POISONING (1949)

(Montague Slater, ed., *The Centenary Poe* [London: Bodley Head, 1949], 34.) In his introduction to an anthology of Poe's works, Montagu Slater claimed that Poe died of alcohol poisoning. The condition occurs when the intake of alcohol exceeds the body's ability to process it and when blood alcohol concentrations reach toxic (or poisonous) levels. Symptoms include lethargy, stupor, pale complexion, clammy skin, confusion, irregular pulse and breathing, vomiting, seizures, ataxia (inability to walk or speak), and loss of consciousness. Dr. Joseph Snodgrass would testify that Poe was exhibiting most of these symptoms when found at the tavern. There can be little doubt that Snodgrass's temperance zeal colored his recollection of events, but he did have a medical credential and his was a firsthand account.

ALCOHOL WITHDRAWAL (2016)

The severity of symptoms can vary based on the sufferer's level of alcohol dependency. Those with a heavy addiction will demonstrate a powerful and prolonged reaction to deprivation known as delirium tremens: confusion, elevated heart rate, fever, profuse sweating, hallucinations, violent tremors, and combative behavior, all of which Poe displayed in the hospital. The condition can be fatal with death occurring within four to six days. In a blind, clinical pathological investigation conducted in 2016, a panel of doctors at the University of Maryland School of Pharmacy were presented these symptoms (although the submitted data may have been flawed) to determine causality and whether modern pharmaceuticals could have saved the unidentified patient. Without consulting among themselves, the panel unanimously concluded the cause to be alcohol withdrawal.

APOPLEXY

Apoplexy is defined as a hemorrhage within a cavity or an internal organ of the body, the difference from edema (or dropsy) being a forced flow usually the result of a ruptured vessel. When in the context of a brain hemorrhage, the term was often used to describe the sudden loss of consciousness before death. Although there were twenty-four recorded deaths due to apoplexy in Baltimore City during 1849, there is no known evidence that Poe was one of them, or that he suffered a cerebral hemorrhage.

BEATING/MUGGING (1857)

(Elizabeth Oakes Smith, "Edgar A. Poe," *United States Magazine* 4, no. 3 [March 3, 1857]: 262–68.) In her magazine article, Smith claimed (without any firsthand knowledge) that Poe was "cruely [*sic*] beaten, blow upon blow, by a ruffian who knew of no better mode of avenging supposed injuries. It is well known that a brain fever followed." However, beating injuries, as a matter of course, were reported to authorities and would have triggered an inquest if resulting in death. An examination conducted by the author in 2019 of coroner inquests for Baltimore City during 1849 produced no document on Poe.

BIPOLAR DISORDER (MANIC DEPRESSION) 1926

(Dr. Harry L. Lyman [PhD], *Baltimore Sun*, January 20, 1926.) Bipolar disorder is a brain illness that causes extreme mood swings and is manifested in alternative periods of mania (and manic activity), followed by, or coupled with, periods of debilitating depression. Symptoms can include euphoria, irritability, unusual talkativeness, abbreviated sleep, loss of ambition, indifference to food, lethargy (physical and mental), and suicide. In his definitive biography, Arthur Hobson Quinn suggests that Poe drank only to escape an inherent "duality" of deep depression and demonstrative exhilaration but does not elevate the condition to a cause of death. Additionally in 1926, Dr. Koopman, a librarian at Brown University, asserted that Poe "was the victim of a form of insanity about which little or nothing was known in his day, but which caused him alternative periods of elation or ecstasy, and [of] the most profound depression." Koopman also claims that "it was to overcome the periods of depression that Poe drank," and that his death was brought about by the alcohol he used to mitigate his "unbalanced state" (this phenomenon of symptomatic drinking to alleviate depression was also presented by Howard Haggard and E. M. Jellinek in their 1942 study of alcoholism, *Alcohol Explored*). Attributing his death *directly* to this disorder would be difficult; however, it would not be as problematic to say that Poe's death could have been knowingly hastened by the poet himself. (See also the listing for Suicide.)

BRAIN CANCER/TUMOR (2006)

Severity and frequency of symptoms can depend on the progression and size of the tumor. These can include headaches, vision and hearing difficulties, loss of balance, confusion, seizures, nausea, and vomiting—Poe's custody of which has not been established. During the process of relocating Poe's grave and the exhumation of his remains in 1875, it was later stated that a hard mass was found to be "rattling" in the skull. Matthew Pearl (author of *The Poe Shadow* [New York: Random House, 2006]) theorized in 2007 that it was a petrified tumor. However, in an article appearing in the *Baltimore Sun* (November 12, 1878) George Spence, who was onsite overseeing the exhumation, indicated that no such thing occurred—calling the story a fabrication. But even had an object been detected at the time it must be observed that Poe's simple coffin (and remains) had suffered twenty-five years of direct exposure in the ground, and a hardened object found within the skull could easily have been something other than calcified organic matter.

BRAIN LESION (1847)

A brain lesion is an abnormality of tissue caused through injury, disease or infection and differs from a tumor that is a growth upon existing tissue. Symptoms can include headaches, vision impairment, fever, loss of appetite, nausea, vomiting, and seizures. When examining Poe in February 1847 after the death of Virginia, his nurse, Marie Louise Shew, believed he was suffering from a brain lesion. Her diagnosis may have been supported by Dr. Valentine Mott, then on the staff of the University Medical College of New York. A corroborating opinion was presented by Poe scholar Thomas Mabbott in his 1969 "Annals," in which he stated that a twist in Poe's face (as shown in a photograph of him) suggested the presence of a brain lesion. Although a cerebral abnormality may explain manic behavior and even sensitivity to alcohol, it cannot be concluded to have contributed to Poe's death without additional support.

CARBON MONOXIDE POISONING (1999)

(Albert H. Donnay, "Poisoned Poe: Evidence that Poe May Have Suffered from Neurasthemia," paper presented at the International Poe Conference, Richmond, Virginia, October 9, 1999.) The symptoms of carbon monoxide poisoning include lethargy, nausea, dizziness, confusion, visual disturbances, and irritability, some of which Poe displayed in the hospital. In 1999, toxicologist Albert Donnay presented his theory that Poe suffered from the effects of the carbon monoxide emitted from gas lamps, the exposure taking place over many years, permeating (and surfacing in) his written works and ultimately killing him. To support his theory, Donnay later arranged to have remnants of Poe's hair tested for elevated concentrations of metals, which proved not to be present.

CEREBRAL EDEMA (1907)

A cerebral edema, or swelling of the brain, can have many causes including physical injury, a tumor, viral or bacterial infection, blood clot, hemorrhage, etc. The resulting intracranial pressure can restrict the flow of fluids within the brain causing permanent damage or death. Symptoms of this serious condition can include headache, dizziness, seizures, stupor, irregular breathing, impaired vision, and a loss of consciousness. For a 1907 feature appearing in the *New York Times*, an unnamed physician opined that Poe's death was the result of a "cerebral oedema." Some of the known symptoms, as given by Dr. John J. Moran, could support this theory, however in his report to Maria Clemm five weeks after Poe's death it is clear that the doctor thought the cause to be something else.

CONGESTION OF THE BRAIN (1849)

Congestion of the Brain or cerebral congestion is an antiquated term that was originally used to describe circulatory abnormalities including apoplexy, cerebral hemorrhage, stroke, coma, headaches, and seizures. During Poe's time it was also used as a euphemism for the manic outbursts, frenzy, and fevered delirium caused by alcohol withdrawal. The October 9, 1849, edition of the *Baltimore Clipper* gave the cause of Poe's death as "congestion of the brain." The Baltimore Board of Health attributed nine deaths in 1849 to "congestion of the brain," but also listed interments for "hemorrhage" (six), "inflammation of the brain" (sixty-seven), "*mania-a-potu*" (five), "nervous fever" (four), and "intemperance" (thirty-three). Poe could have been listed among any of these.

CHOLERA (1849)

(*CL*, 2:820, LTR-323, Letter: Edgar Poe to Maria Clemm, July 7, 1849.) An infection of the gastrointestinal tract, cholera is acquired through drinking-water or food that has become contaminated by bacterium found in fecal matter. Symptoms include lethargy, irritability, acute and sustained diarrhea,

208   *Appendix A*

vomiting (and manifestations of the resulting dehydration), irregular heart rate, and low blood pressure; with death occurring within forty-eight hours, or sooner. Although there were several cholera outbreaks during Poe's time (the cause not identified until 1854) there is no verifiable evidence that it caused his death in Baltimore. In a letter to Maria Clemm while he was in Philadelphia, Poe claimed to "have had the cholera, or spasms quite as bad." But in this instance, he could have been appropriating the sickness to cover for the prolonged aftereffects of a drinking spree, or something worse.

DELIRIUM TREMENS (1992)

(Jeffrey Meyers, *Edgar Allan Poe: His Life and Legacy* [New York: Charles Scribner, 1992], 255.) Frequently used as a synonym for the earlier "mania-a-potu," delirium tremens is an often fatal manifestation or consequence of alcohol withdrawal to sufferers who have acquired the chemical dependence. Symptoms, which usually begin within forty-eight hours of ceasing alcohol consumption, include confusion, elevated heart rate, fever, profuse sweating, hallucinations, violent tremors, and combative behavior—at the time of Poe's death the mortality rate among acute sufferers was estimated to be as high as 37 percent. During his final days in the hospital, Poe exhibited most if not all of these symptoms which *were* originally described by his attending physician, John Moran. In his biography, Meyers seems to infer that an attack of delirium tremens can be brought on by a single alcoholic overdose; however only those who have developed an addiction suffer the condition. Nevertheless, in Poe's case, delirium tremens, or its consequences, endures as the most *probable* cause of death. (See also Toxic Disorder.)

DIABETES (1977)

(David Sinclair, *Edgar Allan Poe* [London: J. M. Dent, 1977], 151–52.) Symptoms of Type 1 Diabetes include chronic thirst and hunger, debilitating fatigue, increased urination, weight loss, and numbness in the extremities. David Sinclair claimed that Edgar Poe, and his brother Henry, inherited the condition, and with their misuse of alcohol suffered a vitamin deficiency (Korsakoff Syndrome) that caused a neurotoxic effect on the brain.

John S. Hill also suggested in the October 1968 issue of the *Poe (Studies) Newsletter* that Poe suffered from diabetes mellitus and died in a diabetic coma. Diabetes and the resulting sugar imbalance certainly could account for a sensitivity to alcohol but the illness (and its symptoms) was recognized during Poe's time and evidence that he exhibited any of the symptoms for an extended period of time has not been discovered.

DIPSOMANIA (1921)

(John W. Robertson, *Edgar A. Poe: A Study* [San Francisco: Bruce Brough, 1921], 4–5, 14.) Dipsomania is an obsolete term for alcoholism and can be described as an involuntary desire for (and consumption of) ardent spirits. In his 1921 book, Robertson (a neurologist) claimed that Poe's alcoholism "was the result of hereditary compulsion." Robertson uses the resulting "fatal delirium" to explain the opinion of brain or meninges inflammation.

In his 1909 magazine article, "Edgar Allan Poe: A Pathological Study," (*The Book News Monthly*, August 1907: 801–3), Dr. Charles Houston Goudiss identifies Poe as a sufferer of dipsomania, but he does not elevate the condition as a cause of the poet's death. That Poe's drinking was, during most of his life, largely episodic seems to be supported by the testimony of those intimate with him. But this would not have precluded a later progression to habitual drinking that resulted in chemical dependence and the inability to abstain.

DRUG OVERDOSE

Before the advent of the hypodermic syringe, opium was taken orally as a cure-all for myriad ailments, as well as recreationally. During Poe's time, procurement was inexpensive and could be obtained without a doctor's permission. It is a popular belief that Poe was a drug user, if not an addict. However, Poe counted many men with medical degrees among his intimate acquaintances, two of which, Dr. John Carter and Thomas Dunn English, categorically rejected the claims of his drug use.

It has also been stated that Poe was given drugs involuntarily: In his book, *The Poe Cult and Other Poe Papers* (New York: Broadway Publishing, 1909), Eugene L. Didier wrote that he was informed by a so-called acquaintance of Poe that the poet was dosed with laudanum (by political thugs wanting to use him as a repeat voter) on the eve of Election Day. However, the California informant was never identified by Didier and the informant's claim is dismissed by most scholars as an attempt to sponge some of Poe's fame.

210   *Appendix A*

ENCEPHALITIS (1875)

(John J. Moran, "Official Memoranda of the Death of Edgar A. Poe," *New York Herald*, October 28, 1875, 4.) Encephalitis is an inflammation of the brain tissue usually the result of a viral (or bacterial) infection. Symptoms can include fever, severe headaches, speech and hearing impairment, confusion, seizures, and coma. In his magazine article, Dr. Moran stated that Professor John C. S. Monkur examined Poe and diagnosed encephalitis, saying "that Poe's death was caused by excessive nervous excitement from exposure, followed by loss of nervous power. The most appropriate name for his disease is encephalitis." This explanation is not without some difficulties the first of which is the source: even though the finding reportedly came from Professor Monkur, we only have Moran's word for it. There is also the elaborate diagnosis given after what could only have been a cursory examination, without the conduct of tests, while the usual result of exposure to the elements is hypothermia or respiratory infections. Yet some of Poe's terminal symptoms are consistent with this condition.

EPILEPSY (1875)

(Francis Gerry Fairfield, "A Mad Man of Letters," *Scribner's Monthly* 10, no. 6 [October 1875]: 691.) Epilepsy is a neurological disorder that is usually manifested by unprovoked, recurrent physical seizures of the body, the result of brain injury, infection, oxygen deprivation, tumor, etc. In 1875, journalist Francis Fairfield suggested that Poe was a lifetime sufferer and it drove him to madness, the proof being his body of work. In 1999, neurologist Dr. Carl Bazil would also theorize that Poe suffered from Temporal Lobe Epilepsy (triggered by alcohol abuse) and "used his experiences from the illness to create memorable tales and poignant poems." Although it is possible that Poe suffered from a form of the disorder, there is no contemporaneous testimony that he "was subject to epileptic attacks" as claimed by Fairfield.

ETHER OVERDOSE

The properties of ether as an anesthetic became known in the eighteenth century and by the 1840s it was in wide use during medical procedures. Ether was also prescribed for various pulmonary and respiratory ailments, and its narcotic effects made it attractive for recreational use. Frequent use produced addiction; Poe's fiancée, Sarah Helen Whitman, may have had such a habit. As with any general anesthetic, an overdose can cause paralysis of the respiratory system and death. Excessive salivation, vomiting, coughing, and convulsions can also indicate an overdose, the sufferer of which can recover when removed from the gas. There is nothing to suggest that Poe was administered ether while in the hospital.

HEART DISEASE (1926)

(Hervey Allen, *Israfel: The Life and Times of Edgar Allan Poe*, 2 vols. [New York: George H. Doran, 1926], 2:841.) There are many types of heart disease that can affect its function or cause complete failure: congenital, arrhythmia, coronary artery disease, cardiomyopathy, heart failure, etc. In his biography, Hervey Allen described Poe's recurring "attacks of heart disease," first diagnosed in him by New York doctor John W. Francis in 1848. Allen ultimately claimed that Poe, excited by the circumstances of his imminent relocation and marriage in the autumn of 1849, required stimulants (alcohol usually acts as a sedative) for his failing heart which would prove disastrous to his brain, and inevitably, fatal. However, Allen's theory of "heart failure" may have resulted from his misinterpretation of a 1920 magazine article; it has never been conclusively established that Poe suffered from any of the various types of heart disease. Other than a "feeble" pulse, Dr. Moran made no specific mention of cardiac irregularities in any of his accounts.

HEMOCHROMATOSIS (2019)

Informally proposed by Laura Anderson during a discussion of this work, hemochromatosis is a genetic disorder that causes a toxic accumulation of iron in crucial organs, principally the liver, heart, and pancreas. Symptoms include joint pain, fatigue, diabetes, impotence, cirrhosis of the liver, and heart failure. Not identified during Poe's time, the disease seems to have no correlation to alcoholism and his custody of these symptoms has not been established.

HYPOGLYCEMIA (1992)

(Meyers, *Edgar Allan Poe*, 255.) Hypoglycemia is a serious condition of low blood sugar that is often linked to diabetes. Symptoms include irregular heart rate, fatigue, pale skin, anxiety, and irritability. If left untreated, cognitive

212   *Appendix A*

issues, blackouts, seizures, and permanent neurological damage can occur. Severe cases are often mistaken for intoxication. Poe demonstrated several of these symptoms during the last years of his life and it has been theorized that he was a chronic sufferer of hypoglycemia. In his biography of Poe, Jeffrey Meyers wrote that the terminal symptoms of the poet were manifestations of the disorder and that he "probably died in a diabetic coma." A sugar imbalance would provide support to the idea that he exhibited sensitivity to alcohol, as would several other conditions including a brain abnormality and chronic alcoholism; however Poe's hyper response (to small quantities of alcohol) has not been proven.

HYPOTHERMIA/NATURAL CAUSES (1899)

(Charles W. Kent, ed., *The Unveiling of the Bust of Edgar Allan Poe in the Library of the University of Virginia* [Lynchburg, VA: J. P. Bell, 1901], 81.) Hypothermia, normally caused by prolonged exposure to cold weather (also water, ice, or snow), occurs when an individual's core body temperature descends to a dangerous level, often triggering cardiac failure. Symptoms that can be mistaken for intoxication include uncontrolled shivering, disorientation (hallucinations), slurred speech, impaired dexterity, and exhaustion. Death as a result of hypothermia can transpire within minutes or hours but has been known to occur even after a period of days. As editor of a volume published to commemorate the dedication of George Zolnay's bust of Poe at the University of Virginia in 1899, Charles Kent wrote, "The real fact is, that Poe's death was due to *natural causes*. His shocking exposure, when thinly clad, to the low temperature of a frosty October night, could have killed a strong man, much less one of his frail and exquisitely delicate structure." Poe was found in clothing that was inadequate for the unseasonably raw weather then occurring (although the length of his exposure is not known), and any measure of alcohol would have facilitated the loss of body temperature. However, in his report to Maria Clemm five weeks following Poe's death, Dr. Moran gave no indication of the associated symptoms.

INFLUENZA

Usually a seasonal (or winter) illness, influenza is a highly contagious viral infection that mainly affects the respiratory system. Symptoms, which are communicated even by those who are unaware they have the illness, can include fever, chills, persistent cough, sore throat, body aches, profound fatigue and malaise, sinus congestion, and headache. On the eve of his planned departure from Richmond, Poe was said to be ill and feverish although the cause of his illness was never identified by those making the claim. Some have presumed that he was still sick upon his arrival in Baltimore, where the weather was reported to be rainy and raw, possibly exasperating his condition which could have facilitated pneumonia. Chris Semtner, curator of the Poe Museum in Richmond, Virginia, had at one point suggested that a high fever might account for his hallucinations and confusion. Yet it is somewhat difficult to believe that the then physically fragile Poe would have had the ambition, indeed the ability, to embark on a trip if stricken with a virus that was then causing conspicuous symptoms.

MALARIA (2017)

(Ralph Giorno, *Decryption of the Death of Edgar Allan Poe* [Middleton, DE: By author, Western Consulting Pathology, 2017], 193.) Malaria is contracted by humans when an infected mosquito injects a parasite into the blood system. Symptoms include shaking (or tremors), high fever, profuse sweating, headache, stomach spasms and other gastrointestinal issues, many of which Poe manifested when in the hospital. Dr. Ralph Giorno makes a compelling argument suggesting that Poe acquired the disease as a young man while in the army and stationed at southern locations. However, he uses Poe's long record of illnesses to bolster his theory which would presume a misdiagnoses during each relapse over those twenty years, this when malaria and its symptoms were well known and already being treated with potions containing quinine.

MALPRACTICE/MISDIAGNOSIS (2017)

(Giorno, *Decryption*, 111.) In his case for malaria, Ralph Giorno suggests that Dr. Moran (Poe's physician of record) not only withheld basic, benign treatments for over-intoxication but also failed to recognize symptoms of malaria. His view is based on Moran's November 15, 1849, letter to Maria Clemm (see appendix D) that includes no mention of curative measures for alcohol abuse, a condition from which he may have been trying to shield Clemm. However, Moran would later describe treatments that were consistent with excessive alcoholic intake.

In his book, *Too Much Moran: Respecting the Death of Edgar Allan Poe* (Eugene, OR: Pacific Rim University Press, 2009, abbr. *Powell*), Michael A.

Powell also claims that malpractice and neglect ultimately killed Poe. Powell's idea that the poet was completely neglected until discovered dead is not likely, however if Poe's identity was not immediately established at the hospital and he went untreated for a length of time in the indigent ward, the delay could have sabotaged any chance of his recovery. (See also Pneumonia.)

MANIA-A-POTU (1849)

(*CL*, 2:825–26, LTR-327, Letter: Edgar Allan Poe to Maria Clemm, July 19, 1849.) *Mania-a-potu* (Latin for manic reaction to drink) was often another name for, or given as a cause of, delirium tremens, a life-threatening reaction to alcohol withdrawal. Symptoms include confusion, fever, delirium, visual and auditory hallucination, violent tremors, combative behavior, rapid pulse, and profuse sweating, all of which Poe exhibited when in the hospital. Poe wrote to Maria Clemm that while in Philadelphia he had suffered an attack of *mania-a-potu* but "had not been drinking a drop." However, his claim of abstinence is difficult to believe in light of what we now know of the episode. Baltimore City's Board of Health Report of Interments for 1849 listed five deaths from *mania-a-potu*.

MENINGITIS

Meningitis is a viral or bacterial infection and inflammation of the membranes surrounding the brain and spinal cord. Symptoms include fever, headache, stiff neck, nausea or vomiting, intolerance to light and sound, confusion, and skin rash. The condition is often fatal. Dr. Moran's description of Poe's symptoms is not completely inconsistent with meningitis and it has been proposed that after a lifetime of exposure to TB, he developed a form of tubercular meningitis (TBM). However, this particularly uncommon disease is usually *progressive* with signaling symptoms such as deafness and partial paralysis, neither of which have been associated with Poe. Though it should be noted that the Baltimore City's Board of Health, to which all deaths were reported, included no such category in their 1849 Report of Interments, instead they listed sixty-seven fatalities from "inflammation of the brain."

MERCURY POISONING (1997)

(Ritchie C. Shoemaker, "Diagnosis of *Pfiesteria*-Human Illness Syndrome," *Maryland Medical Journal* 46 [November/December 1997]: 521–23.) Mercury at abnormal levels is toxic to the human body and can damage organs including the brain. Symptoms of overexposure can include anxiety and irritability, numbness in the extremities, physical tremors, ataxia (impaired muscle coordination), nausea or vomiting, and difficulty with vision, hearing, and speech. Shoemaker theorized that Poe, in an effort to avoid being stricken with cholera, ingested too much calomel (mercury chloride), then an accepted treatment for the illness. Shoemaker then infers that Poe suffered mercury intoxication and ultimately, kidney failure. In 2006, surviving samples of Poe's hair was tested for the presence of toxic metals, including mercury. According to the Edgar Allan Poe Society of Baltimore, notable changes were registered in his exposure over time; however, it was found that the level of mercury detected was 30 times below that associated with poisoning.

MURDER (1998)

(John Evangelist Walsh, *Midnight Dreary: The Mysterious Death of Edgar Allan Poe* [New Brunswick, NJ: Rutgers University Press, 1998], 119–20.) In his book, John Walsh claims that Poe was followed on his final trip from Richmond by the brothers of Elmira Shelton who, because of opposition to the imminent marriage to their sister, assaulted Poe and forced a lethal quantity alcohol into him. As a matter of process, Poe would have (eventually) been examined after his arrival at Baltimore City and Marine Hospital, in order to establish the cause of his condition. Beating injuries, or any indication of foul play, were reported to authorities and would have triggered an inquest if resulting in death. A search, conducted by the author in 2019, of coroner inquests for Baltimore City during 1849 produced no document on Poe. (See also Poisoning.)

NERVOUS BREAKDOWN/EXHAUSTION (1924)

(Sherwin Cody, *Poe: Man, Poet and Creative Thinker* [New York: Boni and Liveright, 1924], 25.) "Nervous Breakdown" is a nonclinical term often used to describe an episode in which an individual's mental distress prevents their function in everyday life and is characterized by uncontrolled anxiety or panic attacks, crying, depression, physical and mental lethargy, as well as thoughts

216   *Appendix A*

of suicide. In his biographical study of the poet, Sherwin Cody opined that "Poe died of nervous break-down rather than the effects of over-indulgence in intoxicants . . . what was supposed to be delirium tremens is more likely to have been attacks of insanity." While this condition usually cannot kill a person directly, the hyperventilation and irregular heart rate experienced during these hysterical outbursts to an individual with underlying health issues can indeed be dangerous.

PATHOLOGIC ALCOHOL REACTION (2009)

(*Powell*) *Pathologische Reaktionsweise auf Alkoholica*, identified and documented in 1869 by Dr. Richard von Krafft-Ebing, is "an exceedingly rare psychosis triggered by the brain's singular metabolism of alcohol," the predisposition to such can be caused by heredity or brain injury. Symptoms can include a spontaneous insanity, disorientation, and other behaviors inconsistent with the sufferer's normal character. In his book, Michael Powell subscribed to the belief that Poe had an unusual sensitivity to liquor, and suffered from a pathologic reaction to it, subjecting him to disorientation and diminished immunity which brought exposure to opportunistic infections such as pneumonia. The evidence of Poe's alcoholic sensitivity (and its immediate effect on him) is largely anecdotal, from Poe himself and sympathetic acquaintances wanting to mitigate his reputation; however, the possibility has not been conclusively disproved.

PHRENITIS (1849)

An antiquated term (even in 1849) referring to the frenzy or delirium *caused by* an inflammation of the brain or meninges and as such, was one of several euphemisms for delirium tremens. A surviving federal census record of deaths occurring within the Third Ward of Baltimore City during 1849 lists an October entry for "E. A. Poe" in which the cause is entered as "Phrenitis." Although records kept by Baltimore City's Board of Health, to which all deaths were reported, included categories for mania, as well as *mania-a-potu* (delirium tremens), there was no listing for phrenitis in 1849.

PNEUMONIA (2009)

(*Powell*, 32.) Symptoms include coughing, colored mucus, fever, sweating, chills, shaking, labored breathing, fatigue, and confusion, a few of which Poe exhibited. Powell believed that upon his arrival at the hospital, Poe was placed in the indigent ward where he laid undisturbed (and untreated) until his death which resulted from pneumonia or its complications ("cardiopulmonary collapse" as he stated in a 2008 interview).

In his 1978 *Maryland Historical Magazine* feature, "Tales of Ratiocination: The Death and Burial of Edgar Allan Poe," Charles Scarlett Jr. also claims "lobar pneumonia" as the cause of Poe's death. Although not seen as a bacterial infection, pneumonia was recognized in 1849 (Baltimore City's Board of Health list of interments show six deaths from pneumonia). As an actual cause of death, pneumonia has a degree of probability; however, Powell's suggestion of (total) neglect has not been substantiated. In addition, no mention was made of coughing, mucal discharges, or chills in Dr. Moran's November 1849 report to Maria Clemm. (See also Pathologic Alcohol Reaction for a related cause.)

POISONING

Indications of arsenic poisoning (arsenicosis) include abdominal pain, nausea and vomiting, muscle cramps, abnormal heart rate, numbness in the extremities, vertigo, confusion, and delirium—symptoms not completely inconsistent with those exhibited by Poe during his final hours. As no external physical injuries to Poe were mentioned at the hospital, poisoning is left as another possible method of attack. Toxins such as arsenic, cyanide, and strychnine had practical uses during Poe's time and were readily available in many forms. In 2006, surviving hair samples from Poe (and his wife) were subjected to analysis by mass spectrometry to detect the presence of toxins, including arsenic. Although the test found levels of the toxin in both samples, they were below that associated with arsenic poisoning (researchers believed that the family ingested similar levels of arsenic from environmental sources, such as their drinking water). It should be observed however that a lethal quantity of poison swallowed by Poe during his final days may not have had time to infiltrate hair extending above the scalp from where the test examples were undoubtedly taken.

218   *Appendix A*

PORPHYRIA (1989)

(Leland S. Rickman and Choong R. Kim, "'Poe-phyria,' Madness, and the Fall of the House of Usher," *JAMA* 261, no. 6 [February 10, 1989]: 863–64.) Named in 1874, Porphyria is a designation given to a group of disorders that result from an excess of porphyrin (essential for the function of hemoglobin), high levels of which can cause excruciating, and even hideous, symptoms. The disease, usually inherited, is suffered in the form of attacks that vary in duration. According to the Mayo Clinic, "There are two general categories of porphyria: acute, which mainly affects the nervous system, and cutaneous, which mainly affects the skin. However there are some forms of the disorder that involve both nervous system and skin. Acute porphyrias can be life-threatening if an attack isn't promptly treated." Symptoms can include extreme sensitivity to light, skin irritations and discolorations, itching, abnormal hair growth in the affected areas of the skin and scalp, abdominal pain, dark or discolored urine, nausea and vomiting, numbness in the extremities, anxiety, confusion, and paranoia. Doctors Leland and Kim suggest that porphyria was the inherited "constitutional and family evil" visited on all members of the Usher family; and because Poe's description of the disorder in his short story was so accurate, he had the intimate knowledge of one who was suffering from it. However, there is no record of the disease's peculiar symptoms in Poe or any mention thereof by those who knew him in life or by Dr. Moran at his death.

RABIES (1996)

(R. Michael Benitez, "Case Records of the University of Maryland and Baltimore VA Medical Centers: A 39-Year-Old Man with Mental Status Change," *Maryland Medical Journal* 45 [September 1996]: 765–69.) Rabies is a deadly encephalitic virus that is usually contracted through the bite or saliva of an infected animal. Symptoms include fever, headache, confusion, hallucination, hydrophobia (fear of water), and hyperactivity. A doctor of cardiology, Michael Benitez claimed that Poe exhibited symptoms of hydrophobia when in the hospital. However, his study relies on flawed information some of which was derived from Dr. Moran who at first indicated that Poe had difficulty swallowing liquids. But then in two separate accounts given later, Moran stated that when administering water and beef-tea to Poe, he drank "without any trouble." Without the presence of hydrophobia, the probability of encephalitic rabies as a cause is negligible.

SUICIDE

After Thomas White's first dismissal of Poe from the *Southern Literary Messenger* in 1835, the magazine publisher reported it to his friend Lucian Minor: "He is in addition [to being a drinker] the victim of melancholy. I should not be at all astonished to hear that he had been guilty of suicide." Perhaps the strongest evidence that Poe was capable of it came from the poet himself who, according to Dr. Moran, when asked on his deathbed about his friends replied, "the best thing his best friend could do would be to blow out his brains with a pistol." Poe also claimed, a year earlier, an attempt to take his own life by overdosing on laudanum, which establishes contemplation even if untrue. Although there can be little doubt that Poe suffered bouts of clinical depression, especially during the years following his wife's passing, to prove his death a suicide, intent as well as the method must be established. (See also Bipolar Disorder.)

SYPHILIS (1997)

(A. G. Gordon, "The Death of Edgar Allan Poe—A Case of Syphilis?" *Maryland Medical Journal* 46, no. 6 [July 1997]: 289–90.) Syphilis is a bacterial infection usually spread by sexual contact and if left untreated can spread to the brain and nervous system (neurosyphilis). Later stage symptoms include paranoia, anxiety, mood swings and changes in personality, severe headaches, ataxia (difficulty with muscle coordination), paralysis, and lingual dementia. Dr. Gordon theorized that Poe had been infected with neurosyphilis, or general paresis, when he was younger and that his terminal symptoms were consistent with the disease. To bolster his claim, he pointed to Lorine Pruette's suggestion that Poe's brain lesion was the result of a syphilitic infection, and also to Poe's protagonist in "The Tell-Tale Heart" and his description of sensitivities conferred by the "disease." In rebuttal, Dr. R. Michael Benitez disputed the symptomatic similarities Poe displayed in the hospital and also pointed out that both forms of the disease Gordon was proposing were "chronic in nature and do not generally cause the acute decline in health which has been associated with Mr. Poe's final days."

TETANUS (1997)

(James E. Starrs, "The Death of Edgar Allan Poe: A Cardiologist Goes to the Heart of It," *Scientific Sleuthing Review* 21, no. 2 [Summer 1997]: 1–5.) The

220   *Appendix A*

tetanus bacillus enters through a break in the skin to cause severe and painful muscle contractions, usually within two weeks of infection. Preliminary
symptoms can include fever, sweating, headache, trouble swallowing, and
abnormal heart rate. In a 1997 magazine article, writer James Starrs believed
that cardiologist, Michael Benitez, in his diagnosis of rabies, overlooked "the
real possibility" of tetanus. Although Starr saw Poe's symptoms as indicators
of the disease, his position seems to be predicated on Dr. Moran's *inconsistent* assertion that the poet had difficulty swallowing. The Baltimore Board of
Health attributed six fatalities to tetanus in 1849 but there was no mention at
the time of this well-recognized condition in association with Poe.

TOXIC DISORDER (1970)

(Birgit Bramsback, "The Final Illness and Death of Edgar Allan Poe: An
Attempt at Reassessment," *Studia Neophilologica* 42, no. 1 [1970]: 57.) In
her article written for the journal identified above, Bramsback refers to the
cause of Poe's death as a *toxic disorder,* embracing the theory of delirium
tremens. But she mistakenly believed the condition is triggered by a single
alcoholic indulgence or develops without a previous excess. Apparently
searching for an exculpatory explanation, she also indicated that it could have
resulted from an acute infection. Indeed there are many illnesses that can trig-
ger derangement; however *delirium tremens* is usually the consequence of
alcohol deprivation to one that has developed a chemical dependency.

TUBERCULOSIS (1953)

(Haldeen Braddy, *Glorious Incense: The Fulfillment of Edgar Allan Poe*
[Washington, DC: Scarecrow Press, 1953], 184.) Pulmonary tuberculosis is a
bacterial infection of the lungs acquired from the aerosol emittances (coughs,
sneezes, shouts, etc.) of an infected individual. Symptoms include persistent
coughing, chest pain, fever, night sweats, chills, fatigue, and progressive
weight loss; many sufferers cough blood from pulmonary hemorrhages. The
condition is usually fatal if untreated. In his book, Braddy theorized that
Poe's death was brought about by the confluence of tuberculosis and alcoholism. He points to the concurring opinion of Dr. Ernest Reuter of Antonio,
Texas, and also to the inaccurate notice appearing in the *New York Morning Express* of December 15, 1846, stating that both Poe and his wife were
"dangerously ill with consumption." Living among tuberculosis sufferers in
close, intimate settings Poe could not have escaped exposure; however, most

of those infected with TB remain disease-free through a natural (perhaps prenatal) immunity.

It has been proposed (by Carole M. Shaffer-Koros in her *First Wednesday Luncheon* series, October 2, 2019, paper, "The Mysterious Death of Edgar Allan Poe," at Echo Lake Country Club, Westfield, New Jersey) that Poe's drinking reactivated a dormant tuberculosis; however, in any of its forms it is difficult to believe the disease would have gone unnoticed, especially by the one stricken. During a time when TB was pandemic no mention was made of its symptoms by *doctors* examining Poe after his wife's death; this includes the several statements made by Dr. Moran who later seemed keen to find an exculpatory cause of death. (See also Meningitis.)

WERNICKE ENCEPHALOPATHY (2014)

Symptoms include ataxia (lack of muscle control), delirium, memory loss, abnormal eye movement, and coma. Wernicke Encephalopathy (WE) is a life-threatening condition caused by alcohol abuse and a resulting thiamine deficiency. This theory was discounted by University of Maryland cardiologist Dr. Michael Benitez, who wrote (in 1995) that because WE is generally associated with ocular palsy, and is "generally progressive rather than relapsing," it was an unlikely cause of Poe's death. There is indeed no record of Poe exhibiting these symptoms over a period of time.

Appendix B

Timeline of Poe's Final Days

Precious little is known of Edgar Allan Poe's final movements within Baltimore City during the days before his discovery there on October 3, 1849. The brief timeline below is provided as a quick reference for the reader and includes only what has been substantiated.

September 27–29: Bound for Philadelphia, Poe departs Richmond, Virginia, aboard one of three steam packets: the *Augusta* (September 27 at 5:30 a.m.), the *Curtis Peck* (September 29 at 5:30 a.m.), or the *Columbus* (September 29 at 4 p.m.). Passage on either the *Augusta* or *Curtis Peck* would have required a transfer to the steamer *Jewess* or *Herald* respectively at Norfolk, while the *Columbus* sailed directly to Baltimore.

September 28–30: Poe lands in Baltimore aboard one of three steam packets: the *Jewess* at approximately 7 a.m. on September 28, the *Herald* at approximately 7 a.m. on September 30, or the *Columbus* at approximately 2 p.m., on the same day. If aboard either of the first two vessels, Poe would have disembarked at the foot of Spear's Wharf (Pratt Street), while the *Columbus* docked at the Light Street wharf on the west side of the harbor.

September 28–30: Poe's disembarkation in Baltimore City is unobserved but he may have given a piece of luggage to a porter at the boat dock. His intentions, whether to immediately board a Philadelphia-bound train or to stay over in the city, are unknown. If taking a train north, Poe would first have to appear at the Philadelphia, Wilmington & Baltimore Railroad ticket depot on Pratt Street and then board a departing train from their terminal almost one mile to the east.

223

224   *Appendix B*

September 28–30: After arriving in Baltimore, Poe may have attempted to call on his friend Nathan C. Brooks at his home at 270 Lexington Street, which would suggest that he did not immediately board the train to Philadelphia that day.

September 28–October 2: Poe disappears and his movements within (or beyond) the city remain unknown. Depending on the date of his arrival, he could have been on the streets for a period of five days.

October 3: Poe is discovered in the afternoon at Gunners' Hall, a tavern in the Old Town section of Baltimore City—it is indicated that he was found sitting *inside* the saloon. Semiconscious, he is conveyed to Baltimore City and Marine Hospital where his identity may not have been immediately established. His condition is believed by those at the hospital to be the result of excessive drinking and he is admitted.

October 4–6: Poe remains in the hospital; his room location and the level of care he receives is not certain. A cousin, Neilson Poe, may have attempted to visit him on or before October 5, but would claim that he was turned away. Visits or communication with the hospital by other relatives have never been substantiated.

October 7: In the early morning, Poe dies at Baltimore City and Marine Hospital from a cause (or causes) that have *become* clouded—whether he articulated any words of coherency or was attended at the time of his death has not been proven. Arrangements are made for his burial the following day by the hospital's administrator, Dr. John J. Moran, and Poe's relatives.

October 8: An open coffin containing Poe's body appears to have been exhibited at the hospital during the morning and early afternoon. At approximately 3 p.m., Poe's coffin leaves the hospital and, followed by a small cortege, is conveyed to the Westminster Presbyterian Cemetery for burial. After an unusually brief ritual witnessed by no more than eight people, Poe's body is interred at the north end of the family lot belonging to David Poe Sr.

Appendix C

Notes on Relevant Individuals Mentioned in the Text

ALLAN, JOHN (1780–1834). Scottish-born Allan emigrated to Richmond, Virginia, sometime around 1794 and after partnering with Charles Ellis to establish an importing business there he married Frances Keeling Valentine (1785–1829) in 1803. When Edgar Allan Poe was orphaned in 1811, the childless couple assumed his care and upbringing but did not formally adopt him. Although not rich at the time, Allan doted on Poe and provided him with a superior education that included schools in England while the family was living abroad. Allan and his family returned to Richmond and five years later (1825) John inherited most of his American uncle's estate to become one of the wealthiest men in Virginia. His guardianship of Poe had grown increasingly contentious by then, but Allan still allowed his ward to attend the University of Virginia. When the undisciplined adolescent accrued enormous gambling debts at the college, Allan refused their assumption and removed Edgar Poe from the school—the episode resulting in their break. After Poe left the family, his beloved foster-mother died and John Allan remarried a woman who provided him with children, all of which effectively severed his ties to Poe.

BROOKS, NATHAN COVINGTON (1809–1898). Maryland-born, Brooks was by avocation an educator, school principal, and administrator. With Dr. Joseph Snodgrass in 1838, he published the short-lived *American Museum of Science, Literature, and the Arts* in Baltimore to which Poe contributed "Ligeia" and "The Haunted Palace." Poe may have attempted to call on Brooks during his final days in Baltimore.

BROWNE, WILLIAM HAND (1828–1912). Browne was a Baltimore native who received a medical degree from the University of Maryland but pursued

225

226   *Appendix C*

a literary career instead, becoming an author, magazine editor, historian, and professor of literature. Also a Poe enthusiast, he became a key resource and correspondent to John Ingram when the latter was writing his redemptive biography of the poet.

CARTER, JOHN FREDERICK, MD (1825–1905). A practicing physician and an acquaintance of the Mackenzie family who had raised Poe's sister Rosalie, Carter befriended the poet during his visit to Richmond, Virginia, in 1849. He claimed that Poe visited his office on the final evening before his departure for Philadelphia.

CARTER, WILLIAM GIBBON, MD (1825–1881). Carter was the brother of Dr. John Carter and husband of Susan Archer Talley's sister, Eliza. He spent time with Poe during his final visit to Richmond and attended him when he suffered an attack of delirium tremens there.

CHIVERS, THOMAS HOLLEY, DR. (1809–1858). Chivers was a well-born Georgian who after receiving a medical degree in 1830, turned to literary pursuits and poetry in particular. An admirer of Poe, he frequently corresponded with the poet whose main interest in *him* seemed to be as a financial backer for his *Stylus* magazine project. Chivers became a posthumous defender of Poe but claimed that "The Raven" and "Ulalume" were plagiarized from his works.

CLARKE, THOMAS COTTRELL (1801–1874). Clarke was a Philadelphia publisher who befriended Poe during his time in the city and agreed to become his partner in *The Stylus* magazine. A temperance observer, he eventually withdrew from the project, perhaps after a drinking spree of Poe's was communicated to him. Yet Clarke was among those who defended Poe after his death.

CLEMM, HENRY (1818–1839?). Little is currently known about Maria Clemm's son who was apparently living with her in Baltimore when Poe was also a member of the family. It is believed that at the time of his family's departure for Richmond (1835) he stayed behind in Baltimore while working in a stonecutter's yard, but by early 1836 returned to sea. In a letter to his second cousin, George W. Poe, in 1839, Edgar Poe included a genealogical table that indicated Henry was then still alive.

CLEMM, MARIA POE (1790–1871). Maria (pronounced "Mariah") was the sister of Edgar's father, David Poe Jr. In 1817, she married Baltimore widower

Notes on Relevant Individuals Mentioned in the Text 227

William Clemm Jr. with whom she had three children: Henry (1818–1839?), Virginia Maria (1820–1822), and Virginia Elizabeth (1822–1847). William Clemm Jr. died in 1826 leaving no estate to Maria who was then also caring for her invalided mother, Elizabeth Cairnes Poe. Around 1831, she also took in her nephew, Edgar Poe, who she came to view as a son even before he married her daughter. After Virginia's death, Edgar and Maria remained together while continuing a hand-to-mouth existence. When Poe died, she assumed (without authority) the executorship of his "estate," consisting only of his written works, which did not rescue her financially. Maria died at the renamed Church Home Hospital and Infirmary in Baltimore, the same building in which Poe spent his last days.

CLEMM, VIRGINIA ELIZA (1822–1847). Virginia was the third child born to William Clemm Jr. (1779–1826) and Maria Poe, Edgar Poe's aunt. When Poe permanently joined his aunt's family in 1831, Virginia was only eight years old and being homeschooled by her mother. Poe's emotional dependence on Virginia and Maria grew to the point that he married his cousin, then at age thirteen, to prevent his separation from the family. While they were living in Philadelphia in January 1842, Virginia suffered a lung hemorrhage that was indicative of pulmonary tuberculosis to which she ultimately succumbed in 1847. The depth of Poe's affection for her and the loss he felt at her death is revealed in the beautiful lines of "Annabel Lee," completed two years later.

CLEMM, WILLIAM T. D. (1814–1895). Tennessee-born, Reverend Clemm was a minister of the Methodist Episcopal Church and a cousin (not uncle) of Poe's wife, Virginia. He officiated at Poe's funeral and maintained that the poet died from delirium tremens.

CULLEN, WILLIAM M., MD (1827–d. unknown). Cullen (or Cullin) received a medical degree from the Washington Medical College (Baltimore) in 1851 and appears to have been serving an internship at Baltimore City and Marine Hospital during the time of Poe's death. After the hospital's administrator, Dr. John J. Moran, made public statements in 1875 describing Poe's final hours, Cullen came forward to repudiate them. Moran would later affirm Cullen's presence at the hospital when Poe was a patient.

DIDIER, EUGENE LEMOINE (1838–1913). Lifelong Baltimorean, Didier was an author and magazine writer whose father, Henry Didier Jr., had taken Poe's older brother under his wing and for a time employed him at his "importing" firm of *D'Arcy and Didier*. Before her death, Eugene befriended

228   *Appendix C*

Maria Clemm after which he produced an early (and considerably inaccurate) biography of the poet, among other works.

D'UNGER, ROBERT, MD (1824?–1908). Maryland-born D'Unger was working for the daily newspaper, the *Baltimore Patriot and Commercial Gazette*, and was first introduced to Edgar Poe in 1846 while at local watering holes for journalists. D'Unger would claim other encounters in subsequent years. Later in life, after getting a medical degree and developing an interest in alcoholism he would volunteer observations of Poe's drinking habits.

ELLET, ELIZABETH FRIES LUMMIS (1818–1877). A published writer and poet, Ellet was one of the New York bluestockings that had begun a literary flirtation with Edgar Poe after the publication of "The Raven." Although married, she apparently felt herself in competition with Frances Osgood for Poe's attention and after his rejection of her (Ellet), initiated a scandal that saw him publicly disgraced and shunned in the city's social circles.

ENGLISH, THOMAS DUNN (1819–1902). By the time of his first encounter with Poe in 1839, English had acquired a medical degree that he would later match with a law credential. Yet he first pursued a career in literature instead, having some success in getting his poetry and tales published. When Poe later attacked him in print, English answered with libelous accusations which brought a successful lawsuit from Poe. Although English remained one of Poe's most vocal enemies, the author and politician defended him (after his death) against allegations of drug use.

EVELETH, GEORGE WASHINGTON (1819–1908). Although the pair never met, Eveleth was one of Edgar Poe's first disciples. The Maine native began an ongoing correspondence with Poe in 1845 while Poe was editing the *Broadway Journal*. Eveleth's enthusiasm did not end with Poe's death as evidenced by his communications with Sarah Whitman, Rufus Griswold, and at least two of the poet's biographers.

FITZGERALD, OSCAR PENN (1829–1911). Fitzgerald's early career was in journalism but he would later become a Methodist clergyman. As a young, twenty-year-old writer for the *Richmond Examiner* in 1849, he attended Poe's final lecture in Richmond and later gave his impressions of the poet to Professor James A. Harrison.

FRANCIS, JOHN WAKEFIELD, MD (1789–1861). Wakefield was a prominent New York physician, author, and patron of the arts who befriended Poe

Notes on Relevant Individuals Mentioned in the Text   229

(first meeting him in 1837 at a dinner given by New York book sellers) and attended him during his time in that city. When examining him at the home of Marie Louise Shew in May 1848, he believed Poe was suffering from heart disease.

FULLER, HIRAM (1814–1880). By 1846, Fuller had become a vociferous critic of Edgar Poe and as editor of the New York daily paper, *Evening Mirror*, used it to wage a relentless war on the poet. When Fuller imprudently printed a libelous attack on Poe by Thomas Dunn English, Poe sued the editors of the publication and was awarded $225 in damages (plus legal costs). Fuller would remain Poe's implacable enemy.

GILDERSLEEVE, BASIL LANNEAU (1831–1924). A Princeton graduate and a professor of ancient literature at Johns Hopkins University, Gildersleeve was in Richmond during the time of Poe's final visit where he sighted Poe "repeatedly" and was among those attending his last lecture at the Exchange Hotel.

GLENN, WILLIAM J. (1821–1902). A tailor and lifelong temperance advocate, Glenn was a member of the Shockoe Hill branch of the Sons of Temperance and as its president in 1849, administered the oath of abstinence to Poe before he left Richmond that autumn.

GOVE, MARY NEAL (1810–1884). A survivor of an abusive marriage, Gove became a woman's health reform advocate, writer, and novelist. After a visit to the Poes' cottage at Fordham in 1846, she called attention to the family's impoverished condition and later wrote about it in a novel and magazine articles.

GRAHAM, GEORGE REX (1813–1894). After first acquiring a law degree, Graham became a Philadelphia magazine editor and publishing entrepreneur. He founded *Graham's Magazine* there in 1840 and employed Poe as his editor the following year. After Poe left his magazine, he continued an amicable relationship with the poet, accepting (and paying for) his contributions. Following Poe's death, Graham became one of his vocal defenders.

GRISWOLD, RUFUS WILMOT (1815–1857). Journalist and anthologist, Griswold first met Edgar Allan Poe in 1841 while he was an editor of *Graham's Magazine*. After Poe publicly criticized his anthology, *The Poets and Poetry of America*, Griswold formed a deep hatred of the poet that he hid beneath a veneer of civility. Immediately after Poe's death, Maria Clemm

230   *Appendix C*

assumed his executorship and directed Griswold to superintend a collection of her nephew's works. Although he did a competent job of organizing and editing the collection, Griswold (eventually) added a surreptitiously malicious memoir of Poe that employed exaggerations and forged documents. The biography stood as the only readily accessible account of Poe's life until 1875, by which time it had succeeded in disseminating a patently negative perception of the poet's personality and habits.

HERRING, ELIZABETH REBECCA (1815–1889). Elizabeth was the daughter of Henry Herring and Elizabeth "Eliza" Poe (1792–1822), the sister of Edgar Poe's father. Poe developed a romantic attraction to her (after his aunt's death) which was disapproved by the remarried Herring and his family. She, however, maintained a fondness for her cousin, visiting him in Philadelphia and New York, as well as claiming to be among those attending his burial.

HERRING, HENRY (1792–1868). Herring was a Maryland native that married Edgar Poe's aunt, Elizabeth Poe, in 1814, and later became a successful lumber dealer in Baltimore. Being an active member of the Whig political party and well known at its headquarters at Gunners' Hall, Herring was one of those called upon for Poe's rescue when he was found there in 1849. He was also among the small contingent at the poet's burial.

HEWITT, JOHN HILL (1801–1890). Hewitt was a nineteenth-century songwriter of some renown, but it was as an editor that he encountered Poe, first as critic of his 1929 collection, *Al Aaraaf, Tamerlane, and Minor Poems*, and then as a competitor in a creative writing contest that his publication promoted. Although Hewitt seems to have never accepted Poe's genius, he was invited to attend the dedication of the poet's monument.

HIRST, HENRY BECK (1813–1874). Hirst was a lawyer and natural history enthusiast, but it is as a minor poet and frequent companion of Poe's during his Philadelphia period that he is chiefly remembered. In later years, after Poe's death, he became a habitué of absinthe that apparently caused his insanity. That Hirst had acquired a manuscript copy of "Annabel Lee" would indicate that he met with Poe during his last visit to Philadelphia.

INGRAM, JOHN HENRY (1842–1916). Ingram was an English writer and biographer who, in 1880, produced the first scholarly examination of Poe's life. In writing his sympathetic (and factually hamstrung) biography, he accumulated an enormous amount of original Poe manuscripts

Notes on Relevant Individuals Mentioned in the Text 231

and correspondence, a collection of which he endowed to the University of Virginia.

KENNEDY, JOHN PENDLETON (1795–1870). Baltimore lawyer, biographer, novelist, and Secretary of Navy (1852–1853), Kennedy was principally responsible for the conferral of the *Baltimore Saturday Visiter* literary award to Edgar Allan Poe in 1833. In ensuing years, Kennedy also offered Poe material assistance and facilitated his first employment in professional literature.

LANE, THOMAS HENRY (1815–1900). Lane was a New York magazine publisher who agreed to help Poe with the floundering *Broadway Journal* but after only a month, served as the publication's liquidator. Lane would also claim that an inebriated Poe spent a night at his uncle's Philadelphia home during the final trip north from Richmond.

LEWIS, ESTELLE ANNA ROBINSON, MRS. (1824–1880). Baltimore-born, Mrs. Lewis was an ambitious but unremarkable poetess who with her husband, attorney Sylvanus D. Lewis, resided near Edgar Poe in New York. Responding to the public attention given to Poe's desperate poverty in 1846, she apparently leveraged financial assistance into critical favor of her work. At the time of Poe's death, Maria Clemm (Poe's aunt) had become dependent on the Lewises who encouraged and advised Clemm in the pursuit of the poet's "estate."

LEWIS, SYLVANUS D. (1826?–1882). Lewis was a New York attorney who facilitated his wife's (Estelle Anna Robinson) ambitions as a poetess. In that endeavor, the couple befriended Poe who was induced to favorably notice Mrs. Lewis's works. After Poe's death, Mr. Lewis acted on behalf of Maria Clemm to secure the services of Rufus Griswold as editor of the poet's works.

LIPPARD, GEORGE (1822–1854). Pennsylvania native, Lippard was a social reformer and labor advocate, as well as a successful writer of historical and moralistic fiction. Although thirteen years younger, he became a disciple of Poe, befriended him during his time in Philadelphia, and rescued him from the streets there on his final visit.

LOCKE, JANE ERMINA STARKWEATHER, MRS. (1805–1859). Locke was a married housewife and one of those responding to the public notice given to Poe's desperate living conditions in 1847 by beginning an adulatory correspondence. When lecturing in her hometown of Lowell, Massachusetts,

232   *Appendix C*

the following year, Poe stayed at her home during which he began a flirtation with her neighbor, Nancy Richmond (also married). Embittered by Poe's transferred attentions, Locke became his vocal detractor.

LONGFELLOW, HENRY WADSWORTH (1807–1882). During Edgar Poe's time, Longfellow became America's most beloved poet. However, Poe nurtured a lingering resentment of what he thought was the inordinate attention given to the New Englander and publicly criticized his work as being imitative. His campaign succeeded in garnering attention to Poe and the publications for which he worked, but also added members to his growing list of enemies.

MACKENZIE, JANE SCOTT (1783–1865). Jane and her husband, William Mackenzie, fostered Poe's sister, Rosalie, after the death of her parents. With the death of her husband, Jane became the head of her family, eventually moving into a large house, on the outskirts of Richmond, that she had built. Known as "Duncan Lodge," Poe spent significant time there during his final visits to that city.

MACKENZIE, JOHN HAMILTON (1806–1875). John was one of the ten children born to William and Jane Mackenzie. After the death of his father, he became the guardian of Poe's sister, Rosalie, whom the family had been caring for since 1811.

MACKENZIE, THOMAS GILLIAT, MD (1821–1867). "Gay young Dr. Tom," as Susan Weiss would refer to him, was a member of the Mackenzie family that fostered Poe's sister, Rosalie. The doctor was one of those said to have attended Poe after he suffered an attack of delirium tremens during his final visit to Richmond.

MITCHELL, JOHN KEARSLEY, MD (1792–1858). Virginia-born and a graduate from the University of Pennsylvania School of Medicine, Kearsley was also an educator and minor poet. He was an acquaintance of Poe prior to treating him (for an unspecified condition) and his wife during the Philadelphia period. Kearsley relabeled Virginia's tuberculosis diagnosis as bronchitis, possibly for the benefit of the sufferer.

MONKUR, JOHN CAVENDISH SMITH, MD (1800–1867). University of Maryland School of Medicine graduate, Monkur was a professor on the faculty of the Washington Medical College (Baltimore) from 1836 through 1851. Moran would claim that he consulted Monkur at the time of Poe's death

Notes on Relevant Individuals Mentioned in the Text 233

and that after an examination of the poet, the professor diagnosed his condition as encephalitis.

MORAN, JOHN J., MD (1820–1888). Maryland native and University of Maryland School of Medicine graduate, Moran was the administrator of the Baltimore City and Marine Hospital at the time of Poe's death there. He later exploited his involvement by writing and lecturing on Poe's final days but the degree of his interaction with the poet has never been established.

MOTT, VALENTINE, MD (1785–1865). Eminent surgeon and professor at the University Medical College of New York, Mott reputedly examined Poe around March 1847 and confirmed the diagnosis of "brain lesion" made by Marie Louise Shew.

OSGOOD, FRANCES SARGENT LOCKE, MRS. (1811–1850). The married Frances Osgood was a poetess and popular member of the New York literati at the time of Edgar Poe's peak celebrity. She became enamored with Poe and the two began an acquaintance and public literary courtship of which there is no evidence of physical intimacy. Although the relationship was approved by Poe's wife, Virginia, they were estranged after Osgood's rival, Elizabeth Ellet, exposed the pair to innuendo and scandal.

PATTERSON, EDWIN H. N. (1828–1880). Patterson was an avid admirer of Edgar Allan Poe and on his twenty-first birthday came into a substantial inheritance which included his father's weekly newspaper, the *Oquawka Spectator*, published in that Illinois town. He contacted Poe with an offer to install him as the sole editor of a new national literary magazine to which the poet seemed to be in accord.

POE, DAVID, JR. (1784–1811?). David Poe Jr., Edgar's father, relinquished the study of law to pursue a career in the theater. There he met and married Mrs. Elizabeth Arnold Hopkins, who had been widowed only five months earlier. Unlike his English-born wife who had been groomed for the stage, David struggled with the profession and there is sufficient evidence that he developed a drinking habit. His disappearance from the historical record in 1809 has perplexed biographers as to the time and place of his death, and whether he ultimately abandoned his wife (and their three children).

POE, ELIZABETH ARNOLD (1788–1811). Edgar Poe's mother, "Eliza" Arnold, was English-born and brought to the United States in 1796 by her actress mother who had groomed the child for the theater—Eliza made her

234 *Appendix C*

debut on the American stage that same year. She met and married fellow actor David Poe Jr. in 1806 and subsequently gave birth to three children: William Leonard (1807), Edgar (1809), and Rosalie (1810). At the time of her premature death from tuberculosis, her husband was no longer a member of the family.

POE, NEILSON (1809–1884). Neilson (pronounced "Nelson") was the grandson of George Poe Sr., brother to David Poe Sr. (Edgar's grandfather.) Neilson began his career as a journalist, eventually acquiring the *Baltimore Chronicle*, a daily Whig newspaper. In 1831, he married his first cousin, Josephine Emily Clemm (1808–1889), who was also the half-sister of Virginia Clemm, the wife of Edgar Allan Poe. The attempt by Neilson and his wife to block Edgar Poe's marriage created enmity between the two cousins, Poe writing privately, ". . . I believe him to be the bitterest enemy I have in the world . . ." After divesting of the Chronicle in 1839, he began the practice of law, and would remain in that profession, ultimately receiving an appointment to the Orphans' Court for Baltimore City. After Poe's death, Neilson was drawn reluctantly into the sphere of the poet's growing fame. During the ceremonies for the dedication of Poe's monument in 1875, Neilson was among those asked to speak, giving a brief statement of appreciation on behalf of the Poe family.

POE, ROSALIE MACKENZIE (1810–1874). Like Edgar Poe, his younger sister was at their mother's side in Richmond, Virginia, at the time of her death. Afterward, she was raised by the family of Mr. and Mrs. William Mackenzie, close friends of Poe's foster-parents, the Allans. As Edgar Allan Poe's closest living relative, she became the poet's legal heir after his death, but challenged by Maria Clemm, Rosalie received nothing but personal belongings and perhaps a quantity of Poe's collected works after they were published.

POE, WILLIAM "HENRY" LEONARD (1807–1831). Born in Boston two years before his famous brother, "Henry" was initially raised by his paternal grandparents in Baltimore, although when their custodianship of him began (and ended) is not clear. He was also fostered by Baltimore businessman, Henry Didier, from whom it is believed he acquired his nickname. William shared Edgar's temperament and literary inclination, as well as his brother's propensity to drink. After spending some time at sea, he returned to live with his grandmother's family in Maryland where he died, it is believed, from a comorbidity of alcoholism and tuberculosis.

Notes on Relevant Individuals Mentioned in the Text   235

QUINN, ARTHUR HOBSON (1875–1960). A native Philadelphian, Quinn attended the University of Pennsylvania where he received a PhD and became a professor of English. His academic studies included American drama and literature, and his 1941 biography, *Edgar Allan Poe: A Critical Biography*, remains the most reliable account of the poet's life. Its frequent citation in the text of this work warranted this entry.

RAWLINGS, GEORGE A. (1819?–1869). Rawlings was for many years a train conductor for the Baltimore and Ohio Railroad and claimed to have returned an incapacitated Poe to Baltimore in the fall of 1849 after discovering him on a Philadelphia-bound train that was *not* operated by the B&O.

REYNOLDS, ELMER ROBERT (1846–1907). Chevalier Reynolds (knighted by Italy's King Humbert in 1887) was a co-founder of the Anthropological Society of Washington, DC, and as an amateur historian of the region, also had an interest in Poe. Reynolds had planned to write a biography of the poet in the pursuit of which he corresponded with Robert D'Unger and W. T. D. Clemm, among others.

REYNOLDS, HENRY R. (1810?–1869). Reynolds was a prominent commercial building contractor based in the Old Town section of Baltimore City. Active politically as well as civically, he was appointed an election judge at the Fourth Ward polls where Poe was found. It was reported that Poe deliriously bellowed the name "Reynolds" during his final hours in the hospital; however, the person's identity has never been conclusively established.

RICHMOND, NANCY LOCKE HEYWOOD, MRS. (1820–1898). During a visit to Lowell, Massachusetts, in 1848, Poe met Mrs. Richmond who was a married housewife and mother to whom he developed a deep (and inexplicable) attraction. In surviving letters that Poe wrote during the last year of his life, he seemed obsessed with her, giving her the pet name "Annie" and *apparently* writing for her his rhythmic depiction of death's threshold, "For Annie."

SARTAIN, JOHN (1808–1897). Sartain was an English-born engraver and publisher who met Edgar Poe in 1840 while they were both involved in the Philadelphia magazine trade. Although Sartain may have later enlarged the degree of their friendship, the engraver was one of those who came to Poe's rescue during the poet's final trip through the city in the spring of 1849.

236 *Appendix C*

SHELTON, SARAH ELMIRA, MRS. (1810–1888). As a teenager, "Elmira" lived near the Allan Mansion in Richmond and secretly gave her consent to marry Poe before his departure for the University of Virginia. The engagement was apparently sabotaged by her parents, after which she married Alexander B. Shelton. By the time of Poe's last visit to Richmond, when both she and he were widowed, they ostensibly planned to wed again.

SHEW, MARIE LOUISE (1821–1877). During Poe's time at Fordham, Shew was an unpaid practical nurse and social worker who devoted herself to the care of the poet's wife throughout her final stages of tuberculosis; also ministering to Poe after her death. An artist of some ability (she provided illustrations for her husband's 1844 book, *Water-cure for Ladies*), Shew rendered the postmortem portrait of Virginia.

SMITH, ELIZABETH OAKES (1806–1893). Born in Maine, Smith was an author, editor, and women's rights advocate, but it was as a published poet that she met Poe in New York City at the literary soirees organized by Miss Anna C. Lynch. After Poe's death she numbered among his defenders.

SNODGRASS, JOSEPH EVANS, MD (1813–1880). Like many who received a medical degree during the antebellum period (his from the University of Maryland in 1836), Snodgrass preferred a career in literature instead. As a Baltimore magazine and newspaper editor, he met and maintained a cordial relationship with Edgar Allan Poe. He was also a lifelong temperance and anti-slavery activist but is most remembered for coming to the poet's rescue in Baltimore during his final days. After suffering in poor health for months, Snodgrass died by his own hand.

SPENCE, GEORGE W. (1824–1899). Spence held the office of sexton at the First Presbyterian Church of Baltimore from 1845 to 1873, and in that capacity, superintended the burial of Poe in 1849 at the Westminster Presbyterian Cemetery. During the disinterment and relocation of Poe's remains in 1875, Spence again supervised the proceedings but in a professional role as undertaker.

STARR, MARY (1816?–1887). Philadelphia-born, Mary Starr was living in Baltimore when she began a romantic relationship with Poe after his dismissal from West Point. In her dotage, she offered recollections of the affair and of other claimed encounters with the poet that were published by her nephew two years after her death.

Notes on Relevant Individuals Mentioned in the Text 237

STODDARD, RICHARD HENRY (1825–1903). Editor and writer, Stoddard was a minor poet living in New York City when he met Poe in person (in 1845) after the latter declined to publish a poem that he had submitted to the *Broadway Journal* and rudely ejected the young man from his office there. Heavily influenced by this negative experience, Stoddard later wrote a memoir of Poe that was patterned after Griswold's poisonous account.

THOMAS, FREDERICK WILLIAM (1806–1866). Thomas began his career as an attorney but later became a novelist and amateur poet. He sought Poe's acquaintance and following a visit with him in Philadelphia in 1840 they became frequent correspondents. After securing a political appointment in Washington, DC, as a treasury clerk in 1841, Thomas acted as a facilitator for Poe who desired the same situation in Philadelphia. Poe failed to win the position but the two remained friends. Thomas reportedly left a manuscript memoir of Poe (cited by James Whitty) the whereabouts of which remains unknown.

THOMPSON, JOHN REUBEN (1823–1873). Thompson received a law degree from the University of Virginia in 1845 but pursued a career in literature and journalism instead. He was editor (and became owner) of Richmond, Virginia's *Southern Literary Messenger* during the time of Poe's final two visits to that city. Afterward, he promoted the theory that the poet's death had been the consequence of political kidnapping.

WEISS, SUSAN ARCHER TALLEY (1822–1917). Poet, author, and artist, Weiss was the talented daughter of noted Richmond couple Thomas Talley and Eliza Frances Archer. When Susan met Poe for the first time in 1849, she was totally deaf, having lost her hearing at age nine from ear infections. Later in life, Weiss would write about her encounter with Poe, much of which is imaginative.

WHITE, THOMAS WILLIS (1788–1843). White was the first owner and publisher of the *Southern Literary Messenger*, a monthly periodical ostensibly devoted to literature and the fine arts, and where Edgar Allan Poe found his first employment in the field of professional literature. Although he initially relied on Poe's scholarship, White became increasingly unhappy with his caustic reviews and drinking habits, dismissing him in January 1837 after only fourteen months in his service.

WHITMAN, SARAH HELEN (1803–1878). Born in Providence, Rhode Island, Whitman was already a published poetess when she became

238 *Appendix C*

enthralled with Poe's writings. After the death of his wife, the two began a literary courtship that resulted in a brief wedding engagement broken off by Whitman when she realized the depth of Poe's drinking problem. One of the first to recognize his literary importance, she became Poe's greatest vocal defender immediately following his death.

WILLIS, NATHANIEL PARKER (1806–1867). Willis was a popular American author, poet, and editor who became an admirer of Edgar Poe. When Poe desperately needed work, Willis gave him employment on the *Evening Mirror* and was the first to publish some of his most celebrated works, including "The Raven." Willis became one the Poe's most steadfast defenders after his death.

WILMER, LAMBERT A. (1805?–1863). A Maryland native, Wilmer studied law but became a journalist, author, and publisher instead. During Poe's Baltimore period, he was an intimate friend of the poet and his brother Henry. When Poe later (in 1843) learned that Wilmer had confided to a shared acquaintance about the poet's growing reputation for the bottle, the two fell out. Yet after Edgar's death, Wilmer remained among Poe's staunchest defenders.

Appendix D

Dr. Moran's Letter to Maria Clemm, November 15, 1849

The following is a transcript of a letter sent from Dr. John J. Moran in reply to a distraught Maria Clemm five weeks after Poe' death. As the administrator of the hospital in which Edgar Allan Poe died, this, his first (surviving) written statement concerning the event, remains one of the most critical documents in relation to the poet's death. The original manuscript survives as part of the Edgar Allan Poe Collection held at the Enoch Pratt Free Library in Baltimore, Maryland (Pratt).

Dr. J. J. Moran to Mrs. Clemm.
Balti. City & Marine Hospital, Nov. 15/1849.
Mrs. Clemm,

My Dear Madam,
I take the earliest opportunity of responding to yours of the 9th Inst. which came to hand by yesterday's Mail.
Your deep solicitude, Madam, in reference to the "last moments" of him of whom you write, does not surprise me. It falls to the lot of but few, to enjoy the extensive popularity that was unquestionably his. Wherever talent—mental worth, nay Genius, was prized there "E. A. Poe" had warm friends. To his rarely gifted mind are we indebted for many of the brightest thoughts that adorn our literature to him is Belles Lettres indebted for the purest gems her Casket Contains. "Poe is gone!" How many hearts have heaved a sigh in uttering these three words! How many thousands will yet, and for years to come, lament the premature demise of this truly great man! Nor can there be found, in the list of his enemies (what great man ever lived without them?) one individual, who will withhold from him the meed of praise to which you refer when you speak of his "nobility of Soul." Posterity will not hesitate to

240 *Appendix D*

award him a place in the Catalogue of those whose pens have strewn flowers in the pathway of life—flowers too, whose fragrance will last for the enjoyment of unborn millions, thereby preserving a memorial more lasting than the Sculptor's Chisel or the Art of the Statuary Could ever fabricate or invent. But now for the required intelligence. Presuming you are already aware of the malady of which Mr. Poe died I need only state concisely the particulars of his circumstances from his entrance until his decease.

When brought to the Hospital he was unconscious of his Condition—who brought him or with whom he had been associating. He remained in this Condition from 5. Ock [*sic*] in the afternoon—the hour of his admission—until 3 next morning. This was on the 3rd Oct.

To this state succeeded tremor of the limbs, and at first a busy, but not violent or active delirium—constant talking—and vacant converse with spectral and imaginary objects on the walls. His face was pale and his whole person drenched in perspiration—We were unable to induce tranquility before the second day after his admission.

Having left orders with the nurses to that effect, I was summoned to his bedside so soon as Consciousness supervened, and questioned him in reference to his family—place of residence—relatives &c. But his answers were incoherent & unsatisfactory. He told me, however, he had a Wife in Richmond (which, I have since learned was not the fact.) that he did not know when he left that City or what had become of his trunk of Clothing. Wishing to rally and sustain his now fast sinking hopes I told him I hoped, that in a few days he would be able to enjoy the Society of his friends here, and I would be most happy to Contribute in every possible way to his Ease & Comfort. At this he broke out with much energy, and said the best thing his best friend could do would be to blow out his brains with a pistol—that when he beheld his degradation he was ready to sink in the earth &c. Shortly after giving expression to these words Mr. Poe seemed to dose [*sic*] & I left him for a short time. When I returned I found him in a violent delirium, resisting the efforts of two Nurses to keep him in bed. This state continued until Saturday evening (he was admitted on Wednesday) when he Commenced Calling for one "Reynolds," which he did through the night up to three on Sunday Morning. At this time a very decided change began to affect him. Having become enfeebled from exertion he became quiet and seemed to rest for a short time, then, gently moving his head he said "Lord help my poor Soul" and expired!

This, Madam, is as faithful an account as I am able to furnish from the Record of his Case.

Mrs. Chapman was not with him, but he lacked nothing which the utmost assiduity of Nurses and myself could supply. Indeed we considered Mr. Poe an object of unusual regard.

Medical Men & Students of the House sympathized earnestly with him. Your imperative request urges me to be candid, else I should not have been thus plain. Rather far would I conceal his errors than even hint a fault of his.

His remains were visited by some of the first individuals of the City, many of them anxious to have a lock of his hair. Those who had previously known him pronounced his corpse the most natural they had ever seen. Z. Collins Lee Esq. and Nelson [*sic*] Poe with many other respectible [*sic*] individuals attended his funeral—The Revd. Mr. Clemm of this City attended officially on the occasion.

I have, thus, complied with your request, Madam, and therefore subscribe myself respectfully yours

J. J. Moran, Res. Phys.

Notes

INTRODUCTION

1. The origin and early proponents of the cooping theory can be found in chapter 5 of this book.

2. Among the first who attempted to "canonize" Poe were Elizabeth Oakes Smith, Susan Archer Weiss, and Dr. John J. Moran, individuals who also initiated questions about the poet's cause of death.

3. Thomas Dunn English, "Reminiscence of Poe [Part 01]," *Independent* (New York), October 15, 1896, 1381.

4. John Ostrom, "Poe and the Bottle: A New Appraisal," *Baltimore Sun*, November 30, 1980, SM51. Ostrom wrote that "Poe seems to have escaped the occasions of alcohol" prior to 1835, an assumption perhaps facilitated by the scarcity of extant documentation or reliable eyewitness testimony from that period.

5. John Ward Ostrom, Burton R. Pollin, and Jeffrey A. Savoye, eds., *The Collected Letters of Edgar Allan Poe*, 2 vols. (New York: Gordian Press, 2008) (hereafter *CL*, by volume:page and letter number), 1:263–64, LTR-109, Letter: Poe to Joseph Snodgrass, April 1 1841: "My sensitive temperament could not stand an excitement which was an everyday matter to my companions."

6. Michael A. Powell, *Too Much Moran: Respecting the Death of Edgar Poe* (Eugene, OR: Pacific Rim University Press, 2009), v (hereafter *Powell*, by page), wrote that Poe demonstrated a pathologic reaction to small amounts of alcohol and thus was incapable of sustained periods of drinking.

7. *CL*, 2:641, LTR-259, Letter: Poe to George Eveleth, January 4, 1848. This passage, originally offered to Eveleth only in private, has in recent times been appropriated, out of context, for use on t-shirts, posters, and various souvenirs, and has colored Poe in way that he probably would not have embraced.

8. Perhaps the most determined argument for Poe's abstinence after taking the pledge was presented by Robert C. Hiden in a piece titled "Poe and his Pledge," that appeared in the March 10, 1895, edition of the *Richmond Times*. Yet in a

daguerreotype that was reportedly taken weeks after he made the promise, Poe appears glassy-eyed and impaired.

9. U.S. National Library of Medicine. Delirium Tremens, https://medlineplus .gov/ency/article/000766.htm.

10. Testimony describing Poe's encounters with delirium tremens while in Philadelphia and Richmond appears in chapter 2 of this book.

11. Philip A. Mackowiak, *Post Mortem: Solving History's Great Medical Mysteries* (Philadelphia: American College of Physicians, 2007), 254. Dr. Mackowiak suggests that the panic attack Poe experienced while visiting Sarah Helen Whitman, seven months before beginning his final trip to Richmond, was symptomatic of delirium tremens.

12. In a letter to Maria Clemm five weeks after Poe's death, Moran gave a detailed description of symptoms that are consistent with delirium tremens. See appendix D.

13. John J. Moran, *A Defense of Edgar Allan Poe: Life, Character and Dying Declarations of the Poet* (Washington, DC: William F. Boogher, 1885), 70–71 (hereafter *Moran*, by page).

14. *CL*, 1:13–16, LTR-007, Letter: Poe to John Allan, December 1, 1828. This letter, from Poe to his foster father, establishes the poet's time at Fort Moultrie.

15. Charles H. Bohner, *John Pendleton Kennedy: Gentleman from Baltimore* (Baltimore: Johns Hopkins Press, 1961), 194.

16. Matthew Pearl, "A Poe Death Dossier: Discoveries and Queries in the Death of Edgar Allan Poe: Part I," *Edgar Allan Poe Review* 7, no. 2 (Fall 2006): 4–29.

17. These unsupported accounts of Poe's whereabouts in Baltimore are detailed and sourced in chapter 3 of this book.

18. *CL*, 2:837–38, LTR-332, Letter: Poe to Maria Clemm, September 18, 1849. In Poe's final letter to Maria Clemm, he gave Philadelphia as the first stop on his trip back to New York. In none of his surviving correspondences does he indicate a stopover in Baltimore.

19. New information on George Rawlings, who had worked as a train conductor for the B&O Railroad, can be found in chapter 3.

20. John R. Thompson became the editor of the *Southern Literary Messenger* and met with Poe during his final two visits to Richmond.

21. Mark Dawidziak, *Mystery of Mysteries: The Death and Life of Edgar Allan Poe* (New York: St. Martin's Press, 2023), 182. Dawidziak expressed the consensus view of Poe scholars when he asked, "Can any of the details offered by Moran be trusted?" And then there is this observation made by Jeffrey Savoye on the Poe Society website: "It is one of the great misfortunes of Poe's biography that Dr. Moran left us chiefly recollections that seem to have come more from his imagination than from what actually happened."

22. From the poem, "Dream-Land," by Edgar Allan Poe.

Notes 245

CHAPTER 1

1. Elijah Stansbury, "The Mayor's Message," *Baltimore Sun*, January 16, 1849, 1. The paper printed a transcription of Mayor Elijah Stansbury's January 15 message to the city council which included a grim description of Baltimore: "For many years . . . the peace of the city has been disturbed. Ordinances have been passed . . . to devise some means to stay the violence . . . Life itself has paid the penalty of the riots[:] an innocent victim has been slain at midday in the public streets, firearms freely used, and the peace of various parts of the city entirely destroyed by scenes of the most disgraceful kind."

2. Letter: Neilson Poe to Maria Clemm, October 11, 1849. Original MS held in the Edgar Allan Poe Collection at the Enoch Pratt Free Library, Baltimore, Maryland, https://collections.digitalmaryland.org/digital/collection/poe (hereafter *Pratt*). The first description of the location of Poe's discovery was provided by Neilson Poe, when writing to Maria Clemm two days following Poe's death: "On Wednesday, he was seen and recognised [*sic*] at one of the places of election in old town." The Lombard Street tavern, where Poe was found, was located in the Old Town section of Baltimore. It was also being used as a polling place that day.

3. Edgar Allan Poe, "The Pit and the Pendulum," *The Gift: A Christmas and New Year's Present 1843* (Philadelphia: Carey & Hart, 1843), 135–51.

4. Geddeth Smith, *The Brief Career of Eliza Poe* (Cranbury, NJ: Fairleigh Dickinson University Press, Associated University Presses, 1988), 22. Eliza's mother, having lost her first husband before embarking on her American venture, arrived in Boston in the company of Charles Tubbs but it has not been established whether the two were then already married.

5. Smith, *Brief Career*, 81. The author wrote that Hopkins contracted the mosquito-borne virus before leaving Fredericksburg, or shortly after arriving in Washington, DC.

6. Smith, *Brief Career*, 82.

7. Arthur Hobson Quinn, *Edgar Allan Poe: A Critical Biography* (New York: D. Appleton-Century, 1941), 19–21 (hereafter *Quinn*, by page). It is a common belief that David Poe left law school in 1803 explicitly to pursue Elizabeth Hopkins. Although it is possible he was in the audience during her performances in Baltimore (Smith, *Brief Career*, 72), records of his first dramatic efforts that year establish that David was with a company in Charleston, South Carolina, while Eliza and her husband were in Norfolk, Virginia. It appears that they did not meet in person before June of 1804 when sharing a stage in Richmond.

8. *Quinn*, 23–24. Although a marriage bond was registered in Henrico County, Virginia (Richmond), on March 14, 1806, the actual day of the couple's wedding remains uncertain.

9. Smith, *Brief Career*, 88.

10. Smith, *Brief Career*, 91.

246 *Notes*

11. *Quinn*, 14–15. In 1777, David Poe Sr. was among those named who had forced a newspaper editor to flee Baltimore. In 1833, his grandson, Edgar Poe, would accost another Baltimore editor who (he believed) unfairly deprived him of a literary award.

12. John Carl Miller, *Building Poe Biography* (Baton Rouge: Louisiana State University Press, 1977), 46–47 (hereafter *Miller*, by page). This appears to have been a family tradition repeated by Maria Clemm in her later years, the veracity of which is not above question.

13. Mary E. Phillips, *Edgar Allan Poe the Man*, 2 vols. (Philadelphia: John C. Winston, 1926), 1:73 (hereafter *Phillips*, by volume:page).

14. *Quinn*, 49. The level to which David Poe Jr. indulged in alcohol is not certain, but Poe seems to have used his father's reputation to explain his lapses.

15. *Quinn*, 30n62. From a transcription of the Allan family bible made by Charles Ellis.

16. *Phillips*, 1:71. Mary Phillips infers that owing to their financial circumstances, Eliza was still bravely performing six days prior to Poe's birth and returned to work only three weeks later.

17. Letter: George Poe Jr. to William Clemm Jr., March 6, 1809. Original MS held in *Pratt*.

18. To understand (and accept) this encounter between David Poe Jr. and his cousin, the entire report to William Clemm Jr. should be read. See *Quinn*, 31–32.

19. *Quinn*, 38.

20. *Quinn*, 37.

21. Smith, *Brief Career*, 114. Smith suggests the possibility that David Poe may have been dismissed by his theatrical manager, Stephen Price, for being troublesome or his persistent poor publicity.

22. *Quinn*, 39. Although he provides no authority, Quinn infers that during the winter of 1809–1810, Eliza, in addition to her two children, may have been caring for an invalid or out-of-work husband.

23. *Phillips*, 1:77. An undated press clipping in the Poeana collection of New York actor, Robert B. Keggereis (or Keggeries), refers to a letter that indicates David Poe Jr. to have been in New York City on July 10, 1810, and also gives his death at Norfolk, Virginia, on October 10, 1810.

24. *New York Columbian*, July 2, 1810, as cited by Smith, *Brief Career*, 118–19. Emphasis of "embarrassments" is mine. If coming before the birth of Rosalie, this notice would seem to suggest that Elizabeth had both Henry and Edgar with her at the time.

25. Dwight Thomas and David K. Jackson, *The Poe Log: A Documentary Life of Edgar Allan Poe, 1809–1849* (Boston: G. K. Hall, 1987), 61–62, (hereafter *PL*, by page), Letter: John Allan to William "Henry" Poe, November 1, 1824. That Allan would raise the question of Rosalie's parentage in light of his transgressions exudes hypocrisy, as well as indecency.

26. George E. Woodberry, *The Life of Edgar Allan Poe*, 2 vols. (Boston: Houghton Mifflin, 1909), 1:363–64 (hereafter *Woodberry*, by volume:page). Benefit performances for individual players were regularly scheduled to allow the theater-going public to reward their favorites. The named actor received the net profits, if any, but

Notes 247

was also required to make up any losses should the promotion fail to attract adequate attendance.

27. Smith, *Brief Career*, 28.

28. Susan Archer Weiss, *The Home Life of Poe* (New York: Broadway Publishing, 1907), 6 (hereafter *Weiss*, by page).

29. *Quinn*, 44–45. Quinn cites the notice appearing in the November 29, 1811, edition of the *Virginia Patriot*: "On this night, Mrs. Poe, lingering on the bed of disease . . . asks your assistance and asks it perhaps for the last time." There is also a letter from theater patron, Samuel Mordecai, written to his sister, Rachael, five weeks before Eliza's death. "Mrs. Poe, who you know is a very handsome woman, happens to be very sick" (Bondurant, 129).

30. *CL*, 1:116, LTR-52, Letter: Poe to Beverley Tucker, December 1, 1835. In this letter, Poe would confess, "In speaking of my mother . . . I myself never knew her."

31. *CL*, 1:185, LTR-79, Letter: Poe to George W. Poe, July 14, 1839. As late as 1839, Poe was apparently still sensitive to his parents' profession, claiming in a letter written to a relative that they "were on a visit to friends in Richmond" when they both died. Yet confliction over his histrionic heritage was evident when declaring it after sympathizing with the playwright and actress, Anna Cora Mowatt, in an 1845 issue of the *Broadway Journal*.

32. Smith, *Brief Career*, 131. Smith suggests the possibility that the foster arrangements with the Allans and Mackenzies may have been made before Eliza died; however, Woodberry (*Woodberry*, 1:16) states that the Poe children were lumped in with the orphans of Richmond's catastrophic theater fire almost three weeks later and not claimed until then.

33. *CL*, 1:58–63, LTR-28, Letter: Poe to John Allan, January 3, 1831. The letter to Edgar's relatives in Baltimore has never been discovered and it may have been invented by Poe to strengthen his position in an argument.

34. *Quinn*, 51–53. Although Quinn describes the Allan's "in comfortable, if not in affluent circumstances," they were at that time living above their store in Richmond.

35. Hervey Allen, *Israfel: The Life and Times of Edgar Allan Poe*, rev. ed. (New York: Farrar & Reinhart, 1934), 77 (hereafter *Allen*, by page). When writing confidentially to his wife about the Allans' return from England, Charles Ellis remarked, "could she [Frances] be as even tempered and as accommodating as she has been sence [since] her return, she would make the path through life much more even to herself." There is also the observation of William Galt Jr. when praising his fiancée who, although a niece of Frances Allan, was "not like her in temper and disposition." See William Galt Jr., Papers, William R. Perkins Library, Duke University, as cited in *PL*, 63.

36. *Allen*, 40–41.

37. *Quinn*, 61.

38. *Quinn*, 90. In regard to John Allan's infidelities, Quinn opined, "It is hard to see how Poe could have remained ignorant of them." It is also not improbable that Frances had difficulty with marital intimacy which would provide another explanation for her barrenness, the perpetual illnesses and her spinster sister's permanent membership to the household. That John Allan successfully fathered children with

248 *Notes*

at least three other women ("Mrs. Collier," Elizabeth Wills and second wife, Louisa Patterson) would also lend credence to the idea.

39. Thomas Ollive Mabbott, *The Collected Works of Edgar Allan Poe*, 3 vols. (Cambridge, MA: Belknapp Press of Harvard University Press, 1969; 1978), 1:533 (hereafter *M*, by volume:page). Mabbott gives the date of Poe's baptism, by the Reverend John Buchanan, as January 7, 1812, however, documentary evidence has proven elusive.

40. *Quinn*, 63–64.

41. William Elijah Hunter, "Poe and His English Schoolmaster," *Athenæum*, October 19, 1878, 496–97.

42. *Quinn*, 54.

43. Among his many accomplishments, Colonel (CSA) John T. L. Preston was instrumental in the creation of the Virginia Military Academy and would serve there as Professor of Modern Languages from 1839–1875, taking a hiatus only for his service during the war between the states.

44. Sara Sigourney Rice, *Edgar Allan Poe: A Memorial Volume* (Baltimore: Turnbull Brothers, 1877), 41.

45. John H. Ingram, ed., *Edgar Allan Poe: His Life, Letters, and Opinions*, 2 vols. (London: John Hogg, 1880), 24.

46. *PL*, 61–62. Letter: John Allan to "Henry" Poe, November 1, 1824. Sometime during the following summer, Henry visited his brother in Richmond.

47. *PL*, 62–63. It is indicated that William Galt's death, and Allan's subsequent inheritance, was not unforeseen. In the months just prior to Galt's passing, Allan amicably dissolved the concern of Ellis and Allan, and he acquired a seat on the board of directors of the Richmond branch of the Bank of Virginia. It is difficult to believe that Allan would not have shared this anticipation with other family members.

48. Notwithstanding Catherine Poitiaux (Frances Allan's godchild and Poe's childhood playmate), and his infatuation of the much older Jane Stith Stanard.

49. James A. Harrison, *The Complete Works of Edgar Allan Poe*, 17 vols. (New York: Thomas Y. Crowell, 1902), 1:62 (hereafter *H*, by volume:page).

50. *Quinn*, 113. Quinn was convinced the shortfall was no accident. Even if true, Allan's purpose in this is still open to discussion.

51. Charles W. Kent, "Poe's Student Days at the University of Virginia," *Bookman*, January 1917, 518. "The faculty-meetings . . . were largely given up to disciplining students guilty of the use of ardent and vinous liquors, or of gambling."

52. Thomas H. Ellis, "Edgar Allan Poe," *Richmond Standard*, May 7, 1881, 2. The figure of $2,500 appears to have been contrived or exaggerated to justify John Allan's subsequent actions. The actual amount will probably never be known.

53. *CL*, 1:20, LTR-9, Letter: Poe to John Allan, February 4, 1829.

54. Douglas Sherley, "Old Oddity Papers," *Virginia University Magazine*, April 1880, 426–45.

55. Letter: Dr. Miles George to E. V. Valentine, May 18, 1880, as cited in *PL*, 69.

56. *CL*, 1:53–54, LTR-25, Letter: Poe to Sergeant Samuel Graves, May 3, 1830.

57. *CL*, 1:58–63. LTR-28, Letter: Poe to John Allan, January 3, 1831. "As to the truth. . . . I leave it to God, and your own conscience."

Notes 249

58. Allan explained his rationale in a letter to Major John Eaton, the Secretary of War, dated May 6, 1829 (as cited by *Quinn*, 136). "He [Poe] left me in consequence of some gambling at the University at Charlottesville, because (I presume) I refused to sanction a rule that the shopkeepers and others had adopted there, making Debts of Honour of all indiscretions."

59. *Allen*, 152–53.

60. Floyd Stovall, *Edgar Poe the Poet* (Charlottesville: University Press of Virginia, 1969), 18. "The full extent of these obligations was not known by Allan until later."

61. *CL*, 1:12, LTR-6, Letter: Poe to Allan, March 20, 1827.

62. Mary Newton Stanard, *Edgar Allan Poe Letters Till Now Unpublished: In the Valentine Museum, Richmond, Virginia* (Philadelphia: J. B. Lippincott, 1925), 181–82. Two years later, when Poe was in Baltimore awaiting his admission to West Point, his trunk was apparently still at Allan's house.

63. *M*, 1:538–39. Although this visit to Baltimore seems likely, evidence for it relies mainly on Poe's extant compositions and his apparent interactions with others there that are difficult to explain in any other way.

64. The exact location of the Clemm/Poe residence in 1827 has not been established.

65. Thomas Ollive Mabbott, *Tamerlane and Other Poems* (Introduction) (New York: Facsimile Text Society, 1941), xii–xviii, xxxiv–xxxvi. Mabbott surmises that Lambert Wilmer adapted the story for his play, *Merlin*, from Poe's broken engagement with Elmira Royster.

66. Lambert A. Wilmer, "Recollections of Edgar A. Poe," *Baltimore Daily Commercial*, May 23, 1866, 1.

67. Mabbott, *Tamerlane*, xiii. Mabbott suggests that Poe could still have been in Baltimore as late as May 1, 1827, and points to the assigned date of his poem found in Octavia Walton's album; however, her dating could be inaccurate if assigned (by her) at a later time.

68. Lewis Leary, "Miss Octavia's Autograph Album and Edgar Allan Poe," *Columbia Library Columns*, February 1968, 15. Leary suggests "that it was in Baltimore, not Boston, where Poe put final touches to the manuscript of the remarkable first volume of poems." See also E. A. Poe, [a.k.a. By a Bostonian], *Tamerlane and Other Poems* (Boston: Calvin F. S. Thomas, 1827).

69. On December 4, 2009, an original 1827 example of *Tamerlane* was sold at auction for $662,000, http://www.christies.com/en/lot/lot-5280770.

70. J. Thomas Russell, *Edgar Allan Poe: The Army Years (USMA Library Bulletin No. 10)* (New York: United States Military Academy, 1972), 5.

71. Carlisle Allan, "Cadet Edgar Allan Poe, U.S.A." *American Mercury* 8 (August 1933): 446–55. When an enlisted soldier in the army "his pay as an artificer became $10 a month, with one ration of whiskey or rum per day, issued in kind."

72. *PL*, 90–91.

73. Russell, *Edgar Allan Poe*, 6–8. Poe first wrote to Allan requesting his assistance for a discharge on December 1, 1828, but was not promoted to the rank of

250 *Notes*

Sergeant Major until January 1, 1829, after which he communicated his West Point ambitions to Allan on February 4.

74. *Richmond Whig*, March 2, 1829. Frances Allan's death, described in this paper as from "a lingering and painful illness," is thought by some to have been the result of tuberculosis."

75. *CL*, 1:50, LTR-23, Letter: Poe to John Allan, November 18, 1829. The particulars of Poe's involvement in the reassignment of "Edwin" to Henry Ridgway (freeman) can be found in the original bill of sale held in the Poe Collection at the Enoch Pratt Free Library.

76. *CL*, 1:69–70, LTR-33, Letter: Poe to John Allan, November 11, 1831. "I was arrested eleven days ago for a debt which I never expected to have to pay, and which was incurred as much on Hy's account as on my own about two years ago."

77. Edgar Allan Poe, *Al Aaraaf, Tamerlane and Minor Poems* (Baltimore: Hatch and Dunning, 1829).

78. Allan was by this time courting (and consorting) again, this preoccupation perhaps mitigating some of his anger toward Poe.

79. *CL*, 1:19–21, LTR-9, Letter: Poe to John Allan, February 4, 1829.

80. Thomas W. Gibson, "Poe at West Point," *Harper's New Monthly Magazine*, November 1867, 754–56.

81. Allan, "Cadet Edgar Allan Poe," 446–55.

82. Allan, "Cadet Edgar Allan Poe," 446–55.

83. *CL*, 1:53–54, LTR-25, Letter: Poe to Sergeant Samuel Graves, May 3, 1830.

84. Scott Peeples, *The Man of the Crowd: Edgar Allan Poe and the City* (Princeton, NJ: Princeton University Press, 2020), 45. Peeples suggests that Poe's motivation for leaving West Point was not due to the harsh discipline but rather John Allan's second marriage to Patterson and the severance of communication (from Allan).

85. *Allen*, 696.

86. Edgar A. Poe, *Poems* (New York: Elam Bliss, 1831). Because many of the poems had been previously published in *Al Aaraaf, Tamerlane and Minor Poems* (1829), Poe noted this work as a "Second Edition."

87. *CL*, 1:43, LTR-19, Letter: Poe to John Allan, August 10, 1829.

88. Stanard, *Edgar Allan Poe Letters*, 277.

89. *CL*, 1:66–67, LTR-31, Letter: Poe to William Gwynn, May 6, 1831.

90. *Quinn*, 198, suggests that at some point he was performing menial tasks for newspapers. See also *CL*, 1:67–68, LTR-32, Letter: Poe to John Allan, October 16, 1831. "I have managed to get clear of the difficulty . . . and am out of debt."

91. Augustus Van Cleef, "Poe's Mary," *Harper's New Monthly Magazine* 78 (March 1889): 634–40.

92. Van Cleef, "Poe's Mary," 634–40.

93. Hervey Allen and Thomas Ollive Mabbott, *Poe's Brother: The Poems of William Henry Leonard Poe* (New York: George H. Doran, 1926), 24.

94. *Quinn*, 192.

95. Genevieve Miller, "A Nineteenth Century Medical School: Washington University of Baltimore," *Bulletin of the History of Medicine* (June 1943): 17n12. Miller

was a founder and president of Washington Medical College (later a university), builders of the hospital in which Poe died.

96. John H. Hewitt, *Shadows on the Wall* (Baltimore: Turnbull Brothers, 1877), 41.

97. Hewitt, *Shadows*, 43.

98. [Robert Thomas Pichett] Allen, "Edgar Allan Poe," *Scribner's Monthly Magazine* 11, no. 1 (November 1875): 142–43. According to this West Point classmate, in 1835 the poet was spotted working in a Baltimore brick-yard "being engaged in wheeling clay in a wheel-barrow." If this is true, his sacrifice would seem to demonstrate genuine concern for the welfare of his new family.

99. L. A. Wilmer, "Recollections of Edgar A. Poe," *Baltimore Daily Commercial*, May 23, 1866, 1.

100. *CL*, 1:90–91, LTR-44, Letter: Poe to Thomas White, June 12, 1835. According to *Matchett's Directory for Baltimore City 1835-1836*, 37, Dr. John Buckler lived on St. Paul Street, south of Saratoga. Buckler may have been compensated for his services by Poe's facility in the publication of Buckler's wife's poem in the *Southern Literary Messenger*.

101. Eugene L. Didier, *The Life and Poems of Edgar Allan Poe* (New York: W. J. Widdleton, 1876), 34.

102. *PL*, .97, 126. Poe is known to have visited the bookstores of Edward Coale and Henry Bool.

103. Sadly, this historic structure was among those destroyed in the great fire of 1904.

104. David F. Gaylin, *Edgar Allan Poe's Baltimore* (Charleston, SC: Arcadia Publishing, 2015), 56. It appears that Poe left Baltimore the first week of August during four days of bloody rioting that had (ultimately) resulted from the failure of the Bank of Maryland.

105. Letter: Margaret Ellis to Charles Ellis, August 19, 1835 as cited by *PL*, 165.

106. David K. Jackson, *Poe and the Southern Literary Messenger* (New York: Haskell House, 1970), 97–98. Letter: Thomas White to Lucian Minor, August 18, 1835. "Poe is here also.—He tarries one month—and will aid me all that lies in his power." Poe's delay may have been due to disappointment, or dissipation.

107. Letter: Poe to Maria Clemm, August 29, 1835. Original MS held in *Pratt*. Poe's instability at the time is painfully evident in this emotional (if not hysterical) letter to his aunt, as well as another sent to John Kennedy a week later on September 11 (*Quinn*, 225–27). It has been suggested that Clemm, perhaps after learning of Poe's attraction to White's eighteen-year-old daughter, used Neilson's offer to manipulate Poe out of fear of losing his support.

108. Jackson, *Poe and the Southern Literary Messenger*, 98. Letter: Thomas White to Lucian Minor, September 8, 1835.

109. Jackson, *Poe and the Southern Literary Messenger*, 100. Letter: Thomas White to Lucian Minor, September 21, 1835.

110. A possible explanation for Maria Clemm's favor of the marriage between Edgar and her daughter may have been that Neilson Poe's offer of shelter only extended to Virginia. This is suggested by Poe's question (in his letter of August 29,

252 *Notes*

1835) to Maria, "If she [Virginia] goes with N. P. what are you to do, my own Aunty?"

111. *Miller*, 52. When writing to Ingram on November 27, 1874, Nathanial H. Morrison (Peabody Institute) stated the ceremony was performed by Rev. John Johns at Christ Church (Baltimore). However, Mabbott (*M*, 546) believed this to be an invention by Maria Clemm and that the ceremony was performed instead by Rev. John Owen at the First Presbyterian Church.

112. *Quinn*, 228–30. Poe's original appeal to White (as well as a follow-up letter) does not survive but they are implied by statements made in White's September 29 letter to Poe.

113. Letter: Thomas White to Poe, September 29, 1835. Original MS in the Griswold Collection, Boston Public Library, as cited by *Quinn*, 228–29.

114. Jeffrey A. Savoye, "Some Updates on Poe's Correspondence, with a New Letter," *Edgar Allan Poe Review* (Spring 2012): 6–17.

115. *Miller*, 52. Letter: N. H. Morison to John Ingram, November 27, 1874.

116. *Allen*, 318–20. In his January 12, 1836 letter requesting financial assistance from George Poe Jr., Poe describes Virginia as his aunt's daughter and a dependent, making no mention that she was his wife.

117. Jackson, *Poe and the Southern Literary Messenger*, 106–7. Letter: White to Minor, December 25, 1835.

118. Jackson, *Poe and the Southern Literary Messenger*, 109–10. Letter: White to Beverly Tucker, December 27, 1836.

119. Dwight Rembert Thomas, "Poe in Philadelphia, 1838–1844: A Documentary Record" (PhD diss., University of Pennsylvania, 1978), 155–57.

120. William Doyle Hull II, "A Canon of the Critical Works of Edgar Allan Poe" (PhD diss., University of Virginia, 1941), 62.

121. *CL*, 1:263–64, LTR-109, Letter: Poe to Joseph Snodgrass, April 1, 1841.

122. Jackson, *Poe and the Southern Literary Messenger*, 111–12. Letter: White to Beverly Tucker, January 19, 1837. "I am so overwhelmed in debt that I scarcely dare think of such an editor as I know I ought to have."

123. *H*, 17:41–42. When they parted, White advanced Poe $20 for future contributions although Poe may have viewed the money as severance pay.

124. William Gowans, *Catalogue of American Books* 28 (1870): 11, as cited by *Quinn*, 267.

125. *PL*, 248.

126. Edgar Allan Poe, *The Narrative of Arthur Gordon Pym* (New York: Harper & Brothers, 1838).

127. John Ward Ostrom, "Edgar A. Poe: His Income as Literary Entrepreneur," *Poe Studies* 15, no. 1 (June 1982): 2. Ostrom wrote that Poe was paid $50 "for his work and name on the tile page" of *The Conchologist's First Book*, and that his total income during the two years after leaving the *Messenger* may have been no more than $143.50.

128. *CL*, 1:175, LTR-77a, Letter: Poe to James K. Paulding, July 19, 1838.

129. Thomas, *Poe in Philadelphia*, 15–16.

Notes 253

130. *Allen*, 377. William Burton was an English-born actor who continued performing in Philadelphia while publishing his magazine. A desire to open his own theater there would eventually impel him to divest of the publication.

131. *PL*, 307. When a Maine subscriber complained to Burton that he had not been receiving his magazines, the publisher blamed it on Poe and his "infirmities." A year later, when writing to Snodgrass in Baltimore, Poe dedicated much of his reply refuting the charges that Burton had been disseminating (*CL*, 1:262–65, LTR-109, Letter: Poe to Joseph Snodgrass, April 1, 1841).

132. Lambert A. Wilmer, *Our Press Gang; Or, A Complete Exposition of the Corruptions and Crimes of the American Press* (Philadelphia: J. T. Lloyd, 1859), 35–36.

133. *PL*, 312.

134. *PL*, 313. The two had corresponded in February 1840 and their acquaintance prior to this "illness" is also indicated by Poe's feature on "Autography" appearing in the December 1841 issue of *Graham's Magazine* which included Mitchell.

135. Edgar Allan Poe, ed., "Maelzel's Chess-Player," *Southern Literary Messenger* 2, no. 5 (April 1836), 318–26.

136. *CL*, 1:237, LTR-97, Letter: Poe to William Poe (Georgia), August 14, 1840. Clemm often acted in the capacity of Poe's secretary: running errands that included delivering his compositions and asking for the attending payment, as well as transcribing his letters (she became quite adept at replicating his signature, a practice that would pay her some dividends after his death).

137. *PL*, 311. Among those paying up front was Nicholas Biddle, president of the United States Bank, who gave Poe an advance of four years' subscription.

138. Albert H. Smyth, *The Philadelphia Magazines and Their Contributors, 1741–1850* (Philadelphia: Robert M. Lindsay, 1892), 217. The tradition that William Burton asked George Rex Graham to keep his "young editor" employed was apparently Graham's well-meaning invention.

139. Baltimore's *Saturday Visiter*, January 1, 1842. Snodgrass, when reviewing *Graham's Magazine* wrote, "we made a hearty supper with Poe's devil-may-care criticisms."

140. *CL*, 1:309, LTR-126, Letter: Poe to Joseph E. Snodgrass, September 19, 1841. "It is not impossible that Graham will join me in The 'Penn.' He has money." The evidence for the idea that Graham would have financed, or even partnered in, yet another periodical (he was then also publishing the *Saturday Evening Post*) rests only with Poe. It is of course possible that Graham made a disingenuous promise to consider such a project when hiring Poe, to which Poe mistook for an agreement.

141. Richard Beale Davis, ed., *Chiver's Life of Poe*, by T. H. Chivers (New York: E. P. Dutton, 1952), 43. Thomas Holley Chivers appears to be the sole authority for Mitchell's white lie, although it was then a common medical practice to provide an avenue for denial in such cases. In his March 25, 1842 letter to Frederick Thomas, Poe stated that he had "strong hope of her [Virginia's] ultimate recovery."

142. Tuberculous is believed to have caused the death of Poe's mother and older brother. That Edgar and his sister never exhibited traditional symptoms *could* suggest a level of immunity acquired in the womb that eluded Henry who was, perhaps, born before his mother acquired the disease.

143. Hervey Allen, *Israfel: The Life and Times of Edgar Allan Poe*, 2 vols. (New York: George H. Doran, 1926), 2:520.

144. *CL*, 1:335–336, LTR-135, Letter: Poe to James Herron, (early) June 1842.

145. *CL*, 1:324–327, LTR-132, Letter: Poe to Frederick W. Thomas, February 3, 1842.

146. *CL*, 1:353–354. LTR-141a, Letter: Poe to J. and H. G. Langley, July 18, 1842. William Ross Wallace was a Kentucky lawyer and aspiring poet (then living in New York City) with whom Poe had become acquainted while with *Graham's*. The mint julep had then become a popular drink in northern US cities.

147. Thomas, *Poe in Philadelphia*, 401. Poe may have also seen Robert Hamilton, editor of *Snowden's Ladies Companion* and found it necessary to pledge his temperance when writing to him later: "I am as straight as judges . . . and, what is more, I intend to keep straight."

148. Van Cleef, "Poe's Mary," 634–40.

149. *CL*, 1:344–45, LTR-138, Letter: Poe to James Herron, June 30, 1842. Poe wrote a brief reply to Herron immediately upon his return acknowledging a "loan" of $20, but a week passed before he could give adequate replies to correspondences that had been accumulating.

150. *CL*, 1:349–50, LTR-140, Letter: Poe to Thomas H. Chivers, July 6, 1842.

151. *CL*, 1:381, LTR-153, Letter: Poe to Frederick W. Thomas, February 25, 1843.

152. William Fearing Gill, *The Life of Edgar Allan Poe* (New York: D. Appleton, 1877), 120–22. In a sloppily written letter sent to Thomas Cottrell Clarke after his arrival in Washington, Poe informs him that his expenses were more than anticipated and asks for more money.

153. Whether Clarke was aware of Poe's quest for a clerkship is not known but this avid pursuit of a "day job" would suggest that he was not wholly committed to the magazine project.

154. Gill, *Life of Edgar Allan Poe*, 120–22.

155. *CL*, 1:389, LTR-156, Letter: Poe to Frederick W. Thomas and Jessie E. Dow, March 16, 1843.

156. Gill, *Life of Edgar Allan Poe*, 121. Baltimore's reputation for lawlessness was then widely accepted but in this case the fear was that Poe would harm himself.

157. *CL*, 1:400–401, LTR-161, Letter: Poe to James R. Lowell, June 20, 1843. "My magazine scheme has exploded—or, at least, I have been deprived . . . of all means of prosecuting it for the present."

158. John Hill Hewitt, *Recollections of Poe*, ed. Richard Barksdale Harwell (Atlanta: Emory University Library, 1949), as cited by Thomas, *Poe in Philadelphia*, 805. The sole authority for this story is Hewitt.

159. Dwight Thomas, "Poe, English and the Doom of the Drinker: A Mystery Resolved," *Princeton University Library Chronicle* (Spring 1979): 257–68. The title of this work is shown in quotation marks (within the text) as it was originally offered to the public in serial form in both the *Cold Water Magazine* and the *Saturday Museum*.

Notes 255

160. Elizabeth C. Phillips, "The Literary Life of John Tomlin, Friend of Poe," PhD diss., University of Tennessee, 1953. As it would happen, Tomlin also developed a drinking habit and died a year after Poe from an attack of delirium tremens.

161. *Woodberry*, 2:42–43.

162. Thomas, *Poe in Philadelphia*, 592.

163. Letter: William Poe to Edgar Poe, June 16, 1843. as cited by *H*, 17:145–146, the original MS held in the Rufus W. Griswold Papers, Boston Public Library Archives and Special Collections, Boston, Massachusetts.

164. Edgar Allan Poe, "Mr. Poe's Reply to Mr. English and Others," *Spirit of the Times*, July 10, 1846.

165. Hervey Allen, *Israfel: The Life and Times of Edgar Allan Poe*, 2 vols. (New York: George H. Doran, 1926), 1:371. "There can be no moral doubt that Poe was using opium, at least from time to time." Woodberry is another who believed that Poe had a drug habit: "The indirect evidence is constant, varied, and convincing." George E. Woodberry, *American Men of Letters; Edgar Allan Poe* (Boston: Houghton Mifflin, 1885), 210–11.

166. Jane Sears, "Henry Herring—Fair Mount," *Maryland Tams Journal* 29, no. 3 (Fall 2008): 10–15. The reason for Henry Herring's move to Philadelphia in 1840 is unclear but may have been an effort to maintain a "low profile" following the failure of his Fair Mount project in Baltimore a few years earlier. By 1842, Henry had returned to Baltimore where he reestablished himself in the city's lumber trade: *Matchett's Baltimore Directory for 1842*, 202; *Baltimore Sun*, November 23, 1842, 2. After remarrying, Elizabeth went to live in Woodville, Virginia.

167. It has been stated that this "Miss Herring" was Elizabeth's younger sister, Mary Estelle Herring; however, the reference to being a widow in 1840 could only apply to Elizabeth.

168. *Woodberry*, 2:428–30.

169. It appears this testimony was provided by the daughter of Neilson Poe and not his twin sister.

170. Thomas Dunn English, "Reminiscences of Poe," *Independent* (New York), October 15, 1896, 2.

171. John Sartain, *The Reminiscences of a Very Old Man, 1808–1897* (New York: D. Appleton, 1899), 224. The use of absinthe, with its herbal flavor and high alcohol content, became popular in the nineteenth century as an alternative to traditional drinks.

172. Donald W. Goodwin, *Alcohol and the Writer* (New York: Penguin Books, 1988), 29. Dr. Goodwin wrote that Poe was *probably* an absinthe drinker but provided no support for his theory.

173. Thomas, *Poe in Philadelphia*, 893–94. There are too many traditions concerning the genesis and construction of "The Raven" to recount. Most are poorly supported at best, including its rejection by *Graham's Magazine* in 1843.

174. *Delaware State Journal*, January 2, 1843, 2.

175. Joseph Evans Snodgrass, "The Facts of Poe's Death and Burial," *Beadle's Monthly* (May 1867): 283–87.

176. *Allen*, 464.

177. Thomas Dunn English, "Reminiscences of Poe [Part 02]," *Independent* (New York), October 22, 1896.

178. *CL*, 1:437–439, LTR-174, Letter: Poe to Maria Clemm, April 7, 1844; written c. May 1849.

179. Jacob E. Spannuth, ed., *Doings of Gotham: Poe's Contributions to The Columbia Spy* (Pottsville, PA: Jacob E. Spannuth, 1929).

180. Letter: N. P. Willis to George P. Morris, October 17, 1858, as cited by *PL*, 473.

181. N. P. Willis, "The Death of Edgar A. Poe," *Home Journal*, October 20, 1849.

182. Poe sold the poem, perhaps in late December 1844, to George H. Colton, the editor of the *American Review*; however, the timing of the transaction prevented the poem's publication there before the February number. The daily paper, the *Evening Mirror*, of which Poe was a staff member, gained permission from Colton for a "preview" of the work in their January 29 edition.

183. *PL*, 508.

184. *CL*, 1:475, LTR-189, Letter: Poe to Frederick W. Thomas, January 4, 1845.

185. Mukhtar Ali Isani, "Reminiscences of Poe by an Employee of the Broadway Journal," *Poe Studies* 6, no. 2 (December 1973): 34. Besides claiming to witness Poe's intoxication when appearing for work, Alexander T. Crane would also recall being one of "scarcely a dozen" that went to the lecture.

186. Heyward Ehrlich, "The Broadway Journal: Brigg's Dilemma and Poe's Strategy," in *The Collected Writings of Edgar Allan Poe: Vol. IV: Broadway Journal*, ed. Burton Pollin (New York: Gordian Press, 1986), xviii–xix.

187. Edgar Allan Poe, "Longfellow's Waif" (part I), *Evening Mirror*, January 13, 1845.

188. *Quinn*, 453–55.

189. The venue for this lecture was the Odeon Theatre on Federal Street where Poe's parents had been performing when he was born.

190. Thomas Dunn English, "A Card: Mr. English's Reply to Mr. Poe," *Evening Mirror*, June 23, 1846.

191. Walt Whitman, *Specimen Days and Collect* (Glasgow, Scotland: Wilson & McCormick, 1883), 17.

192. Richard H. Stoddard, "Edgar Allan Poe," *Lippincott's Monthly Magazine*, January 1889, 107–15. Although Poe may have been "ill" at the time, his conclusion that Richard Stoddard had borrowed too much of the work may have been justified.

193. Sidney P. Moss, *Poe's Major Crisis: His Libel Suit and New York's Literary World* (Durham, NC: Duke University Press, 1970), 3. Moss inferred that it was fear of the letter's contents being used for material in Poe's upcoming gossip column, "The Literati of New York City," that had prompted Ellet's actions.

194. *CL*, 2:731, LTR-290, Letter: Poe to Sarah Helen Whitman, November 24, 1848. Poe would confess his breach of propriety to Sarah Whitman: "I permitted myself to say what I should not have said—I had no sooner uttered the words, than I felt their dishonor."

Notes 257

195. "Fought the Poet and Won," *Washington Post*, February 15, 1892, 6. John H. Tyler (nephew of President John Tyler), one of those separating the two combatants, reported that "Poe got the worst of it."

196. Perhaps for strategic reasons, Poe arranged for his doctor, John Francis, to write and deliver his letter that claimed an attack of mental illness.

197. *PL*, 633–34.

198. *PL*, 726. When explaining to Sarah Whitman why Poe had been banished from her soirees, Anne Lynch would write, "he is in such bad odour with most persons who visit me that if I were to recieve [*sic*] him, I should lose the company of many whom I value more."

199. J. H. Whitty, ed. *The Complete Poems of Edgar Allan Poe* (Boston: Houghton Mifflin, 1911), lvii.

200. Letter: Mary Hewitt to Poe, April 15, 1846, Rufus W. Griswold Papers, Boston Public Library, as cited by *Quinn*, 506n22.

201. "Edgar A. Poe, Esq." *Baltimore Sun*, May 5, 1846, 2. Reports of Poe's "insanity" reached the papers in Baltimore, where it was reported, "Mr Poe has been elected Anniversary Poet, by the University of Vermont, but has been obliged to decline on account of continued ill health. He is sojourning in a retired part of Long Island [Fordham], where he is still severely suffering from an attack of 'brain fever.'" Louis A. Godey found it necessary, albeit for commercial reasons, to repudiate published reports of Poe's mental instability in his *Lady's Book*: "we have letters from him of very recent dates . . . which show anything but feebleness either of body or mind."

202. *CL*, 1:602, LTR-241, Letter: Poe to George Eveleth, December 15, 1846. "I had no other design than critical gossip."

203. *Quinn*, 497.

204. Thomas Dunn English, "A Card: Mr. English's Reply to Mr. Poe," *Evening Mirror*, June 23, 1846.

205. *PL*, 689. During the trial Poe's troubles with alcohol were exposed when his own character witnesses were made to say that he was "occasionally addicted to intoxication."

206. Edgar Allan Poe, "Mr. Poe's Reply to Mr. English and Others," *Spirit of the Times*, July 10, 1846.

207. *Quinn*, 674. Letter: Mary E. Hewitt to Frances Osgood, December 20, 1846.

208. Poe's protracted illness during this period has never been identified but his resulting inactivity precluded any income for months.

209. Mary Gove Nichols, *Reminiscences of Edgar Allan Poe* (New York: Union Square Book Shop, 1931; repr. *Sixpenny Magazine* [London], February 1863), 13. In 1855, Nichols wrote a novel in which she included Poe as a character and described this visit to his home at Fordham. Her "reminiscences" written later in 1863 and claiming several visits to the cottage, seems to contain just as much fiction.

210. *New York Morning Express*, December 15, 1846, 2.

211. *CL*, 1:611–12, LTR-246, Letter: Poe to Nathaniel P. Willis, December 30, 1846. In this letter to Willis, Poe indicates that he was not suffering from "consumption."

212. *Miller*, 94–106.

258   *Notes*

213. *Evening Mirror*, June 7, 1847, as cited in *PL*, 701.

214. John E. Reilly, "Robert D'Unger and His Reminiscences of Edgar Allan Poe in Baltimore," *Maryland Historical Magazine* 88 (Spring 1993): 60–72.

215. Letter: Louis A. Godey to George Eveleth, August 6, 1847, as cited by *PL*, 703.

216. *CL*, 2:632, LTR-255, Letter: Poe to Robert T. Conrad, August 10, 1847.

217. *CL*, 2:647–49, LTR-263, Letter: Poe to George W. Eveleth, February 29, 1848.

218. Mary Elizabeth (nee Bronson) LeDuc, "Recollections of Edgar A. Poe," *Home Journal* (New York), July 21, 1860, 3. In a letter Poe wrote to her father, C. P. Bronson, in the fall of 1847, he indicated the poem, "Ulalume," was written at Mr. Bronson's suggestion.

219. LeDuc, "Recollections," 3, "I mean to start for Richmond on the 10th March."

220. *Miller*, 101–2. There is an unsupported story that was given by the Reverend John H. Hopkins, decades later, that he and Roland Stebbins Houghton (Marie Shew's future husband) were summoned to the poet's side to find him "crazy drunk in the hands of the police" after going on a spree with the publisher's advance; however, this may have been confused with the incident described by Hiram Fuller a year earlier.

221. *CL*, 2:669–70, LTR-268, Letter: Poe to Charles Astor Bristed, June 7, 1848. "Will you forgive me, then, if I ask you to loan me the means of getting to Richmond?"

222. *CL*, 2:725, LTR-287, Letter: Poe to Edward Valentine, November 20, 1848. In the reply to Poe's emissary (Susan Talley Weiss), Valentine would write, "It is not in my power to aid Mr. Poe. I have a large sum of money to raise by Spring." Poe may have construed from this that Valentine would be able to help him after the spring.

223. Frederick W. Coburn, "Poe as Seen by the Brother of 'Annie.'" *New England Quarterly*, September 1943, 470. When describing Poe's lecture as one who had attended, Amos Bardwell Heywood would write, "Twas a brilliant affair."

224. John E. Reilly, "Robert D'Unger and His Reminiscences of Edgar Allan Poe in Baltimore." *Maryland Historical Magazine* 88 (Spring 1993): 60–72. D'Unger claimed that during this trip in 1848, Poe stopped in Baltimore long enough to be seen drinking.

225. *CL*, 2:683–84, LTR-275a, Letter: Poe to Maria Clemm, August 5, 1848.

226. Letter: John R. Thompson to E. H. N. Patterson, November 9, 1849, as cited by *Quinn*, 569–70.

227. *CL*, 2:683–84, LTR-275a, Letter: Poe to Maria Clemm, August 5, 1848.

228. J. H. Whitty, "Literary Reputation made in Richmond," *Times-Dispatch* (Richmond), January 17, 1909, as cited by *Woodberry*, 2:443–45.

229. *PL*, 786. When later noticing Poe's engagement to Sarah Whitman in the *Semi-Weekly Examiner*, John M. Daniel would offer marital advice that included, "We also hope he will leave off getting drunk in restoratives, and keep his money in his pockets."

230. Letter: John R. Thompson to Philip Pendleton Cooke, October 17, 1848, as cited by *Quinn*, 568. In this letter written more than a month after Poe returned to New York, Thompson appears irritated.

Notes   259

231. *CL*, 2:671–74, LTR-270, Letter: Poe to Miss Anna Blackwell, June 14, 1848.

232. John Carl Miller, *Poe's Helen Remembers* (Charlottesville: University Press of Virginia, 1979),193. When correcting Poe's biographer, John H. Ingram, Whitman would curiously write, "If I had never seen Poe intoxicated, I should never have consented to marry him."

233. *CL*, 2:721–25, LTR-286, Letter: Poe to Annie L. Richmond, November 16, 1848.

234. Richard Henry Stoddard, *Select Works of Edgar Allan Poe, Poetical and Prose* (New York: W. J. Widdleton, 1880), cxxxvi (hereafter *Stoddard*, by page).

235. Miller, *Poe's Helen Remembers*, 348. Letter: Sarah H. Whitman to John H. Ingram, October 25, 1875.

236. *PL*, 766.

237. Philip A. Mackowiak, *Post Mortem: Solving History's Great Medical Mysteries* (Philadelphia: American College of Physicians, 2007), 254. The author suggests that the panic attack Poe suffered at the Whitman house was symptomatic of delirium tremens.

238. Stanley Thomas Williams, "New Letters About Poe," *Yale Review* 14 (July 1925): 763. Letter: Sarah H. Whitman to Mary E. Hewitt, September 27?, 1850. According to Whitman, they were to be wed on the ensuing Sunday following her mother's consent that was given on December 22. However, the *Poe Log* (*PL*, 779) gave the date of the proposed marriage as Monday, December 25, which was actually a Tuesday.

239. *H*, 17:413, Letter: W. J. Pabodie to R. W. Griswold, June 11, 1852. "At the invitation of the Prov. Lyceum; and, on the evening of his arrival, he delivered a lecture on American Poetry before an audience of some two thousand persons."

240. *CL*, 2:766–67, LTR-303, Letter: Poe to Mrs. Annie L. Richmond, February 8, 1849. "Since I returned from Providence—six weeks ago. I have not suffered a day to pass without writing from a page to three pages. Yesterday, I wrote five, and the day before a poem considerably longer than 'The Raven.'"

241. *CL*, 2:802, LTR-315, Letter: Poe to George P. Putman, May 18, 1849. In this attempt to convince Putman to print a second edition of Lewis's poems, Poe sounds very much like the woman's press agent: "Mrs Lewis . . . has been highly praised by the critics [mostly Poe], is very popular as an authoress and daily growing more so."

242. *CL*, 2:766–67, LTR-303, Letter: Poe to Mrs. Annie L. Richmond, February 8, 1849.

243. That Maria Clemm did not accompany him implies financial constraints.

244. Michael J. Deas, *The Portraits and Daguerreotypes of Edgar Allan Poe* (Charlottesville: University Press of Virginia, 1989), 48.

245. Kenneth Silverman, *Edgar A. Poe: Mournful and Never-Ending Remembrance* (New York: Harper Collins, 1991), 411.

246. *CL*, 2:792–94, LTR-312, Letter: Poe to E. H. N. Patterson, ca. April 30, 1849.

247. Edward Wagenknecht, *Edgar Allan Poe: The Man Behind the Legend* (New York: Oxford University Press, 1963), 72. "First he put off pursuing Patterson in order to pursue Mrs. Whitman." Wagenknecht inferred that Poe actually received

260   *Notes*

(and read) Patterson's proposal in December 1848 but incredibly delayed his reply until the spring of 1849, months after his break with Whitman.

248. *CL*, 2:799, LTR-313, Letter: Poe to John R. Thompson, May 10, 1849. "I shall probably be in Richmond about the 1rst of June."

249. *CL*, 2:809–10, LTR-319, Letter: Poe to Annie L. Richmond, June 16, 1849.

250. Ingram, *Edgar Allan Poe*, 2:215.

251. "Quoth the Raven: A Catalog of the Exhibition." Prepared by Col. Richard Gimbel, *Yale University Library Gazette*, April 1959, 33:184. Eight days following Poe's death, Maria Clemm assumed executorship of his estate and, with the aid of Sylvanus Lewis, drew up a written agreement directing Rufus Griswold to produce a collection of the known works of her nephew. Her written appointment of Griswold appears in the opening of the first volume.

252. *The Works of the Late Edgar Allan Poe*, 4 vols, edited by Rufus W. Griswold (New York: J. S. Redfield, 1850–1856), 3:vii–xxxix. Griswold had the first two volumes of Poe's collected works ready for publication by the end of 1850. Within a year, he produced the third volume containing Poe's "Literati" and "Marginalia" series, as well as his vitriolic "memoir" of the poet. A fourth volume containing "The Narrative of Arthur Gordon Pym" and miscellaneous short stories was added in 1856, but Griswold's malicious biography would be included in all subsequent editions and run largely uncontested until 1875.

CHAPTER 2

1. *CL*, 2:830–32, LTR-330, Letter: Poe to Maria Clemm, August 29, 1849. "You know we could easily pay off what we owe at Fordham." Also, *CL*, 2:837–38, LTR-332, Letter: Poe to Maria Clemm, September 18, 1849. "It will be better for me not to go to Fordham—don't you think so?"

2. *Quinn*, 611–12.

3. *Miller*, 199–201. Mrs. Lewis first stated in 1854 that Poe left her Brooklyn home at 5 p.m. following the meal. Later, in 1880, she would tell John Ingram that Poe and Maria Clemm spent the night of June 29 at her house and he left the following morning. However, her earlier version, only four years following these events, is better trusted.

4. Letter: Maria Clemm to N. P. Willis, as cited in his article in the (New York) *Home Journal*, October 20, 1849. The spelling of Clemm's nickname for her nephew, "Eddie," is confirmed.

5. W. Williams, *Appleton's Railroad & Steamboat Companion for 1849* (New York: D. Appleton, 1948), 224.

6. Letter: George Lippard to Rufus Griswold, November 22, 1849. Rufus W. Griswold Papers, Boston Public Library Archives and Special Collections, Boston, Massachusetts. Lippard states that he received a letter from Poe dated July 19, requesting a search for the missing valise, this being after his declaration to Maria Clemm on July 14, that the bag had been recovered.

Notes 261

7. John Sartain, *The Reminiscences of a Very Old Man, 1808–1897* (New York: D. Appleton, 1899), 210–12. *Quinn*, 617n3, found no record of Poe's confinement at the Philadelphia County Prison but a brief detention there may have precluded any recording.

8. Sartain, *Reminiscences*, 210.

9. John Sartain, *Boston Evening Transcript*, February 25, 1893. *Quinn*, 616, is skeptical of this story, perhaps thinking of the Thompson daguerreotype that shows Poe with a mustache in Richmond. However, the photograph was taken more than two months after these events, time enough for it to grow back in.

10. Sartain, *Reminiscences*, 205–12.

11. *CL*, 2:820–21, LTR-323. Letter: Poe to Maria Clemm, July 7, 1849: "I have been taken to prison once since I came here for getting drunk; but then I was not. It was about Virginia."

12. *CL*, 2:825–26, LTR-327, Letter: Poe to Maria Clemm, July 19, 1849. His continued drinking during the missing days is inferred by his declaration, "I have not drank anything since Friday morning." One possible explanation of his whereabouts is that after being found in a "condition," the poet was taken to the home of a Philadelphia relative of Thomas H. Lane (Poe's partner at the *Broadway Journal*) only to leave the following morning against the wishes of his host. *Quinn*, 637–38, however, believed this to have occurred when Poe was on his way back north in the fall.

13. George Lippard, "Edgar A. Poe," *Dodge's Literary Museum* (Boston) 9, no. 20 (October 21, 1854): 315–16.

14. Letter: George Lippard to Rufus Griswold, November 22, 1849. Rufus W. Griswold Papers, Boston Public Library Archives and Special Collections, Boston, Massachusetts. See also *Philadelphia Evening Telegraph*, January 19, 1909.

15. *CL*, 2:820–821, LTR-323, Letter: Poe to Maria Clemm, July 7, 1849.

16. *CL*, 2:825–826, LTR-327, Letter: Poe to Maria Clemm, July 19, 1849.

17. Philip A. Mackowiak, *Post Mortem: Solving History's Great Medical Mysteries* (Philadelphia: American College of Physicians, 2007), 254.

18. *Quinn*, 619–20. Quinn states he left Philadelphia on Friday, July 13, and arrived in Richmond the very next day. The travel guides and schedules establish that this trip, via railroad and steam packet, could not have been completed in less than thirty-eight hours. At that time, an "overnight passage" from Philadelphia to Richmond (by rail or boat) was not being offered. Had such an express service been available, it is most certain that Poe could not have afforded it. If Poe actually left Pennsylvania on the evening of July 13, he could not have landed in Richmond before Sunday afternoon, July 15.

19. *Richmond Enquirer*, September 11, 1849, 2. The Powhatan Line's *Pocahontas* left Baltimore on Saturdays at 4 p.m. It was a direct cruise and reached Richmond five hours earlier than the Baltimore Steam Packet that left from Spear's Wharf at the same time. Had Poe taken the latter boat he would have, after transferring at Norfolk, arrived at Richmond in late afternoon or early evening.

20. *CL*, 2:822–823, LTR-325, Letter: Poe to Maria Clemm, July 14, 1849.

21. J. Disturnell, *Disturnell's Railroad, Steamboat, and Telegraph Book* (New York: J. Disturnell, 1850), 9.

262 *Notes*

22. George Lippard, *Quaker City*, October 20, 1849.

23. *CL*, 2:823–824, LTR-326, Letter: Poe to Maria Clemm, July 14, 1849.

24. Alexander Crosby Brown, *The Old Bay Line, 1840–1940* (New York: Bonanza Books, 1940), 36. Passenger steamers that ran between Norfolk and Baltimore had saloons as an advertised amenity.

25. *CL*, 2:825–26, LTR-327, Letter: Poe to Maria Clemm, July 19, 1849.

26. *CL*, 2:808–809, LTR-318, Letter: Poe to John R. Thompson, June 9, 1849.

27. Letter: George Lippard to Rufus W. Griswold, November 22, 1849. Griswold Collection, Boston Public Library. Lippard states that he received a letter from Poe dated July 19 requesting a search for the missing valise.

28. Susan Archer Talley Weiss, "The Last Days of Edgar A. Poe," *Scribner's Magazine* 12 (March 1878): 707–16.

29. Letter: Miss Susan Archer Talley to Poe, November 29, 1848, as cited in *H*, 17:324. Poe's new arrangement with Edwin H. N. Patterson should have rendered Valentine's support unnecessary.

30. Mary Wingfield Scott, *Old Richmond Neighborhoods* (Richmond, VA: Whittet & Shepperson, 1950), 157. "Talavera," the Richmond mansion of the Talley family, was still standing in 1950 at 2315 West Grace Street.

31. Weiss, "Last Days," 707–16.

32. *Weiss*, 158. Weiss gives varying dates (in different accounts) for Mackenzie's matrimonial advice; however, the 1848 visit to Richmond appears the most likely.

33. *Quinn*, 629.

34. Completed letter: Poe to Maria Clemm, August 29, 1849. The Edgar Allan Poe Society of Baltimore, see https://www.eapoe.org/works/letters/p4908280.

35. *Weiss*, 199–200.

36. *Powell*, 120–29. Elmira Shelton to Edward V. Valentine, November 19, 1875, as transcribed by Michael Powell. One possible motive for this hasty marriage with the well-off widow could have been to avoid his partnership with Edwin Patterson and a promised trip to St. Louis. Producing a magazine (on his own) at Richmond would certainly have been a more attractive prospect to him.

37. *PL*, 819.

38. *Quinn*, 657, cited from the original manuscript in the Simon Gratz Collection, Historical Society of Pennsylvania, Philadelphia.

39. *CL*, 2:828–29, LTR-329, Letter: Poe to E. H. N. Patterson, August 7, 1849.

40. *Times-Despatch*, January 1909. The veracity of Poe's 1848 "duel" with John M. Daniels, as provided by James H. Whitty (from an interview with Judge Robert W. Hughes), appears questionable.

41. Daniel, 220. Daniel's brother wrote that at the time of Poe's death, the poet had promised to "furnish literary articles" to the *Examiner.*

42. John Moncure Daniel, "[Obituary of Edgar A. Poe]," *Richmond Semi-Weekly Examiner*, October 12, 1849, 2.

43. *Phillips*, 2:1433–34.

44. Weiss, "Last Days," 713–14.

45. *H*, 1:316.

46. *H*, 1:315–16.

Notes   263

47. Poe's use of a cane while in Richmond will be shown to have significance.

48. Weiss, "Last Days," 707–16.

49. *Miller*, 31–32.

50. Weiss, "Last Days," 712.

51. *H*, 1:311–12.

52. J. H. Whitty, ed., *The Complete Poems of Edgar Allan Poe* (Boston: Houghton Mifflin, 1911), lxxxi.

53. *PL*, 826.

54. Completed letter: Poe to Maria Clemm, August 29, 1849. The Edgar Allan Poe Society of Baltimore, https://www.eapoe.org/works/letters/p4908280.

55. Weiss, "Last Days," 710. His reluctance in publicizing the pending marriage would not be not hard to fathom. If Patterson learned of the wedding, he could have thought that Poe was fizzling on him and the magazine venture. Poe could have also simply wanted to prevent any interference this time.

56. *CL*, 2:723, LTR-286, Letter: Poe to Annie L. Richmond, November 16, 1848.

57. Completed letter: Poe to Maria Clemm, August 29, 1849. The Edgar Allan Poe Society of Baltimore, see https://www.eapoe.org/works/letters/p4908280.

58. Weiss, "Last Days," 712.

59. *Quinn*, 624.

60. John P. Little, *History of Richmond* (Richmond, VA: Dietz Printing, 1933), 104.

61. *PL*, 830–31.

62. William Glenn, "Letters from William and Mary College," *Virginia Magazine of History and Biography* (April 1921): 143n10. When writing to Edward V. Valentine, Glenn reiterated "the consensus of opinion of the Temperance men was that he [Poe] had kept his pledges inviolate up to that time."

63. *CL*, 2:830–31, LTR-330, Letter: Poe to Maria Clemm, August 29, 1849.

64. *CL*, 2:766–67, LTR-303, Letter: Poe to Mrs. Annie L. Richmond, February 8, 1849. In this letter Poe makes it clear that he and his aunt had been making plans to leave New York. Had the Lewises given Clemm the money to go south, it is probable that neither one would have returned.

65. *PL*, 815.

66. *Phillips*, 2:1467–69. After his arrival in Norfolk, Poe was apparently invited to stay at the Hygeia Hotel as a guest of Mr. and Mrs. D. French.

67. Anonymous, "She Lives Over an Evening with Poe," *New York Herald*, February 19, 1905, 4.

68. *CL*, 2:837–838, LTR-332, Letter: Poe to Maria Clemm, September 18, 1849.

69. *CL*, 2:841, LTR-334, Letter: Poe to Mrs. Marguerite St. Leon Loud, September 18, 1849.

70. Thomas Dimmock, "Notes on Poe," *Century Illustrated Magazine* 50 (June 1895): 315–16.

71. John F. Carter, MD, "Edgar Poe's Last Night in Richmond," *Lippincott's Monthly Magazine* 70, November 1902: 562–66.

72. James A. Harrison, *New Glimpses of Poe* (New York: M. F. Mansfield, 1901), 43.

264 *Notes*

73. James A. Harrison, "New Glimpses of Poe." *Independent*, September 20, 1900, 2259–62.

74. John Ward Ostrom, "Edgar A. Poe: His Income as Literary Entrepreneur," *Poe Studies* 15, no. 1 (June 1982): 6. Ostrom believed that Poe may have received a small honorarium for one or more of his final three lectures in Virginia and that the total amount realized from the appearances there did not exceed $75.

75. Letter: Elmira Shelton to Maria Clemm, September 22, 1849. Original MS in *Pratt*. It is clear from this communication that Shelton had by then become aware of Poe's drinking.

76. *CL*, 2:837–838, LTR-332, Letter: Poe to Maria Clemm, September 18, 1849. In his last known letter to Maria Clemm, Poe indicates that a date for the wedding had not then been set: "Nothing is yet definitely settled and it will not do to hurry matters."

77. *CL*, 1:836, LTR-331a, Letter: Poe to Maria Clemm from Old Point Comfort, Virginia, September 10, 1849.

78. Weiss, "Last Days," 713–14.

79. Letter: John R. Thompson to Rufus W. Griswold, October 10, 1849, original MS in the Simon Gratz Collection, Historical Society of Pennsylvania. The contents of the original letter Thompson gave to Poe (if it ever existed) is unknown but is assumed to have contained material for Rufus W. Griswold's new edition of *The Poets and Poetry of America*. In his October 10 letter to Griswold, Thompson describes Poe's visit as "some three weeks since" which certainly was not the evening before he left Richmond.

80. *PL*, 842–43.

81. *Woodberry*, 2:341.

82. John F. Carter, MD, "Edgar Poe's Last Night in Richmond," *Lippincott's Monthly Magazine*, November 1902, 562–66.

83. Letter: Rosalie Poe to R. W. Griswold, August 20, 1850, Free Library of Philadelphia, Gimbel Collection; quoted by Jeffrey A. Savoye, "Two Biographical Digressions: Poe's Wandering Trunk and Dr. Carter's Mysterious Sward Cane," *Edgar Allan Poe Review* 5 (Fall 2004): 15–42. It is possible that the Mackenzies retrieved the trunk from Poe's hotel after learning of his death but this does not agree with Rosalie's claim that her brother entrusted it to her personally.

84. Hervey Allen, *Israfel: The Life and Times of Edgar Allan Poe*, 2 vols. (New York: George H. Doran, 1926), 2:839. The story of the broken lamp and Rosalie's remark, "that no complaint should be made as it was broken by a poet," had been told to sculptor Edward V. Valentine, by an unidentified lady who claimed to have been present; see Allen's footnote 921. Mary Phillips (2:1486) placed this event at the home of the Talley's and gave the name of the witness as Valentine's sister, E. A. V. Gray.

85. *CL*, 1:10–13, LTR-5, Letter: Poe to Allan, March 19; LTR-6, Letter: Poe to Allan, March 20, 1827; See also *CL*, 1:42–45, LTR-19, Letter: Poe to Allan, August 10, 1829. It is not clear whether Allan ever complied with Poe's repeated requests for the trunk or if Poe managed to retrieve it at later date.

Notes 265

86. *CL*, 2:823–824, LTR-326, Letter: Poe to Maria Clemm, July 14, 1849: "My clothes are so horrible." There is also Poe's letter to Clemm (LTR-330, Completed letter: Poe to Maria Clemm, August 29, 1849. The Edgar Allan Poe Society of Baltimore, https://www.eapoe.org/works/letters/p4908280), describing his arrival in Richmond: "without clothes, and in every way in despair," both indicating that he was then traveling without luggage. See also George Lippard's communication to Rufus Griswold (Letter: Lippard to Griswold, November 22, 1849. Griswold Collection, Boston Public Library) establishing that Poe had asked Lippard to search for his missing valise (in Philadelphia) after the poet had arrived in Richmond.

87. Mary Newton Stanard, *Edgar Allan Poe Letters Till Now Unpublished: In the Valentine Museum, Richmond, Virginia* (Philadelphia: J. B. Lippincott, 1925), 179.

88. It has been the tradition (albeit an unsupported one) that Poe had a steamer trunk with him when he landed in Baltimore. But as discussed, if he left a chest behind in Richmond it seems improbable that he would have acquired a second trunk for his brief trip north.

89. John F. Carter, MD, "Edgar Poe's Last Night in Richmond," *Lippincott's Monthly Magazine*, November 1902, 562–66.

90. Inferred in a letter from R. W. Griswold to J. R. Thompson, October 25, 1849, MS in the J. K. Lilly Collection of Edgar Allan Poe, Lilly Library at the University of Indiana, Bloomington, Indiana, cited by *Quinn*, 656. John H. Ingram also states in his 1880 biography, "Upon his arrival [at Baltimore] he gave his trunk [bag] to a porter"; however, he cites no authority. See Ingram, *Edgar Allan Poe: His Life, Letters, and Opinions*, 2 vols. (London: John Hogg, 1880), 2:235.

91. Duncan Lodge, at what is today 1800 West Broad Street, Richmond, Virginia, was considered the "country" in 1849 and was over two miles from Sadler's Restaurant at Sixteenth Street. Rockett's Landing was another mile away in the opposite direction, the total distance to be covered being five miles—in the dark. However, if Poe instead had his trunk stored at the Madison House, there would have been ample time to stow the cane there and still make his early morning departure.

CHAPTER 3

1. Henry W. and Albert A. Berg Collection, New York Public Library, New York, cited in *PL*, 844.

2. *Richmond Enquirer*, September 11, 1849, 2. The schedules of these boats are shown in an advertisement. Built in 1829, the *Pocahontas* was the oldest in the Powhatan Line's fleet and was growing increasing unreliable. On September 28, when Poe could have been steaming up the bay from Norfolk, the *Baltimore Sun* reported that after leaving Baltimore the *Pocahontas* was "ashore" at Kent Island, meaning it had run aground or had experienced a mechanical failure. The same paper would report at the end of October that the steamer had been taken out of service for overhaul at a shipyard in Fells Point.

3. J. Disturnell, *Disturnell's Railroad, Steamboat, and Telegraph Book* (New York: J. Disturnell, 1850), 9.

Notes

4. As Poe referred to Thomas Moore's work in his lectures, it is not improbable that he left a copy of the music book with John Carter, especially if he had another example, or could easily acquire a replacement.

5. *Quinn*, 755. The word "Augusta" appears in quotation marks on Carter's copy of Moore's *Irish Melodies* suggesting the appellation of a vessel rather than someone's name; but coming from Dr. John Carter, this story must be viewed with caution.

6. Disturnell, *Disturnell's Railroad*, 9.

7. *Quinn*, 755.

8. Alexander Crosby Brown, *The Old Bay Line, 1840–1940* (New York: Bonanza Books, 1940), 36.

9. Charles Cobb, *American Railway Guide & Pocket Companion for the United States: 1851* (New York: Curran Dinsmore, 1851), 119. The boat trip from Norfolk to Baltimore was advertised as thirteen hours but depending on the boat's cargo, number of passengers, and amount of unscheduled stops, the voyage could be lengthened by a couple hours, yet would still arrive in plenty of time for the 9 a.m. train to Philadelphia.

10. R. J. Matchett, *Matchett's Baltimore Directory for 1849-1850* (Baltimore: Matchett, 1849), p. 14, appendix.

11. Charles P. Dare, *Philadelphia, Wilmington and Baltimore Railroad Guide, 1856* (Philadelphia: King & Baird, 1856), 19. The arrangement of shared premises with the Baltimore & Ohio (B&O) would end the following year when the new Philadelphia, Wilmington & Baltimore (PW&B) Railroad station was completed on President Street; the passenger terminal survives today as the Civil War Museum.

12. Inferred in a letter from R. W. Griswold to J. R. Thompson, October 25, 1849, MS in the Poe Collection, Lilly Library at the University of Indiana, cited by *Quinn*, 656. John Ingram also states in his 1880 biography, "Upon his arrival [at Baltimore] he gave his trunk [bag] to a porter"; however, he provides no authority (Ingram, *Edgar Allan Poe: His Life, Letters, and Opinions*, 2 vols. [London: John Hogg, 1880], 2:235).

13. United States Census Bureau (website): https://www2.census.gov/library/working-papers/1998/demographics/pop-twps0027/tab08. The figure of 515,547 is given for the population of New York City for 1850.

14. Anonymous, "Commerce of Baltimore." *Baltimore Sun*, October 3, 1849. "Arrivals at the port of Baltimore during the month of September . . . 178 [ships] of which 162 were American, 11 British, 3 Russian, 1 Genoese and 1 Danish."

15. Edward Hungerford, *The Story of the Baltimore & Ohio Railroad, 1827–1927*, 2 vols. (New York: G. P. Putnam's Sons, 1928), 2:72. Although the city permitted no locomotives on Pratt Street between the B&O and PW&B Railroad stations, tracks were laid to allow the horse-drawn transfer of individual train cars, which added even more congestion around the harbor.

16. Francis F. Beirne, *The Amiable Baltimoreans* (New York: E. P. Dutton, 1951), 142.

17. Clinton McCabe, *History of the Baltimore Police Department, 1774–1907* (Baltimore: Fleet-McGinley, 1907), 20.

Notes 267

18. *McCabe,* 24. See also Clayton Colman Hall, *Baltimore: Its History and Its People,* 3 vols. (New York: Lewis Historical Publishing, 1912), 45–46.

19. Hollingsworth, along with Ellicott and Grant Streets (that ran north and south between Light and Calvert Streets), were alleys that resulted when the original docks north of Pratt Street were cut off from the harbor and the slips between the piers filled in. The resulting buildings and warehouses were completely destroyed in the great fire of 1904 after which the opportunity was taken to eliminate these narrow alleyways.

20. Eugene L. Didier, *The Poe Cult and Other Poe Papers* (New York: Broadway Publishing, 1909), 176–77. This story of the Widow Meagher's (which also includes a tale of Poe's "cooping") was given to Didier in a letter dated December 8, 1879, by Baltimore attorney, Alexander Hynds, who identified his source only as a "prominent man of San Francisco." The original MS letter is in the Poe Collection at the Enoch Pratt Free Library in Baltimore, Maryland.

21. Danl. H. Craig, *Craig's Baltimore Business Directory and Baltimore Almanac, for 1842* (Baltimore: J. Robinson, 1842), p. 123.

22. *Woodberry,* 2:342.

23. Pearl, "A Poe Death Dossier," 4–29.

24. "A Card," *Baltimore Sun,* September 27, 1849, 2.

25. "Local Matters," *Baltimore Sun,* September 24, 1849, 1.

26. *Miller,* 245.

27. Pearl, "A Poe Death Dossier," 7–8.

28. In 1859, Nathan Brooks received an honorary LLD degree (Doctor of Laws in English, the same degree conferred to Woodberry) but at the time of Poe's death he did not have the credential.

29. R. L. Polk, *R. L. Polk & Company's Baltimore City Directory for 1887* (Baltimore: A. Hoen, 1887), 94. Brooks's home in 1849 was at 270 Lexington Street in Pascault Row. In 1886, the street address was changed to 657 West Lexington Street. Although repurposed as apartments, this impressive row home, built in 1819, was still standing in 2021.

30. William Oberhardt, "Edgar Allan Poe," *Cosmopolitan Magazine* (February 1909): 252. A slightly different account appears in the *St. Louis Globe-Democrat,* January 17, 1909.

31. Fortunately this account would not be included in Sara Sigourney Rice's book (*Edgar Allan Poe: A Memorial Volume* [Baltimore: Turnbull Brothers, 1877]).

32. Letter: Mrs. D. H. Carroll to Sara Sigourney Rice (undated but believed to be c. 1876), Original MS in the Poe Collection, Enoch Pratt Free Library, Baltimore, Maryland. Reverend Clemm's eyewitness testimony is generally trustworthy; however, here he was only repeating a story heard from others. Indeed this detail of Poe passed out at Lexington Market was not included in his recollection of the conversation with Moran as given to E. R. Reynolds in 1889.

33. Matchett, *Matchett's Baltimore Directory for 1849-1850,* lists John S. Macher as a carpenter and living at 115 S. Eutaw Street. His acquaintances are given by Mrs. Carroll only as "Mr. Crane" and "Mr. Turner" for which there is no reliable information.

268   *Notes*

34. Richard H. Stoddard, "Edgar Allan Poe," *Harper's Monthly Magazine* 45 (September 1872): 557–68.

35. Letter: George B. Coale to Richard H. Stoddard, April 26, 1871, Anthony Street Collection, Manuscript Division, New York Public Library, New York.

36. John J. Moran, "Official Memorandum of the Death of Edgar A. Poe," *New York Herald*, October 28, 1875, 4.

37. Matchett, *Matchett's Baltimore Directory for 1849-1850*, 319. "Rawlings George, Conductor R. Road conductor, 87 S Paca."

38. *Moran*, 60.

39. Hungerford, *Story of the Baltimore & Ohio Railroad*, 1:196. What may have been the first railroad train ferry in the world began crossing the Susquehanna River in 1837, from Havre de Grace to Perryville, and would continue in practice until the river was bridged after the Civil War.

40. *Moran*, 58–61.

41. *Baltimore Sun*, March 26, 1849, 2. In March, "Capt. George W. Rollins" [Rawlings] was presented a gold-topped cane by the B&O as recognition for his years of service after which (*Baltimore Sun*, April 12, 1849, 2) it was announced that he was with the Merchant's and People's Transportation Company. A classified advertisement for the freight company placed by him in December (*Baltimore Sun*, December 3, 1849, 4) appears to show him still engaged there. By 1853 ("A Faithful Officer Properly Remembered," *Baltimore Sun*, April 29, 1853, 1), he was back with the B&O where he lost his pocket watch while ministering to passengers after a train accident.

42. Ingram, *Edgar Allan Poe*, 2:236–37.

43. *Powel*, vi.

44. John Evangelist Walsh, *Midnight Dreary: The Mysterious Death of Edgar Allan Poe* (New Brunswick, NJ: Rutgers University Press, 1998), 113. It is certain that Elmira Shelton's family opposed the marriage to Poe, her mother and children in particular. However, the disapproval of her brothers toward the union has never been recorded and any interaction they may have had with Poe after he left Richmond remains without support.

45. *Quinn*, 637.

46. T. C. Duncan Eaves, "Poe's Last Visit to Philadelphia," *American Literature*, March 1954, 50nn. In his paper, Eaves also suggested that this episode could have occurred during his July visit to the city.

47. Pearl, "A Poe Death Dossier," 24.

CHAPTER 4

1. "Local Matters," *Baltimore Sun*, October 3, 1849, 1. "Yesterday . . . was one of the most disagreeable days . . . experienced for a long season. . . . Successive showers of rain came down whilst the atmosphere was cold, raw and misty, and the thermometer standing all day at 56 degrees. . . . The northeast wind which prevailed indicated a continuance of falling weather." That the rain continued on Election Day (October 3) is confirmed by a report in the *Baltimore Sun* the following day: "The

Notes 269

Election – The genius of patriotism was yesterday put to her umbrella and over shoes, for the atmosphere partook sensibly of the spongy character."

2. In yet a later account (*Moran*, 59), John J. Moran would describe the bench as a plank resting across the top of two barrels.

3. John J. Moran, "Official Memoranda of the Death of Edgar A. Poe," *New York Herald*, October 28, 1875, 4.

4. John H. Ingram, ed., *Edgar Allan Poe: His Life, Letters, and Opinions*, 2 vols. (London: John Hogg, 1880).

5. The Horse You Came In On Saloon, "Our Story," 2020, https://www.thehorse-baltimore.com/story (accessed October 2020).

6. R. J. Matchett, *Matchett's Baltimore Directory for 1849-1850* (Baltimore: Matchett, 1849), 35. When street numbers in Baltimore City were rationalized to the present system in 1886, the address of 64 Thames Street was changed to 1626 (the current location of "The Horse You Came in On Saloon"). However, directories reveal that from 1845 to 1851, Mr. John Bennet operated a grocery store at 64 Thames Street. As late as 1860, the location was still shown as a confectionery and boarding house.

7. Letter: Neilson Poe to Maria Clemm, October 11, 1849, original manuscript in *Pratt*.

8. "Suicide," *Baltimore Sun*, May 28, 1880, 3.

9. *Miller*, 84–85. Letter: Wm. Hand Browne to John Ingram, October 16, 1880. According to Browne, Snodgrass's letters had by then suffered much damage and their condition was such that the need for transcription was seen as immediate in order to preserve their contents.

10. Edward Spencer, "The Memory of Poe: Unpublished Letters of the Poet to Dr. Snodgrass," *New York Herald*, March 27, 1881, 8.

11. Letter: Wm. Hand Browne to John Ingram, February 22, 1909. John Henry Ingram's Poe Collection, University of Virginia, Charlottesville, Virginia, ca. 1829–1915. When Ingram later questioned the note's authenticity (and the fidelity of the transcription), Browne provided a detailed description: "It was in pencil, on course paper, no doubt he [Walker] got at Ryan's. It was written in a good round hand, accurately spelled and punctuated, as one would expect from a printer, and the signature was free and flowing, as a man signs his own name." Browne further added, "you may take your oath the copies I sent you are correct to the comma."

12. See John Henry Ingram's Poe Collection, University of Virginia, Charlottesville, Virginia.

13. Mary Markey and Dean Krimmel, "Poe's Mystery House: The Search for Mechanics Row," *Maryland Historical Magazine* (Winter 1991): 387–95.

14. Pearl, "A Poe Death Dossier," 8.

15. Matchett, *Matchett's Baltimore Directory for 1849-1850*, 405.

16. J. E. Snodgrass, "E. A. Poe's Death and Burial," *Spiritual Telegraph* (New York), January 26, 1856, 155.

17. Snodgrass's misspelling of Thomas J. Coath's last name indicates the accepted pronunciation.

270   *Notes*

18. John Heywood, *A Dialogue Conteinyng the Number in Effect of all Prourbes in the Englishe Tongue*, 2 vols. (London: Thomas Berthelet, 1546), 2:chap. 1. The idiom, "the worse for wear" dates at least to its appearance in Heywood's book of 1546 ("Al thing is the wors for the wearyng") but its euphemistic application for "the worse for drink" is more contemporary.

19. 1850 United States Federal Census: https://www.ancestryheritagequest.com (website). In the 1850 Federal Census, Ryan is shown as being fifty-two years old, and his occupation is given as "Tavern Keeper."

20. R. L. Polk, *R. L. Polk & Company's Baltimore City Directory for 1887* (Baltimore: A. Hoen, 1887), 97. In 1886, street numbers in Baltimore City were rationalized to the present system. The Polk directory for the following year lists all old street numbers along with the corresponding new number—the address of 44 East Lombard Street was changed to 912 East Lombard Street. The original address of the hotel is given as No. 46 from various newspaper listings.

21. *Baltimore Sun*, July 12, 1848, 3.

22. *Baltimore Sun,* November 17, 1843, 3; March 6, 1852, 3; April 10, 1868, 1.

23. The tavern was located on the north or sunny-side of Lombard Street where most businesses then erected awnings to shelter patrons as well as their sidewalk annexes from the sun.

24. Joseph Evans Snodgrass, "The Facts of Poe's Death and Burial," *Beadle's Monthly* (May 1867): 283.

25. Snodgrass, "Facts," 284.

26. Joseph Evans Snodgrass, Letter (reprint), *New York Reformer* (Watertown, NY), July 26, 1855, 2. Snodgrass's letter was reprinted in full from an earlier, 1855 edition of the *Women's Temperance Paper*.

27. Ingram's Poe Collection, University of Virginia, ca. 1829–1915. In the doctor's defense, it appears he was writing from memory; that he did not have (or could not find) Joseph Walker's note to use as reference is indicated by the incorrect month (November) he gave. William Hand Browne suggested that Snodgrass had forgotten that he had tucked the note into one of the other letters in his collection.

28. Elizabeth Oakes Smith, "Autobiographic Notes: Edgar Allan Poe," *Beadle's Monthly* (February 1867): 147–56.

29. Snodgrass, "Facts," 283–87.

30. Snodgrass, "Facts," 283–87.

31. Edward Spencer, "The Memory of Poe: Unpublished Letters of the Poet to Dr. Snodgrass," *New York Herald*, March 27, 1881. Spencer's first publication of Joseph Walker's note to Snodgrass in the *New York Herald* was not to establish Poe's whereabouts, but to discredit Snodgrass's account as those of a temperance zealot.

32. *CL*, 1:263, LTR-109, Letter: Poe to Joseph Snodgrass, April 1, 1841. Poe himself would confer his confidence in Snodgrass's medical acumen: "You are a physician, and I presume no physician can have difficulty in detecting the drunkard at a glance."

33. Snodgrass, "Facts," 283–87.

34. J. E. Snodgrass, "Death and Burial of Edgar A. Poe," *Life Illustrated* (New York), May 17, 1856, 24.

Notes 271

35. Snodgrass, "Death and Burial," 24. Snodgrass indicated that he encountered two of Poe's relatives at Gunners' Hall, Henry Herring and perhaps his [Henry's] uncle, George Herring.

36. *Baltimore Sun*, January 21, 1847, 2: A meeting at Gunners' Hall was called by citizens of the Fourth Ward to organize collection of funds for the poor. Henry Herring was assigned to the second district. See also: Jane Sears, "Henry Herring—Fair Mount," *Maryland Tams Journal* 29, no. 3 (Fall 2008): 12. Herring had also been a member of the Vigilant Fire Company that was stationed directly across the street from Gunners' Hall.

37. Peter Ackroyd, *A Life Cut Short* (New York: Doubleday, 2008), 3. Still another version claims that Henry Herring was not summoned to Gunners' Hall but just happened to be there on "electoral business."

38. Snodgrass, "Facts," 283–87.

39. "From our Correspondent," *Baltimore Sun*, December 8, 1840, 4. The widely used term "hack cab" is somewhat of a contradiction: "hacks" (hackney coaches) had four wheels with side doors and were much slower than a "cab" (French cabriolet or Hansom Cab) that rolled on two wheels and opened at the front.

40. Mary Newton Stanard, *Edgar Allan Poe Letters Till Now Unpublished: In the Valentine Museum, Richmond, Virginia* (Philadelphia: J. B. Lippincott, 1925), 179. As worded, Stanard's assertion would mean that Poe remained in the soiled clothing (in which he was found) for the four days he was in the hospital and that no one there examined him during his admittance.

41. *Allen*, 673. Hervey Allen was one the biographers accepting this story of the trunk key. Also in 2021, the trunk was being publicly exhibited at the Poe Museum in Richmond, Virginia along with a plaque that read: "The key to the trunk was found in Poe's pocket after his death."

42. Inferred in a letter from R. W. Griswold to J. R. Thompson, October 25, 1849, original manuscript in the J. K. Lilly Collection of Edgar Allan Poe. Lilly Library, University of Indiana, Bloomington, Indiana, cited by *Quinn*, 656. John H. Ingram also states in *Edgar Allan Poe: His Life, Letters, and Opinions*, 2 vols. (London: John Hogg, 1880), "Upon his arrival [at Baltimore] he gave his trunk to a porter to convey it." However, Ingram provides no authority for the declaration, writing only that "it is stated" (2:235). As discussed, it was probably not his steamer trunk.

43. *Woodberry*, 2:343.

44. *Weiss*, 207. Also in an 1878 article for *Scribner's Magazine*, Susan Archer Weiss would mention the cane, as well as Poe's September 26 visit to Dr. John Carter's office. The synchronization of their stories is not surprising as Weiss was related to Carter by marriage.

45. *Phillips*, 2:1502, and also *Allen*, 673.

46. Snodgrass, "Facts," 283–87.

47. *Moran*, 62–63. The doctor claimed to have paid the cab driver himself.

48. "Local Matters." *Baltimore Sun*, October 2, 1849, 1. On October 1, Snodgrass had attended and spoke publicly at a meeting of The Friends of the Sunday Law that was being held to withdraw their support of Mr. John Watchman, a temperance candidate for the House of Delegates, who had been seen drinking at a tavern.

272   *Notes*

49. W. Williams, *Appleton's Railroad & Steamboat Companion for 1849* (New York: D. Appleton, 1948), 272. For those fares within the city limits, from Green Street to the Jones Falls, hack cab operators charged 37-1/2 cents. Old Town was outside these boundaries as was the hospital on Broadway where the fee was increased to 50-cents. Additional passengers were 12-1/2 cents more, all of which added incentive to send Poe alone.

CHAPTER 5

1. Snodgrass's house, at what is today 25 N. High Street, no longer survives.
2. Pearl, "A Poe Death Dossier," 8.
3. *CL*, 1:98–101, LTR-047, Letter: Poe to William Poe, August 20, 1835. "Mr. Henry Herring of Baltimore, a man of unprincipled character." This remark to another relative, whether justified or not, demonstrates the apparent reciprocal animosity Poe and his Baltimore relations had for each other.
4. *Powell*, 49.
5. Richard Franklin Bensel, *The American Ballot Box in the Mid-Nineteenth Century* (Cambridge: Cambridge University Press, 2004), 168.
6. See note 14.
7. Daniel Walker Howe, *The Political Culture of the American Whigs* (Chicago: University of Chicago Press, 1979), 14.
8. Howe, *Political Culture*, 15.
9. Bensel, *American Ballot Box*, 9.
10. Letter: Wm. Hand Browne to John Ingram, January 13, 1909. John Henry Ingram's Poe Collection, University of Virginia, Charlottesville, Virginia, ca. 1829–1915.
11. Bensel, *American Ballot Box*, 20.
12. Bensel, *American Ballot Box*, 9–13.
13. "The New Police Bill," *Baltimore Sun*, December 26, 1856, 1. A bill was finally passed that abolished the system of watches and reorganized the municipal police force, increasing the number of officers, and requiring day and night duty from all. In place of the watch-houses, the city was divided into four districts and foot patrols, or "beats" were assigned to now uniformed officers. Side arms were also approved for the first time but funding would prevent widespread implementation until 1858.
14. "Captured and Cooped," *Baltimore Sun*, October 1, 1850, 2. When an elderly woman went to the police "office" to complain that her husband had been "rudely assailed" and kidnapped by a gang of "rowdy politicians," the constable advised her to make the complaint at city hall.
15. Bensel, *American Ballot Box*, 18–19.
16. Bensel, *American Ballot Box*, 182.
17. Edward Spencer, "The Memory of Poe: Unpublished Letters of the Poet to Dr. Snodgrass," *New York Herald*, March 27, 1881, 8.
18. Spencer, "Memory of Poe," 8.

Notes 273

19. "Lawlessness," *Baltimore Sun*, October 15, 1850, 2.

20. J. Thomas Scharf, *Chronicles of Baltimore: Being a Complete History of "Baltimore Town" and Baltimore City* (Baltimore: Turnbull Brothers, 1874), 567. The practice of political kidnapping in the city would perhaps reach its "peak" in the violence-plagued presidential election of 1859. "Is there no way to arrest these savage doings?" asked a *Baltimore Sun* contributor when describing the abduction of husbands, "Law, Order, Justice and Humanity," *Baltimore Sun*, November 1, 1859, 1.

21. "The Election," *Baltimore Sun*, October 4, 1849, 2.

22. *Republican and Argus*, October 1, 1849, 2.

23. *Republican and Argus*, October 1, 1849, 2.

24. "The Election," *Baltimore Sun*, October 4, 1849, 2.

25. Jeffrey A. Savoye, "The Mysterious Death of Edgar Allan Poe," Edgar Allan Poe Society of Baltimore, https://www.eapoe.org/geninfo/poedeath.htm (accessed July 5, 2023). "A legitimate question is why there seems to have been very little attention to the 'cooping' theory of Poe's death until J. R. Thompson began his lecture tour."

26. Edgar Allan Poe, *The Works of the Late Edgar Allan Poe*, 4 vols. ed. by Rufus W. Griswold (New York: J. S. Redfield, 1850–1856), 3:vii–xxxix.

27. Elizabeth Oakes Smith, quoted in "Edgar A. Poe," *United States Magazine*, March 3, 1857, 262–68.

28. Joseph Evans Snodgrass, "The Facts of Poe's Death and Burial," *Beadle's Monthly*, May 1867, 283–87.

29. John R. Thompson, *The Genius and Character of Edgar Allan Poe* (Richmond, VA: Garrett & Massie, 1929).

30. An examination of John R. Thompson's original manuscript (held at the Poe Museum in Richmond, Virginia) containing the first description of Poe's "cooping," revealed attached newspaper clippings from 1860 to which he referred. From this it appears likely his original lectures included the cooping theory. It is also indicated that Thompson delivered at least one presentation in Richmond during the Civil War (Anonymous, "Latest News from the South," *Baltimore Sun*, February 12, 1862, 1) as a fundraiser "for the benefit of volunteers in the field." The number of lectures he presented after the war remains unclear as he spent some time in England.

31. Thompson, 42.

32. *H*, 17:404, Letter: John R. Thompson to E. H. N. Patterson, November 9, 1849.

33. *H*, 17:404.

34. Spencer, "Memory of Poe," 8.

35. Eugene L. Didier, *The Poe Cult and Other Poe Papers* (New York: Broadway Publishing, 1909), 177–78. Many years after Poe's death, Didier received indirect testimony from an anonymous man claiming to have been cooped with him. Likewise, the eyewitness accounts from Louis Passano and George Rawlings were offered only after Poe's name had become a household word.

36. Letter: George B. Coale to Richard H. Stoddard, April 26, 1871, in Anthony Street Collection, Manuscript Division, New York Public Library, New York. It is not known whether the request for discretion, "it is not necessary to say this," came

274   *Notes*

from Neilson Poe or Coale, or what was meant by it. It could have been an attempt to protect Poe's reputation, or perhaps, having no authority for the story, Neilson Poe wanted to avoid becoming its source.

37. Eugene L. Didier, *The Life and Poems of Edgar Allan Poe* (New York: W. J. Widdleton, 1876), 120. After receiving a letter from Baltimore attorney Alexander Hynds in 1879, Didier would expand the story and include it in a second book, *The Poe Cult and Other Papers* (New York: Broadway Publishing, 1909). In this unsubstantiated version, Hynd's nameless acquaintance claimed that he, along with Poe and two others, was "nabbed" by the Democrats and imprisoned in their coop on Calvert Street, after which they were voted at thirty-one locations on election day. The original letter is held in *Pratt*.

38. Elisabeth Ellicott Poe, "Poe, The Weird Genius," *Cosmopolitan Magazine* (February 1909): 252.

39. Elisabeth Ellicott Poe and Vylla Poe Wilson, *Edgar Allan Poe: A High Priest of the Beautiful* (Washington, DC: Stylus Publishing, 1930), 79.

40. Anonymous, "Fourth Ward—Relief of the Poor," *Baltimore Sun*, January 16, 1849, 2. In this announcement, Lewis Passano is shown to be a member of the Collecting Committee for the Lombard Street district. Other listed members of this Whig organization included Harry [Henry] R. Reynolds, Edward G. Starr, and Richard Lilly, all of whom would serve as election judges at Gunners' Hall on the day Poe was found there.

41. Anonymous, "Large Gathering of the People," *Baltimore Sun*, November 1, 1859, 1. Louis Passano is nominated as an officer of the Reform Committee for the Fourth Ward.

42. Spencer, "Memory of Poe," 8.

43. John J. Moran, "Official Memoranda of the Death of Edgar A. Poe," *New York Herald*, October 28, 1875, 4.

44. *Moran*, 55–56.

45. *Miller*, 78–79. Letter: Wm. Hand Browne to John Ingram, December 3, 1875. Written testimony from Alnutt remains undiscovered although it appears he may have been acquainted with Henry R. Reynolds, a political advocate in Baltimore's Fourth Ward ("Local Matters," *Baltimore Sun*, July 16, 1852, 1).

46. *Miller*, 86. Letter: Wm. Hand Browne to John Ingram, October 25, 1880.

47. Spencer, "Memory of Poe," 8. Spencer, a writer for the *Baltimore Sun*, reported that the notorious "Fourth Ward Club" on High Street held as many as 140 captives.

48. Edgar Allan Poe, "Mellonta Tauta" (1849), *H*, 6:209.

49. *CL*, 1:287, LTR-117, Letter: Poe to Frederick Thomas, June 26, 1841. US President William Henry Harrison died after only one month in office after which his vice president, John Tyler, succeeded him.

50. R. J. Matchett, *Matchett's Baltimore Directory for 1849–1850* (Baltimore: Matchett, 1849), 325. Henry Reynolds operated the building firm of H. R. & J. R. Builders (later H & J Reynolds Architects & Builders). Henry's residence is shown as 23 South High Street, two blocks from Gunner's Hall.

51. "Local Matters," *Baltimore Sun*, October 3, 1849, 1.

52. Pearl, "A Poe Death Dossier," 14.

Notes

53. William T. Bandy, "Dr. Moran and the Poe-Reynolds Myth," in *Myths and Realities: The Mysterious Mr. Poe*, ed. Benjamin Franklin Fisher (Baltimore: Edgar Allan Poe Society, 1987), 26–36. One wonders that if Poe was invoking the name of his relative in the hospital, why he would not have called out "Henry" instead of "Herring." Other theories that have Poe bellowing the name of another author seem farfetched, although Burton R. Pollin's idea that he was conjuring Frederick Mansel Reynolds, author of Miserrimus, is not as easy to disqualify. See Burton R. Pollin, *Discoveries in Poe* (Notre Dame, IN: University of Notre Dame Press, 1970), 189–204.

54. Mayne Reid, "A Dead Man Defended," *Onward* (April 1869): 305–8. Reid's description of Poe's indifference to articles of his clothing after becoming intoxicated is very revealing.

55. John Sartain, *Boston Evening Transcript*, February 25, 1893. Quinn, 616.

56. Of course Poe *could* have been expelled and brought back inside by Walker.

CHAPTER 6

1. The University of Maryland was more than a mile to the west through the center of town, while the state-operated Maryland Hospital (where Johns Hopkins is today) treated only the insane. There was also the Baltimore Infirmary (the city's almshouse on West Lombard Street) but even Herring could have seen that choice as cruel.

2. Before the advent of taximeters, fares were set rates and even in Baltimore, drivers always took the shortest route.

3. William N. Batchelor's book, *Recollections of the East Building before it was Church Home & Infirmary*, ed. Frederick T. Wehr (Baltimore: Church Home and Hospital, 1982), 6, gives the location of the hoist as being on the exterior of the rotunda at the northeast corner, or turret. An 1858 newspaper article that lists improvements made to the building for its new owners describes a steam-powered lift or "dumb waiter that passes up through the corridors" ("Church Home and Infirmary – A Free Hospital," *Baltimore American and Commercial Advertiser*, January 20, 1858, 1). Although the building had been heated by steam boilers from the beginning, the steam-powered hoist was evidently not added until many years after Poe's death.

4. Letter: Moran to Maria Clemm, November 15, 1849. Original MS, *Pratt*: "When brought to the Hospital he was unconscious of his condition—who brought him or with whom he had been associating."

5. *Moran*, 59. This detail would be accepted and repeated by others including Poe's Philadelphia friend John Sartain, as well as Charles Scarlett Jr. in a poorly researched article appearing as "A Tale of Ratiocination: The Death and Burial of Edgar Allan Poe," *Maryland Historical Magazine* 73 (Winter 1978): 360–74.

6. "Washington University of Baltimore." *Baltimore Sun*, September 28, 1839, 4. Period newspaper advertisements for Washington University Hospital specified varying accommodation and care based on paid fees. As subsequent ads verify, this policy was maintained when Baltimore City and Marine Hospital took over the premises. Moran was tasked with making the enterprise profitable and his decisions as to patient

276 *Notes*

care would have been affected by such pecuniary considerations. As he would later admit, "It was not a charity hospital; my support depended alone upon the receipts of the house" (*Moran*, 77).

7. Eugene L. Didier, "Poe's Last Days and Death." *Indianapolis Journal*, January 14, 1895, 3. Didier wrote, "His last hours were passed in the charity ward of a public hospital" but cited no authority for this statement. However, Didier had by this time communicated with Dr. William M. Cullen who informed that he was Poe's actual caregiver.

8. *Powell*, vii.

9. Genevieve Miller, "A Nineteenth Century Medical School: Washington University of Baltimore," *Bulletin of the History of Medicine* 14, no. 1 (June 1943): 17n12.

10. Harold J. Abrahams, *The Extinct Medical Schools of Baltimore, Maryland* (Baltimore: Maryland Historical Society, 1969), 1–9.

11. Judith Robinson, *Ensign on a Hill: The Story of the Church Home and Hospital and Its School of Nursing, 1854–1954* (Baltimore: Barton & Gillet, 1954), 41.

12. Abrahams, *Extinct Medical Schools*, 8. This declaration seems to suggest that in addition to the number of deceased sailors the school was processing, some of the bodies were the result of a generally high mortality rate in Baltimore.

13. Batchelor, *Recollections*, 3.

14. "Notice Is Hereby Given," *Baltimore Sun*, July 15, 1848, 4. A notice appeared in this paper that the university had by then been in arrears of a paving tax (in the amount of $692.59) for four months.

15. "Trustee's Sale of Valuable Property," *Baltimore Sun*, September 22, 1849, 2.

16. Abrahams, *Extinct Medical Schools*, 1–9.

17. This hospital is not to be confused with Baltimore Marine Hospital that once operated at Wyman Park near Johns Hopkins University.

18. "Baltimore City and Marine Hospital," *Baltimore Sun*, July 4, 1849, 2.

19. The university directors may have been correct in thinking the location too distant from the city for a medical center. At the time of Poe's death, the hospital still sat amid mostly undeveloped land, especially to the east.

20. John J. Moran, "Five Dollars Reward," *Baltimore Sun*, July 4, 1850, 3. One of "J. J. Moran's" tenants had lost a cow that was also being stabled at the hospital, prompting Moran, acting as property manager, to place an ad in the paper for the animal's recovery.

21. Robinson, *Ensign on a Hill*, 27. One who was both poor and elderly, Maria Clemm became a resident at Church Home in the spring of 1863. She would remain until February 1871, dying in the same building where her famous nephew and son-in-law spent his last days, twenty-two years earlier.

22. Charles E. Rosenberg, *The Care of Strangers: The Rise of America's Hospital System* (New York: Basic Books, 1987), 305. "Private hospitals could to some extent choose their clientele; city and county hospitals could not." Especially at public facilities, alcohol cases were often seen in the same light as patients suffering from venereal disease; both as pariahs and deserving of less-than-equal treatment.

23. Appendix D. During his time as the "authority" on Poe's final days, Moran would give varying descriptions of the interment, as though he had attended. Yet

when referring to the "funeral," Moran may have been thinking not of the burial but rather the viewing and funeral service that he arranged at the hospital.

24. Mark Dawidziak, *Mystery of Mysteries: The Death and Life of Edgar Allan Poe* (New York: St. Martin's Press, 2023), 182. When referring to this letter, Dawidziak wrote, "The inescapable conclusion is that Moran was doctoring the truth all along"; and when reviewing Kenneth Silverman's *Edgar A. Poe: Mournful and Never-ending Remembrance*, for the March 1993 issue of *Science Fiction Studies* (113), David Ketterer called Moran's missive "notorious unreliable," to cite only two examples of those questioning the truthfulness of Moran's letter.

25. In Baltimore City during this period, hospital case records involving mortalities were sent to the Board of Health who collated these as Reports of Interments. A search made at the city archives by the author in 2019 produced no record on Edgar Allan Poe.

26. The church was just three blocks southwest of the hospital and its proximity may have been the reason Neilson Poe deputed Moran. However, it was usual for the family of the deceased to make such arrangements and Moran could have volunteered these accommodations (and others) out of a sense of responsibility.

27. *Moran*, 18.

28. James A. Harrison, "A Poe Miscellany," *Independent*, November 1, 1906, 1044–51. This exchange between William Clemm and Chevalier E. R. Reynolds (knighted in 1887 by Humberto I, King of Italy) took place in 1889, after Moran's book on Poe's final hours, of which Reynold's is known to have acquired, had been published. The asterisk in the first sentence was added by Harrison to mark a footnote that identified Moran's 1885 book.

29. *H*, 1:321.

30. Matthew Warner Osborn, *Rum Maniacs: Alcoholic Insanity in the Early American Republic* (Chicago: University of Chicago Press, 2014), 51. It was not uncommon to see a hospital patient admitted with a typical injury or sickness only to later explode into an episode of delirium tremens, causing havoc within the building. For this reason it was recommended that administrators ascertain the drinking habits of the patient at the time of admittance.

31. *Moran*, 65. Michael Powell also agrees that Moran's 1885 description of Poe's room that included barred windows was a mental slip (*Powell*, 15).

32. A daguerreotype taken of East Baltimore by Henry H. Clark in 1849 shows the hospital but from a distance too far away to determine whether any windows were screened or barred, although bars could have been fitted from the inside.

33. John Alexander Joyce, *Edgar Allan Poe* (New York: F. Tennyson Neely, 1901), 199–202.

34. Robinson, *Ensign on a Hill*, 27.

35. Caroline Ticknor, *Poe's Helen* (New York: Charles Scribner, 1916), 170, Letter: Maria Clemm to Sarah Helen Whitman, June 16, 1863, "I am now in the house where my Eddie breathed his last, and I think it one of my greatest privileges that I can go unto the room where he died."

36. John Alexander Joyce, *Edgar Allan Poe* (New York: F. Tennyson Neely, 1901), 202.

278 *Notes*

37. *Moran*, 60. "I had him placed in a small room in the turret part of the building where patients were put who had been drinking freely." An illustration in Moran's book identifies a second floor room in the southwest tower.

38. Clara Dargan Maclean, "Some Memorials of Edgar Allan Poe," *Frank Leslie's Popular Monthly* (April 1891): 457–64.

39. Batchelor, *Recollections*, 7. The eighteen-month period of William Batchelor's residence in the building was prior to the renovations made by Church Home and Infirmary. There is also an 1849 daguerreotype taken by Henry H. Clark which reveals that the southwest turret of the rotunda had no windows on it western wall (in contrast to the opposing tower), indicating it then housed a staircase instead of individual rooms.

40. "Church Home and Infirmary–A Free Hospital," *Baltimore American and Commercial Advertiser*, January 20, 1858, 1.

41. Robinson, *Ensign on a Hill*, 3.

42. John J. Moran, "Official Memoranda of the Death of Edgar A. Poe," *New York Herald*, October 28, 1875, 4. The question of Poe's accommodations while in the hospital apparently became an important one for Moran: "He [Poe] seemed to revive, and opened his eyes, fixing his gaze upon the transom over his room door, each room having transoms over the door for ventilation and air. He kept them moved for more than a minute. He was lying directly polite [below] this transom." Moran's emphasis on a transom in this "recollection" seems to be deliberately made as though he had felt pressure to prove that Poe had placed in a private room.

43. *H*, 1:337–38.

44. *Moran*, 60.

45. *Moran*, 21. Abrahams assigns 300 beds but this is one of the few occurrences where Moran is better trusted (*Moran*, 9).

46. John J. Moran, "Baltimore City and Marine Hospital," *Baltimore Sun*, October 5, 1849, 1.

47. *Moran*, 77–78. Moran's claim, "Nor did anyone ever pay a single penny for his [Poe's] expenses while in my care" came after Neilson Poe's death when there was no one left to challenge it.

48. Letter: Neilson Poe to Maria Clemm, October 11, 1849, original manuscript in *Pratt*. Much has been made of the incorrect day of the week given here for Poe's death. It could have been an honest mistake by the distracted barrister, or perhaps an attempt by him to support a disingenuous offer of notification to Clemm.

49. Kenneth Silverman, *Edgar A. Poe: Mournful and Never-Ending Remembrance* (New York: Harper Collins, 1991), 434.

50. Notwithstanding the family legend of George Poe alerting Neilson after encountering Edgar passed out at Barnum's Museum on the evening of October 3, as discussed in chapter 3.

51. *Moran*, 78.

52. *Powell*, 2.

53. "Local Matters," *Baltimore Sun*, October 5, 1849, 1.

54. An evening visit made after regular hours, would better explain the forbiddance to see Poe. Neilson's attempt may have also been repulsed by one of Moran's

Notes   279

assistants who failed to report the visit, but Neilson gave no indication of either sequence.

55. 1850 United States Federal Census: https://www.ancestryheritagequest.com [website]. In the Federal Census record for 1850, William M. Cullen's listing appears among others residing at the "Baltimore City and Marine Hospital," including John J. Moran. The entry in the record gives his age as twenty-three, his place of birth as Ireland, and spells his surname as "Cullin."

56. Abrahams, *Extinct Medical Schools*, 26.

57. Charles Scarlett Jr., "A Tale of Ratiocination: The Death and Burial of Edgar Allan Poe," *Maryland Historical Magazine* 73 (Winter 1978): 366. Scarlett cited no authority for his statement, but if Moran had in fact requested Dr. John C. S. Monkur's assistance, or just consulted with him on the case, it would seem to confirm that he was by then aware of his patient's importance.

58. Eugene L. Didier, *The Life and Poems of Edgar Allan Poe* (New York: W. J. Widdleton, 1876).

59. Eugene L. Didier, "Poe as a Man and as a Poet," *Literary World* (Boston, MA), November 6, 1880, 393–94.

60. *Moran*, 81. Although Moran's list of twenty-seven individuals in the funeral cortege is obviously fictitious, some of those named could have attended a viewing at the hospital that the doctor seems to have arranged.

CHAPTER 7

1. "Washington University of Baltimore," *Baltimore Sun*, March 26, 1849, 2.

2. *Moran*, 21.

3. Moran wrote a lengthy article on Poe's death that was published in the October 28, 1875, edition of the *New York Herald*. In 1882, he gave several lectures in the mid-Atlantic region of the United States on the subject, and three years later authored a small book on Poe and his final hours.

4. 1880 United States Federal Census: https://www.ancestryheritagequest.com [website]. Although Moran is an Irish name, the doctor and his parents were American-born, and it is not likely that he had much of an Irish accent when speaking.

5. Eugene Fauntleroy Cordell, *Historical Sketch of the University of Maryland, School of Medicine, 1807–1890* (Baltimore: Press of Isaak Friedenwald, 1891), 189.

6. Bandy, 33.

7. "Local Matters," *Baltimore Sun*, December 4, 1847, 2.

8. "Special Dispatch from Frederick: Washington, Saturday, Oct. 18," *New York Times*, October 16, 1862, 1. Moran became newsworthy in 1862 after he was arrested by agents of the federal government for misusing his office as Examining Surgeon (for the draft) in Frederick County.

9. "Washington University of Baltimore," *Baltimore Sun*, March 26, 1849, 2. "Those gentlemen who may be desirous of attending the SUMMER COURSE OF LECTURES, at the university, will assemble at the Lecture Rooms of the Hospital Building, Broadway, on THIS DAY, the 26th instant, at 12 o'clock PM. . . . The

280 *Notes*

Resident Physician and Surgeon of the house, Dr. Moran will be at the building . . . to communicate with any who may be unable to attend punctually."

10. "Local Matters," *Baltimore Sun*, April 8, 1882. Moran and his family may have remained on the property until October 1855.

11. *Baltimore Sun*, January 2, 1854, 1.

12. "Appointments," *Baltimore Sun*, January 12, 1856, 4.

13. Dr. J. J. Moran, noted in "Frederick County (MD) Fair," *American Farmer* 14, no. 6 (1858): 146–47. At the 1858 Frederick Agricultural Fair, Moran exhibited some of his prize vegetables and poultry.

14. "The Enrollment in Maryland," *Baltimore Sun*, August 23, 1862, 1.

15. "Arrest of Surgeon Moran at Frederick," *Baltimore Sun*, October 16, 1862, 2.

16. "Special Dispatch from Frederick," *New York Times*, October 16, 1862, 1.

17. "The Draft in Maryland," *Baltimore Sun,* October 23, 1862, 1.

18. John A. Marshall, *American Bastille* (Philadelphia: Thomas W. Hartley, 1871), 415.

19. Moran, "Share Farmers Advertisement," *Baltimore Sun*, January 2, 1863, 3. Moran placed an advertisement in the *Baltimore Sun* looking for "share farmers" to work his farm in Frederick. Applicants were to reply to "Mrs. L. [Lydia] Green," the mother of Moran's wife.

20. John W. Woods, *Woods' Baltimore City Directory, 1865–'66* (Baltimore: J. W. Woods, 1865–1866), 300, 560.

21. "Local Matters," *Baltimore Sun*, August 31, 1866, 1.

22. "Local Matters," *Baltimore Sun*, September 28, 1867, 1.

23. "Local Matters," *Baltimore Sun*, October 22, 1867, 1.

24. In 1865, Moran was among a group of investors that purchased a property in Mount Washington (then a suburb of Baltimore) that was serving as a female college, only to "flip" it two years later. During that same year he is also shown to have sold a twenty-acre estate in the same area for $18,000. *Baltimore Sun*, April 8, 1867, 1.

25. United States, Patent Office, *Annual Report of the Commissioner of Patents for the Year 1869* (Washington, DC: Government Printing Office 1871), 205, 38.

26. John W. Woods, *Woods' Baltimore City Directory, 1870* (Baltimore: J. W. Woods, 1870), 426, 498.

27. *Boston Weekly Globe*, December 19, 1888, 5. Moran some fifteen years ago gave up entirely the practice of medicine.

28. Melvin Lee Steadman Jr., *Falls Church by Fence and Fireside* (Falls Church, VA: Falls Church Public Library, 1964), 79–80. Moran served as mayor from April 13, 1875, to July 1, 1876, during which he seems to have proposed no petitions or ordinances. Following his brief term as mayor he apparently retained a seat on the council.

29. "Senatorial Convention. Nomination of W. H. F. Lee. Harmony and Good Feeling," *Alexandria Gazette and Virginia Advertiser*, October 18, 1876, 1. Moran represented Alexandria County at the Conservative Senatorial Convention to nominate a candidate to fill an unexpired term in the state senate.

Notes 281

30. J. J. Moran, "Letter: J. J. Moran to Hon. Fitzhugh Lee, February 20, 1886," *Journal of the Senate of the Commonwealth of Virginia, 1885-1886* (Richmond: Baughman Brothers, 1885), Senate Doc. No. 40, 2.

31. An amount of $2,316,123 was originally presented to Virginia Governor Fitzhugh Lee (by Moran) in 1886; however, the figure was apparently reduced to $447,059 which still equates to $12,070,593 at current values.

32. "The Moran Contract," *Baltimore Sun*, March 23, 1899, 8.

33. Virginia General Assembly, *Acts and Joint Resolutions Passed by the General Assembly of Virginia: During the Extra Session of 1902-3-4* (Richmond: J. H. O'Bannon, 1904), 42–43.

34. "A Staunch Friend of Poe," *Baltimore Sun* December 15, 1888, 1.

35. "Died," *Baltimore Sun*, April 1, 1889, 2.

36. Letter: Moran to Maria Clemm, November 15, 1849, original manuscript in *Pratt*.

37. Letter: Maria Clemm to John J. Moran, March 2, 1850, original manuscript in the Colonel Richard A. Gimbel Collection of Edgar Allan Poe, Free Library of Philadelphia, Philadelphia, Pennsylvania. Moran included a forged version of this communication from Clemm in John J. Moran, *A Defense of Edgar Allan Poe: Life, Character and Dying Declarations of the Poet* (Washington, DC: William F. Boogher, 1885), 16–17. Clemm's original wording, "I received a letter from Neilson Poe saying that he had in his possession my son's trunk" was changed to read "I received a letter from Neilson Poe saying that you had placed in his possession my son's trunk." Maria Clemm, having died in 1871, was not around to expose Moran's forgery.

38. Edgar Allan Poe, *Poems by Edgar Allan Poe, Complete* (New York: W. J. Widdleton, 1874).

39. Richard H. Stoddard, "Edgar Allan Poe," *Harper's Monthly Magazine* 45 (September 1872): 557–68.

40. Richard H. Stoddard, "Edgar Allan Poe," *Independent*, February 12, 1885, 10–11. According to Stoddard, Moran also made the claim of having handled Poe's trunk in his 1875 pitch to *The World*.

41. "Local Matters," *Baltimore Sun*, October 16, 1875, 5. The publication of Moran's "Official Memoranda" was intended to coincide with the monument's dedication ceremonies in Baltimore, originally scheduled for October 27, but postponed until November 17. Although he had not been invited to participate in the ceremonies, Moran later claimed to have been contacted by the committee for information on the poet's death, and also expressed disappointment (and some resentment) that he had not been consulted before: "Without vanity permit me to say I firmly believe that had they called upon me for statements . . . when he died, I could have been instrumental" (*Moran*, 11). Moran was speaking here in hindsight of Griswold's venomous memoir and of being able to nip it in the bud, but his real complaint seems to be the disregard for his authority.

42. Anonymous, "The Monument to Edgar Allan Poe." *New York Herald*, October 28, 1875.

282 *Notes*

43. R. H. Stoddard, *Select Works of Edgar Allan Poe, Poetical and Prose* (New York: W. J. Widdleton, 1880), clxviii. Harrison would also state that according to Neilson Poe, while in the hospital "he [Poe] never regained consciousness" (*H*, 1:332). Unfortunately, Harrison did not cite his source for Neilson's statement.

44. John J. Moran, "Edgar Allan Poe," *Baltimore Sun*, October 29, 1875, 1.

45. Eugene L. Didier, "Poe as a Man and as a Poet," *Literary World* (Boston, MA), November 6, 1880, 393.

46. "Where Edgar Allan Poe Died," *Baltimore American and Commercial Advertiser*, December 18, 1881, 4.

47. John J. Moran, "Official Memoranda of the Death of Edgar A. Poe," *New York Herald*, October 28, 1875, 4; emphasis on "transcript" is mine.

48. John J. Moran, quoted in *Harrisonburg-Rockingham Register*, December 12, 1878, 3.

49. *Rockingham Register*, July 23, 1883. In a letter written to this publication Moran claimed, "I have made it my business for some years to gather every fact and incident of his life, to enable me to take the field in his defense." There is also this description of Moran in his *Baltimore Sun* obituary that was probably provided by a family member: "His enthusiasm for Poe and his writings became a strong factor in his after-career. He was able to repeat all of Poe's poems. "A Staunch Friend of Poe," *Baltimore Sun*, December 15, 1888, 1.

50. "Letter from Washington," *Baltimore Sun*, February 3, 1882, 4.

51. *Moran*, 80. In his book, the doctor reverted to the October 9 date.

52. "Local Matters," *Baltimore Sun*, April 8, 1882, 6. Moran's revised chronology of Poe's hospital arrival on the morning of October 7, and his death sixteen hours later, is a clear contradiction of the timeline he gave to Maria Clemm in November 1849 and informs his lack of recall of the communication, as well as the absence of any records in his possession.

53. Letter: Moran to Edward Abbott, February 27, 1882, cited by *Allen*, 718. Moran would also claim a second, four-hour interview with Shelton in his 1885 work, *A Defense of Edgar Allan Poe* (21). Although there appears to be no independent confirmation of either meeting, Moran's elevation of her status as the true "Annabel Lee" could suggest compensation for her time.

54. "Local Matters," *Baltimore Sun*, April 8, 1882, 6. Moran's call at the Church Home and Infirmary building on April 7 is stated to be his first since his employment there; however, his visit with John Joyce in 1869 (and an earlier one suggested by Joyce) reveals yet another of the doctor's fibs.

55. "Dr. John J. Moran, of Falls Church," *Evening Critic* (Washington, DC), April 12, 1882, 2.

56. John J. Moran, *Rockingham Register*, July 23, 1883. In a letter to this publication Moran stated, "I have lectured in but three cities up to the present . . . in Baltimore, Washington and Richmond."

57. *Moran*, 18. "My professional experience has been assailed, my veracity and even my own identity have been disputed." It was also probably not a coincidence that Neilson Poe, the one person remaining who could expose Moran, had died the year before the book's publication.

Notes   283

58. *Moran*, n.p.

59. *Moran*, 55. It is clear that Moran had some communication with Neilson Poe and also contacted Reverend Clemm to conduct Poe's service; however, exchanges between him and other family members took place weeks and months later, and then only by their initiation. Moran's identification of Poe's hotel and acquisition of his trunk are not supported by fact.

60. *Moran*, 56. As demonstrated, Poe was discovered in Baltimore on Election Day, October 3. Moran was then contesting the historical record of which he must have been aware.

61. *Moran*, 60–61. Neilson Poe received an appointment to Baltimore City's orphan's court in 1878 and retained the position until 1883.

62. *H*, 1:321, Letter: W. J. Glenn to James A. Harrison, December 4, 1900.

63. *Moran*, 66.

64. *Moran*, 72–74.

65. Mary E. Phillips, *Edgar Allan Poe the Man*, 2 vols. (Philadelphia: John C. Winston, 1926), 2:1508.

66. *H*, 1:314.

67. *Powell*, 92.

68. *Moran*, 77; R. J. Matchett, *Matchett's Baltimore City Directory for 1851* (Baltimore: Matchett, 1841), 198. "Namuth Fredk. T. cabinet maker and undertaker, 14. N Frederick." Namuth's statement in Moran's book is shown to have been witnessed by William James Dew who is listed in the 1881 Baltimore directory as a patternmaker living on South Stricker Street.

69. Henry Herring, "Edgar Allen [*sic*] Poe," *Baltimore American and Commercial Advertiser*, October 11, 1865, 4. In 1865, Herring claimed that he furnished "a neat mahogany coffin." Perhaps to counter his decision to consign the dying poet to strangers, he may have later wanted it known that he did all he could.

70. *Moran*, 76. Mary Moran was a very talented seamstress who exhibited her work at agricultural fairs. Two of her quilts are now a part of the collection of the National Museum of American History at the Smithsonian Institute.

71. *Moran*, 78.

72. Reverend W. T. D. Clemm, "He Buried Edgar A. Poe." *Indianapolis News,* May 9, 1894, 8.

73. *Moran*, 62–63. Moran claimed that he volunteered payment after discovering the cab driver sitting at the hospital's front door, which at that time was at the east end of the building on Broadway. However, if he was parked behind the facility it is just as likely the driver had come inside to remind the doctor.

74. "In the Poet's Corner," *Baltimore Sun*, May 5, 1885, 1. The impressive sculpture by Richard Henry Park is currently on display at the Edgar Allan Poe Museum in Richmond, Virginia, where it is on long-term loan by the Metropolitan Museum of Art.

75. Notwithstanding any responsibility that he (or his facility) had for Poe's death, in the absence of verifiable evidence he deserves the benefit of the doubt.

76. Oscar Wilde, "Art and the Handicraftman," in *Essays and Lectures*, 4th ed. (London: Methuen, 1913), 195.

284 *Notes*

77. *The Works of the Late Edgar Allan Poe*, 4 vols., edited by Rufus W. Griswold (New York: J. S. Redfield), 1850–1856. In the biography that he wrote for the third volume of Poe's works, Griswold includes correspondences that he forged in order to make Poe appear petty and unprincipled.

78. "The Enrollment in Maryland," *Baltimore Sun*, August 23, 1862, 1. Moran's appointment as Examining Surgeon was by Maryland Governor Augustus Bradford and not by any member of the federal government.

CHAPTER 8

1. Birgit Bramsback, "The Final Illness and Death of Edgar Allan Poe: An Attempt at Reassessment," *Studia Neophilologica* 42, no. 1 (1970): 40–59. For her 1970 analysis of Poe's death, Bramsback conducted an exhaustive search for an official record but had no success. My pursuits in 2019 proved equally as fruitless.

2. *PL*, 851. The source for the *Baltimore Clipper's* "congestion of the brain" has not been established but it could have been provided by the city's health commissioner, J. F. C. Hadel.

3. Edna A. Kanely, ed., *The Unveiling of the Bust of Edgar Allan Poe in the Library of the University of Virginia* (Lynchburg, VA: J. P. Bell, 1901), v. "Church records are spotty in their coverage. Doubtless many events went unrecorded due to lack of cooperation of the persons involved and due to the laxity of church officials in performing their duty. The situation was then compounded by the ravages of time in the disappearance of registers."

4. Maryland State Archives, http://guide.msa.maryland.gov/pages/viewer=death-testing.

5. *Baltimore City Health Department: The First Thirty-Five Annual Reports, 1815–1849* (Baltimore: Commissioner of Health of Baltimore, Maryland, 1953), introduction, n.p.

6. "Health Office," *Baltimore Sun*, October 9, 1849, 2.

7. United States Census Bureau [website]: https://www.census.gov/programs-surveys/decennial-census/technical-documentation/questionnaires/1850/1850-instructions.html.

8. State of Maryland, "Persons who Died during the Year ending 1st June, 1850, in 3rd Ward Baltimore City." Poe's listing in the ledger can be found on page 47, eighth from the top.

9. Robert James, *A Medicinal Dictionary* (London, England: T. Osborn, 1743). "In a Phrenitis, the Patient is afflicted with an acute Fever; his Pulse is hardly perceptible on the Surface of the Body. . . . His face is inflated and full . . . his Rest is disturb'd; he is seized with a kind of turbulent Madness . . . and a Privation of Reason. . . . Among the antecedent Causes of a Phrenitis . . . drinking Wine too copiously . . . remaining long exposed to the Sun . . . a Phrenitis, and delirious Fevers, are highly incident to those afflicted with long Grief, or Care, who fatigue their minds by profound Meditation and Study . . . who surfeit themselves with strongly hopt Malt-liquors . . . [and] who are addicted to Wine."

Notes 285

10. The territories of census marshals were assigned by political district and the resulting statistics were thus organized.

11. Considering that these ledgers were transcriptions of field reports made by individuals who were in most cases unacquainted with their subjects, such errors should come as no surprise; it is not difficult to envision the census marshal (or the transcriber of his report) confusing the occupation of the interviewee with the deceased.

12. Letter: Neilson Poe to R. W. Griswold, November 1, 1849. Original MS held at the Henry W. and Albert A. Berg Collection. New York Public Library, New York, cited in *PL*, 844. Emphasis of "single indulgence" was made by Neilson Poe.

13. Rufus Griswold's malicious "Memoir" did not appear until September 1850, in vol. 3 of Poe's edited works and was so appended to subsequent editions for the next twenty-five years.

14. *H*, 1:321. This story rests on the written statement of William J. Glenn who was an officer in the Shockoe Hill (Richmond) Chapter of the Sons of Temperance and was the person who had administered the oath of abstinence to Poe when he joined the organization there in July 1849. In a letter to James A. Harrison, dated December 4, 1900, Glenn stated that a "gentleman by the name of Benson . . . went to the hospital at which he died, and had a talk with the doctor . . . who told him that Poe had not been drinking . . . but was under the influence of a drug." A search of the *Richmond Directory* for 1855 found only one listing for a W. H. Benson, a merchant tailor trading at 110 Main Street, and residing on 19th St. ("Benson, W.H. merchant tailor, 110, Main st. res. 19th st." Butters, 29). It was probably no coincidence that Glenn was also a tailor.

15. *The Works of the Late Edgar Allan Poe*, 4 vols., edited by Rufus W. Griswold (New York: J. S. Redfield, 1850–1856), xxx.

16. Letter: Moran to Maria Clemm, November 15, 1849. Original MS in *Pratt*.

17. *H*, 1:321.

18. John J. Moran, "Official Memoranda of the Death of Edgar A. Poe," *New York Herald*, October 28, 1875, 4. Having died nine years prior to the publication of this article, Dr. John Monkur was not around to support (or challenge) Moran's account.

19. "Local Matters," *Baltimore Sun*, April 8, 1882, 6.

20. *Moran*, 70–71. Moran's final version (of Poe's cause of death) would appear in is 1885 publication, "Dr. Monkur gave it as his opinion that Poe would die from excessive nervous prostration and loss of nerve power, resulting from exposure, affecting the encephalon, a sensitive and delicate membrane of the brain."

21. Elizabeth Oakes Smith, "Edgar A. Poe," *United States Magazine*, March 3, 1857, 262–68.

22. Elizabeth Oakes Smith's belief that Poe died as a result of a beating is discussed in chapter 4 of this book.

23. John Evangelist Walsh, *Midnight Dreary: The Mysterious Death of Edgar Allan Poe* (New Brunswick, NJ: Rutgers University Press, 1998).

24. Joseph Evans Snodgrass, "The Facts of Poe's Death and Burial," *Beadle's Monthly* 3, no. 5 (May 1867): 283–87.

286 *Notes*

25. A coroner's inquest was an investigative hearing similar to a grand jury but usually presided over by a medical officer who presented the evidence (medical or otherwise) and if available, witness testimony, to a panel of common citizens who then returned an opinion as to cause. A coroner's report was then created and, in the case of culpable death, presented to the authorities. An inquest often served the purpose of an autopsy when the remains had already been interred.

26. Science History Institute Museum & Library [website]: https://sciencehistory .org/stories/magazine/an-everyday-poison/#:~:text=White%20arsenic.

27. In all three versions of the treatment he administered to Poe, Moran gave no indication of a poisoning or performing a stomach purge.

28. James Marsh, "Account of a Method of Separating Small Quantities of Arsenic from Substances With Which it May Be Mixed," *The Edinburgh New Philosophical Journal*, April–October 1836, 229–36.

29. As explained by the Great Plains Laboratory, "Metals Hair Test by Great Plains Laboratory," *Integrative Psychiatry* [Internet], https://www.integrativepsychiatry.net/shop/the-great-plains-laboratory/metals-hair-test-great-plains/ (accessed June 6, 2020). "As protein is synthesized in the hair follicle, elements are incorporated permanently into the hair with no further exchange with other tissues . . . and because it grows an average of one to two cm per month, it contains a 'temporal record' of element metabolism and exposure to toxic elements. . . . Therefore, hair is the tissue of choice for detection of recent exposure to elements such as arsenic, aluminum, cadmium, lead, antimony, and mercury."

30. Albert H. Donnay, "Poisoned Poe: Evidence that Poe May Have Suffered from Neurasthemia," paper presented at the International Edgar Allan Poe Conference, Richmond, Virginia, October 9, 1999.

31. "Testing Poe's Hair," press release from April 9, 2006, cited by the Edgar Allan Poe Society of Baltimore, https://www.eapoe.org.

32. *Boston Evening Transcript*, February 25, 1893. Sartain also stated, without attribution, that Poe "had evidently been drugged," this in a newspaper account written forty-four years later and which appears to have been purposed to argue against Poe's drinking.

33. Eugene L. Didier, *The Poe Cult and Other Poe Papers* (New York: Broadway Publishing, 1909).

34. Edward Spencer, "The Memory of Poe: Unpublished Letters of the Poet to Dr. Snodgrass," *New York Herald*, March 27, 1881, 8.

35. John J. Moran, "Official Memoranda of the Death of Edgar A. Poe," *New York Herald*, October 28, 1875. Moran to Poe: "I must administer an opiate to give you sleep and rest."

36. *Woodberry*, 429. One of these was Poe's cousin, Elizabeth Herring, who in her dotage would make the astonishing claim "that she had often seen him decline to take even one glass of wine, but . . . that, for the most part, his periods of excess were occasioned by a free use of opium." Herring also added that when residing in Philadelphia in 1841 she recalled making visits to the Poe's while Edgar was suffering from the effects of his drug use and that the family endeavored to conceal it.

Notes   287

37. Hervey Allen, *Israfel: The Life and Times of Edgar Allan Poe*, 2 vols. (New York: George H. Doran, 1926), 1:371–72; emphasis on "suspicion" is mine.

38. *PL*, 555 A critic for the *Richmond Compiler* of July 30, 1845, reduced Edgar Allan Poe's *Tales* (New York: Wiley and Putnam, 1845) to the "the strange outpourings of an opium eater, while under the influence of that stimulating drug."

39. *Woodberry*, 2:430.

40. Thomas Dunn English, "Reminiscences of Poe," *Independent* (New York), October 15, 1896, 2.

41. George E. Woodberry, *American Men of Letters; Edgar Allan Poe*, ed. Charles Dudley Warner (Boston: Houghton Mifflin, 1885), 210–11.

42. *Weiss*, 127–28. In this highly questionable account, Weiss places many of Rosalie's phrases in quotation marks but does not indicate where or when this information was acquired; however, Weiss's "while he . . . begged for morphine" does not appear in quotes and could have been her invention.

43. *CL*, 2:721–25, LTR-286, Letter: Poe to Mrs. Nancy Richmond, November 16, 1848 (from a transcript of the original MS letter made by Mrs. Richmond and sent to Poe biographer John Ingram). The letter that Poe claimed to have written Mrs. Richmond while in Boston, as well as the name of the friend who came to his aid, has never been discovered.

44. Allen, *Israfel* (1926), 2:841–42.

45. Theodore Pease Stearns, "A Prohibitionist Shakes Dice with Poe," *Outlook*, September 1, 1920. Support for the meeting between Murdock and Poe relies only on Stearns magazine story; however, Allen's discovery of this article, as well as one by Dr. William Elliot Griffis for the (New York) *Home Journal* in 1884, is indicated by his description of Poe's purported trip to Saratoga.

46. Allen, *Israfel* (1926), 2:540.

47. Allen, *Israfel* (1926), 2:540.

48. Allen, *Israfel* (1926), 1:362. "During the latter part of 1834 . . . Edgar himself was in ill health, approaching one of those periods of utter depression, due to nerve strain and a weak heart."

49. *Miller*, 99. Letter: Marie Louise Shew to John Ingram, January 23, 1875. When recalling this years later, Shew would write that Poe had not been drinking but collapsed from illness.

50. *Miller*, 139. Letter: Marie Louise Shew to John Ingram, May 16, 1875.

51. *CL*, 2:699, LTR-278, Letter: Poe to Sarah Helen Whitman, October 1, 1848.

52. *Baltimore Clipper*, October 9, 1849, 2. "Died: —. On the 8th instant of congestion of the brain, Edgar A. Poe, Esq. aged 38 years. Mr. Poe was well known as a writer of great ability" (as cited in *Quinn*, 644).

53. *Moran*, 71.

54. Charles Scarlett Jr., "A Tale of Ratiocination: The Death and Burial of Edgar Allan Poe," *Maryland Historical Magazine* 73 (Winter 1978): 366. In this inaccurate and poorly documented essay, Scarlett also claimed that Poe was ministered under Monkur's direction but cited no authority for the statement.

55. Scarlett, "Tale of Ratiocination," 336.

56. In his 1875 account appearing in the *New York Herald*, Moran claims that he gave Poe a glass of beef-tea and two cordials, one of which was infused with opium. And in his book published ten years later, the doctor states that when he offered water, Poe "drank half a glass without any trouble" (*Moran*, 71).

57. Susan Archer Talley Weiss, "The Last Days of Edgar A. Poe," *Scribner's Magazine* 15 (March 1878): 712.

58. Letter: Moran to Maria Clemm, November 15, 1849. Original MS in *Pratt*.

59. *CL*, 2:721–23, LTR-286, Letter: Poe to Annie L. Richmond, November 16, 1848.

60. Sartain, *Reminiscences*, 205–12.

61. Hannah J. Dean and Ryan L. Boyd, "Deep into That Darkness Peering: A Computational Analysis of the Role of Depression in Edgar Allan Poe's Life and Death," *Journal of Effective Disorders* 1 (April 2020): 482–91.

62. Dean and Boyd, "Deep," 482–91.

63. *Powell*, vi–vii.

64. Scarlett, "Tale of Ratiocination," 365. In his confused and imaginative paper on Poe's death for the *Maryland Historical Society*, Charles Scarlett also believed that the cause was "lobar pneumonia" but offers little foundation.

65. *Powell*, vii. When providing a possible reason for the hospital's neglect Powell wrote that they believed Poe "to be sleeping off the effects of delirium tremens (from which it was not possible for Poe to have suffered)."

66. *Powell*, 33.

67. *Woodberry*, 2:341.

68. Hunting Williams, "Table B, Reports of Interments," December 31, 1849, n.p., in *Baltimore City Health Department: The First Thirty-Five Annual Reports, 1815–1849* (Baltimore: Commissioner of Health of Baltimore, Maryland, 1953).

69. University of Maryland Thesis 1845 (Internet Archive), https://archive.org/details/universityofmary45unse/page/n281/mode/2up.

70. If Poe had suffered an attack of delirium tremens, it is probable that it began after he was admitted to the hospital and not at the tavern. Snodgrass described the man he found as semiconscious, not unhinged.

71. *CL*, 2:825–26, LTR-327, Letter: Poe to Maria Clemm, July 19, 1849. Poe wrote of this only after reaching Richmond.

72. Matthew Warner Osborn, "Diseased Imaginations: Constructing Delirium Tremens in Philadelphia, 1813–1832," *Social History of Medicine* 19, no. 2 (August 2006): 196.

73. Howard Wilcox Haggard and E. M. Jellinek, *Alcohol Explored* (Garden City, NY: Doubleday, Doran, 1942), 234.

74. Abdul Rahman and Manju Paul, "Delirium Tremens (DT)," in StatPearls [Internet] (Treasure Island, FL: StatPearls Publishing, 2020), https://www.ncbi.nlm.nih.gov/books/NBK482134/ (accessed May 2021).

75. Matthew Warner Osborn, *Rum Maniacs: Alcoholic Insanity in the Early American Republic* (Chicago: University of Chicago Press, 2014), 173–74.

76. Osborn, "Diseased Imaginations," 195, 199.

77. Benjamin H. Coates, qtd. in Osborn, *Rum Maniacs*, 142.

Notes 289

78. John Romano, "Early Contributions to the Study of Delirium Tremens," *Annals of Medical History* 3, no. 2 (March 1941): 132. Acute alcoholic hallucinosis can occur during heavy intoxication but usually in drinkers with underlying psychiatric conditions.

79. Letter: Moran to Maria Clemm, November 15, 1849, original MS in *Pratt*.

80. Charles E. Rosenberg, *The Care of Strangers: The Rise of America's Hospital System* (New York: Basic Books, 1987), 40.

81. "City Mortality of the Week," *New York Daily Times*, August 22, 1853, 4.

82. "City Mortality," *Baltimore Sun*, May 23, 1845, 4. During 1844, New York attributed sixty-four deaths to delirium tremens alone.

83. "Health Office," *Baltimore Sun*, December 29, 1857, 2. In the last weekly report of interments for 1857, health commissioner Dr. J. W. Houck was still listing mortalities from "congestion of the brain."

84. Hunting Williams, "Table B, Reports of Interments."

85. "Report of the Select Committee on the License Law," *Baltimore Sun*, February 19, 1847, 1. Thomas O. Sollers, warden of the Baltimore City and County jail, had estimated that of the "three-fourths of the entire number placed in his custody, intemperance has been the direct, and in many others the remote cause of commitment. . . . Frequent have been the cases of delirium tremens."

86. William N. Batchelor, *Recollections of the East Building Before It Was Church Home & Infirmary*, ed. Frederick T. Wehr (Baltimore: Church Home and Hospital, 1982), 7, claimed that when his family first explored the then vacant building in 1855, they found body parts, bones, and surgical tools strewn about the dissection theater on the fourth floor; however, the recollection of a five-year-old, colored by decades of family embellishments, may not be the most trustworthy.

87. Unauthorized dissections or postmortem examinations at the medical school were reserved for the unclaimed remains of sailors and unidentified, indigent cases, while Poe's identity had certainly been established by the time of his death.

88. Leslie S. King and Marjorie C. Meehan, "A History of the Autopsy," *American Journal of Pathology* 73, no. 2 (November 1973): 535–36.

89. Francis Delafield, *A Handbook of Postmortem Examination and Morbid Anatomy* (New York: William Wood, 1872).

90. Baltimore City Archives, *Suspicious Deaths in Mid-19th Century Baltimore* (Silver Spring, MD: Family Line Publications, 1986), iii. Although Baltimore City was then under county authority, the city maintained a separate coroner's office which was sustained on their collected fees. When the murder count was low, the office undertook investigations of deaths caused by disease, drownings, and other accidents, to which the city council complained.

CHAPTER 9

1. James A. Harrison, "A Poe Miscellany," *Independent*, November 1, 1906, 1044–51. According to William T. D. Clemm, it was at this meeting that John J. Moran confided to him that Poe's death was the result of delirium tremens.

290   *Notes*

2. Mary Ellen Hayward and R. Kent Lancaster, *Baltimore's Westminster Cemetery & Westminster Presbyterian Church* (Baltimore: Westminster Preservation Trust, 1984), 3.

3. *H*, 1:337–338. "I made his shroud and helped to prepare his body for burial." This statement by Mary Moran was offered to James A. Harrison by her nephew, Mr. J. B. Green, after she had died.

4. Henry Herring, "Edgar Allen [*sic*] Poe," *Baltimore American and Commercial Advertiser*, October 11, 1865, 4.

5. Thomas Ollive Mabbott, *The Collected Works of Edgar Allan Poe*, 3 vols. (Cambridge, MA: Belknapp Press of Harvard University Press, 1969), 1:569n10.

6. R. J. Matchett, *Matchett's Baltimore City Directory for 1851* (Baltimore: Matchett, 1851), 198.

7. *Moran*, 77–78. "Not one came forward to represent POE or to look after his welfare . . . nor did any one ever pay a single penny for his expenses while in my care."

8. "Buried Edgar A. Poe: The Minister Who Officiated at the Funeral Still Living," *Indianapolis News*, May 9, 1894, 8. Although much of this testimony given by William T. D. Clemm in the year before his death is based on hearsay, I find no reason to distrust his eyewitness account of Poe's obsequies.

9. *Moran*, 78.

10. Letter: Mrs. D. H. Carroll to Sara Sigourney Rice (undated but believed to be c. 1876), in *Pratt*. In this letter, transcribed by Mrs. D. H. Carroll, Clemm stated that "the funeral [procession] . . . took place from the infirmary."

11. George P. Clark, "Two Unnoticed Recollections of Poe's Funeral," *Poe's Newsletter* 3, no. 1 (June 1970): 1–2.

12. R. L. Polk, *R. L. Polk & Company's Baltimore City Directory for 1887* (Baltimore: A. Hoen, 1887), 112. Herring and his family were then living in a house at 128 East Pratt Street, changed in 1886 to 1134 East Pratt.

13. "Says Obsequies of Poet Poe Were Held On Pratt Street," *Baltimore Sun*, November 10, 1936, 9. Among other items presented by Miss Warden to the Poe Society in 1936 was a Poe-autographed copy of *The Gift*, ed. Miss Leslie (Philadelphia: Carey & Hart, 1840) (an 1840 anthology containing his tale "William Wilson,") and two trinkets believed to have belonged to Poe's wife Virginia which consisted of a small smelling salts bottle and a miniature goblet.

14. George Spence would later claim (*The Critic*, July–August 1898, 39–45) that Elizabeth Herring Smith and her husband Edmund also attended Poe's burial. However, they would have had to travel to the cemetery in a second coach that went unmentioned in most testimony.

15. In 1849, prior to construction of the Westminster Presbyterian Church, carriages entering the cemetery's main entrance on Greene Street could cross the field on an "avenue" that lead to a back gate which opened at an alley then on the east side of the graveyard.

16. May Garrettson Evans, "Poe's Burial and Grave: The Story of the Simple Ceremony in Baltimore," *New York Times*, February 26, 1893, 10.

17. *Moran*, 81. In his 1885 publication, Dr. John J. Moran would provide a list of twenty-seven individuals who were at the burial. While his roster is an obvious

Notes 291

fabrication, it is not inconceivable that some of those named attended a viewing that Moran appears to have arranged at the hospital.

18. Colonel J. Alden Weston, qtd. in "He Saw Poe's Burial," *Baltimore Sun*, March 30, 1909, 14. It is possible that Elizabeth Herring Smith and her husband trailed the hearse and Neilson's hack in a third vehicle but became separated from the cortege en route.

19. "The Day of Poe's Burial," *Baltimore Sun*, June 3, 1949, 14.

20. *Moran*, 81.

21. "The Day of Poe's Burial," *Baltimore Sun*, June 3, 1949, 14.

22. Letter: Neilson Poe to Maria Clemm, October 11, 1849. Original MS held in *Pratt*.

23. "He Buried Edgar A. Poe," *Indianapolis News*, May 9, 1894, 8. Clemm would later recall, "I merely read the burial service of the Methodist Episcopal Church at the grave. Then the coffin was lowered into the earth."

24. Christopher Scharpf, "Where Lies the Noble Spirit?—An Investigation into the Curious Mystery of Edgar Allan Poe's Grave in Baltimore," in *Masques, Mysteries, and Mastodons: A Poe Miscellany*, ed. Benjamin F. Fisher (Baltimore: Edgar Allan Poe Society, 2006), 200–2. In a letter from Baltimore realtor, James Tucker, to amateur historian, William M. Marine (c. 1904) the writer, stated that when leaving the cemetery after his grandfather's burial there in 1849, the fresh grave of Edgar Poe was pointed out to him by friends and that he would never forget their remarks "that it was fitting for Mr. Poe to be buried next to the pastor."

25. Like the large monument under which Poe's remains now rests, Orrin Painter's 1913, raven-topped cenotaph, created to mark the original spot, was also too wide to be placed in the narrow gap between the graves of David Poe Sr. and the Reverend Patrick Allison. Its current location, at the southern edge of the family lot, actually marks the grave of Edgar's older brother, William Henry Leonard Poe.

26. "Where Lies the Noble Spirit?" 208. The number "80" had no correlation to the cemetery plot of David Poe which is identified as number 27 in church records.

27. Stephen J. Vicchio, "Baltimore's Burial Practices, Mortuary Art and Notions of Grief and Bereavement, 1780–1900," *Maryland Historical Magazine* 81, no. 2 (Summer 1986): 145–46.

28. *Baltimore Evening Sun*, September 22, 1950. In this same article, it was reported that the city passed an ordinance that required the removal of all downtown graveyards "unless a place of worship existed in the same lot"; however, a record of this ordinance has proved elusive.

29. Hayward and Lancaster, *Baltimore's Westminster Cemetery*, 8.

30. Not all of the Poe family escaped being covered over by the church. The lot (no. 129) of George Poe Jr., who was the nephew of Edgar's paternal grandfather, David Poe, included at least ten members, one of which was Jane McBride Poe, Edgar's great-grandmother and matriarch of the Baltimore Poe family. The unmarked graves are located near the current entrance to the "catacombs."

31. St. Louis Republican Correspondent, "Grave of Edgar A. Poe," *New York Times*, August 23, 1854, 1.

292   *Notes*

32. Letter: "Stella" Anna Lewis to George W. Eveleth, January 3, 1854, reprinted in *Miller*, 197–98. Mrs. Lewis's plan also included relocating the remains of Poe's wife from the cemetery of the Dutch Reformed Church at Fordham to the Green-Wood Cemetery in Brooklyn.

33. Letter: Maria Clemm to Neilson Poe August 19, 1860; repr. *Miller*, 46–49.

34. Neilson Poe, qtd. in "Bogus Relics of the Poet Poe," *Baltimore Sun*, November 12, 1878, 1.

35. Thomas Dimmock, "Notes on Poe," *Century Magazine* o.s. 50 (June 1895): 315–16. The timing of Neilson Poe's purchase of a headstone, if it actually occurred, is uncertain. Dimmock describes a visit to Baltimore in February 1860 during which he was told that a marker for Poe's grave was in the works. However, Maria Clemm's letter to Neilson, was sent in August of that year, suggesting it was not the impetus.

36. A pencil-sketch of the stones was made by Charles M. Dimmock, but as they are described as "proposed," the rendition was most likely created from a verbal description.

37. Dimmock, "Notes on Poe," 315–16.

38. Sara Sigourney Rice, *Edgar Allan Poe: A Memorial Volume* (Baltimore: Turnbull Brothers, 1877), 45–46.

39. "Literary Entertainment in [*sic*] Behalf of the Poe Memorial Fund," *Baltimore Sun*, November 8, 1865, 2. "A reading will be given on the evening of November 10 by graduates of the Western Female High School in the school building." An encore program was held on December 7 at Concordia Hall in Baltimore.

40. "The Poet Edgar Allan Poe; Dedication of a Monument to His Memory," *Baltimore Sun*, November 18, 1875, 1, 4. Among these contributions would be $54 from the Troy Female Seminary, a school that Sarah Ann Lewis had attended as a girl.

41. "The Poet Edgar Allan Poe," *Baltimore Sun*, November 18, 1875. A careful examination of the monument's funding demonstrates that no more than $52 could have been generated by school students (this figure would be shown as $152 in Rice's memorial volume but that included two $50 donations from anonymous individuals). Professor Henry E. Shepherd, who had been the superintendent of Baltimore City schools at the time, would later deny that such a student program provided substantive capital for the project, stating that "the greater part of the money was the gift of Mr. G.W. Childs." *Baltimore Sun*, February 19, 1924, 10.

42. "Poe's Two Funerals," *Baltimore Sun*, February 3, 1903, 9. The decision to place the memorial at Poe's burial site may have been influenced by an 1873 visit to the cemetery by poet, Paul H. Hayne, who after having difficulty finding the grave was quoted as saying, "In the name of art, of patriotism, of common gratitude and the benefactions of genius . . . let a monument be erected over the poet's 'first couch of rest' worthy in all respects of his country and himself!"

43. Rice, *Edgar Allan Poe*, 46.

44. Rice, *Edgar Allan Poe*, 47. Only $879.55 had been collected by the monument committee by the end of 1874.

45. Rice, *Edgar Allan Poe*, 46

46. Rice, *Edgar Allan Poe*, 63–64.

47. "Exhumation of the Poet Poe's Remains," *Baltimore Sun*, October 1, 1875, 4.

Notes

48. "Poe's Monument," *Baltimore Sun*, October 2, 1875, 4.

49. "Local Matters," *Baltimore Sun*, October 15, 1875, 4.

50. "Local Matters," *Baltimore Sun*, October 16, 1875, 5. It is not clear whether a better location had been promised to some of those who had donated money.

51. "Local Matters," *Baltimore Sun*, October 16, 1875, 5.

52. "The Poe Monument," *Baltimore Sun*, October 29, 1875, 4. The new date for the monument's dedication was given as November 10, but would be pushed one final time to the following week.

53. Rice, *Edgar Allan Poe*, 47 fn.

54. Scharpf, "Where Lies the Noble Spirit?" 219n28.

55. William P. Meany, "Edgar Allan Poe's Grave," *Celtic Monthly*, September 1879, 140. In this magazine article, Meany relies on Snodgrass's statement that no coffin liner was used and George Spence's subsequent description of one "proved" the wrong grave had been excavated.

56. "Bogus Relics of the Poet Poe." *Baltimore Sun*, November 12, 1878, 1. "Mr. Spence afterwards regretted this burning, as many friends have applied to him for pieces of the coffin as relics."

57. Evans, "Poe's Burial and Grave," *New York Times*, February 26, 1893, 2.

58. "Poe's Brain Petrified," *St. Louis Republican*, November 8, 1878.

59. "Bogus Relics of the Poet Poe," *Baltimore Sun*, November 12, 1878, 1.

60. William Reynolds, *A Brief History of the First Presbyterian Church of Baltimore* (Baltimore: Waverly Press, 1913), 124.

61. Meany, "Edgar Allan Poe's Grave," 140.

62. "The Poet Edgar Allan Poe," *Baltimore Sun*, November 18, 1875, 1.

63. "The Poet Edgar Allan Poe," *Baltimore Sun*, November 18, 1875, 1. It was reported that 2,000 invitations were extended which included Maryland's governor and the mayor of Baltimore, as well as members of the city council and school board. Also, in his description of the ceremonies for the *New York Daily Tribune*, Eugene Didier stated that tickets to the event were limited to 1,000: "The Poe Monument," *New York Daily Tribune*, November 18, 1875, 2.

64. Eugene Didier, "The Poe Monument," *New York Daily Tribune*, November 18, 1875, 2. In the opening address delivered by Professor William Elliott Jr., three individuals who attended the original burial were stated to be in attendance.

65. "The Poet Edgar Allan Poe," *Baltimore Sun*, November 18, 1874, 1.

66. "Walt Whitman at the Poe Funeral," *Baltimore Sun*, November 19, 1875, 4.

67. "The Poet Edgar Allan Poe," *Baltimore Sun*, November 18, 1874, 1, 4.

68. "The Poet Edgar Allan Poe," *Baltimore Sun*, November 18, 1875, 4.

69. "Poe Monument the First," *Baltimore Sun*, April 15, 1907, 12.

70. William Fearing Gill, "Edgar A. Poe and His Biographer, Rufus W. Griswold," in *Lotos Leaves: Original Stories, Essays and Poems*, ed. William Fearing Gill (Boston: William Gill, 1875), 277–306. It is probable that it did not occur to Maria Clemm that Griswold would supplement the memoirs of Willis and Lowell with one of his own at a later date.

71. Jeffrey A. Savoye, "Edgar Allan Poe and Rufus Wilmot Griswold," Edgar Allan Poe Society of Baltimore, January 22, 2009, https://www.eapoe.org.

Bibliography

ARCHIVES

Anthony Street Collection. Manuscript Division. New York Public Library, New York.

Colonel Richard A. Gimbel Collection of Edgar Allan Poe, Free Library of Philadelphia, Philadelphia, Pennsylvania.

Edgar Allan Poe Collection. Enoch Pratt Free Library, Baltimore, Maryland. https://collections.digitalmaryland.org/digital/collection/poe.

Edgar Allan Poe Society of Baltimore. https://www.eapoe.org.

Henry W. and Albert A. Berg Collection. New York Public Library, New York.

J. K. Lilly Collection of Edgar Allan Poe. Lilly Library, University of Indiana, Bloomington, Indiana.

John Henry Ingram's Poe Collection. University of Virginia. Charlottesville, Virginia.

Maryland State Archives. http://guide.msa.maryland.gov/pages/index.aspx.

Poe Museum, Richmond, Virginia.

Rufus W. Griswold Papers. Boston Public Library Archives and Special Collections, Boston, Massachusetts.

Simon Gratz Collection. Historical Society of Pennsylvania, Philadelphia.

U.S. National Library of Medicine. https://medlineplus.gov/.

SOURCES

Abrahams, Harold J. *The Extinct Medical Schools of Baltimore, Maryland.* Baltimore: Maryland Historical Society, 1969.

Ackroyd, Peter. *Poe: A Life Cut Short.* New York: Doubleday, 2008.

Allen, Hervey. *Israfel: The Life and Times of Edgar Allan Poe*, 2 vols. New York: George H. Doran, 1926.

296   *Bibliography*

————. *Israfel: The Life and Times of Edgar Allan Poe*, rev. ed. New York: Farrar & Reinhart, 1934.

Allen, Hervey, and Thomas Ollive Mabbott. *Poe's Brother: The Poems of William Henry Leonard Poe*. New York: George H. Doran, 1926.

Baltimore City Archives. *Suspicious Deaths in Mid-19th Century Baltimore*. Silver Spring, MD: Family Line Publications, 1986.

Bandy, William T. "Dr. Moran and the Poe-Reynolds Myth." In *Myths and Realities: The Mysterious Mr. Poe*, edited by Benjamin Franklin Fisher, 26–36. Baltimore: Edgar Allan Poe Society, 1987.

Batchelor, William N. *Recollections of the East Building Before It Was Church Home & Infirmary*. Edited by Frederick T. Wehr. Baltimore: Church Home and Hospital, 1982.

Beirne, Francis F. *The Amiable Baltimoreans*. New York: E. P. Dutton, 1951.

Benitez, R. Michael. "Case Records of the University of Maryland and Baltimore VA Medical Centers. A 39-Year-Old Man with Mental Status Change," *Maryland Medical Journal* 45 (September 1996): 765–69.

Bensel, Richard Franklin. *The American Ballot Box in the Mid-Nineteenth Century*. Cambridge: Cambridge University Press, 2004.

Bohner, Charles H. *John Pendleton Kennedy: Gentleman from Baltimore*. Baltimore: Johns Hopkins Press, 1961.

Bondurant, Agnes M. *Poe's Richmond*. Richmond, VA: Poe Associates, 1978.

Bonner, Charles H. *John Pendleton Kennedy: Gentleman from Baltimore*. Baltimore: Johns Hopkins University Press, 1961.

Braddy, Haldeen. *Glorious Incense: The Fulfillment of Edgar Allan Poe*. Washington, DC: Scarecrow Press, 1953.

Bramsback, Birgit. "The Final Illness and Death of Edgar Allan Poe: An Attempt at Reassessment," *Studia Neophilologica* 42, no. 1 (1970): 40–59.

Brown, Alexander Crosby. *The Old Bay Line, 1840–1940*. New York: Bonanza Books, 1940.

Butters' Richmond Directory for 1855. Richmond: H. K. Ellyson's Steam Presses, 1855.

Cobb, Charles. *American Railway Guide & Pocket Companion for the United States: 1851*. New York: Curran Dinsmore, 1851.

Cody, Sherwin. *Poe: Man, Poet and Creative Thinker*. New York: Boni and Liveright, 1924.

Cordell, Eugene Fauntleroy. *Historical Sketch of the University of Maryland, School of Medicine, 1807–1890*. Baltimore: Press of Isaak Friedenwald, 1891.

Craig, Danl. H. *Craig's Baltimore Business Directory and Baltimore Almanac, for 1842*. Baltimore: J. Robinson, 1842.

Daniel, Frederick S. *The Richmond Examiner During the War; or The Writings of John M. Daniel*. New York: printed for the Author, 1868.

Dare, Charles P. *Philadelphia, Wilmington and Baltimore Railroad Guide, 1856*. Philadelphia: King & Baird, 1856.

Davis, Richard Beale, ed. *Chiver's Life of Poe*, by T. H. Chivers. New York: E. P. Dutton, 1952.

Bibliography

Dawidziak, Mark. *Mystery of Mysteries: The Death and Life of Edgar Allan Poe.* New York: St. Martin's Press, 2023.

Dean, Hannah J., and Ryan L. Boyd. "Deep into That Darkness Peering: A Computational Analysis of the Role of Depression in Edgar Allan Poe's Life and Death," *Journal of Effective Disorders* 1 (April 2020): 482–91.

Deas, Michael J. *The Portraits and Daguerreotypes of Edgar Allan Poe.* Charlottesville: University Press of Virginia, 1989.

Delafield, Francis. *A Handbook of Postmortem Examination and Morbid Anatomy.* New York: William Wood, 1872.

Didier, Eugene L. *The Life and Poems of Edgar Allan Poe.* New York: W. J. Widdleton, 1876.

———. *The Poe Cult and Other Poe Papers.* New York: Broadway Publishing, 1909.

Disturnell, J. *Disturnell's Railroad, Steamboat, and Telegraph Book.* New York: J. Disturnell, 1850.

Donnay, Albert H. "Poisoned Poe: Evidence that Poe May Have Suffered from Neurasthemia." Paper presented at the International Edgar Allan Poe Conference, Richmond, Virginia. October 9, 1999.

Edgar Allan Poe Society of Baltimore. http//eapoe.org.

Erlich, Heyward. "The Broadway Journal: Brigg's Dilemma and Poe's Strategy." In *The Collected Writings of Edgar Allan Poe: Vol. IV: Broadway Journal,* edited by Burton Pollin, xviii–xix. New York: Gordian Press, 1986.

Gaylin, David F. *Edgar Allan Poe's Baltimore.* Charleston, SC: Arcadia Publishing, 2015.

Gill, William Fearing. "Edgar A. Poe and His Biographer, Rufus W. Griswold." In *Lotos Leaves: Original Stories, Essays and Poems,* edited by William Fearing Gill, 277–306. Boston, William Gill, 1875.

———. *The Life of Edgar Allan Poe.* New York: D. Appleton, 1877.

Giorno, Ralph. *Decryption of the Death of Edgar Allan Poe.* Middleton, DE: By author, Western Consulting Pathology, 2017.

Goodwin, Donald W. *Alcohol and the Writer.* New York: Penguin Books, 1988.

Gordon, A. G. "The Death of Edgar Allan Poe—A Case of Syphilis?" *Maryland Medical Journal* 46, no. 6 (July 1997): 289–90.

Great Plains Laboratory. "Metals Hair Test by Great Plains Laboratory." *Integrative Psychiatry.* 2020. https://www.integrativepsychiatry.net/shop/the-great-plains-laboratory/metals-hair-test-great-plains/ (accessed January 6, 2020).

Haggard, Howard Wilcox, and E. M. Jellinek. *Alcohol Explored.* Garden City, NY: Doubleday, Doran, 1942.

Hall, Clayton Colman (editor). *Baltimore: Its History and Its People,* 3 vols. New York: Lewis Historical Publishing, 1912.

Harrison, James A., ed. *The Complete Works of Edgar Allan Poe,* 17 vols. New York: Thomas Y. Crowell, 1902.

———. *New Glimpses of Poe.* New York: M. F. Mansfield, 1901.

298   *Bibliography*

Hayward, Mary Ellen, and R. Kent Lancaster. *Baltimore's Westminster Cemetery & Westminster Presbyterian Church*. Baltimore: Westminster Preservation Trust, 1984.

Hewitt, John H. [Hill]. *Recollections of Poe*. Edited by Richard Barksdale Harwell. Atlanta: Emory University Library, 1949.

———. *Shadows on the Wall*. Baltimore: Turnbull Brothers, 1877.

Heywood, John. *A Dialogue Conteinyng the Nomber in Effect of all Prourbes in the Englishe Tongue*, 2 vols. London: Thomas Berthelet, 1546.

The Horse You Came In On Saloon. "Our Story." 2020. https://www.thehorsebaltimore.com/story (accessed October 24, 2020).

Howe, Daniel Walker. *The Political Culture of the American Whigs*. Chicago: University of Chicago Press, 1979.

Hull, William Doyle, II. "A Canon of the Critical Works of Edgar Allan Poe." PhD diss., University of Virginia, 1941.

Hungerford, Edward. *The Story of the Baltimore & Ohio Railroad, 1827–1927*, 2 vols. New York: G. P. Putnam's Sons, 1928.

Ingram, John H., ed. *Edgar Allan Poe: His Life, Letters, and Opinions*, 2 vols. London: John Hogg, 1880.

Isani, Mukhtar Ali. "Reminiscences of Poe by an Employee of the Broadway Journal," *Poe Studies* 6, no. 2 (December 1973): 33–34.

Jackson, David K. *Poe and the Southern Literary Messenger*. New York: Haskell House, 1970.

James, Robert. *A Medicinal Dictionary*. London, England: T. Osborn, 1743.

Joyce, John Alexander. *Edgar Allan Poe*. New York: F. Tennyson Neely, 1901.

Kanely, Edna A. *Directory of Maryland Church Records*. Silver Spring, MD: Family Line Publications, 1987.

Kent, Charles W., ed. *The Unveiling of the Bust of Edgar Allan Poe in the Library of the University of Virginia*. Lynchburg, VA: J. P. Bell, 1901.

King, Leslie S., and Marjorie C. Meehan. "A History of the Autopsy." *American Journal of Pathology* 73, no. 2 (November 1973): 514–44.

Little, John P. *History of Richmond*. Richmond, VA: Dietz Printing, 1933.

Mabbott, Thomas Ollive. *The Collected Works of Edgar Allan Poe*, 3 vols. Cambridge, MA: Belknap Press of Harvard University Press, 1969; 1978.

———. *Tamerlane and Other Poems* (Introduction), New York: Facsimile Text Society, 1941.

Mackowiak, Philip A. *Post Mortem: Solving History's Great Medical Mysteries*. Philadelphia: American College of Physicians, 2007.

Marshall, John A. *American Bastille*. Philadelphia: Thomas W. Hartley, 1871.

Matchett, R. J. *Matchett's Baltimore Directory for 1849-1850*. Baltimore: Matchett, 1849.

———. *Matchett's Baltimore City Directory for 1851*. Baltimore: Matchett, 1851.

McCabe, Clinton. *History of the Baltimore Police Department, 1774–1907*. Baltimore: Fleet-McGinley, 1907.

Meyers, Jeffrey. *Edgar Allan Poe: His Life and Legacy*. New York: Charles Scribner, 1992.

Miller, Genevieve, "A Nineteenth Century Medical School: Washington University of Baltimore." *Bulletin of the History of Medicine* 14, no. 1 (June 1943): 14.

Miller, John Carl. *Building Poe Biography*. Baton Rouge: Louisiana State University Press, 1977.

———. *Poe's Helen Remembers*. Charlottesville: University Press of Virginia, 1979.

Moran, John J. *A Defense of Edgar Allan Poe: Life, Character and Dying Declarations of the Poet*. Washington, DC: William F. Boogher, 1885.

Moss, Sidney P. *Poe's Major Crisis: His Libel Suit and New York's Literary World*. Durham, NC: Duke University Press, 1970.

Nichols, Mary Gove. *Reminiscences of Edgar Allan Poe*. New York: Union Square Book Shop, 1931; Reprint. *Sixpenny Magazine* [London], February 1863.

Osborn, Matthew Warner. "Diseased Imaginations: Constructing Delirium Tremens in Philadelphia, 1813–1832," *Social History of Medicine* 19, no. 2 (August 2006): 191–208.

———. *Rum Maniacs: Alcoholic Insanity in the Early American Republic*. Chicago: University of Chicago Press, 2014.

Ostrom, John Ward. "Edgar A. Poe: His Income as Literary Entrepreneur," *Poe Studies* 15, no. 1, (June 1982): 1–7.

Ostrom, John Ward, Burton R. Pollin, and Jeffrey A. Savoye, eds. *The Collected Letters of Edgar Allan Poe*, 2 vols. New York: Gordian Press, 2008.

Pearl, Matthew. "A Poe Death Dossier: Discoveries and Queries in the Death of Edgar Allan Poe: Part I," *Edgar Allan Poe Review* 7, no. 2 (Fall 2006): 4–29.

———. "A Poe Death Dossier: Discoveries and Queries in the Death of Edgar Allan Poe: Part II," *Edgar Allan Poe Review* 8, no. 1 (Spring 2007): 8–31.

———. *The Poe Shadow*. New York: Random House, 2006.

Peeples, Scott. *The Man of the Crowd: Edgar Allan Poe and the City*. Princeton, NJ: Princeton University Press, 2020.

Phillips, Elizabeth C. "The Literary Life of John Tomlin, Friend of Poe." PhD diss., University of Tennessee, 1953.

Phillips, Mary E. *Edgar Allan Poe the Man*, 2 vols. Philadelphia: John C. Winston, 1926.

Poe, Edgar Allan. *Al Aaraaf, Tamerlane and Minor Poems*. Baltimore: Hatch and Dunning, 1829.

———. *The Gift*. Edited by Miss Leslie. Philadelphia: Carey & Hart, 1840.

———. *The Gift: A Christmas & New Year's Present*. Philadelphia: Carey & Hart, 1842; 1843.

———. *The Narrative of Arthur Gordon Pym*. New York: Harper & Brothers, 1838.

———. *Poems by Edgar Allan Poe, Complete*. New York: W. J. Widdleton, 1874.

———. *Tales*. New York: Wiley and Putnam, 1845.

———. [a.k.a. By a Bostonian]. *Tamerlane and Other Poems*. Boston: Calvin F. S. Thomas, 1827.

———. *The Works of the Late Edgar Allan Poe*, 4 vols. Edited by Rufus W. Griswold. New York: J. S. Redfield, 1850–1856.

Poe, Elisabeth Ellicott, and Vylla Poe Wilson. *Edgar Allan Poe: A High Priest of the Beautiful*. Washington DC: Stylus Publishing, 1930.

Polk, R. L. *R. L. Polk & Company's Baltimore City Directory for 1887*. Baltimore: A. Hoen, 1887.

Pollin, Burton R. *Discoveries in Poe*. Notre Dame, IN: University of Notre Dame Press, 1970.

Powell, Michael A. *Too Much Moran: Respecting the Death of Edgar Poe*. Eugene, OR: Pacific Rim University Press, 2009.

Quinn, Arthur Hobson. *Edgar Allan Poe: A Critical Biography*. New York: D. Appleton-Century, 1941.

Rahman, Abdul, and Manju Paul. "Delirium Tremens (DT)." In *StatPearls [Internet]*. Treasure Island, FL: StatPearls Publishing, 2020. https://www.ncbi.nlm.nih.gov/books/NBK482134/ (accessed 2020).

Reynolds, William. *A Brief History of the First Presbyterian Church of Baltimore*. Baltimore: Waverly Press, 1913.

Rice, Sara Sigourney. *Edgar Allan Poe: A Memorial Volume*. Baltimore: Turnbull Brothers, 1877.

Rickman, Leland S., and Choong R. Kim. "'Poe-phyria,' Madness, and the Fall of the House of Usher," *JAMA* 261, no. 6 (February 10, 1989): 863–64.

Robertson, John W. *Edgar A. Poe: A Study*. San Francisco: Bruce Brough, 1921.

Robinson, Judith. *Ensign on a Hill: The Story of the Church Home and Hospital and Its School of Nursing, 1854–1954*. Baltimore: Barton & Gillet, 1954.

Romano, John. "Early Contributions to the Study of Delirium Tremens." *Annals of Medical History* 3, no. 2 (March 1941): 128–39.

Rosenberg, Charles E. *The Care of Strangers: The Rise of America's Hospital System*. New York: Basic Books, 1987.

Russell, J. Thomas. *Edgar Allan Poe: The Army Years (USMA Library Bulletin No. 10)*. New York: United States Military Academy, 1972.

Sartain, John. *The Reminiscences of a Very Old Man, 1808–1897*. New York: D. Appleton, 1899.

Savoye, Jeffrey A. "The Mysterious Death of Edgar Allan Poe." Edgar Allan Poe Society of Baltimore. https://www.eapoe.org/geninfo/poedeath.htm (accessed July 5, 2023).

———. "Two Biographical Digressions: Poe's Wandering Trunk and Dr. Carter's Mysterious Sword Cane." *Edgar Allan Poe Review* 5 (Fall 2004): 15–42.

Scharf, J. Thomas. *Chronicles of Baltimore: Being a Complete History of "Baltimore Town" and Baltimore City*. Baltimore: Turnbull Brothers, 1874.

Scharpf, Christopher. "Where Lies the Noble Spirit?—An Investigation into the Curious Mystery of Edgar Allan Poe's Grave in Baltimore." In *Masques, Mysteries, and Mastodons: A Poe Miscellany*, edited by Benjamin F. Fisher, 194–222. Baltimore: Edgar Allan Poe Society, 2006.

Scott, Mary Wingfield. *Old Richmond Neighborhoods*. Richmond, VA: Whittet & Shepperson, 1950.

Sears, Jane. "Henry Herring—Fair Mount." *Maryland Tams Journal* 29, no. 3 (Fall 2008): 10–15.

Shoemaker, Ritchie C. "Diagnosis of *Pfiesteria*-Human Illness Syndrome." *Maryland Medical Journal* 46 (November/December 1997): 521–23.

Silverman, Kenneth. *Edgar A. Poe: Mournful and Never-Ending Remembrance.* New York: Harper Collins, 1991.

Sinclair, David. *Edgar Allan Poe.* London: J. M. Dent, 1977.

Slater, Montagu, ed. *The Centenary Poe.* London: Bodley Head, 1949.

Smith, Geddeth. *The Brief Career of Eliza Poe.* Cranbury, NJ: Fairleigh Dickinson University Press, Associated University Presses, 1988.

Smyth, Albert H. *The Philadelphia Magazines and Their Contributors, 1741–1850.* Philadelphia: Robert M. Lindsay, 1892.

Spannuth, Jacob E., ed. *Doings of Gotham: Poe's Contributions to The Columbia Spy.* Pottsville, PA; Jacob E. Spannuth, 1929.

Stanard, Mary Newton. *Edgar Allan Poe Letters Till Now Unpublished: In the Valentine Museum, Richmond, Virginia.* Philadelphia: J. B. Lippincott, 1925.

Starrs, James E. "The Death of Edgar Allan Poe: A Cardiologist Goes to the Heart of It." *Scientific Sleuthing Review* 21, no. 2 (Summer 1997): 1–5.

Steadman, Melvin Lee, Jr. *Falls Church by Fence and Fireside.* Falls Church, VA: Falls Church Public Library, 1964.

Stoddard, R. H. [Richard Henry]. *Select Works of Edgar Allan Poe, Poetical and Prose.* New York: W. J. Widdleton, 1880.

Stovall, Floyd. *Edgar Poe the Poet.* Charlottesville: University Press of Virginia, 1969.

Thomas, Dwight Rembert. "Poe in Philadelphia, 1838–1844: A Documentary Record." PhD diss., University of Pennsylvania, 1978.

Thomas, Dwight, and David K. Jackson. *The Poe Log: A Documentary Life of Edgar Allan Poe, 1809–1849.* Boston: G. K. Hall, 1987.

Thompson, John R. *The Genius and Character of Edgar Allan Poe.* Richmond, VA: Garrett & Massie, 1929.

Ticknor, Caroline. *Poe's Helen.* New York: Charles Scribner, 1916.

United States. Patent Office. *Annual Report of the Commissioner of Patents for the Year 1869.* Washington, DC: Government Printing Office 1871.

Virginia General Assembly. *Acts and Joint Resolutions Passed by the General Assembly of Virginia: During the Extra Session of 1902-3-4.* Richmond: J. H. O'Bannon, 1904.

Wagenknecht, Edward. *Edgar Allan Poe: The Man Behind the Legend.* New York: Oxford University Press, 1963.

Walsh, John Evangelist. *Midnight Dreary: The Mysterious Death of Edgar Allan Poe.* New Brunswick, NJ: Rutgers University Press, 1998.

Weiss, Susan Archer. *The Home Life of Poe.* New York: Broadway Publishing, 1907.

Whitman, Walt. *Specimen Days and Collect.* Glasgow, Scotland: Wilson & McCormick, 1883.

Whitty, J. H., ed. *The Complete Poems of Edgar Allan Poe.* Boston: Houghton Mifflin, 1911.

Wilde, Oscar. "Art and the Handicraftman." In *Essays and Lectures*, fourth ed. London: Methuen, 1913.

302 *Bibliography*

Williams, Huntington. *Baltimore City Health Department: The First Thirty-Five Annual Reports, 1815–1849.* Baltimore: Commissioner of Health of Baltimore, Maryland, 1953.

Williams, Stanley Thomas. "New Letters About Poe," *Yale Review* 14 (July 1925): 755–73.

Williams, W. *Appleton's Railroad & Steamboat Companion for 1849.* New York: D. Appleton, 1948.

Wilmer, Lambert A. *Our Press Gang; Or, A Complete Exposition of the Corruptions and Crimes of the American Press.* Philadelphia: J. T. Lloyd, 1859.

Woodberry, George E. *American Men of Letters; Edgar Allan Poe.* Edited by Charles Dudley Warner. Boston: Houghton Mifflin, 1885.

———. *The Life of Edgar Allan Poe,* 2 vols. Boston: Houghton Mifflin, 1909.

Woods, John W. *Woods' Baltimore City Directory, 1865–'66.* Baltimore: J. W. Woods, 1865–1866.

———. *Woods' Baltimore City Directory, 1870.* Baltimore: J. W. Woods, 1870.

Index

Publications and page references for figures are italicized

absinthe, 43, 230, 255
Al Aaraaf, Tamerlane and Minor Poems, 26, 28, 230, 250, 299
alcohol dehydrogenase, 203
alcohol poisoning, 204
alcohol withdrawal, 5, 68, 182, 184, 204, 207, 208, 214
Allan, Carlisle, 27, 249
Allan, Frances, 19–20, 26, 55, 247–48, 250
Allan, John, 18–24, 26–28, 37–38, 85, 225; letter to, 244, 246–48, 250
Allen, Hervey, 2, 34, 85, 125, 174, 176, 211, 247, 250, 254–55, 265, 271, 287
Allison, Patrick, 291
Alnutt, James W., 125, 274
"Annabel Lee," 1, 31, 44, 59, 79, 83, 159, 227, 231, 234, 282
apoplexy, 204–5, 207
army, 6, 25–26, 213, 249, 300
assault, 145, 171, 215
autopsy, 184–85, 286, 289, 298

Baltimore & Ohio Railroad (B&O), 89, 98–99, 235, 244, 266, 268, 298
Baltimore City and Marine Hospital, 131, *134*, 135–36, 137, *140*, *142*, *143*, 144, 146, 149–50, 152, 158, 167, 169, 215, 224, 227, 233, 275–76, 278–79
Baltimore Custom House, *158*
Baltimore Marine Hospital, 276
Baltimore Steam Packet Company, *88*, 261
Bandy, William, 128
Basil, John, 195
Batchelor, William, 134–36, 142, 275, 276, 278, 289, 296
beating/mugging, 171, 205, 215, 285
"The Bells," 44, 59
Benitez, Michael, 178, 218–21, 296
Benson, Oscar, 187
Benson, W. H., 170, 285
bipolar disorder/manic depression, 205, 219
Blackwell, Anna, 57; letter to, 259
Booth, Edwin, *165*
Boston Lyceum, 48, 50
Boyd, Ryan L., 179–80, 288, 297
brain cancer/tumor, 199, 205–6, 210
brain fever, 50, 121, 171, 183, 205, 257
brain lesion, 52, 206, 219, 233
Bransby, John, 20
Briggs, Charles, 47

304 *Index*

Bristed, Charles Astor, 55, 258
bronchitis, 38, 232
Bronson, Mary, 54, 258
Brooks, Nathan, 7, 28, 36, 93, *94–95*, 97, 106, 115, 200, 224, 225, 267
Browne, William Hand, 104–*5*, 118, 125, 225–26, 270; letter from, 269, 272, 274
Buckler, John, 30, 251
Burr, Chauncey, 67, 71
Burton, William, 36–37, *38*, 253

cane (Carter's), 83–85, 112, *126*, 264–65, 271, 300
carbon monoxide, 172, 206–7
Carpenter, William, 104–5
Carroll, Mrs. D. H., 96, 267, 290
Carter, Dr. Gibbon, 77, 226
Carter, John, 75, 80, 83–85, 88, 112, 174, 209, 226, 263–66, 271, 300
case record (Poe's hospital), 136, 167, 203
census (1850), *168*, 216, 266, 270, 279, 284–85
cerebral edema, 207
Childs, George, 196, 292
Chivers, Thomas, 40, 56, 226, 253–54, 296
cholera, 29, 67, 73, 152, 172, 178, 207–8, 215
Church Home and Hospital, 227, 275–76, 289, 296, 300
Church Home and Infirmary, 136, *137*, 140–41, 160, *188*, 275, 278, 282
Clark, Joseph H., 20, 200
Clarke, Thomas Cottrell, 40–41, 226; letter to, 254
Clemm, Henry, 33, 226
Clemm, Maria, 4, 9, 25–*27*, 30, 33, 35, 37, 44–45, 52, 54, 61, 63, 65, 67, 70, 72, 76, 78, 80, 82–83, 101, 104, 128, 136, 140, 154, 156, 158–59, 163, 170, 177, 180 181, 183, 189, 191–94, 197–98, 207–8, 212–14, 217, 226–27, 228–29, 231, 234; letter to,

239–41, 244, 246, 251, 256, 258–65, 269, 275–78, 281–82, 285, 288–93
Clemm, William T. D., 96, 138–39, 156, 164, 187, 189, 235, 277, 283, 289, 290
Coale, George, 97–98, 123, 274; letter from, 268, 273
Coates, Benjamin, 183, 288
Coath, Thomas, 106–7, 117, 269
coffin (Poe's), 163–64, 187–89, 198–99, 206, 224, 283, 291, 293
congestion of the brain, 165, 168, 177, 184, 207, 284, 287, 289
Conrad, Robert, 53, 258
coop (holding cells), 119–20, 123, *126*, 274
cooping (theory), 3, 8–9, 119–21, 123, 125–29, 156, 173, 243, 267, 273
coroner inquest, 171, 185, 205, 215, 286
Cullen, William, 145, *146*–47, 157, 227, 276, 279

Daniel, John, 56, 74, 258, 262, 296
Davidson, Robert, 199
Dean, Hannah J., 179–80, 269, 288, 297
death certificate, 6–7, 167, 203
Delafield, Francis, 185, 289, 297
delirium tremens/*mania-a-potu*, 3, 5–6, 67–68, 76, 136, 139, 156, 161, 167, 173, 178–84, 181–82, 204, 207–8, 214, 216–17, 220, 226–27, 232, 244, 255, 259, 277, 288–89, 299, 300
Democrats, 116, 120, 123, 125, 153, 274
diabetes, 208–9, 211–12
Didier, Eugene, 92–93, 123, 145, 157, 173, 202, 209–10, 227 –28, 251, 267, 273–74, 276, 279, 282, 286, 293, 297
dipsomania, 209
Dow, Jessie, 40–41; letter to, 254
drugs/opium/laudanum, 42, 57, 103, 112, 116, 121, 123, 170–71, 173–76, 178–79, 209, 219, 228, 255, 286–88
Duncan Lodge, 71, 75, 77, 85, 111, 232
D'Unger, Robert, 53, 228, 235, 258

Ellet, Elizabeth, 49–50, 171, 228, 233, 256
Elliott, William, 165, 197, 200, 201, 293
Ellis, Charles, 225, 247; letter to, 251
Ellis & Allan (business), 19–20, 248
encephalitis, 3, 6, 168, 170–71, 177–78, 210, 233
English, Thomas Dunn, 4, 41–42, 44, 48–50, 171, *174*, 175, 209, 228, 243, 254–57, 287
epilepsy, 210
ether, 210–11
Evans, May Garrettson, 191, 290
Eveleth, George W., 5, 54, 228; letter to, 243, 257, 258, 292

Fair Mount (Baltimore), *134*, 255, 271, 300
Fairmount Water Works (Philadelphia), 66, *68*, 179
Fitzgerald, Oscar, 75, 81–82, 228
Fordham (Poe's cottage), 50–54, 56, 61, 63, *64*, 175, 229, 236, 257, 260
Fourth Ward Hotel, 8, 107, 115, 131, 138
Francis, John, W., 176–77, 211, 228–29, 257
French, John C., 191
Front Street Theater, 152
Fuguet, Dallet, 100–101
Fuller, Hiram, 53, 229, 258
funeral/viewing, 97, 138, 156, 162, 187–90, 227, 241, 277, 279, 290, 291–93

Galt, William Sr., 22, 247–48
Garfield, James A., 159
George, Miles, 23, 248
Gibson, Thomas, 27, 250
Gildersleeve, Basil, 75, 81, 229
Gill, William F., 191, 200, 202, 254, 293, 297
Giorno, Ralph, 2, 213, 297
Glenn, William, 76, 78, 229, 263, 285; letter from, 283

Godey, Louis, 53, 67, 257–58
Gove, Mary, 51, 229, 257, 299
Gowans, William, 35, 252
Graham, George, 37–*38*, 229, 253
Graves, Samuel, 26–27, 248, 250
Griswold, Rufus, 43, 61, 71, 73, 83–84, 87, 101, 121, 155, 165, 169–*70*, 202, 228, 229–30, 237, 260, 264–65, 273, 281, 284–85, 293, 299; letter from, 266, 271; letter to, 259, 261–62, 264–65, 285
Gunners' Hall, 7, 43, 104–8, 110–12, 116, 119, 124, 127, 129, 224, 230, 271, 274
Gwynn, William, 28, 250

Haggard, Howard, 182, 205, 288, 297
Harrison, James A., 76, 143, 163, 228, 248, 263–64, 274, 277, 282–83, 285, 289–90, 297
Hawks, Francis, 35
heart disease, 6, 176–77, 211, 229
heart failure, 176, 211
hemochromatosis, 211
Herring, Elizabeth, 42, *173*, 230, 255, 286, 290–91
Herring, George W., 110, 152
Herring, Henry, 10, 43–44, *110*–13, 128, 134, 145, 164, 187–89, 230, 255, 271–72, 275, 283, 290, 300
Hewitt, John, 30, 41, 159, 200, 230, 251, 254, 298
Hewitt, Mary, 51; letter from, 257; letter to, 259
Heywood, Amos Bardwell, 60, 258
Hirst, Henry, 43, 230
Holladay, Frederick, 153–54
Holliday Street Theater, *15*
The Horse You Came In On Saloon, 103, 269, 298
Howard, Joshua, 26
Hubner, William, 189
hypoglycemia, 211–12
hypothermia, 210, 212

306 *Index*

Independent Order of Good Templars, 139, 153, 158

influenza, 212

Ingram, John, 2, 21, 33, 99, 103–5, 118, 125, 176, 191, 202, 226, 230–31, 248, 260, 265–66, 268–72, 295, 298; letter to, 252, 259, 269, 272, 274, 287

Ingram, Susan, 79

intemperance, 5, 36, 54, 79, 100, 136, 184, 207, 289

Jameson, Horatio, 133

Jellinek, E. M., 182, 205, 288, 297

Jones, Timothy, 27

Joyce, John, 140–41, 277, 282, 298

Kennedy, John P, 4, 7, *29*, 30, 32, 231, 244, 251, 296

King, Lester S., 185

Lane, Thomas H., 48, 101, 231, 261

Langley, James & Henry G., 254

Latrobe, John, 30, 200–201

lecture (Moran's), 141, 149, *159*, *160*–61, 279, 282–83

lecture (Poe's), 40, 43–44, 46, 48, 54–55, 57, 59–60, 63–65, 70–71, 74, 76, 77–83, 228, 229, 256, 258–59, 264, 266

lecture (Thompson's), 8, *121*, 173, 273

Lee, Z. Collins, 189, 241

Lewis, Sarah "Estelle" Anna, 52, 56, 59, 63, 79, 193, 231, 241, 260, 263, 292

Lewis, Sylvanus, 56, 63, 79, 231, 260

Lexington Market, 7, *96*–97, 103, 267

Lilly, Richard, *124*, 127, 274

Lippard, George, 43, 67, 69, *71*, 231, 261–62, 265; letter from, 260–62, 265

Locke, Jane Ermina, 52, 55, 231–32

Lombard Street, 8, 13, 15, 97, 103, *104*, 106–7, 117, 125, 135, 245, 270, 274, 275

Longfellow, Henry, 47–48, 201, 232, 256

Loud, John, 78, 80, 100, 101

Mabbott, Thomas Ollive, 2, 187, 206, 248–50, 290, 296, 298

Mackenzie (family), 18, 71, 75–76, 83–85, 111, 247, 264; Jane Scott, 19, 71, 76, 232; John H., 56, 72, 122, 232; Thomas G., 77, 232

Maclean, Clara, 141, 278

Madison House, 78–80, 84–85, 265

malaria, 2, 6, 172, 213

malpractice/misdiagnosis, 6, 213–14

marriage (to): Sarah Elmira Shelton, 73–74, 77, 80, 82, 100, 171, 176, 179, 211, 215, 262–63, 268; Sarah Helen Whitman, 57, 238; Virginia Clemm, 33–34, 234, 245, 251–52

Maxwell, Susan, 79

Meehan, Marjorie, 185, 289, 298

meningitis, 3, 214, 221

mercury poisoning, 172, 215, 286

Miller, James H., 30, 133

Minor, Benjamin, 122

Minor, Lucian, 32, 219, 251

Mitchell, John Kearsley, 37–38, 176, 232, 253

Monkur, John C. S., 6, 145, 163, 170–71, 177–*78*, 210, 232–33, 279, 285, 287

monument (Poe's), 9, 96, 156, 190, 194–99, *200–201*, 202, 230, 261, 291–93

Moran, John J., 4, 6, 9, 97–99, 103, 111–13, 124–25, 128, 131–32, 135–36, 138–47, 149–51, *152*, 153–60, *161*–66, 170–73, 177–79, 181, 183–85, 187–89, 191, 207–8, 210–14, 217–21, 224, 227, 232–33, 239–41, 243–44, 267–69, 271, 274–91, 296, 299–300; letter from, 239, 275, 281–82, 288–89

Moran, Mary J., 143, *153*, 283, 290

Moran, Washington Ellis, 154

Index

Mosher, Phillip, 198
Moss, James, 101
Mott, Valentine, 53, 206, 233
Moyamensing Prison, *65–67*
murder, 2, 100, 124, 171, 215
Murdock, E. M., 176, 287

Namuth, Frederick, 164, 187, 283
The Narrative of Arthur Gordon Pym, 36, 260, 299
nervous breakdown/exhaustion, 215–16
New York University, 48, 50
Nye, W. A. R., 76

Old Capitol Prison, *151*
Osgood, Frances, *49*, 50, 52, 228, 233; letter to, 257

Pabodie, William, 58; letter from, 259
Painter, Orrin, 201, 291
Passano, Lewis, 123, *124*, 273–74
pathologic alcohol reaction, 5, 180, 216–17, 243
Patterson, Edwin, 60–61, 70, 73, 122, 233, 258, 260, 262, 263; letter to, 259, 262, 273
Patterson, Louisa, 28, 248, 250
Patterson, Samuel, 67
Paulding, James K., 36, 252
Pearl, Matthew, 2, 93–94, 106, 110, 115, 127, 199, 206, 244, 267–69, 272, 274, 299
The Penn (Poe's magazine project), 37, 253
Philadelphia, Wilmington & Baltimore Railroad (PW&B), 89, *98*, 99, 105, 115, 223, 266, 296
Phillips, Mary E., 2, 125, 163, 191, 246, 262–64, 271, 283, 299
phrenitis, 168, 183, 216, 284
pneumonia, 3, 6, 19, 180–82, 213–14, 217, 288
Poe, Amelia Fitzgerald, 42
Poe, David Jr., 14–18, 226, 233–34, 245–46

Poe, David Sr., 14, 187, 191–93, 224, 234, 246, 291
Poe, Elisabeth Ellicott, 95, 123, 274, 299
Poe, Eliza Arnold, ix, *14*, 15–18, 233–34, 245–47, 301
Poe, Elizabeth Cairnes, 14, 25, 28, 32, 227
Poe, George Jr., 17, 246, 252
Poe, George W., 33, 226, 247
Poe, John Prentiss, 165
Poe, Neilson, xiv, 32, 34, 84, 87, 95–98, 104, 111, 123, 138, *144–45*, 155–56, 162, 165, *169*, 187, 189, 191–95, 197, 200–201, 224, 234, 245, 251, 255, 274, 277–79, 281–83, 285, 291–92; letter from, 245, 269, 278, 285, 290–91; letter to, 292
Poe, Rosalie Mackenzie, *17*–19, 56, 71–72, 74, 76, 84, 111, 122, 175, 226, 232, 234, 246, 264, 287; letter from, 264
Poe, Virginia Clemm, 25, 30–*31*, 32–34, 38–39, 44–45, 51–52, 96, 172, 176–77, 206, 227, 232–34, 236, 251–53, 261
Poe, William (second cousin), 42; letter from, 255; letter to, 253, 272
Poe, William "Henry" Leonard, 15–16, 18–19, 25–26, 28, 29, 208, 234, 238, 246, 248, 250, 253, 291, 296; letter to, 248
Poems (Elam Bliss), 28, 250
poison, 171–72, 204, 206, 215, 217, 286, 297
Poitiaux, Catherine, 76, 248
police, 53, 89, 116, 118, 258, 266, 272, 298
porphyria, 218
Powell, Michael, 2, 99, 115, 132, 145, 163, 180–81, 214, 216–17, 243, 262, 272, 276, 277–78, 283, 288, 300
Power, Anna, 58
Powhatan Line (steam packet), 87–88, 261, 265

308   *Index*

Preston, John, 21, 248

Quinn, Arthur Hopson, 2, 16–17, 20, 35, 50, 63, 78, 100–101, 112, 125, 191, 205, 235, 245–52, 256–58, 260–63, 265–66, 268, 271, 275, 287, 300

rabies, 177–78, 218, 220
"The Raven," 7, 43–44, 46, 48, 79, 81, 108, 159, 226, 228, 238, 255, 259
Rawlings, Dr. George, 76
Rawlings, George (train conductor), 98–99, 163, 235, 244, 268, 273
Reynolds, Elmer R., 138, 235, 267, 277
Reynolds, Henry, *124*, 127, 128, 138, 183, 235, 240, 274, 296
Rice, Sara Sigourney, 96–97, 165, *195*–97, 200, 202, 248, 267, 290, 292–93, 300
Richmond (period image), 69
Richmond, Nancy "Annie," 55, 57, 59–61, 77, 175, 232, 235; letter to, 259–60, 263, 287, 288
Robbins, Henry R., 152
Rockett's Landing, 56, *84*–85, 87, 265
Rosenberg, Charles, 136, 276, 289, 300
Russell, J. Thomas, 25, 249, 300
Ryan, Cornelius, 105, 107, 115, 125, 127, 129, 269–70

Sadler's Restaurant, 83, 85, 265
Sargeant, William, 106, 107, 117
Sartain, John, 43, 65, *66*–68, 100, 129, 171, 179, 235, 261, 275, 286, 288, 300
Savoye, Jeffrey, 108, 120, 202, 243–44, 252, 264, 273, 293, 299, 300
Seven Stars Tavern, 32
Shelton, Sarah Elmira Royster, 22, 72–73, *74*, 77–78, 82–83, 86, 100, 159, 163, 171, 179–80, 215, 236, 249, 268; letter from, 262, 264
Shew, Marie Louise, 51, *52*–53, 176–77, 206, 229, 233, 236, 258; letter from, 287

Silverman, Kenneth, 2, 259, 277–78, 301
Sisson, Hugh, 194–96, 292
Smith, Elizabeth Oakes, 109, 121, 171, 205, 236, 243, 270, 273, 285
Snodgrass, Joseph, 7–8, 36, 44, 94, 104–6, 108–13, 115, 121, 128, 152, 171, 189, 200, 204, 225, 236, 243, 255, 267–73, 285–86, 288, 293; letter to, 243, 252–53, 270
Sons of Temperance, 78, 86, 229, 285
Spear's Wharf, 89, *92*, 223, 261
Spence, George, *190*–92, 197–200, 206, 236, 293
Spencer, Edward, 105, 119, 123, 125, 173, 269–70, 272–74, 286
Stanard, Jane, *21*, 74, 248
Stanard, Mary Newton, 85, 111, 249–50, 265, 271, 301
Stanard, Robert, 74
Starr, Edward, *124*, 127, 274
Starr, Mary, 28, 39, 236
Stedman, E. C., 165
Stoddard, Richard, 48, 97, 99–100, 156–57, 237, 256, 259, 268, 281–82, 301; letter to, 273
The Stylus (Poe's magazine project), 40, 55, 71, 226
suicide, 57, 66, 104, 121, 175, 179–80, 205, 216, 219, 269
Suter, Charles, 187
Sutton, Thomas, 182
Swan Tavern, 71, 76–78, *79*, 85
syphilis, 219, 297

Talavera, 75, 262
Tamerlane and Other Poems, 25–26, 28, 230, 249–50, 298–99
tetanus, 219–20
Thomas, Frederick, 38, 40, 46, 53, 127, 237, 253; letter to, 254, 256, 274
Thompson, John R., xiv, 56, 60–61, 73, 83, 121–*22*, 124, 129, 173, 181, 237, 244, 273, 301; letter from, 258, 264; letter to, 260, 262, 265–66, 271

Index

Tomlin, John, 41, 255, 299
toxic disorder, 208, 220
trunk (Poe's), 25, 78, 83–85, 111, 119, *155*, 162, 240, 249, 264–66, 271, 281, 283, 300
tuberculosis, 4, 17, 18, 29, 38, 51–52, 220–21, 227, 232, 234–36, 250
Tucker, Thomas, 23
Tyler, Robert, 40, 127

University of Maryland, 150, 166, 178, 204, 218, 221, 225, 232, 233, 236, 275, 279, 288, 296
University of Virginia, 22, 24, *24*, 105, 122, 212, 225, 230, 236, 237, 248, 252, 269–70, 272, 284, 295, 298

Valentine, Edward, 55, 71–72, 262–64; letter to, 248, 258
Volck, Frederick, 197

Walker, Joseph, 104–10, 125, 128, 269–70, 272, 275
Walsh, John, 2, 100, 163, 171, 215, 268, 285, 301
Warden, Ella, 189, 289
Washington Medical College, 133–35, 178, 184, 227, 232, 251
Washington University (hospital), 6, *132*–35, 137, 145–46, 149, 250, 275–76, 279, 299
Weiss, Susan Archer Talley, 71–72, 75–77, 80, 83, 112, 125, 175, 226, 232, 237, 243, 247, 258, 262, 271, 288, 301; letter from, 262
Wernicke Encephalopathy, 221
Western Female High School, 195–96, *199*, 200, 292
Weston, J. Alden, 191, 291
Westminster Presbyterian Church, 188, 192, *193*, 195, 198, 200, 224, 236, 290–91, 298
West Point, 25–29, 236, 249–51
Whigs, 107, 110, 116, 120, 123–25, 127, 230, 272, 274, 298
White, Thomas W., 30, 32–*33*, 34–35, 219, 237, 251–52; letter from, 251–52; letter to, 251
Whitman, Sarah Helen, *55*–59, 72, 177, 182, 211, 228, 237–38, 244, 256–60; letter from, 259; letter to, 256, 277, 287
Whitman, Walt, 48, 201, 256, 293, 301
Whitty, James, 56, 237, 257–58, 262–63, 301
Widow Meagher, 90, 92–*93*, 267
Willis, Nathaniel P., 45, *47*, 238, 256, 293; letter from, 256; letter to, 257, 260
Wilmer, Lambert, 25, 29–30, 36, 41–42, 238, 249, 251, 253, 302
Woodberry, George, 2, 42, 93–95, 112, 125, 174–75, 246–47, 255, 258, 264, 267, 271, 286–88, 302
Worth, W. J., 26

About the Author

David F. Gaylin is a retired business owner from Baltimore, Maryland, where the shadow of Edgar Allan Poe is ever-present. A lifelong student and collector of Poe, his passion for the poet produced the book, *Edgar Allan Poe's Baltimore* (2015). When he is not writing books and poetry, David volunteers at the Edgar Allan Poe House where he is the senior docent. He is also a member of the Poe Studies Association and is currently serving as president of the Edgar Allan Poe Society of Baltimore.